VERSATILE VICTORIAN
Selected Writings of George Henry Lewes

VERSATILE VICTORIAN

Selected Writings of George Henry Lewes

Edited with an Introduction by

ROSEMARY ASHTON

Bristol Classical Press

First published in 1992 by
Bristol Classical Press
an imprint of
Gerald Duckworth & Co. Ltd
The Old Piano Factory
48 Hoxton Square, London N1 6PB
Tel: 071 729 5986
Fax: 071 729 0015

A catalogue record for this book is available
from the British Library

ISBN 1-85399-090-6

Printed in Great Britain by
The Cromwell Press, Melksham, Wiltshire

Contents

Introduction

In the January 1879 issue of the *Fortnightly Review*, Anthony Trollope paid tribute in touching terms to the 'peculiarly valuable literary life' of his friend, G.H. Lewes. 'On Wednesday the 4th of December', he wrote, 'a few loving friends stood over the grave in Highgate Cemetery which received the body of George Henry Lewes, who was the first Editor of this Review.'[1] Lewes, best known as the companion for nearly thirty years of George Eliot, was in his lifetime both admired and, on occasion, disdained for his extraordinary versatility. Francis Espinasse described him as 'the prince of journalists', and recalled that Lewes had once claimed to have published articles in every serious magazine 'except the damned old *Quarterly*.'[2] This was scarcely an exaggeration, for in the space of forty years Lewes wrote well over five hundred articles in journals ranging from the lighthearted, like *Douglas Jerrold's Shilling Magazine*, in the 1840s, to the serious monthly and quarterly periodicals, such as the *Edinburgh Review*, the *Westminster Review*, and in the 1860s and 1870s the *Fortnightly Review* and the *Cornhill Magazine*.

Lewes not only edited the *Fortnightly Review* during its first year (1865-6), but was editorial adviser to W.M. Thackeray and the publisher George Smith in the *Cornhill* venture in 1860, and had been co-founder and editor of the best liberal weekly newspaper to be published in the Victorian period. This was the *Leader*, whose literary editor Lewes was from 1850 until he left for Germany with Marian Evans in July 1854.

If the number of papers willing to publish his work was large – the *Quarterly Review* was so politically and aesthetically conservative that Lewes never petitioned its editors for column space – the range of topics he covered in his prolific journalistic life was equally so. As Trollope wrote, 'there was no form of literary expression in which he did not delight and instruct.' Nor was there any subject on which he did not touch, from the plays of Sophocles to the most recent novels, English, French, German and Italian, from the mid-century craze for table-rapping and spirit-summoning to the theories of Charles Darwin and Thomas Henry Huxley, from Plato and Aristotle to the positivist philosophy of Auguste Comte and his English disciples.

In the *Leader* during 1853 Lewes published simultaneously a series of articles translating and explaining Comte's 'Philosophy of the Sciences' (in which he introduced Comte's term *altruisme* into English) and a regular witty column on the London theatre, using the pseudonym 'Vivian'. These drama

1

criticisms were popular and durable enough to be reprinted in a volume in
1896, long after Lewes' death;[3] reviewing the collection, George Bernard
Shaw admitted that Lewes was a sort of model for his own regular drama
criticism in the *Saturday Review*. He valued Lewes' 'variety of culture,
flexibility, and fun', adding, 'I consider that Lewes in some respects anticipated me, especially in his free use of vulgarity and impudence whenever
they happened to be the proper tools for his job'.[4] No doubt Shaw had in
mind such essays as the one Lewes wrote in February 1852 when the
actor-manager Charles Kean, annoyed by adverse criticism, stopped sending
Lewes free press tickets for his shows. The mock-sorrowful essay, reprinted
here, is called 'Vivian in Tears (All along of Mr Kean)'; in it Lewes robustly
declares that he will henceforth pay for his own ticket and continue to criticise
Kean's performances in an independent spirit (see p. 36). Such fearlessness
was the hallmark of Lewes the critic. Shaw praised his 'rare gift of integrity',
as well as declaring him 'the most able and brilliant [dramatic] critic between
Hazlitt and our own contemporaries'.[5] In the Vivian essays, some of which
are included in this selection, Lewes' fun coexists easily with serious, if brief,
assessments of drama, such as his astute remarks on *Hamlet* in the course of
a review of a visiting German company in 1852 (see p. 37).

Lewes' essays, with the exception of the Vivian papers, a volume of
articles republished from the *Pall Mall Gazette* entitled *On Actors and the
Art of Acting* (1875),[6] and his *Fortnightly Review* series *The Principles of
Success in Literature* (1885),[7] have not previously been collected. Thus
important essays on Dickens, Thackeray, Charlotte Brontë, Spinoza, Goethe,
Darwin and others are not readily available to readers unable to gain access
to the nineteenth-century periodicals in which they appeared. On the other
hand, it is noticeable that editors of volumes in the *Critical Heritage* and
Casebook series, collecting criticisms of individual authors and works, have
invariably included extracts from Lewes' reviews as examples of the best,
and often the most original, Victorian criticism. The *Critical Heritage*
volumes on Jane Austen, Thackeray, Dickens, the Brontës, and Arnold are
cases in point.[8]

Wherever scholars of nineteenth-century intellectual life have probed,
looking for intelligent responses in matters literary, philosophical, historical,
or scientific, they have come across G.H. Lewes. Had he been less prolific,
and less of a generalist, his work might well have been better known today.
Even during and immediately after his lifetime, praise for his omnicom-
petence tended to be qualified by suspicions of shallowness. 'Dined at the
Athenaeum with John Morley, meeting M. Arnold and Frederic Harrison [the
leading English Comtist]', wrote Grant Duff in his diary for 16 December
1878:

> The conversation turned much upon George Lewes, whose death the
> other day took us all by surprise. Morley, I observed, put him very high

as a philosopher, Huxley as a physiologist; Arnold thought him strongest as a dramatic critic. Both Morley and Harrison seemed to think that he would appear a more considerable person to posterity than he did to his contemporaries. I have always thought that it was the fashion to underrate him quite absurdly. I have certainly myself come across very few people who do so many different things so well.[9]

Jack-of-all-trades though Lewes was, he was master of a surprising number of them. As Trollope noted, shrewdly turning Lewes' early disadvantages into an asset, 'his education was desultory, but wonderfully efficacious for the purposes of his life'. Like Trollope himself, like Dickens and later Hardy, Lewes was not university educated. Born in 1817, grandson of Charles Lee Lewes, a comic actor of some fame, son of a more obscure literary man who disappeared when Lewes was a child, stepson of a Captain Willim, whom he disliked, Lewes, with his two brothers, attended different schools in London, Jersey and France. Possibly the family moved around in this way because of financial difficulties; if so, Lewes' upbringing was again similar to Dickens' and Trollope's. His knowledge of French, dating from his schooldays in the 1820s, drew much admiring comment from those who knew him in later life. It also opened to him early on the world of French literature. As a young man, he wrote unusually knowledgeable articles on Balzac, George Sand, Hugo and Dumas, and became an ardent, if temporary, disciple of Comte.

After school, Lewes may have begun medical studies in London. An oblique reference to himself in the article on Spinoza he wrote for the *Fortnightly Review* in April 1866 (see p. 269) suggests this: 'a sixth [member of a student club in Red Lion Square in the 1830s] studied anatomy and many other things, with vast aspirations, and no very definite career before him'. His interest in anatomy and physiology, though remaining that of an amateur, bore fruit in the years of his life with George Eliot. A series of clearly written popularising science books was published, first in magazines, then in volume form: *Sea-Side Studies at Ilfracombe, Tenby, the Scilly Isles, and Jersey* (1858; first published in *Blackwood's Magazine*, 1856-7), *The Physiology of Common Life* (1859-60; first published in *Blackwood's Magazine,* 1858), and *Studies in Animal Life* (1862; first published in the *Cornhill Magazine*, 1860). Though none of these works could lay claim to original discoveries, they were based on firsthand experience, for Lewes was an enthusiastic collector and experimenter, as well as an avid reader of the works of the great English, French and German physiologists of the day. *The Physiology of Common Life*, in the Russian translation of 1861, so impressed the young student Pavlov by its clear empirical method that he later named it as influential on his development of the theory of conditioned reflexes.[10] Lewes' work crops up again, also in a Russian context, in Dostoevsky's *Crime and Punishment* (1866), in the pub conversation between the starving student Raskolnikov and the drunken civil servant Marmeladov (ch. 2).

Though Darwin and Huxley came to respect Lewes' scientific studies – the former writing to thank him for his appreciative articles in the *Pall Mall Gazette* in 1868 – Lewes was more than once subjected to professional snobbery from career scientists. Indeed, Huxley himself had sneered at his 'mere book-knowledge' in a review of Lewes' *Comte* (1853),[11] and Lewes' professorial collaborators on the late Victorian periodical *Mind* (founded in 1876) were markedly unenthusiastic about his last published work, the ambitious *Problems of Life and Mind* (1874-9).[12] It was a subject on which Lewes was uncharacteristically touchy. In an article on 'Goethe as a Man of Science' (*Westminster Review*, 1852), later incorporated into his *Life and Works of Goethe* (1855), he wrote sympathetically of the suspicion which greeted Goethe's efforts in plant morphology and optics:

> When Goethe claimed a hearing on abstruse and comprehensive questions of positive science, the world at large very naturally prejudged the matter, and somewhat superciliously regarded his efforts as those of a poet dabbling in science; while professional men, with professional contempt, shrugged their shoulders at the 'amateur'.[13]

While robustly defending Goethe's interest in, and contribution to, the progress of science, Lewes could take comfort in sharing his sense of injustice at the hands of experts.

In more than one way, Lewes' work on Goethe was central to his career. An autodidact from the start, Lewes taught himself German and set off for Berlin in 1838, at the age of twenty-one, armed with letters of introduction from the chief mentor of Lewes' generation, Thomas Carlyle. It was Carlyle's enthusiastic, robust, quasi-mystical proselytising of German literature, and Goethe in particular, which encouraged Lewes, as it did George Eliot, Arnold and John Stuart Mill, among others, to become acquainted with German culture.[14] Through Carlyle's offices, he met and interviewed Goethe's friends Johann Eckermann and Varnhagen von Ense, and began collecting materials for his biography of Goethe.

This was the work which would establish his reputation. It was to be further researched and written in Weimar and Berlin during 1854 and 1855, when Lewes and Marian Evans were beginning their life together.[15] The book was, in a sense, a collaborative effort, since Marian not only discussed it with him but also helped to translate the extracts from Goethe's works. Goethe was the single most important European author for both of them. Lewes valued Goethe's many-sidedness, his tolerance, his stress on the importance of self-culture (*Bildung*). Goethe is accordingly quoted by Lewes more than any other source throughout his career. He was also to be a fruitful influence on George Eliot, forming the subject of a thoughtful essay, 'The Morality of *Wilhelm Meister*' (*Leader*, July 1855, timed to precede the appearance of Lewes' *Life* a few months later), and suggesting the term 'elective affinities' for involuntary human attraction which she was to use, problematically, in *The Mill on the Floss* (1860). Lewes' *Life of Goethe* was an instant success in both England and Germany. He could claim in the preface to the second edition (1864) that it had already sold 13,000 copies in the two countries. The work is lucid, thorough, and unprejudiced, particularly in the passages in which Lewes defends Goethe against the usual charges of immorality. The chapter on *Wilhelm Meister*, that epoch-making but controversial archetype of the *Bildungsroman*, is reproduced here, as representative of Lewes' writing on Goethe (pp. 217-25).

If Carlyle was an important influence on the young would-be *littérateur* in the 1830s – and Lewes' early style shows signs, as his friend Mill pointed out, of uneasy imitation of 'Carlylese'[16] – another was Leigh Hunt, Carlyle's near-neighbour in Chelsea. Hunt, a relic from Regency days and the height of English Romanticism, was in the mid-1830s a grand old man of letters to whom those with literary, republican or sceptical leanings still turned. Admired for his bold attacks on the Prince Regent in the 1810s, revered for his closeness to the late Byron and Shelley – he was with the latter in Italy when he drowned – sought out for his anecdotal acquaintance, Hunt presided over a circle of young men who idolised Shelley to the point of apeing his open-necked appearance and worshipping his atheism and anti-monarchism. Lewes was one of these. A sceptic in religion, a liberal, if not radical, in politics, he gravitated naturally towards Leigh Hunt and bohemianism. Hunt encouraged his first attempts at essay-writing, publishing some slight pieces in the *Monthly Repository* in 1837, and it was through Hunt that Lewes petitioned Mary Shelley to be allowed to write a life of Shelley. Permission was not granted, for Mary Shelley wished to play down her husband's unorthodoxy, not least because she depended on her father-in-law, Sir Timothy Shelley, for financial support, and Sir Timothy had vetoed all publicity about his reprobate son.

Hunt's friendship was to be as important for Lewes as Carlyle's, though in a different way, for Lewes became fast friends with Thornton, Hunt's eldest son. Together they set up the *Leader* in 1850, with Thornton Hunt as political editor and Lewes in charge of the literary pages. And Thornton Hunt was to contribute to the situation which later made it impossible for Lewes and Marian Evans to marry. Lewes' wife, Agnes, following the Shelleyan principle of free love, also embraced by Lewes and Hunt, bore four children to Thornton Hunt between 1850 and 1857. Once Lewes had registered the first two of these as his own, he was debarred from seeking a divorce. When he met Marian Evans in October 1851, he may already have been living apart from Agnes, though he was still running the *Leader* with Hunt.

Though on the face of it the union with Marian Evans was an odd one – Lewes ex-bohemian, flippant, cosmopolitan, and Marian earnest, provincial, and plain – the couple had in fact a great deal in common. They were part of radical literary London, moving in the circle surrounding the freethinking publisher John Chapman, with whom Marian boarded when she came to London from Coventry in 1850. Both were agnostics, both were widely read in European literature, both admired Goethe, both saw Comte's positivism as helping to fill the gap left by religious belief, both had discovered the neglected philosophy of Spinoza. Intellectually, therefore, they were well suited. Emotionally, it seems, they were equally so. Lewes, having found his previous life unsatisfactory, gained in Marian both a sympathetic listener and a woman honest and loyal towards those she loved. She, though at first repelled by his manner and appearance ('a sort of miniature Mirabeau'), soon found that he was 'a man of heart and conscience wearing a mask of flippancy'.[17]

Lewes considered his relationship with Marian a true marriage; they brought up his three sons, and they supported Agnes and her four children by Hunt. In his essay on Comte (*Fortnightly Review*, 1866), Lewes writes feelingly about marriage: 'It may prove an inestimable blessing, the subtle influences of which will permeate every hour of the day', or it may 'prove a desolating evil, numbing the sympathies, irritating and scattering the intellectual energies, distorting the life' (see p. 248). Comte's circumstances somewhat paralleled his own. His wife had left him when he met and fell in love with Clotilde de Vaux, whose husband was a criminal jailed for life. Both, though 'morally free', were 'legally bound'.

When Lewes set out for Weimar with Marian in July 1854, he had recently published his book, *Comte's Philosophy of the Sciences, Being an Exposition of the Principles of the Cours de philosophie positive* (1853), republished from his *Leader* articles. With Mill and Harriet Martineau he was among the first English enthusiasts of positivism. He had met Comte in Paris in 1842 and had been involved in the attempt of well-meaning public men to help Comte financially. His first book, the extraordinarily successful *Biographical History of Philosophy* (1845-6), placed Comte as the honourable heir of Aristotle and Bacon in the line of empirical philosophy which Lewes saw as the true march of progress in thought. Bacon's and Comte's were experimental methods; they observed and verified, unlike the idealist philosophers from Plato to Descartes and beyond. Comte proposed a 'scientific' study of society. His was therefore *the* philosophy of the nineteenth century with its religious scepticism, its interest in science, and its rapid industrial advance.

Though by 1866 Lewes was calling himself a 'reverent heretic' and dissociating himself from Comte's later work, with its 'religious cultus', he could write gratefully of the effect of Comte's philosophy on him and his generation. The 1866 essay is included here (pp. 244-68) for several reasons. Firstly, it is a lucid exposition of the positive philosophy which, although now scarcely regarded as important, seemed to many European liberal thinkers to hold the key to the philosophical, religious and social problems of the age. Secondly, the essay is – unusually for Lewes – both directly and indirectly autobiographical. Thirdly, it is a fine example of the Victorian periodical essay of the 'life and works' variety.

In 1854 Lewes had an agreement, as he thought, with the publisher Bohn (who had brought out Lewes' *Comte* in his 'Scientific Library' series) for a translation of Spinoza's *Ethics*.[18] He had discovered Spinoza during his short spell as a medical student (official or unofficial). The student club he attended in Red Lion Square included a watchmaker named Cohn, who introduced his fellows to Spinoza's works. Lewes became an immediate admirer of Spinoza's humanism, and a sympathiser with his difficult life. In the *Westminster Review* in 1843 he wrote one of the earliest appreciations of Spinoza in English. The translation of the *Ethics* was handed over to Marian while Lewes finished his work on Goethe in Weimar. She, too, had come to admire Spinoza's lucid ethical thinking, particularly his stress on sympathy and imagination as important springs of human action. Having just finished her translation of Ludwig Feuerbach's *Essence of Christianity*, which was published by John Chapman during her absence in Germany, she was eminently qualified to translate the thinker who lay behind Feuerbach's secularising of religious belief. Both philosophers dealt in the vocabulary of human morality independent of religious faith. In her novels George Eliot would show imaginatively one character acting beneficently on the life of another (Dorothea and Lydgate, Daniel Deronda and Gwendolen) in terms close to those of Feuerbach and Spinoza.

Lewes returned to Spinoza in an article, reprinted here, which he wrote for the *Fortnightly Review* immediately after the Comte essay of January 1866. Once more, he is strikingly personal in his assessment, as well as giving a full and accurate account of Spinoza's life and work. For Lewes, as for George Eliot, it was important to undermine 'the rooted prejudice that morality is inseparable from certain special dogmas which, if rejected, leave the man a prey to all animal and ignoble passions' (see p. 282). These two *Fortnightly Review* essays, on Comte and Spinoza, represent Lewes in his best mature style, and – with his many times reprinted *Biographical History of Philosophy*[19] – give a fair idea of his claim to have contributed to the history of philosophy in the nineteenth century.

It was also in the *Fortnightly Review* that Lewes attempted to give a philosophical view of literature in a series of six articles entitled 'The Principles of Success in Literature' (May-November 1865). True to his embracing of the empirical, scientific method in philosophy, by which we must limit ourselves to asking only those questions which can be answered by reference to experience, he applies the scientific method to literature. Not surprisingly, the result is not always convincing, though the informative idea is interesting:

No one, it is to be presumed, will imagine that I can have any pretension of giving recipes for Literature, or of furnishing power and talent where nature has withheld them. I must assume the presence of the talent, and

then assign the conditions under which that talent can alone achieve
real success. No man is made a discoverer by learning the principles
of scientific Method; but only by those principles can discoveries be
made; and if he has consciously mastered them, he will find them
directing his researches and saving him from an immensity of fruitless
labour. It is something in the nature of the Method of Literature that I
propose to expound. Success is not an accident. All Literature is
founded upon psychological laws, and involves principles which are
true for all peoples and for all times. These principles we are to consider
here.[20]

In the application of this confident assertion in the essays which follow,
Lewes is not always able to sustain his method. He has valuable things to say
about literature, but he is manifestly better at making particular critical points
than at applying rules. He is, in fact, somewhat hampered by his subdivision
of the 'laws of literature' into three – the principle of Vision (or imagination),
the principle of Sincerity, and the principle of Beauty. His discussions tend
to mix the categories he has been at pains to distinguish.

Nevertheless, the essays are interesting, and the third, 'Of Vision in Art'
(July 1865), is reprinted here for its thesis that imagination and experience
are not opposed, but linked phenomena. Lewes here gives a new slant to the
Romantic theory of literature as represented particularly by Coleridge, whom
he half-quotes on the imagination and memory being both involved, the first
turning into active employment the materials presented to the passive memory.[21] It is clear that Lewes does this with the theory and practice of his
consort in mind. Indeed, he more than once quotes 'a very imaginative writer'
from the *Westminster Review*; this was George Eliot writing in January 1857
on the eighteenth-century poet Edward Young. The Victorian age was not,
on the whole, an age rich in literary theory; a naive realism pervaded literary
criticism in the periodicals. Only Lewes, George Eliot, and Ruskin wrote
more thoughtfully about the relationship between literature and 'reality' as
one more complex than a mere copying procedure. Lewes' essays were taken
up in America, where they were first reprinted in 1885 by Albert Cook, 'for
the use of students of the University of California', and were later reprinted
in London, with an introduction by T. Sharper Knowlson (1898). Geoffrey
Tillotson, in his prefatory remarks to the 1969 reprint of the *Principles*, while
noting Lewes' unfulfilled ambition to describe the laws of literature, declares
that of all the critical writings of the mid-nineteenth century 'none are more
brilliant and thoughtful than Lewes'.'[22]

Lewes' claims on our attention as a critic must rest chiefly on his reviews
of contemporary literature. There was no new work of value which Lewes
did not discuss, and no author who has since become a classic whose genius
Lewes did not at once recognise. With the exception of the late Wordsworth,
to whose *Prelude* he gave a lukewarm welcome in the *Leader* in 1850 –

though he redeemed himself in 'The Principles of Success in Literature' in 1865 (see pp. 233-6) – Lewes judged, and judged fairly, each production of poets and novelists old and new. He hailed Browning as robust and original, while asserting that he was not a 'singer' and was too often obscure. In a review of Browning's poem 'Christmas Eve and Easter Day' (*Leader*, 27 April 1850), Lewes admires 'the bold and artful mingling of the ludicrous with the intensely serious', in which he thinks Browning resembles Carlyle, but warns that 'Realism in Art has Truth as an aim, Ugliness as a pitfall' (see p. 123). As for Elizabeth Barrett Browning, she *is* 'a born singer', but Lewes objects mildly to the insubstantial nature of her subject matter. He employs a phrase which George Eliot was to make much use of in her essays and novels as descriptive of her kind of realism – 'the workaday world':[23] '[Elizabeth Barrett Browning] has allowed her phantasy to move amidst the reveries and unrealities of a silent life, instead of seeking to rebaptize in beauty the thoughts and sufferings of our work-day world' (see p. 129). Tennyson is 'our greatest living poet' (see p. 124), and Arnold writes better when he ceases to imitate the ancients he so admires (see p. 138). Some of Lewes' assessments of contemporary poetry, mainly short articles in the *Leader*, are included here. They sometimes bear the marks of weekly journalism (as when he quotes at disproportionate length), but are nevertheless intelligent and consistent.

Many of Lewes' best essays in his early years, before his life with George Eliot, were published in the *British Quarterly Review*. In November 1847 he contributed an amusing, if rather too lengthy, estimate of Browning's poetry, finding *Pippa Passes* frequently obscure, and defining *Sordello* as a set of 'Sybilline incoherences'.[24] Two essays on Charles Lamb in 1848 claim a scoop. Benefiting from his friendship with Leigh Hunt, Lewes includes unpublished letters and personal anecdotes from Lamb's life. Specifically, in the first article (May 1848, reprinted here) he discusses for the first time in public the murder of Lamb's mother by his sister Mary and Lamb's heroic decision to devote his life to caring for his periodically insane sister. In November 1848 Lewes returns to the subject in a review of T.N. Talfourd's edition of Lamb's letters, in which the correspondence relating to the family tragedy is printed as a result of its having been aired in the *British Quarterly Review* in May. Lewes boasts, 'We are satisfied with this result of our labours. The public is indebted to us for a precious gift. The history of man is enriched by a new and curious contribution to psychological experience.'[25]

Other essays in the *British Quarterly Review* include an entertaining debunking of Alexandre Dumas, reprinted here (pp. 202-15) for its author's extraordinary knowledge of Dumas' innumerable works, its fun, its interesting comments on literature generally, and its prescient remarks about the mass of the French people, who were to rise up in revolution in the very month in which this article was published – February 1848. Lewes' own political views are to be inferred – for he never wrote a direct political essay, though he was proud to be associated with the liberal socialism of the *Leader* in the 1850s – from two slashing articles in the *British Quarterly Review*. The review of the first two volumes of Macaulay's *History of England* (*British Quarterly Review*, 1849) is too repetitive and lengthy to include. That of the third and fourth volumes (1856), which is reprinted here, is a bold attack on Macaulay's confidence and 'deficiency of speculative power' and an astute analysis – half admiring, half contemptuous – of the historian's amazing tricks of rhetoric. Lewes is perhaps a little too hard, but he makes out a strong case against Macaulay, partly by means of a telling comparison with Carlyle.

The second of Lewes' destructive articles included in this selection is on Disraeli. Ostensibly a review of the fifth edition of Disraeli's novel *Coningsby* (1849), it is in fact a strong condemnation of Disraeli as both novelist and politician. He anticipates the emphasis he was later to put on authorial honesty and seriousness in 'The Principles of Success in Literature' when he accuses Disraeli of a 'want of truthfulness' in art, as in politics. Interestingly, in view of Lewes' own versatility, he makes short work of Disraeli's pretensions to shine at epic and drama, as well as fiction: 'he made one gallant dash at the dramatic laurel wreath, feeling himself called upon to "revive English tragedy"' (see p. 162). Only a few months before writing the article, Lewes had taken his own tragic drama, *The Noble Heart*, to Manchester, where it was given three performances at the Theatre Royal in April 1849. The play, with Lewes in the role of Don Gomez, the honourable father who sacrifices his own for the sake of his son's happiness, was as good as many of the pseudo-Elizabethan productions which appeared on the Victorian stage, but was not a success. It had a brief run in London in 1850, but Lewes, who seriously contemplated following his grandfather into the acting profession at this time, was discouraged. As Shaw slyly noted in his assessment of Lewes' drama criticism, 'he wrote plays of the kind which, as a critic, he particularly disliked'.[26]

Lewes wrote no more tragedies and did no more acting, though he translated and adapted several comedies from French originals during the 1850s. His experiences as an actor, first with Dickens' amateur company in 1847, then as Shylock and Don Gomez in Manchester, bore fruit in his series of articles in the *Pall Mall Gazette* in 1865, 'On Actors and the Art of Acting'. And the difficulties of a playwright trying to get managers to put on his work are amusingly remembered in 'The Miseries of a Dramatic Author' (*Cornhill Magazine*, 1863), reprinted here (pp. 42-56). One might have expected him to be more sympathetic towards Disraeli's attempt, but his article makes clear his dislike for Disraeli's assumption of excellence in every sphere, and his 'want of self-knowledge' in thinking himself dramatically gifted.

On Disraeli the novelist Lewes is even more withering: 'The prose run mad of "Alroy" was too extravagant even for the Minerva press. The philosophico-poetico-"psychological Romance" of "Contarini Fleming" was unendurable to men and boys', and so on (see p. 164). Here again Lewes was a shrewd and unsparing critic of another's failure; again he was himself the recent author of two unsuccessful efforts in the genre. He wrote two bad novels, *Ranthorpe* (1847), about the ups and downs of a struggling young writer, and *Rose, Blanche, and Violet* (1848), with its complicated plot turning on the love problems of three sisters. Jane Carlyle minced no words in calling the latter 'execrable'; and Lewes himself found *Ranthorpe* an embarrassment in later life.[27] In a review of German fiction in 1858, he took Otto Ludwig to task for his incessant narrative 'psychologising' instead of showing characters' motives in action (*Westminster Review*, October 1858). The criticism applies precisely to his own novels.

Being a poor novelist himself by no means disqualified Lewes as a critic and judge of others' talent in the genre; not for nothing did he see in Marian's essay writing in the mid-1850s the qualities which would make her a good novelist, and he duly encouraged her to try her hand at fiction. Lewes was also an able critic of the best novelists writing before George Eliot made her *début* with *Scenes of Clerical Life* in 1858. His intelligent welcoming of the early works of Dickens, Thackeray and Charlotte Brontë brought letters of thanks from each of these authors, beginning literary friendships of importance not only to Lewes but also to them.

The relationship with Dickens was the earliest, the longest, and the most volatile of the three. One of Lewes' earliest review articles was one in the minor magazine, the *National Magazine and Monthly Critic*, which ran for only two volumes in 1837-8. This was a masterly effort by the twenty-year-old Lewes, in which he shrewdly and generously analysed the success of Dickens' earliest works, *The Pickwick Papers*, *Oliver Twist*, and *Sketches by Boz* (see pp. 57-61). Dickens was pleased with the review and, as Lewes recalled in his last article on his old friend (published in the *Fortnightly Review* in 1872, after Dickens' death), asked Lewes to visit him. A friendship ensued. Lewes' letters to Dickens are lost, but he elicited interesting replies from Dickens, some, at least, of which survive. Thus Dickens explained to him in a letter probably written in June 1838, presumably in response to a query about the creative frame of mind:

> With reference to that question of yours concerning Oliver Twist I scarcely know what answer I can give you. I suppose like most authors I look over what I write with exceeding pleasure and think (to use the words of the elder Mr. Weller) 'in my innocence that it's all wery capital.' I thought that passage a good one *when* I wrote it, certainly, and I felt it strongly (as I do almost every word I put on paper) *while* I wrote it, but how it came I can't tell. It came like all my other ideas, such as they are, ready made to the point of the pen – and down it went. Draw your own conclusion and hug the theory closely.[28]

Lewes did hug the revelation closely until he came to write his retrospective review of Dickens' achievement in 1872. In this odd article, excellent and grudging by turns, Lewes reveals Dickens' method, remembering conversations in which Dickens had talked of the power of his dreams and of his having 'distinctly *heard*' every word his characters spoke. Lewes, half-anticipating Freud's view of the literary imagination as an expression of neurosis and of dreams as holding the key to our subconscious, builds up an intelligent discussion of Dickens' peculiar genius as powered by a kind of sane hallucinating. Though Dickens' biographer, John Forster, took umbrage at this and subsequently pilloried Lewes in his *Life* of Dickens (1872-4), it is in fact a highly intelligent and not at all damaging criticism.

Unfortunately, though, Lewes, in two minds about the products of Dickens' undeniable genius, becomes harsh about the unreality of Dickens' characters. He is surely right to see in Dickens' works 'human character and ordinary events pourtrayed [sic] with a mingled verisimilitude and falsity altogether unexampled'. But he comes down too heavily on Dickens' lack of 'the reflective tendency': 'I do not suppose a single thoughtful remark on life or character could be found throughout the twenty volumes'. Presumably his criticism here results from a silent comparison with George Eliot's very different genius. While Forster saw in this only 'the scattering of rubbish over an established fame',[29] Trollope more correctly called the essay 'the best analysis we have yet had of the genius of that wonderful man'. Having known both Lewes and Forster, and having discussed the row between them with Lewes, Trollope could declare, 'On behalf of Lewes I find myself bound to say that his was the simple expression of his critical intellect dealing with the work of a man he loved and admired, – a work which he thought worthy of the thoughtful analysis which he applied to it'.[30] I think that, on the whole, Trollope was right, and therefore reprint the essay in this selection.

Between 1837 and 1872, when Lewes made his first and last pronouncements on Dickens, much of interest happened in their relationship. In 1847, Dickens began getting together an amateur acting company with the specific purpose of raising money to help the ageing and ever impecunious Leigh Hunt, whom Dickens was later rather cruelly to preserve in *Bleak House* (1853) as Harold Skimpole, 'a romantic youth who had undergone some unique process of depreciation' (ch. 6). Knowing that Lewes was a friend of Hunt's, and presumably knowing also of his theatrical antecedents, Dickens approached Lewes in June 1847:

> You know what we are going to do for Leigh Hunt, and how we purpose acting in London on the 14th. and 19th. of July, and in the country on the 24th. and 28th. or thereabouts. You have a hearty sympathy for Hunt, and are, I am told, an excellent Actor. The characters to let, are, the Host in *The Merry Wives of Windsor* (a very good part), and old Knowell in *Every Man in his Humour*.[31]

In the event, the plays were not put on in London, but *Everyman in his Humour* was performed in Manchester and Liverpool in July, with Lewes duly acting old Knowell, as well as taking a role in the accompanying farce. The following year, Lewes played the part of the garrulous Welshman, Sir Hugh Evans, in *The Merry Wives of Windsor*, which was put on in London and the provinces in aid of 'the Fund for the Endowment of a Perpetual Curatorship of Shakespeare's House'.[32] Some newspaper reviews of the 1848 performances singled out Lewes for praise as a comic actor, though he was widely thought to have tried too hard, and lapsed into caricature. One unidentified newspaper cutting in the collection made by John Forster, also one of the troupe and at this time quite friendly with Lewes, includes the remark that 'the Hugh Evans of Mr. G.H. Lewes was one of the best "hits" in the piece', though there was a 'trifling tendency towards exaggeration', offset however by 'an unwearied intelligence'. Another alluded to Lewes as – already – a man of many parts:

> Mr. Lewis [sic] played well, effectively, and funnily, though he caricatured somewhat. His appearance too was in his favour. He played the Welsh parson...and skipped about the stage and snapped his fingers, and contorted his little wizzened [sic] figure in the grotesquest way. A good deal of laughter greeted the 'biographer of philosophy' as he led his troop of little sham devils in their dance around Falstaff and Herne's Oak.[33]

Dickens' acting company came together again in 1850, to perform Bulwer Lytton's play, *Not So Bad as We Seem*, but this time without Lewes, who had in the meantime unsuccessfully tried out an acting career in *The Merchant of Venice* and his own tragedy and was now busy editing the *Leader*.[34] There is no evidence that the relationship between Lewes and Dickens had changed from the friendly one suggested by Dickens' letters of 1847 and 1848, though Dickens did allow himself a sardonic smile at Lewes' high hopes as a tragic dramatist and actor: 'I understand the Noble Heart says that "nothing has been seen like it, since the days of Kean." I should think not'.[35] But something did occur two years later to sour the friendship. Curiously, it was a case of Lewes offending Dickens in the same way that Lewes himself felt affronted by the professional scientific fraternity. He accused Dickens of scientific ignorance.

The cause was *Bleak House*, which appeared in monthly instalments between March 1852 and September 1853. At the end of Part Ten, published in December 1852, Dickens has the drunken Mr Krook, 'the Lord Chancellor of the Rag and Bottle shop', die of 'Spontaneous Combustion' (ch. 32). Lewes, reviewing the novel so far in the *Leader* of 11 December, objected to Dickens' use of a 'vulgar error' for the purposes of art. He took it upon himself to lecture Dickens on physiological fact and probability, rubbing the wound with the rather condescending remark that 'as a novelist he is not to be called to the bar of science; he has doubtless picked up the idea among the curiosities of his reading from some credulous adherent to the old hypothesis, and has accepted it as not improbable'. Lewes rightly concluded that spontaneous combustion was 'only admissible as a metaphor' (see p. 63).

Dickens, sensitive about his learning, took the unwise course of ignoring the let-out Lewes thus offered, and going on the offensive in the very next chapter of the novel. Part Eleven, published in January 1853, opens with the inquest of Krook, and Dickens observes with aggressive sarcasm, born of uneasiness, that though some 'men of science and philosophy' deny the possibility of spontaneous combustion, there are a great many authorities to support it. He rather airily names a few of these (see p. 63). Uncharacteristically, though understandably in view of his own sensitivity on the subject of scientific credentials, Lewes returned to the attack on 5 February 1853. He cited well-known scientists such as Liebig and his friend the anatomist Richard Owen, and poured scorn on the cases Dickens had adduced (see pp. 63-6). The following week he added to the weight of evidence against the possibility of spontaneous combustion occurring, and required Dickens to 'make some qualifying statement in the preface to *Bleak House*, so as to prevent the incident of Krook's death from promulgating an error'. Though stern here, Lewes kept the tone of his letter friendly, observing that Dickens' genius 'has moved with beneficent power in so many other directions than that of Physiology', and that it would 'cost [Dickens] nothing to avow a mistake'.[36]

However, the price was too great for Dickens' pride. On 7 February, just after the first of Lewes' February articles, he wrote to his friend Dr John Elliotson, a mesmerist estranged from the orthodox medical community, thanking him for 'fortifying' Dickens with examples of the phenomenon, and protesting that he could not understand 'how people [could] reject such evidence'.[37] He also wrote Lewes a partly conciliatory, partly defiant letter, showing his annoyance that Lewes 'rather hastily assumed that I knew nothing at all about the question – had no kind of sense of my responsibility – and had taken no trouble to discriminate between truth and falsehood'. On the contrary, 'I looked into a number of books with great care, expressly to learn what the truth was. I examined the subject as a Judge might have done'. Finally:

...so far from making any qualifying statement in the Preface to Bleak House I can only say that I have read your ingenious letters with much pleasure [!] – that I champion no hypothetical explanation of the fact – but that I take the fact upon the testimony, which I considered quite impartially and with no preconceived opinion.[38]

True to his word, Dickens published no retraction when the novel was brought out in a volume in September 1853. Indeed, he went out of his way to argue with his adversary, 'my good friend Mr Lewes', answering him with the same discredited sources he had used in Part Eleven of the novel, which he had got from Dr Elliotson (see pp. 66-7). Lewes replied once more, on 3 September, but briefly and with the obvious intention of closing the affair:

> We need not again expose the questionable nature of the evidence, and its authorities; we confine ourselves to the simple *morale* of the case, and declare that while he was at liberty to cite all the authorities in his favour, he was not at liberty to disregard and pass over in silence the names of Liebig, Bischoff, Regnault, Graham, Hofmann, and Owen; and against that omission we protest.[39]

This debate, though it may be said to have dragged on too long, is of interest for what it tells us of both Dickens' and Lewes' prickliness about their lack of formal education. Both were men of undistinguished origins now in positions of influence in the literary world. Lewes may have taken Dickens' 'mistake' too seriously, though he would probably have let the matter drop if Dickens had not insisted on his scientific authorities. But then, Lewes was concerned that literature, when not employing language symbolically, should use it correctly. Inasmuch as literature, especially the novel, reflects the world and has a wide influence on its readers, its practitioners should take care to be truthful and, where they claimed to inform, to inform accurately. Again we can see why it was that Lewes later recognised and encouraged George Eliot. In her novels she took pains to 'get it right' in matters legal (as in *Felix Holt*), historical (as in *Romola*), and scientific (as in *Middlemarch*). And for both Lewes and George Eliot it was an important element of the organic unity of human endeavour that the method of both literature and science be the scrupulous application of both imagination and verisimilitude. In the debate about spontaneous combustion, part of which is reproduced here, lie the seeds of Lewes' later disparagement of Dickens, while at the same time he continued to pay homage to Dickens' brilliant imaginativeness.

Though Lewes and Dickens kept up a friendly, gentlemanly tone in their private and public letters during 1852-3, it is probable that relations cooled thereafter. Only when Dickens, generously admiring *Adam Bede* (1859), sought in July 1859 to persuade the new novelist George Eliot to write a work of fiction to be serialised in his periodical *All the Year Round*, did the correspondence between the two men resume. Dickens, probably as part of his angling for George Eliot, asked Lewes to contribute a few light popularising articles on science [!] to both his papers, *Once a Week* and *All the Year Round*, between 1859 and 1861. The article 'Magic and Science' (*All the Year Round*, March 1861), in which Lewes distinguishes between real and pseudo-science by rapping the rappers, is included here as a good example of Lewes' ability in the lighter kind of journalism (see pp. 290-8). From this time until Dickens' death in 1870, the two men met socially, but Lewes, moving away from literary criticism in the 1860s, did not review any more of Dickens' works as they appeared, and, probably as a peace gesture, omitted entirely the *Bleak House* controversy when he once more dealt with the spontaneous combustion question in an article in *Blackwood's Magazine* in April 1861. His final words on Dickens are, as Trollope saw, the product of a critical mind both appreciative of Dickens' genius and clear-sighted about his faults.

The same is true of Lewes' equally intense, though perforce much briefer, relationship with Charlotte Brontë (who died in 1855). As with Dickens, Lewes' side of the correspondence has been lost, but Charlotte Brontë's preserved. Again, we find an author responding with gratitude to a discerning critic; again, Lewes' lost letters elicited interesting replies revealing an author's view of his (or her) creative process. When Smith, Elder & Co. accepted the unknown Currer Bell's novel *Jane Eyre* for publication in 1847, their reader William Smith Williams sent a copy to Lewes for review. Lewes later remembered, in response to Mrs Gaskell's request for help with her biography of Charlotte Brontë (1857), what had been his impression on reading the novel:

> When *Jane Eyre* first appeared, the publishers courteously sent me a copy. The enthusiasm with which I read it, made me go down to Mr. Parker, and propose to write a review of it for *Frazer's Magazine*. He would not consent to an unknown novel – for the papers had not yet declared themselves – receiving such importance, but thought it might make one on 'Recent Novels: English and French' – which appeared in *Frazer*, December, 1847. Meanwhile I had written to Miss Brontë to tell her the delight with which her book filled me; and seem to have 'sermonised' her, to judge from her reply.[40]

The relationship between novelist and critic which ensued is so interesting that, as with Dickens, I have decided to include part of the correspondence as well as some of Lewes' articles. Thus Charlotte Brontë's reply (6 November 1847) to Lewes' sermonising, with its obliging point-by-point answer to his lost but reconstructible remarks, is reprinted here (see pp. 87-8). It seems that in his letter, as well as in the *Fraser's* article in December, he praised her where she was true to experience and castigated her for what he saw as lapses from that standard. He opens his article on 'Recent Novels: French and English' with a general plea for 'truth in the delineation of life and character', singling out Fielding and, more particularly, Jane Austen for favourable comment (see p. 82). Then he launches into a paeon of praise for the 'reality' and the power of *Jane Eyre*: 'it fastens itself upon your attention, and will not leave you'. He sees at once that the novel is autobiographical, 'not, perhaps, in the naked facts and circumstances, but in the actual suffering and experience'. While mildly objecting to moments of melodrama and to the delineation of St John Rivers, the missionary, as having 'a touch of the circulating-library', he unequivocally tells the author, whom he assumes to be female, to 'persevere; keep reality distinctly before you, and paint it as accurately as you can' (see p. 87). A glance at other contemporary reviews of *Jane Eyre*, with their shocked tone and talk of immorality and coarseness, confirms how far ahead of his fellow reviewers Lewes was in his critical sense.[41]

Charlotte Brontë, a tyro in the matter of publishing, living in country isolation, viewed the London literary world, of which Lewes was such an established member, with awe tempered by mistrust. She responded directly to Lewes' praise and to his criticisms. After his first letter to her, she procured a copy of his novel *Ranthorpe* and wrote to him, eagerly overpraising it as a work which 'fills the mind with fresh knowledge' and which predisposed her to take his forthcoming review of *Jane Eyre* very seriously. 'You will be severe; your last letter taught me as much. Well! I shall try to extract good out of your severity.'[42]

She did. Thanking him on 12 January 1848 for his kind words in *Fraser's*, she soon got on to his criticisms, implied and actual. While she would try, in her next novel, to avoid melodrama, as he instructed her to, she was not inclined to take the suggested (ignominious) comparison with Jane Austen lying down. 'Why do you like Miss Austen so very much?' she asked. Never having read any of her predecessor's novels, she had taken Lewes' hint and read *Pride and Prejudice*. There follows one of Charlotte Brontë's now famous remarks about Jane Austen's 'accurate, daguerrotyped' portraits (see p. 89). Less than a week later a second letter tumbled out, adding to her critique of Jane Austen. In short, it was Lewes' criticism which piqued her into first reading Jane Austen (and later Balzac and George Sand, whose books Lewes lent her in 1850), then distinguishing her own talent from her rival's.

During 1848 and 1849, Charlotte Brontë kept in touch with Lewes' doings through Smith Williams. She was almost obsessed with the idea of this London critic who 'must be a man of no ordinary mind', who had a 'strange sagacity' and yet was, she felt, 'not always right'. She devoured his second novel, *Rose, Blanche, and Violet*, and felt able to criticise it (at least to Smith Williams) for the 'slightness' of its story and 'a touch too much of dogmatism'. Her fascination with Lewes emerges again: 'G.H. Lewes is, to my perceptions, decidedly the most original character in the book'.[43] A year later, in April 1849, she heard of Lewes' acting *début* in Manchester:

What you tell me of Mr. Lewes seems to me highly characteristic. How sanguine, versatile, and self-confident must that man be who can with ease exchange the quiet sphere of the author for the bustling one of the actor! I heartily wish him success; and, in happier times, there are few things I would have relished more than an opportunity of seeing him in his new character.[44]

Lewes' efforts on the stage must indeed have seemed remote from Charlotte, whose brother Branwell had died in September 1848, with her sister Emily following in December, and whose only remaining sister, Anne, had been diagnosed as terminally ill with consumption. Anne died in May 1849.

Unfortunately, the relationship with Lewes, so fruitful up to now, was to become strained with Lewes' next critical utterance on her work. No doubt she was now even more sensitive than before the family tragedies. Lewes, unaware of her situation, gave her next novel, *Shirley*, rather too rough a notice in the *Edinburgh Review* in January 1850. His article opened with some rather bitter humour about the possibility of women being equal to men in various walks of life, including authorship. A long paragraph on women's 'grand function' as 'maternity' ends with the odd question, 'What should we do with a leader of opposition in the seventh month of her pregnancy? or a general in chief who at the opening of a campaign was "doing as well as could be expected"? or a chief justice with twins?'[45] Presumably the mother-hood issue, though scarcely relevant to the literary of all professions, was much in Lewes' mind, for as this review was being written, Agnes was six months pregnant with her first child by Thornton Hunt, Edmund, born on 16 April 1850.

So one unhappy person wounds another. Lewes goes on to find *Shirley* not a 'pleasant' book, but one of 'over-masculine vigour' amounting even to 'coarseness'. Though praising the author's power in certain passages, he ends by exhorting Charlotte Brontë to aim at a gracefulness in her writing more suitable to her sex and more likely to allow her to 'take the rank within her reach'.

It is an uncharacteristically grudging review, and one of which Lewes was probably ashamed in later years. Indeed, after having generously lent Mrs Gaskell all Charlotte's letters to him for her use in the *Life*, he gently rebuked her for her adverse comments on the *Edinburgh Review* article:

> I have nothing but thanks for the way you have managed my slight episode. There is however one thing I could have wished, – and perhaps in a second edition, if your own judgement goes that way, you might insert a phrase respecting the 'Edinburgh' article, intimating that it is *not* a disrespectful article to women, although maintaining that in the *highest* efforts of intellect women have not equalled men. Lord Jeffrey tampered with the article, as usual, and inserted some to me offensive sentences, but the main argument – as far as I recollect it – is complimentary to women, not disrespectful.[46]

There is in this remonstrance some fudging, conscious or unconscious, for Francis Jeffrey had in 1850 long ceased to edit the *Edinburgh Review*, though it is true that he kept a close eye on its editorial affairs until his death in 1850.

Whatever his feelings about the *Shirley* review, Lewes magnanimously allowed Mrs Gaskell to print all Charlotte Brontë's letters to him, including her two bruised responses to his criticism. The first is brief, reading in its entirety:

> To G.H. Lewes, Esq.
> I can be on my guard against my enemies, but God deliver me from my friends!
>
> Currer Bell.

Thinking this rather unreasonable, Lewes wrote to her and received in reply a letter showing naked hurt but a proud desire to rise above it. She thought he had judged her not as an author, but as a woman, which made her 'grieved' and 'indignant'. Then follows a bold passage of criticism, *de haut en bas*, in which she presumes to characterise the man by whom she is fascinated at a distance, and whom she has never met:

> However, I will not bear malice against you for it; I know what your nature is: it is not a bad or unkind one, though you would often jar terribly on some feelings with whose recoil and quiver you could not possibly sympathise. I imagine you are at once sagacious and careless; you know much and discover much, but you are in such a hurry to tell it all you never give yourself time to think how your reckless eloquence may affect others; and, what is more, if you knew how it did affect them, you would not much care.
>
> However, I shake hands with you: you have excellent points; you can be generous. I still feel angry; but it is the anger one experiences for rough play rather than for foul play. I am yours, with a certain respect, and more chagrin,
>
> Currer Bell.[47]

Charlotte Brontë's interest in the man whom she thus astutely anatomised from afar did not abate. References to him as 'coarse' and 'conceited', but also as the author of articles she admires in his new paper, the *Leader*, pepper her letters to Smith Williams. Then in June 1850, on her second visit to London, she met Lewes at her publisher George Smith's house, and found, to her surprise, that he looked 'so wonderfully like Emily – her eyes, her features – the very nose, the somewhat prominent mouth, the forehead – even at moments the expression: whatever Lewes does or says I believe I cannot hate him.'[48]

This odd and touching comment was not quite her last respecting Lewes. She returned his Balzac and George Sand in October 1850, duly criticising Balzac's minuteness of detail and George Sand's aptness to be misled by her feelings. Her last letter to Lewes, on 23 November 1850, contains a hysterical, bitter onslaught on his and Thornton Hunt's liberal stance *vis-à-vis* the setting up of a Roman Catholic Archbishopric in London. Giving a taste of the anti-Catholic fervour which was to inform her last novel, *Villette*, she wrote:

> I have one pleasing duty to perform which I must not forget ere I conclude this letter – that is to congratulate you and all others whom it may concern on the pious disposition evinced by the *Leader* to walk bodily back to the True Fold....You ask me to write to your 'Open Council' [the *Leader*'s letters column]. I couldn't presume to do such a thing – but in another year – perhaps your columns will be consecrated by contributions from the Cardinal and letters from Father John Henry Newman.
> ...Wishing you and Mr. Thornton Hunt and all of you much felicity of speech in your first experiment in auricular confession, and a very full absolution from your awful heresies together with no heavier penance than the gravity of the case (which will be pretty stringent) shall seem absolutely to demand, – I am, Yours sincerely,
>
> C. Brontë.[49]

What Lewes the well-known freethinker made of this extraordinary letter, we do not know. Mrs Gaskell wisely omitted it from her biography, and Lewes himself heroically avoided any mention of Charlotte's ferocious anti-Catholicism in his review of *Villette* in the *Westminster Review*, April 1853. The article, included in this selection, divides its attention between Mrs Gaskell's *Ruth* and *Villette*, and has shrewd things to say about both. He calls the latter 'a work of astonishing power and passion' and openly admires its author's 'contempt of conventions in all things, in style, in thought, even in the art of story-telling' (see p. 101). Though not always happy with Charlotte Brontë's metaphors, which he says she 'runs to death sometimes', he pays tribute to the novel as 'prose poetry of the very highest order' (see p. 106).

Charlotte Brontë seems not to have responded to this review. Indeed, Lewes figures no more in her letters up to her death early in 1855. But their brief relationship, from 1847 to 1850, is one of the strangest and most interesting in literary history. And Lewes, in spite of his slip in the article on *Shirley*, remains her best contemporary critic.[50]

In his discussion of *Villette* and *Ruth*, Lewes addresses the question, 'Should a work of Art have a moral?' His answer is interesting. After quoting George Sand on, and adducing Goethe as an example of, the novelist as one whose narrative can 'prove nothing', being merely an illustration of a particular case, he goes on to suggest that, nevertheless, the reader's moral sense requires to be gratified. But this need not happen through what George Eliot was to call 'copybook morality' in an essay grappling with the same problem in 1855.[51] Indeed, it is best if the novel 'carry within it, not one but many moral illustrations, naturally arising out of the way the incidents are grouped, and the way the characters express themselves' (see p. 92). This describes precisely what Lewes himself had failed to do as a novelist and what George Eliot was soon to become preeminent at doing. Meanwhile, Lewes praises *Ruth* for largely succeeding in carrying its moral in the story. Though the 'fallen woman' is here made perhaps too innocent, according to Lewes, Mrs Gaskell's instinct to show tolerance and allow natural feelings to emerge from unhappy wrongdoing is correct. Lewes' own tolerance is on display here, and is of particular interest given his situation in 1853, living in friendly estrangement from his wife and supporting the children she continued to have by Thornton Hunt.

The last of the great contemporary novelists whose works Lewes reviewed was Thackeray. With him Lewes had a cordial relationship from beginning to end. As with the others, Lewes began with a pleasant review and was rewarded by a letter of thanks. In Thackeray's case, it was Lewes' discussion of *The Book of Snobs* and *Vanity Fair* in the *Morning Chronicle* in March 1848 which drew a response. In his short review, reprinted here, he praised Thackeray's satirical genius, while finding 'something terrible' in the impartiality of Thackeray's laughter. He complained, though in a friendly way, that 'all the people' in *Vanity Fair* are 'scamps, scoundrels, or humbugs' (see p. 109). This led Thackeray, in his letter of thanks for the 'sincere goodwill of my critic', to admit the 'dismal roguery' of *Vanity Fair*, but to claim that the world was pretty much like that (see p. 113).

Lewes returned to the subject of *Vanity Fair* in an article in the *Athenaeum* in August 1848, in which, while again giving due praise to Thackeray's wit, he complained that Thackeray was a careless constructor of plot and lacked passion – a 'serious deficiency' in a writer of fiction.[52] Lewes once again goes to the heart of Thackeray's strengths and weaknesses as a novelist, giving evidence of his early and consistent emphasis on the necessity of taking fiction seriously, and the necessity for fiction to be both imaginative and true to life, both entertaining and earnest. In his review of *Pendennis* in December 1850, reprinted here, Lewes again complains of Thackeray's 'want of respect for his art', while finding that, like Goethe, Thackeray writes in both a loving and a mocking spirit (see p. 116).

Lewes and Thackeray met socially during the 1850s and in 1860 they collaborated on George Smith's new periodical, the *Cornhill Magazine*. Thackeray edited it, Trollope serialised his novels in it, and Lewes wrote the scientific articles. His *Studies in Animal Life* appeared in six-monthly parts during 1860. Early in 1862 Thackeray, both too ill and too neurotic to be an effective editor of a magazine (he could not bring himself to reject contributions unequivocally), resigned.[53] Smith, like Dickens before him having his eye on George Eliot, offered Lewes the editorship. Lewes, also ill and wishing to devote his time to physiological and psychological studies, refused. But he did become 'chief literary adviser' at a salary of £600 per annum. (And George Eliot did take the bait this time; she accepted the unprecedented offer of £10,000 for her next novel. *Romola* was duly published in parts in the *Cornhill* in 1862-3.[54]) Thackeray died in 1863. Lewes continued to write lighthearted popular science articles for the *Cornhill Magazine*.

He also wrote more serious scientific articles, particularly in the *Fortnightly Review*, which he edited in 1865 and 1866, and to which he continued to contribute, after giving up the editorship on health grounds. The *Fortnightly Review* broke new ground among British periodicals by insisting on its articles being signed. It also included, under Lewes' management, a regular editorial column headed 'Causeries'. In these pages Lewes covered current affairs in general literature and in science – much as he had done anonymously in the *Leader* in the 1850s – with particular emphasis on science. In September 1866 he noticed, and quoted from, the Proceedings of the British Association for the Advancement of Science (to which he had himself contributed three papers in 1859). In his 'Farewell Causerie' in December 1866, before handing over the editorship to John Morley, he reviewed the year's events, singling out Huxley's *Lessons in Elementary Physiology* as a good clear textbook for pupils and teachers.

It is also worth recording that, though Lewes was in 1866 not a particularly political animal, he picked out of all the international events of the year the meeting of the Karl Marx-inspired First International as the most 'historic'. Here is how Lewes presciently describes it:

> A study of history will...disclose to the philosophic eye certain characteristics which give significance to phenomena seemingly unimportant; and this study will enable us to see something eminently significant in one of the events of 1866, – not noisy at all, not discussed in newspapers and public meetings, but certain to be one day referred to as the starting-point of a new epoch. What is this? Ask the press what have been the great topics of this year of noises. They have been the cattle-plague, the [financial] panic, the disclosures of railway mismanagement, the agitation for Reform, the Fenians, the conflict of the President with Congress, the Seven Days' War, ending in the expulsion of Austria from Germany, and the freedom of Italy from a foreign yoke. These are, some of them at least, events of importance, but the philosophic student will probably see far more significance in an event which was neither imposing in outward aspect, nor suggestive in its prophecies to the ordinary mind: that event is the Congress of Workmen in Geneva.[55]

Though Lewes bowed out as editor on this impressive note, he remained a frequent contributor to the *Fortnightly Review*. In 1868 he wrote four intelligent essays on 'Mr. Darwin's Hypotheses', the first of which is reproduced here. These articles undertake to explain natural selection and other elements in Darwin's theory of species by reference to the history of thought and Darwin's uniquely valuable contribution to it: 'No work of our time has been so general in its influence' (see p. 299). Lewes also criticises some of Darwin's suggestions, particularly in the later essays not included here. In the main, where Lewes differs he does so on Lamarckian grounds, seeming to accept the now discredited hypothesis of Lamarck that species may inherit acquired characteristics. (An example of this non-Darwinian view would be that giraffes have over the years acquired, and passed on to their descendents, long necks by dint of stretching to reach the leaves on the tallest trees; the accepted view is rather that those with long necks survived because of their ability to reach tall trees.) But Lewes staunchly upholds Darwin's 'Development Hypothesis' as 'the best hypothesis at present before the world' (see p. 301).

These papers on Darwin, with some earlier brief reviews of his *Variations of Animals and Plants under Domestication* (1868), caused Darwin to seek Lewes out. The three notices of this work appeared in February 1868 in George Smith's daily newspaper, the *Pall Mall Gazette*. Darwin wrote to his friend Hooker, saying he was 'excessively pleased' by the first notice on 10 February: 'If by any chance you should hear who wrote the article in the *Pall Mall*, do please tell me; it is some one who writes capitally, and who knows the subject'. He signs the letter, 'Your cock-a-hoop friend, C.D'.[56] Darwin and Lewes became friendly, with the former introducing the latter to the Linnaeus Society in 1869.

In January 1874 both men were present, as sceptical observers, at a spiritualist séance, the 1870s' successor to the table-rapping craze of the 1850s, held at Darwin's brother's house. Darwin reported the event:

> We had grand fun, one afternoon, for George [Wedgwood] hired a medium, who made the chairs, a flute, a bell, a candlestick, and fiery points jump about in my brother's dining-room, in a manner that astounded every one, and took away all their breaths.... I went away before all these astounding miracles, or jugglery, took place.... The Lord have mercy on us all, if we have to believe in such rubbish.[57]

Lewes commented more tersely in his diary for 16 January 1874: 'After lunch we went to a spiritualist séance at Erasmus Darwin's. The Charles Darwin family, Myers, Mrs. Bowen, Galton &c there. But as complete darkness was insisted on we left in disgust.'[58]

Lewes continued to be an admiring supporter of serious science and a mocker of pseudo-scientific enthusiasms. The last article he wrote, reproduced here, was a clear but passionate defence of science as a 'bringer of aid' and a 'bringer of light'. In this essay, 'On the Dread and Dislike of Science' (*Fortnightly Review*, June 1878), he combats popular fears of scientific advance. The immediate cause of the article was the topical debate on vivisection. A Royal Commission had been set up in 1875 to report on the treatment of animals in laboratories. Anti-vivisection societies sprang up and successfully lobbied Parliament, resulting in the Cruelty to Animals Act of 1876, which, while allowing experiments on live animals, sought to regulate the conditions under which they were carried out. Agitation on both sides continued, with Darwin and Lewes, among other scientists, on the side of vivisection.[59] Lewes contributed on the topic to *Nature*, a weekly illustrated journal of science, in 1876.

In his *Fortnightly Review* article Lewes makes the trenchant point that while cruelty to animals for the sake of scientific and medical advance for the many creates an outcry, fox-hunting and other pursuits carried out for the sake of the pleasure of the few are approved or silently condoned. Having exposed the hypocrisy of this, Lewes opens out the discussion to include a historical review of thought, going back to the old conflict between science and theology. The article is a suitable one with which to finish this selection of Lewes' critical writings, for in it he shows a consistency in his thinking from the earliest writings on philosophy, history and science. Comte is once more invoked. The empirical method is once again embraced as the one true way of advancing knowledge. The last essay of a sick man of sixty-one ends on a ringing note of optimism based on faith in scientific progress (see p. 326):

> When Science has fairly mastered the principles of moral relations as it has mastered the principles of physical relations, all Knowledge will be incorporated in a homogeneous doctrine rivalling that of the old theologies in its comprehensiveness, and surpassing it in the authority of its credentials.

The chief characteristics of this selection are two. The emphasis just placed on Lewes' consistency of view and purpose must share our attention with an equal emphasis on his extraordinary range of interest and ability, his quite unusual versatility. It was this which his contemporaries noticed more than anything else. According to Frederick Greenwood, the editor of the *Pall Mall Gazette*, Lewes could 'get up' any subject, 'so versatile was he, so lucid, so sparkling and adept'.[60] The essays reproduced here show these qualities again and again, as well as giving us a privileged insight into the multifarious concerns of the Victorian period, from the ephemera of table-rapping and séances to the lasting influences of a Dickens in literature and a Darwin in science.

Notes to Introduction

1. Trollope, Anthony, 'George Henry Lewes', *Fortnightly Review*, XXV, new series (January 1879), p. 15.
2. Espinasse, Francis, *Literary Recollections* (London, 1893), p. 276.
3. *Dramatic Essays by John Forster and George Henry Lewes*, (ed.) William Archer and Robert Lowe, (London, 1896).
4. Shaw, George Bernard, *Saturday Review* (20 June 1896); reprinted in *Our Theatres in the Nineties*, 3 vols (London, 1932), II, p. 161.
5. Shaw, George Bernard, *Saturday Review* (5 June 1897), ibid., III, p. 155.
6. *On Actors and the Art of Acting* (published by Smith, Elder & Co, 1875; reprinted by H. Holt & Co., New York, 1878, and twice reprinted more recently by Grove Press, 1957, and by Greenwood Press, 1968).
7. *The Principles of Success in Literature* (published by Bosqui, San Francisco, 1885, followed by several new editions, English and American, up to 1969, when Gregg International Publishers Ltd reissued it with an introduction by Geoffrey Tillotson).
8. Southam, B.C. (ed.), *Jane Austen: The Critical Heritage* (London, 1968). Southam is typical, claiming that 'Lewes' superiority to his fellow-critics is not in doubt', pp. 28-9.
9. Rt. Hon. Sir Mountstuart E. Grant Duff, *Notes from a Diary 1873-1881*, 2 vols (London, 1898), II, p. 88.
10. See Pavlov, Ivan Petrovitch, *Lectures on Conditioned Reflexes*, tr. W. Horsley Gantt, 2 vols (London, 1963), I, p. 13, and II, p. 170n.
11. Huxley, Thomas Henry, *Westminster Review*, V, new series (January 1854), p. 256.
12. See Robertson, J.C. (ed.), *Mind* (January 1876, January 1878, October 1881).
13. Lewes, G.H., 'Goethe as a Man of Science', *Westminster Review*, II, new series (October 1852), p. 479.
14. See Ashton, Rosemary, *The German Idea: Four English Writers and the Reception of German Thought 1800-1860* (Cambridge, 1980).
15. George Eliot changed her name from Mary Ann to Marian Evans during her first years in London, 1850-1. See Haight, G.S. (ed.), *The George Eliot Letters*, 9 vols (New Haven, Connecticut, 1954-6, 1978), vol. I. After 1854 she called herself Marian Lewes.
16. See J.S. Mill to G.H. Lewes, late 1840, about his Shelley article for the *Westminster Review*, in *The Earlier Letters of John Stuart Mill*, (ed.) F.E. Mineka, vol. XIII (Toronto, 1963), pp. 448-9; *Collected Works* in progress.
17. George Eliot to Charles Bray (8 October 1851), and to Caroline Bray (16 April 1853), *The George Eliot Letters*, I, p. 367, II, p. 98.

18. Bohn and Lewes disputed the terms of their agreement, and Marian's translation of the *Ethics* remained unpublished until it was printed with an introduction by Thomas Deegan (Salzburg, 1981).

19. By 1857 the *Biographical History of Philosophy* had sold 40,000 copies, and a new edition was prepared. Lewes went on revising and reprinting the work until 1871.

20. Lewes, G.H., 'The Principles of Success in Literature', No. I, *Fortnightly Review*, (May 1865), I, pp. 86-7.

21. See p. 239. Compare Coleridge's famous definition of the Imagination in ch. 13 of *Biographia Literaria* (1817): 'The imagination...dissolves, diffuses, dissipates, in order to re-create; or where this process is rendered impossible, yet still, at all events, it struggles to idealize and to unify.... The fancy is indeed no other than a mode of memory emancipated from the order of time and space.... But equally with the ordinary memory it must receive all its materials ready made from the law of association', *The Collected Works of Samuel Taylor Coleridge*, see Coburn, Kathleen (ed.), 16 vols (Princeton, New Jersey, 1969-), VII.1 (1983), pp. 304-5.

22. Tillotson, Geoffrey (ed.), *The Principles of Success in Literature* (London, 1969), p. ii.

23. See, for example, *Adam Bede*, chs 27 and 50, and the Introduction to *Felix Holt*.

24. Lewes, G.H., 'Browning and the Poetry of the Age', *British Quarterly Review* (November 1847), VI, pp. 497ff.

25. Lewes, G.H., 'Charles Lamb and his Friends', *British Quarterly Review* (November 1848), VIII p. 382.

26. Shaw, George Bernard, *Our Theatres in the Nineties*, II, p. 162.

27. Jane Welsh Carlyle to Thomas Carlyle (13 April 1848), in *Letters and Memorials of Jane Welsh Carlyle*, (ed.) J.A. Froude, 3 vols (London, 1883), II, p. 34. As early as 1852 Lewes wrote to R.H. Horne that he 'disavowed' *Ranthorpe* (MS Harry Ransom Humanities Research Center, University of Texas at Austin).

28. Dickens to Lewes (9 June 1838), in *Letters of Charles Dickens*, (ed.) Madeleine House, Graham Storey, *et al.* (Oxford, 1965-; 6 vols so far), I, p. 403. Henceforth referred to as the Pilgrim Edition.

29. Forster, John, *The Life of Charles Dickens*, 3 vols (London, 1872-4), III, p. 304.

30. 'George Henry Lewes', *Fortnightly Review*, XXV, new series (January 1879), pp. 22-3.

31. Dickens to Lewes (15 June 1847), in *Letters of Charles Dickens*, Pilgrim Edition, V, p. 91.

32. For Lewes' part in Dickens' company, 1847-8, see ibid., V, pp. 91ff, and Walter Dexter, 'For One Night Only: Dickens's Appearances as an Amateur Actor', *The Dickensian*, (1940), XXXVI, pp. 20-32.

33. Cuttings in the Forster Collection, Victoria and Albert Museum. The reference to Lewes' shortness of stature draws attention to one reason why Lewes failed as a tragic actor: his physical presence was not strong. See his remarks on an actor's need for 'physical advantages' in his celebration of Macready in the *Leader* (1851), p. 31.

34. Lewes' review of Bulwer's play in the *Leader* (21 June 1851) is reprinted here (see pp. 33-5).

35. Dickens to Sheridan Muspratt (4 June 1849), *Letters of Charles Dickens*, Pilgrim Edition, V, p. 550.

36. *Leader* (12 February 1853), p.163.

37. Dickens to Elliotson (7 February 1853), in *The Letters of Charles Dickens*, (ed.) Walter Dexter, 3 vols (London, 1938), II, pp. 446-7.

38. Dickens to Lewes (25 February 1853), in G.S. Haight, 'Dickens and Lewes on Spontaneous Combustion', *Nineteenth Century Fiction* (1955-6), X, pp. 58, 60. See also Trevor Blount, 'Dickens and Mr. Krook's Spontaneous Combustion', *Dickens Studies Annual* (1970), I, pp. 183-213; E. Gaskell, 'More About Spontaneous Combustion', *The Dickensian*, (1973), LXIX, pp. 25-35; and Peter Denman, 'Krook's Death and Dickens's Authorities', *The Dickensian* (1987), LXXXIII, pp. 131-141.

39. *Leader* (3 September 1853), p. 858.

40. Gaskell, Elizabeth, *The Life of Charlotte Brontë* (London, 1857; reprinted Everyman's Library, 1971), p. 233.

41. See Allott, Miriam (ed.), *The Brontës: The Critical Heritage* (London, 1974).

42. Charlotte Brontë to Lewes (22 November 1847), in *The Brontës: Their Lives, Friendships and Correspondence*, (ed.) T.J. Wise and A.J. Symington, 4 vols (Oxford, 1932), II, p. 156.

43. Charlotte Brontë to William Smith Williams (11 December 1847 and 26 April 1848), ibid., II, pp. 159, 206.

44. Charlotte Brontë to Smith Williams (5 April 1849), ibid., II, p. 322.

45. Lewes, G.H., 'Currer Bell's Shirley', *Edinburgh Review* (January 1850), XCI, p. 155.

46. Lewes to Mrs Gaskell (15 April 1857), *The George Eliot Letters*, II, pp. 315-6.

47. Charlotte Brontë to Lewes (undated letter, January 1850), *The Brontës*, III, pp. 67, 68.

48. Charlotte Brontë to Ellen Nussey (12 June 1850), ibid., III, p. 118.

49. Charlotte Brontë to Lewes (23 November 1850), ibid., III, pp. 183-4.

50. See Miriam Allott's comments in the introduction to *The Brontës: The Critical Heritage*, p. 24. For an interesting account of part of Lewes' relationship with Charlotte Brontë see Franklin Gary, 'Charlotte Brontë and George Henry Lewes', *Publications of the Modern Language Association of America* (June 1956), LI, pp. 518-42.

51. Eliot, George, '*Westward Ho!* and *Constance Herbert*', *Westminster Review* (July 1855), *Essays of George Eliot*, (ed.) Thomas Pinney, (New

York, 1963), p. 134.

52. Lewes, G.H., review of *Vanity Fair*, *Athenaeum*, No. 1085 (12 August 1848), p. 795.

53. There is a series of unpublished letters from Thackeray to George Smith about his troubles with the editorship (Manuscript Department, National Library of Scotland).

54. See Haight, G.S., *George Eliot: A Biography* (Oxford, 1969), p. 354ff.

55. Lewes, G.H., 'Farewell Causerie', *Fortnightly Review* (December 1866), VI, pp. 891-2.

56. Darwin to J.D. Hooker (10 February 1868), in *The Life and Letters of Charles Darwin*, (ed.) Francis Darwin, 3 vols (London, 1887), III, p. 76.

57. Darwin (letter of 18 January 1874), ibid., III, p. 187.

58. Lewes's diary for 1874 (MS Beinecke Library, Yale University).

59. See *Vivisection in Historical Perspective*, (ed.) Nicolaas Rupke, (London, 1987).

60. See Robertson Scott, J.W., *The Story of the 'Pall Mall Gazette'* (London, 1950), p. 148.

'Vivian': Dramatic Criticism
in the Leader (1851-2)

Was Macready a Great Actor? (8 February 1851)

The greatest—incomparably so—of all living tragedians concluded his farewell performances at the Haymarket, on Monday last, amidst the frantic bravos of a loving and regretting public. Although his farewell to the public will be bidden on the occasion of his benefit (fixed for the 26th instant), yet we may say that on Monday last he bade farewell to the stage. He has left it for ever. His career as an Actor is closed. We may select his niche in the Pantheon. The Actor is dead, and can no longer strut his brief hour on the stage. The curtain drops—the house empties—the lights are extinguished—silence, cold and cheerless, succeeds to the loud acclamations which made the vaulted roof reverberate erewhile—the Tragedian is washing the paint off his face, and in another hour will be in the retired privacy of his quiet happy home! The mask is laid aside—and for ever.

Considering Macready, then, as dead—as I am bound to consider him in a theatrical sense—I will try to answer the questions which my children and their friends are sure to ask me some day when I am running down *their* idolised tragedian, and try to spoil their pleasures by cheapening their 'dear delightful Mr_____,' and assuring them I had seen 'Edmund Kean and Macready in that part,'—the question, namely, 'Was Macready a great Actor?' '*To say nothing but good of the dead*,' is a maxim for which I have always felt but a mediocre respect, mainly, perhaps, because the medal bears on the reverse side, '*To say nothing but evil of the living*.' While a statesman or an artist lives, envy and all uncharitableness assail him; no sooner does the bell toll for his funeral than those who yesterday were foremost to assail, now become elegiac in their grief and hyperbolic in their eulogium. It has always seemed to me that the contrary would be the more generous as well as the more advantageous method. When blame ceases to give pain I see no reason why it should be spared; when adverse criticism can 'instruct the public' and yet not hurt an artist's fortunes, then is the time for the critic to speak without reservation—*then* let us have the truth in all its energy!

Do not suppose this to be a preface to an 'attack' upon the fine actor who has just quitted the scene. My purpose is far from polemical. I merely wish, in the way of conversation, to jot down such hints towards an appreciation of his talent as have occurred to me; and as, with all my admiration, I must

29

still qualify the praise by advancing objections which thorough-going admirers will pronounce heresies, I claim, at the outset, the right of saying of the dead all the evil I think, and not of garlanding the tomb with artificial flowers.

It is a question often mooted in private, whether Macready was a *great* actor, or only an intelligent actor, or (for this, too, is not unfrequently said) an intrinsically bad actor. The last opinion is uttered by some staunch admirers of Kemble and Young, and by those critics who, looking at the drama as an *imitation of Nature*, dwell upon the exaggerations and other false colours wherewith Macready paints, and proclaim him, consequently, a bad artist. Now, in discussing a subject like the present, it is imperative that we understand *the point of view* from which we both look at it.

I am impressed with the conviction that the majority mistakes Art for an *imitation* of Nature. It is no such thing. Art is *representation*. This is why too close an approach to Reality in Art is shocking; why coloured statues are less agreeable—except to the vulgarest minds—than the colourless marble.

Without pausing to expound that principle, I beg the reader will, for the present at least, take my word for its accuracy, that I may be able to place him at my point of view. Taking Art as a Representative rather than as an Imitative process (including imitation only as one of its *means* of representation), I say that the test of an actor's genius is not 'fidelity to Nature', but simply and purely his power of exciting emotions in you respondent to the situation—ideal when that is ideal, passionate when that is passionate, familiar when that is familiar, prosaic when that is prosaic. A bad actor mouths familiar prose as if it were the loftiest verse; but a good actor (such as Bouffé or Charles Mathews), if he were to play ideal characters with the same familiarity and close adherence to Nature as that which makes his performance of familiar parts charming, would equally sin against the laws of Art.

Let me go some distance back for an illustration. In Greek tragedy, acting, as we understand it, was impossible. Addressing an audience of thirty thousand (I give you the number on the authority of Plato), all of whom, like true democrats, insisted on hearing and seeing, the unassisted voice and the unaided proportions of the actor would of course have been useless. A contrivance considerably raised and amplified the man's stature, while his voice was assisted by a bronze mask with a round hole at the mouth, through which the actor spoke as through a speaking-trumpet. Now I ask you to place yourself upon stilts and shout 'To be or not to be,' through a speaking-trumpet, and *then* answer me whether acting were possible under *such* conditions!

This mask gives me the image I am in want of to convey my meaning. The Latin word *persona* is derived from thence, and *dramatis personae* may be translated '*The masks through which the actors speak.*' Whether the actor dons a veritable mask of bronze, or whether he throws it aside and makes a mask of his own face, he is still only personating, *i.e.* speaking through a mask, *i.e.* representing. The Greeks had twenty-six different classes of masks, and bestowed immense pains on them. 'There be actors that I have seen play, and heard some applaud too,' who had but *one* invariable mask—and that a bad one—for every part. *Ma non ragioniam di lor!*

Taking, then, the masks as types of the various characters an actor has to play (to *personate*, as we correctly say), you see at once what a very different thing it was for the Greek actor to go to some antique Nathan and choose his mask, and for the modern who has to invent and make up his own mask with his own limited materials! Many actors, nay, the vast majority, do still go to some Nathan's and borrow a *traditional* mask; just as many poetasters go to the common fund for images, similes, rhymes and rhythms, or as politicians re-issue the old and well-worn currency of sophisms, facts, and paralogisms. So few men can compose their own masks.

To compose a mask, or, if you like it, to personate a character, there are three fundamental requisite conditions, which I will call—(1) *Conceptual Intelligence*; (2) *Representative Intelligence*; (3) *Physical Advantages*. The first condition is requisite to *understand* the character; the two last are requisite in different degrees to *represent* the character. High poetic culture, knowledge of human nature, sympathy with elemental states of passion, and all that we understand by a fine intellect, will assist the actor in his *study* of the character, but it will do no more. The finest intellect in the world would not enable a man to play Hamlet or Othello finely. Shakespeare himself couldn't do it; but wisely cast himself (Oh! the lesson to actor-managers!) as the Ghost. There are other requisites besides conception. There is the second requisite (what I have called representative intelligence), under which may be included the intelligent observation and reproduction of *typical* gestures, looks, tones—the mimetic power of imitating pecularities. This requisite is possessed by actors oftener than the first. Without fine intellect it makes respectable actors; carried to a certain degree and accompanied with certain physical advantages it makes remarkable actors, especially in the comic line. The third requisite, which I have named physical advantages, includes person, deportment, voice, and physical power. Too little consideration is devoted to that, yet it is enough of itself to make or mar an actor. All the intellect in the world, all the representative intelligence in the world, could not enable a man with a weak voice, limited in its compass, unless compensated by some peculiar effects in tone, to perform Othello, Macbeth, Shylock, etc., with success. Whereas a noble presence, a fine voice, and a moderate degree of representative intelligence, with no appreciable amount of conceptual intelligence, have sufficed to draw the town ere now, and make even critics believe a great actor has appeared.

Having thus briefly indicated what I conceive to be the leading principles in the philosophy of acting, I proceed to apply them to Macready; and first say that, inasmuch as he possesses in an unusual degree the three requisites laid down, he must be classed among the *great* actors. His conceptual

intelligence every one will acknowledge. Even those to whom his peculiarities are offensive admit that he is a man of intellect, of culture. But I do
not go along with those who exalt his intellect into greatness. I am not aware
of any manifestation of greatness he has given. His conception always
betrays care and thought, and never betrays foolishness. On the other hand,
I never received any light from him to clear up an obscurity; my knowledge
of Shakespeare is little increased by his performances. I cannot point to any
one single trace of illumination—such as Edmund Kean used to flash out.
This may be my fault; but I am here recording individual impressions, and I
say that Macready's knowledge of Shakespeare and his art, unquestionable
though it be, does not prove to me the greatness of intellect which his ardent
admirers assume for him. The intelligence most shown by Macready is that
which I have named representative intelligence, and which he possesses in
a remarkable degree. Certain pecularities and defects prevent his representing the high, heroic, passionate characters; but nothing can surpass his
representation of some others; and connecting this representative intelligence with his physical advantages, we see how he can execute what he
conceives, and thus become an actor. His voice—one primary requisite of
an actor—is a fine one, powerful, extensive in compass, and containing tones
that thrill, and tones that weep. His person is good, and his face very
expressive. So that give him a character within his proper range and he will
be great in it; and even the greatest of actors can only perform certain
characters for which their representative intelligence and physical organisation fit them.

'I wish I had not seen Macready in *Macbeth*. I saw him in Werner, and
came away with such an impression of his power that I regret having seen
his Macbeth, which completely destroys my notion of him.' That was the
phrase I heard the other day at dinner, and it seemed to me a good text for a
criticism on Macready; for if the real test of an actor be that he raises emotions
in you respondent to the situation, then assuredly does Macready stand this
test whenever the situation be *not* of a grand, abstract, ideal nature. The
anguish of a weak, timid, prostrate mind he can represent with a sorrowing
pathos, as great as Kean in the heroic agony of Othello; and in all the touching
domesticities of tragedy he is unrivalled. But he fails in the characters which
demand impassioned grandeur, and a certain *largo* of execution. His Macbeth and Othello have fine touches, but they are essentially unheroic—their
passion is fretful and irritable, instead of being broad, vehement, overwhelming. His Hamlet is too morbid, irritable, and lachrymose. Lear is his finest
Shakespearian character—because the fretfulness and impatience of the old
man come within the range of Macready's representative powers, of which
the terrible curse may be regarded as the climax. King John, Richard II, Iago
and Cassius are also splendid performances; in each we trace the same
characteristic appeal to the actor's peculiar powers. Although you can see
him in no part without feeling that an artist is before you, yet if you think of

him as a great actor, it is as Werner, Lear, Virginius, Richelieu, King John, Richard II, Iago—not as Othello, Macbeth, Hamlet, Coriolanus. Nor is this any ground of objection. Every actor is by nature fitted for certain characters, and unfitted for others. I believe Macready to be radically unfitted for ideal characters—for the display of broad elemental passions—for the representation of grandeur, moral or physical; and I believe him peculiarly fitted for the irritable, the tender, and the domestic; he can depict rage better than passion, anguish better than mental agony, misery better than despair, tenderness better than the abandonment of love. But the things he can do he does surpassingly well; and for this, also, I must call him a great actor.

The tricks and mannerisms which others copy, and which objectors suffer to outweigh all other qualities, I need waste no words on here. He was great in spite of them, as Kean was in spite of his.

Summing up these remarks into a compact sentence, I answer the question put by my imaginary questioners thus: 'Yes, Macready *was* a great actor. Though not a man of genius, he was a man of intellect, of culture, of representative talent, with decided physical advantages, capable of depicting a wide range of unheroic characters with truth and power, an ornament to his profession, the pride of his friends, and the favourite of the public. He gained his position when Kean and Young were on the stage; when they left it he stood alone. His departure left a blank. There was no successor; none capable of bending the bow of Ulysees.'

Before I conclude this incomplete notice let me, in extenuation of what may seem severity, observe that I have throughout criticised according to an abstract standard of the Art, and not according to the present condition of the stage. I might easily and conscientiously have written a panegyric; but there would have been half the real compliment in it there is in the foregoing attempt at philosophic analysis, though blame may have been 'precipitated' by the analysis. True, very true, the adage, 'Art is difficult, Criticism easy'; but there is something far easier than Criticism, and that is panegyric!

Not so Bad as We Seem[1] (21 June 1851)

You never read Petronius Arbiter, of course: he is too improper! I have. But to the pure all things are pure! This, however, I will say, that although scholars may prize the *Satyricon* for its pictures of Roman life and its occasional glimpses of elegance and poetry, the careful parent will *not* place it in the hands of his daughters. Among the few things I noted in that chaos of pruriency was one passage about the poverty of authors, where our ill-clad poet proudly drapes himself in his rags, and answering the question of wherefore he is so ill-clad, replies with a dignified sadness—Because the love of letters never yet made men wealthy. *Quare ergo, inquam, tam male vestitus es? Propter hoc ipsum, ait; Amor ingenii neminem unquam divitem fecit.* That has been true of all times, and is likely to continue so; but if we cannot keep authors from being poor, cannot we do something towards making them more *provident*? Such is the thought at the bottom of the scheme for a *Guild of Literature and Art*; and although doctors may differ as to the details of the scheme itself, there will, I suppose, be but one sentiment with respect to the original intention and the generosity of its promoters.

A crowded audience at the Hanover Square Rooms, on Wednesday, assembled to see the amateurs in their new play; unfortunately there were but few who could sit or see comfortably, owing to the cramped space, and the platform not being raised. This may have had something to do with the effect of weariness which attended the performance; but the great fault was in the comedy itself. It may seem indelicate to criticise too closely a play written for such an object and under such circumstances; indeed, were the author less able to afford objection than Sir Edward Lytton, I should not whisper it; but he has been too successful not to perceive himself that the present comedy is too slow in its movement, and too hazy in its plot; nor will I pay him the bad compliment of saying it is to be reckoned among his successes—except for an occasional touch, and for the spirit which prompted him in writing it. Curiously enough, too, the amateurs are for the most part less admirable in these characters written for them than in those written two centuries ago! The reader has not now to be told what excellent actors some of these amateurs are, nor how charming the effect is of a play performed by men of education and refinement, so that even the insignificant parts have a certain *cachet d'élégance*; but to those who have seen these actors in *Not so Bad as We Seem*, for the first time, it is but just to say that no adequate idea of their powers can be formed. Frank Stone, indeed, is richer in the Duke of Middlesex than in any part he has yet attempted; but Dickens, except in the personation of Curl, where he gave a glimpse of his humour, and Lemon, and Forster, and Jerrold, and Costello, and Topham, and Egg, were incomparably better in *Every Man in his Humour*, or *The Merry Wives of Windsor*.[2] I do not think a company of actors could be now found to play *these* pieces with greater charm of ensemble.

I am told that the farce *Mr Nightingale's Diary* is a scream, and that therein Dickens and Lemon show what they are capable of; but I was forced to leave after the comedy, having 'to fry some *feesh*,' as a German lady of my acquaintance used to say.

It is a pleasant sight to see these authors and artists assembled together in such a cause; and the buzz of friendly curiosity, as each new actor comes upon the stage, keeps the audience on the alert. The scene in Will's Coffee-house, for example, allowed the public to see their benefactor, Charles Knight, as Tonson, the celebrated bookseller; and Peter Cunningham bodily present in a scene he inhabits mentally; and Horne as the terrible Colonel (a capital bit of acting, by the way!), and Marston, whose Sir Thomas Timid was a bit of nature.

The stage is extremely pretty, and the scenery, dresses, and general getting up, betray the vigilance and taste of artists. The figures all looked like portraits. Forster seemed as if he had just the instant before jostled Walpole; Lemon reminded me forcibly of Dr Johnson; and Egg looked quite grand as the poor proud author.

Vivian in Tears! (7 February 1852)
(*All along of Mr Kean*)

What a thing is Life! The remark is novel and profound—its application you will appreciate on hearing my appeal. Yesterday I was the gayest of the gay, blithe and joyous as a young bird before family cares perplex it in its calculations of worms; to-day you see me struck from that sunny altitude into the gloom of immeasurable despondency! Weep! weep with me, ye that have any tears! Let me, like a Prometheus of private life, fling my clamorous agonies upon the winds, and call upon every feeling heart to listen to my 'billowy ecstasy of woe!'

Hear it, ye winds—Charles Kean has cut me off the Free List!

No more! never never more, am I to enjoy the exquisite privilege of seeing that poetic eye, 'in fine foolishness rolling!'—no more! never never more, am I to listen to that musical utterance of verse, that delicate expression given to subtle meanings! I am banished. Charles Kean closes his door upon me! He courted me, and courted my criticism—then I was happy! then I was proud! then I knew where to spend an intellectual evening; but now, alas! that glory is departed; it now appears that he did not like my criticism, and he cruelly robs me of my only enjoyment—the privilege of seeing him act! He humbles me, he saddens me, he leaves me no refuge but misanthropy! Oh, *why* didn't I write more glowingly about his genius; *why* did I not, by some critical alchemy, convert his peculiarities into talents; *why* did I not discover eloquence in his pauses, variety and expression in his gestures, and intelligence in his conceptions? Fool that I was! I might have laughed at him amongst his friends, as remorselessly as they do, and still have preserved my precious privilege of free admission to the Princess' Theatre; but now!...As the not more unfortunate Philoctetes, banished from his loved Hellas, roamed disconsolate about the isle, so I pace Oxford Street with pale wistful glances, exclaiming:

αλλ οι μεν εκβαλοντες ανοσιως εμε
γελωσι σιγ εχοντες η δ εμη νοσος
αει τεθηλε, καπι μειζον ερχεται.[3]

(That bit of Greek is especially meant for Mr Kean—the immense intelligence displayed in his handling of English verse placing beyond question the assumption that he must be very strong indeed upon Greek verse, and, therefore, I won't translate it.)

Let me for a moment stop the flood of grief and review my position (though my tears). When Charles Kean was about to take the Princess' Theatre, he asked me if I would support him; because, he added, it was useless to embark in such a speculation unless he could get the Press to back him. I gave him the only promise I could give—I promised to do my best. I was glad to see a gentleman in the position. It looked well for the drama; and no one will dispute that it *has* been a great advantage—that he has made the Princess' a first-class theatre in every respect; and as far as the public is concerned, he has been an excellent manager. Hitherto I have kept my promise; but I told him at the time that it was one thing to support a theatre by all friendly offices, and another to praise actors or pieces which I did not approve. Now mark! because I was silent in a case where, if I had spoken at all, it could only have inflicted a needless wound—because I do *not* think Charles Kean a tragic actor, and never would say I did—because in short, while feeling and (as all who know me will testify) *expressing* a personal liking for him, I exercised towards him a privilege I do not withdraw even with regard to dearest friends—that, namely, of uttering my opinion—because, I say, my friendly articles were not fulsome eulogies, Charles Kean declared me 'one of his bitterest enemies'; and now, I presume, because I said last week that Helen Faucit was the greatest of our tragic actresses (a fact about which there are not two opinions), the 'bitterest enemy' is told he cannot be admitted any more.

Poor fellow! poor fellow! to be so sensitive—and an actor! One hears of hens, in a soil where chalk is deficient, laying eggs without shells—nothing but a thin membrane to protect the embryo chick; how unpleasant to be such a chick!

As for me, I confess I have long expected to be cut off the free list by some irate manager or other, but do not respect the sagacity which has so exercised the managerial power. Can Mr Kean suppose that by suppressing *free admissions* he suppresses *free speech*? Or does he think that no critic would be mad enough to rush into the utter extravagance of *paying* for a place to see him act? Let him undeceive himself. I shall be there on first nights as of old; the only difference will be this—that until he declared open war I still preserved my original position; henceforth I shall remember that kindly silence is interpreted as insult, and shall speak out just what I think. In concluding, let me say that whereas I would not suffer my criticism to be eulogistic when urged by *interest* (in the vulgar sense of the term—Mr Kean will understand me), so likewise I have too much pride to allow this last act to *pique* me into injustice.

Hamlet and the German Actors (19 June 1852)

I once had a maternal uncle (had, alas! vixit!) whose views on the drama were freely communicated to me in the high and buoyant days when five-act tragedies in swelling verse were the dream and occupation of my life. He resided in Bungay, where he adorned a large domestic circle with all the virtues of a citizen, and earned the eternal gratitude of mankind by his improvements in soap!

In soap! Imagine Vivian in connection with saponaceous commerce! But biography has no delicacy, and facts are shattering to all illusions; and the fact is as I state. This free-spoken uncle was an anticipation of the Fast School of Critics. He snored at five-act dramas, and was merciless to mine. Shakespeare was his personal enemy. I think I see him now, rubbing his fat fingers through his scanty hair, as he authoritatively delivered himself of this favourite remark: '*Hamlet*, sir? If *Hamlet* were produced to-morrow, *Hamlet* would be d—d, sir.' After uttering that he would relapse into his chair, complacent, authoritative, obese.

I have since heard the remark from others, especially from actors, although, in *fact*, no play is so popular as *Hamlet*. It amuses thousands annually. It stimulates the minds of millions. Performed in barns, in minor theatres, and Theatres Royal, it always attracts. The lowest and most ignorant audiences delight in it; partly, no doubt, because of its profundity and sublimity—for the human soul can *feel* a grandeur which it cannot understand, and the dullest will listen with hushed awe and sympathy to those outpourings of a great meditative mind obstinately questioning fate and existence; to the lowest as the highest it is, *To be or not to be!* But *Hamlet* mainly delights the crowd by its wondrous dramatic and theatric art.

Consider for a moment the variety of its effects. The Ghost—the tyrannous murderer—the faithless wife and queen—the melancholy hero doomed to such an awful fate—the poor Ophelia, broken-hearted, and dying mad—the play within a play, entrapping the conscience of the King—the grave-diggers in ghastly mirth—the funeral of Ophelia, and the quarrel over her grave—and finally, the hurried bloody *dénouement*. Here are elements for several Fast dramas. Let us add thereto the passion and the poetry—let us note how Shakespeare by his art has made intensely interesting that which in other hands would have been insufferably tedious—I mean *Reverie*. *Hamlet* is a tragedy of thought; there is as much reflection as action in it. It is the representation of a great *meditative* soul struggling against circumstance; and in this respect it is a theatrical paradox, for it makes Scepticism, Reverie, Reflection, *dramatic*. Here the *activity* of thought supplies the place of action, and hurries the audience along with it.

The peculiarity of *Hamlet* is its indissoluble union of refinement with

horrors, of thought with tumult, of high and delicate poetry with gross
theatrical effects. Only pause for a moment to consider the machinery of this
play. What a tissue of horrors it is! the ghostly apparitions—the incestuous
adultery and murder—Hamlet half mad—Ophelia raving mad—Polonius
killed like a rat behind the arras—grave-diggers casting skulls upon the stage,
and descrating the churchyard with their ribaldry—a funeral interrupted by
a furious quarrel between the two who loved the dead most dearly—murder
planned—poisonings and stabbings to close this history,—and all these as
the machinery for the most thoughtful and philosophic of poems! In this
respect, as in so many others, it resembles *Faust*: that, also, is a poem wild,
fantastic, brutal in its machinery; lofty, refined, and impassioned in its spirit.

I think, then, there is good reason for siding with fact against avuncular
dogmatisms, and for declaring that *Hamlet* is not only a marvellous poem,
but a great play. And this great play was performed here in London by the
'great Germans', who discovered Shakespeare, and who have taken out a
patent for the correct appreciation of him. I have much to say on this
hypothetical superiority of German appreciation; but for the present my
business is with Herr Devrient, as the acknowledged Hamlet of Germany at
this moment. The expectation raised was immense. Before venturing an
opinion on the performance, it will be well to fix the point of view.

There are three capital aspects in the representation of Hamlet—(1st), The
princely elegance of a sorrowing, profoundly meditative man. (2nd), The
fitful wildness of madness only half assumed. (3rd), The lover of Ophelia.
On the first point there is no dispute. On the second and third points critics
are not agreed. Now, did the occasion warrant it, I could prove Hamlet to be
in such a state of cerebral excitement, that its outward manifestations should
be those of madness, whether we consider him really mad or not; so that, as
regards the actor, it matters very little what view he takes of this vexed
question, he must depict the wildness and fitfulness proper to the scene, and
not, as Charles Kean does, preserve the same settled gloom and contempla-
tive quiet *after* the interview with the Ghost which served to express his
mental condition *before* the interview. On this point I shall venture to repeat
what two years ago I said when noticing Charles Kean's *Hamlet*:

'At the opening of the play Hamlet is grave with the gloom of a father's
sudden death, and the gloom is deepened and embittered by the indelicate
marriage of his mother with his uncle. The world has become weary, flat,
stale, and unprofitable to him. Woman has, in the person of his mother, been
smitten from the pedestal whereon his love had placed her, to fall down and
worship, and her name has become the synonym of Frailty. Were it not that
God had 'fix'd his canon gainst self-slaughter,' this gloom and bitterness
would seek an issue in death; but he resolves to suffer all in silence. In the
representation of this settled sorrow, Charles Kean is unsurpassed. The tones
of his voice in which he answers, 'Ay, madam, it is common', and 'I prithee
do not mock me, fellow-student; I think it was to see my mother's wedding',

together with the look of painful disbelief of Horatio—as if his soul, throwing off its load for a while to interest itself in friendship, was suddenly checked, and flung back again upon the woe it tried to escape—were most effective touches. But this state of Hamlet's mind is only preparatory. It bears the same relation to the subsequent acts as the solemn, ghostly opening scenes, with their awful revelations, bear to the scenes of madness and crime which follow. The play opens on the platform of the castle of Elsinore. It is the depth of midnight; the sentinel pacing to and fro is nipped with cold, and shivering with vague terrors: not a mouse stirring! The silence is broken only by the regular footstep on the platform, and the hoarse sullen murmurs of the Baltic raving below. On this scene appears the Ghost. He reveals the crime which sent him from the world, and then the storm and terror of the play begins; then come the madness of Hamlet, the conviction of the King, the murder of Polonius, the ravings of Ophelia, the grave-diggers casting skulls upon the stage and desecrating the graveyard with their jesting, Ophelia's funeral interrupted and disgraced by a hideous quarrel, and, finally, the general massacre of the last scene! The same ascension from settled gloom to wild and whirling horror and madness may be seen in Hamlet. After the visitation of the Ghost, Hamlet is a *changed man*. His sorrowing nature has been ploughed to its depths by a horror so great that his distended brain refuses every alternate moment to credit it: the shock has unsettled his reason. If he is not mad, he is at any rate in such a state of irrepressible excitement that to feign madness seems the only possible relief to him. This is the point where our differences from Charles Kean's version take their rise. He may not agree with us that Hamlet was really mad; though, unless Shakespeare is to be set down as a bungler, we think that we could bring a mass of evidence wholly irresistible to prove that Hamlet was in a state of cerebral excitement not distinguishable from insanity; but we waive the point, and admit that he was perfectly sane, and still the fact remains that, *after* the revelations of the Ghost, Hamlet must be in a totally different condition of mind from what he was before. That difference Charles Kean does not represent. The *same* gloom over-shadows him when alone; the *same* expression of face accompanies him. Instead of the agonised soul of a son in presence of an adulterous mother and a murderous uncle, he exhibits the concentrated sorrow of the first act, diversified only by the outbreaks of assumed madness. He does not depict the hurrying agitation of thoughts that dare not settle on the one horror which, nevertheless, they cannot escape. The excitement, even as simple excitement, is not represented; and thus neither the meaning of the assumed madness, nor the effects of the Ghost's revelations are apparent in his acting.'

According to the view taken of Hamlet's madness, his demeanour towards Ophelia will be somewhat modified. That he loved her is clear enough; his treatment of her is not so clear if he were sane, though explicable upon the assumption of his derangement. At any rate, in their great scene there is a mingled tenderness and bitterness which affords the actor great scope: he should always *look* the contrary of what he utters, and his ferocity should have that restless wildness in it which would excuse it in her eyes. If he is assuming madness, he would wish her to believe him mad, and *so* interpret his harshness; if he is really mad, the wildness is natural.

I have thus established, as it were, some definite grounds of philosophic criticism on the representations of Hamlet. Setting details aside, I call your attention to the three central points in the character: if the actor rightly seize them, we may pass over imperfections of detail; if he miss them, no excellence of detail will compensate. And now I am prepared to answer the question, How did Emil Devrient succeed in *Hamlet*? Indifferently. The princely elegance was never represented; indeed, I thought him ungainly, but those around me thought him graceful, so let him have the benefit of their admiration. The sorrowing of a profoundly meditative nature I caught no glimpse of; it was more like dyspepsia than sorrow, and as unlike meditation as it was unlike reality. In fact, the first scene was very inferior to that played by Charles Kean, who does represent the settled sorrow of Hamlet, if he represent little else. While, in his interview with the Ghost, Herr Devrient had more the demeanour of a frightened school-boy than of the sceptical student and affectionate son. Let me say, once for all, that I see no trace of superior intelligence in Emil Devrient's reading of his part, but very many evidences of careless, superficial interpretation, such as will bear no examination. There is too much of what may be called *haphazard emotion*—*i.e.*, emotion not following a thorough study of identification with the character, but arising from a sort of guess at what should be the feeling of the moment. To give an example: He asks the players if they can perform a certain piece which he has in his eye, and moreover, if they will insert some dozen lines that he will write. I am ashamed to be forced into such an obvious remark as that Hamlet must be thoroughly aware of the peculiar *bearing* of the play he has chosen, and has already determined upon the use he will make of it to catch the conscience of the King; but I am forced to make the remark, because Herr Devrient, in the soliloquy which followed—

'O what a rogue and peasant slave am I,' etc.,

made a great point of suddenly conceiving this idea of using the play as a means of testing the King; he smacked his forehead, paused a long while, tried to throw speculation into his eyes, and in low, mysterious accents announced to himself this very determination. Now this is what I call haphazard emotion. The slightest consideration of the character as a *whole* will serve to exhibit repeated instances of the same kind. Of all characters on the stage, Hamlet most demands from its performer a subtle sympathy and an appreciation of intellect, which certainly are not with Herr Devrient's nature. Whatever else there may be in his acting, there is not intense mental vigour. Were it not that space and time are wanting, I would undertake to go through any scene, and point out proofs of what I say. Having, however, expressed my opinion with a frankness demanded by the occasion, and by the enormous praise which has greeted Herr Devrient, with more hospitality than discernment, let me now turn to what was excellent in his performance.

The second aspect which the character presents—viz., that of Hamlet half-mad, was forcibly given. Herr Devrient—probably according to German tradition—preserves the significant phrases addressed to the Ghost, 'How now, old mole! dost work i' the earth so fast,' etc., and taking the plain hint given in such language, he represents the reason of Hamlet as completely unsettled by the revelations of the Ghost—he *is* the madman he affects to be. This one scene was sufficient to show that a new version of Hamlet, more consistent with the text, would be far more effective than our English versions. Herr Devrient was wild, fitful, and impressive. The change from the earlier manner was complete. Perhaps in the subsequent scenes a more intelligent actor would have been less monotonous in his wildness; but, at any rate, it was something to see the mad view of the part seriously taken up. As Ophelia's lover—the third aspect of the part—Herr Devrient wanted tenderness altogether (he always does), but he played without the harshness which usually spoils this scene; and, indeed, it only wanted a little tenderness to make it perfect. The elegance, the pathos, the fluctuating passion, and the thought of Hamlet, were but poorly represented; but, on the other hand, the madness was thoroughly grasped; and very many of the speeches which one has been accustomed to hear ranted and mouthed, were spoken with a naturalness far more effective. To sum up in a phrase: Herr Devrient has not a spark of *genius*, but he is a practised actor, capable of giving effect to certain passages; and his Hamlet has some scenes one can honestly praise, though not one passage that roused any enthusiasm in me.

The Polonius of Herr Limbach, on the contrary, was a fine piece of acting. He conceived Polonius rather as a stupid than a senile man, and in so far he erred, I think; nevertheless, this is almost hypercriticism on his excellent performance, which was admirable within its own limits. He was 'made up' like a Vandyke; and the unconscious garrulity and feebleness of intellect were naively and quietly hit off.

The Miseries of a Dramatic Author

From the *Cornhill Magazine* (October 1863)

All professions have their pleasures and their pains; and the artistic temperament, by reason of its excessive sensitiveness, is peculiarly organised for
pain. But although long familiarity with the dramatic art has made me
conversant with the minor miseries incidental to it, I never thoroughly
realised to myself how much more the dramatist had to suffer than poets and
novelists, until the other day, when, in a conversation on the delight which
an orator must feel in swaying an audience, some one observed:

'A friend of mine says he can conceive nothing equal to the pleasure of
being a dramatic author. He gets the applause *paid down.*'

'Whoever said that,' I answered, laughing, 'was assuredly *not* a dramatist.
He spoke from the outside.'

'That's true. Still he knows dramatists; and any one can appreciate the
value of the applause being instantaneous and concentrated, instead of
dribbling in at slow intervals. Moreover, the praise of a novel or a poem is
given to the work as a whole; only a few of its details are noticed, and the
author generally finds that the critics pass over his best things.'

'Yes, yes—we all know that. As a wit once said, the only criticism to
satisfy an author is unqualified praise and all extracted!'

'Well, the dramatist has "all extracted". Every passage tells; every single
good thing gains applause.'

'I admit that an author's self-love is more energetically stimulated by the
volleying plaudits of a delighted pit, than by the scattered and not over-in-
telligent praises of critics, or the vague warmth of congratulations from
acquaintances. It is one thing to read a column of commonplaces, even when
eulogistic, or to hear Brown, Jones, and Robinson declare they have been
"delighted" with your charming work, and another thing to hear every good
speech welcomed by the bravos or the laughter of a full house. It is one thing
to get a note from your publisher announcing that the edition will soon be
run out, and a second must be thought of; another thing to have the 'pit rise
at you'. But this excess of triumph is dearly purchased. The dramatist has to
endure what the poet or the novelist is happily shielded from.'

'Nevertheless, it is evident that the pleasure preponderates. If the applause
did not repay the author for his tribulations, the drama would be deserted;
whereas, it is notorious that a man who has once had the applause ringing in
his ears, is eager to try for it again and again.'

'Don't lay too much stress on that. Men who have *never* been applauded, and never will be—men who have been foiled in all their efforts to get their works put on the stage, are found dauntlessly besieging the theatre. In fact, there is a fascination about the drama which no amount of failure, no amount of irritation can destroy. I remember one case of an author, now dead, who had wasted his energies and his fortune in the hopeless effort to gain dramatic success. He published tragedy after tragedy which no manager was mis-guided enough to accept. He engaged a theatre for the purpose of producing his works, one of which was indeed performed amidst yells of laughter, at the cost of his remaining fortune; and he passed the rest of his days in a miserable garret writing plays, calm amid the wreck of his fortunes, and declaring that he would rather live in a garret and write plays, than live in prosperity excluded from the drama. This is an extreme case; but it indicates the fascination.'

'Are you not supporting the very proposition you began by contradicting?'

'Not at all. I never denied the attraction which draws men of poetic sensibility, and men of irritable ambition, to the stage; especially when they are innocent of all the vexations which throng the avenues. I simply affirmed that it was a mistake to estimate the career of a dramatist from the superficial view of its one compensating pleasure. Admitting the fact that the applause is greater, more concentrated, heartier, I add that it is purchased by a far greater amount of anxiety, irritation, and disgust; and not only so, but that even on the very night of triumph, we over-estimate the pleasure. We have seen nothing of what preceded the victory; we know nothing of the wounds inflicted in the very moment of success.'

'That is true of all authorship. The poet's crown may be splendid, but, as the Pope said, *ça brille, mais ça brûle.*'

'It is peculiarly the case in dramatic authorship, even when successful. Consider for a moment. You have written your play—I speak, of course, of a real work of art, not a thing patched up from a novel, or translated from the French, but a serious effort at tragedy or comedy. If you have written it in ignorance of the stage, or without thought of its being performed, the pleasures of composition are indeed unalloyed; but then the chances of its being represented are proportionately lessened, and the certainty of your vexation increased. If you already know the stage and its requirements, then the exquisite delight in dramatic composition will be thwarted by having to sacrifice your cherished intentions to the inexorable demands of actors and managers. You must mould your work not according to your conceptions of art and nature, but according to the capabilities of the actors, or the prejudices of the stage.'

'Well, I don't see much hardship in this; nothing, at least, that may not be matched among the vexations of other forms of art.'

'If you were a dramatist you would not speak in that way. But let it pass. Suppose your play written, and sent in. Unless you are already known as a successful writer, your manuscript is deposited with scores of rivals, the very sight of the mass causing the manager to feel uncomfortable, knowing, as he does, that there will be scarcely one piece in a hundred which is not either utterly absurd, or wholly impracticable. You cannot possess yourself of the idea that the manager has not plenty of time to look at your piece; nor dispossess yourself of the idea that if he would only look at it he would at once see that it was a masterpiece, certain to be 'a hit'. You fret impatiently at the inevitable delay. A couple of hours he might surely spare for your *chef-d'oeuvre?* Yet these hours, which to you seem so easily spared, are claimed by scores of rivals. Meanwhile he has quite other things to occupy him. Your piece slumbers with the others. You write, and get no answer, or are informed that your piece will be read and considered as soon as possible. The season passes, and you get no reply. Indignant, you withdraw your piece, and present it to a rival theatre—with similar results.'

'I don't deny that such things occur; but as far as my experience goes it is only the mediocre or impracticable works—plays or novels—which ever suffer from neglect. There is a wide-spread notion that managers and publishers can with difficulty be brought to look at the work of an unknown author; and I am constantly appealed to "to use my influence" —as if publishers were mysteriously opposed to their own interest, and had to be persuaded to accept a work which will bring them profit! as if publishers and managers were not, on the contrary, only too anxious to secure any work having the least promise! But the fact is such heaps of trash are offered, and very properly declined—while every work is confidently believed by its author to be certain of success—that these repeated rejections encourage the idea of a silent opposition to their own interest on the part of managers and publishers. It's all nonsense! If my play is a good one, I shall not find any difficulty in getting it accepted.'

'What you say is undoubtedly true of publishers, but I assure you that managers are in general too busy to find time for reading many pieces.'

'Yet pieces *are* read, I suppose, since they are occasionally produced?'

'True; only you have little idea how long an unknown author has to wait even for a reading. I say nothing of your feelings when the piece has been read, and is returned to you with a polite note, praising its literary qualities, but intimating that it is not suited to the company; or that the manager's engagements leave him little hope of producing it, and therefore, not to stand in your way, he begs to forward it to you. Of course this is mere varnish. The piece is a bad one—or the manager thinks so, which is the same thing. Your self-love will not let you see through the excuse; and you present the play to another manager, to undergo a repetition of the delay and the vexation.'

'All this the unsuccessful novelist has to endure. But we are considering the successful writers. Let us suppose the play is accepted; all the difficulties are forgotten then?'

'Forgotten? It is then that the real troubles *begin.*'

My friend looked incredulous, so I rehearsed some of the more obvious vexations which beset the dramatist; and as the narrative surprised him, I will repeat it here in fuller detail.

The dramatist hears with no little satisfaction that his work is to be produced, but hears with no little mortification that some alterations will be necessary. Alterations! The work which has cost him so much labour, so much anxious thought, every exit and entrance having been pondered with severe attention, every speech polished and polished with fastidious care, has to be altered, as if it had been put together by a carpenter. He goes to his interview with the manager, resolved not to disturb a line of this 'work of art'. He is received with gracious and agreeable courtesy, is complimented warmly, but is told with firm friendliness, much like a surgeon's gentleness, that some of his most original and characteristic details are 'impracticable'. If he is obstinate, he argues the point—not with the slightest success. If he is complying, he sits in grim silence, while the manager's experience of the stage is brought to enlighten him; and he learns that the situation which he has always calculated on as thrilling is in imminent danger of being ridiculous on the stage. The word 'impracticable' is freely used; but poets require considerable experience before they learn to distinguish between what is and what is not practicable. Thus I have known an important situation made to depend upon a pathetic song which the lover had to sing. In a drama to be read, there was no difficulty in this; the reader can imagine the young lover singing as easily as talking. In the drama to be acted, there is this difficulty: the tragic actor is not a Mario; if he ever had a voice, he has probably ranted it away; at any rate, the rare accomplishment of singing well enough can hardly be counted on. Thus, either the part must be played by a singer, for the sake of the song; or the song must be cut out. I mention this as an illustration of the kind of impracticabilities which an inexperienced author is liable to fall into.

By the time his interview with the manager is at an end, it is lucky if all that the author most prizes for its originality has not been ruthlessly condemned; and his piece, from being a well-considered work of art, is mutilated into commonplace. What he has suffered under this surgery I leave you to imagine. However, rather than be frustrated entirely, he sadly consents to alter his work, to destroy its fair proportions, and make it 'actable'.

Then comes the reading in the green-room. Great moment! Long wished-for occasion! When I used to hear of an author reading his piece to the actors, it sent an imaginative thrill through me, and I pictured my delight should ever such a moment of triumph be mine. When the moment did arrive, it was not at all like my anticipations. In a state of fluttering depression I reached the theatre, and found actors and actresses standing about the dark stage. I was presented to them, feeling mingled pleasure at being thus brought into contact with artists long admired on the stage, and anxiety at the idea of their co-operation being essential to my success. How civil I was to them all! Into the dingy green-room we went, and I was quickly seated at the table, my mouth dry and my pulse throbbing. Unrolling the manuscript with great nervousness, I cleared my voice, and began. Of course I read detestably (most authors do, and have no suspicion of the fact), and was very anxious to impress upon the actors clear conceptions of their several parts.

Those were the days of innocence, when faith in art (especially in my own) made me imagine that actors and actresses were intensely interested in the play as a work of art, and not simply interested in their parts. I little suspected the truth, that according to his part will each actor judge of the play. If his character is one which seems to offer him opportunities of display he will be enthusiastic about the drama; if he has misgivings about his part, he will be despondent about the play; and if he positively dislikes his part he will predict a fiasco. And this is perfectly natural. The *amour propre* of the actor is no less engaged than that of the dramatist. Success to him also is the breath of life. He cannot help viewing the piece solely in relation to himself. It pains you when first you make the discovery; but if you are wise you will admit that is is quite excusable. He is indifferent to art, you think, and ought to be interested in your success. But are not you equally indifferent to his success, thinking only of your own?

As I said, the reading began. At first all were attentive, expectant. I got over my nervousness, and began to read better. But very shortly I became aware that the actors were trying to discover which parts were intended for them; and having discovered this, their attention slackened in all those scenes from which they were absent. This was a small torture. In vain I threw fresh fervour into the reading; from the corner of my eye I perceived that while the lovers were having their interview, the villian, the heavy father, the comic servant, and the pert soubrette, were wholly insensible to my impassioned dialogue, quite unmoved by the delicacies of style. If you have ever read a work of your own to an inattentive audience, you may imagine the sensations of one who is reading a play to the actors upon whose interest and co-operation his fate depends, and observes the villian's eye wandering from the ceiling to his boots, the comic servant intent upon the condition of his finger-nails, and the soubrette scanning the bonnet of the leading actress.

Nor is this the worst. It may happen, very probably will happen, that as the reading proceeds you become vaguely aware of a certain mute opposition which is quite disheartening. The leading actor who was at first full of hope begins to feel his part ineffective, or perceives the part of his rival becoming too effective. The principal actress finds herself too long absent from the scene, or present during scenes when others make long speeches to her, which she has to 'feed' with interjections, or feeble inquiries. No sooner are such discoveries made than you read the discontent in their faces. Instead of radiant sympathetic listeners, the leading actor becomes gloomy and abstracted, or fidgets in his seat; the actress pinches her mouth with ominous reserve, and keeps her eyes downcast.

At last this stage of torture is over. You close the manuscript to the sound of obligatory applause. If the parts have interested several of the actors, the applause is genuine and hearty; for so long as their vanity is not in danger, actors are very sympathetic, and take a real delight in anything admirable. They are a pleasant set of human creatures; and if their infirmities sometimes cause you pain, you cannot see much of them without liking and respecting them. If only one or two have been pleased with their parts, the applause rings hollow, and you know the effect you have produced. Then the parts are distributed. Each actor receives in silence a small manuscript containing the 'words' of the part allotted to him. He puts it in his pocket without comment, and quits the room, joining the other malcontents on the stage, or in the porter's hall, freely canvassing the play, or predicting its failure. Somehow the author always knows this: partly he *feels* it, partly he divines it, and partly his attention is pointed to it by the remarks of the actors who, being satisfied with their parts, remain to compliment him: they laughingly remark that 'B is not over-pleased', and that 'C will throw up his part'.

You quit the theatre with strange noises in your head, and heavy forebodings at your heart. You tell your wife all. That sympathetic woman stigmatizes the conduct of the malcontents in terms of great energy; but consoles herself and you with the reflection that 'the piece will be played, let B and C like it or dislike it.' She may be wrong here. The piece may *not* be played, even after having been rehearsed. In my early days, I remember getting a brief note from a manager, requesting me to step down to the theatre, as he wished to speak with me on the subject of my comedy. With some uneasiness I entered his room, dimly apprehending an unpleasant communication. Judge of my feelings on hearing that the leading actor had thrown up his part! To make the misfortunes greater, there was no other man then on the stage to whom the part could have been entrusted. I was advised to call on the recusant, and try my power of persuasion; though I daresay the manager knew well enough the hopelessness of the attempt. Sick at heart, I jumped into a cab, went, was politely received, and quietly but firmly assured that the part was not one the distinguished actor could consent to play. I argued and entreated, in vain. 'There are *no laughs* in the part,' was the inexorable answer.

'But, my dear sir,' I pleaded, 'it is not *meant* to be a part to excite laughter so much as admiration for intellectual subtlety and quiet finesse. It is a sort of Talleyrand; it is high comedy.'

'Yes, I know, I know; monstrous clever, and all that; but without laughs it is no *part*. If I were a young man beginning my career I might jump at such a chance; as it is, I really can't play it. I must have laughs.'

'What is to be done? No one can touch the part but yourself.'

'No one. Without me the piece would be damned.'

'Surely you will not, by refusal, prevent my piece being played?'

'I am very sorry, very; but I can't play it, and without me the piece would be damned.'

This was the constant *refrain*. I quitted the house, boiling with indignation. Such cruel egoism! to blight a young author's prospects merely because
the admiration of the audience for the artist did not suffice for the vanity
which craved the vulgar applause of laughter!

Yet, now I look back on those days, I see that my indignation was simply
my own egoism reproaching him for his. He was doubly right. Right in
perceiving that the part was *not* one which could be effective, consequently
one which a fine actor ought not to be asked to play; and right in preferring
his own interest to mine—as I preferred mine to his. If I could have had such
clear vision then, I should have thought less unworthily of him, and have
made less bad blood in fuming at my own mistake. To give the finishing
touch to this anecdote, I will add that on my reporting my ill success to the
manager, he completed my despair by asking—if I couldn't alter the part into
one for Keeley?

It may perhaps be objected that had my piece been better I should have
escaped this; which is true. I only mentioned the case as an illustration of the
vexations to which the dramatist is specially liable. When the novelist has
secured the acceptance of his work, his initiatory troubles are at an end.
Publishers, to begin with, are far from being so troublesome as managers.
Indeed, after a long experience of both, I can conscientiously say that except
in one instance, I never met with anything but courtesy, liberality, and ready
attention from publishers, whereas of only one manager can I say all this. No
doubt the chief reason is that the manager is so much more harassed than the
publisher, and the production of a new play is to him so much greater a *risk*
than the production of a new book. But let us suppose that the initiatory
troubles and vexations are equal up to the point of acceptance: at this stage
the novelist is at ease; the MS goes to the printer, proofs arrive; the book is
published, and speaks directly to the public, certain to meet with the success
which its adaptation to public taste can secure for it. Not so with the accepted
drama. The serious difficulties begin, as I said, at rehearsal. Unlike a book,
a drama cannot directly speak to the public; it has to address audiences
through the medium of a *representative* art. Instead of calculable elements—
such as printer's types—it employs the incalculable elements—human
actors, mutable, capricious, imperfect. If I write a fine verse, the printers will
set it forth in types which everywhere, and at all seasons, will carry that verse
directly home to the intelligent mind; but the actors who are charged with
speaking that verse—publishing it for me—may mangle or mouth it, so that
the audience shall be moved to laughter or contempt. If the printer's proof is
sent to me with imperfections I can easily correct them; but how can I correct
the actor's proof—which is rehearsal—unless I am dealing with a very
intelligent and complying actor? Now it is unnecessary to say that not all
actors are very intelligent and very complying. Even when intelligent, they
are human beings, subject to the mutable motives and caprices of men. They

have their interests to attend to, and their vanity to misguide them. Rehearsal brings these out. First let me note that it is only good actors who ever act at rehearsal; the others gabble over the words, and when by emphasis or manner they unmistakingly betray some misapprehension of the part, they answer your objections with the one invariable formula: 'It will be all right at night.' You have horrible misgivings that it will be all wrong at night; but what can you do? Bad actors are unteachable, incorrigible. They will take no hint; they resent advice. I remember once trying to convince an actor that the whole effect of his exit in a pathetic situation would be ruined unless he spoke his few words in a faltering tone of subdued emotion, instead of 'taking the stage' and ranting his farewell. He haughtily informed me that he had been on the stage five-and-twenty years—and *that*, of course, was an answer to everything. Being unable to persuade him that 'farewell' was never pronounced '*far*well' off the stage, I was obliged to cut the word out.

Among smaller irritations, you have to endure the endless suggestions of the actors to have their parts altered—a speech put in for them here, or 'written up' there. One man, whose only qualification I ever could discover was the 'bend in his back', of which he was not a little proud, pestered me day after day to have some confidence in him. He wanted, especially, a 'dying scene'; he was certain he could produce a great effect with a death; but, as the structure of the piece required him to live, I could hardly confide in him to that extent. This seemed a hardship; he was so sure of 'bringing the house down' with a good dying scene. Had there been a chance of its breaking his back, I might have been tempted. You are also continually plagued for 'exit speeches'. No actor willingly quits the scene without a point, or something to raise a laugh—'something to take him off', as the phrase goes. It matters not how little relation this speech may have to the business of the scene; the one imperious desire is for an exit speech. A manager once drew a friend of mine aside, and with some earnestness, said—

'I wish you could give B an exit speech in this scene; his position in the theatre demands it.'

'Perhaps so; but his position in the play doesn't admit of one.'

'Oh, anything will do—just something to get him off.'

'But, I ask you, *what* can he say?'

'H'm! I don't know—Why not a curse? *B.'s position in the theatre demands a curse.*'

'Oh,' said the author, laughing, 'two curses if you like.'

'The very thing! *B. would like two curses!*'

Another friend was pestered by a comic servant for an exit speech in a scene when he had to hurry off the stage—summarily dismissed by his master. He was told that the occasion did not possibly admit of a speech. He was silent; but imagine the author's feelings at night when he saw the actor toss the half-crown he had received at an earlier part of the scene, and exclaim—'Welcome, little stranger!'

In Victor Hugo's memoirs, just published, there are several stories of the vexations to which he had to submit during the rehearsal of his plays, and these are the more illustrative because he was an author of immense reputation. Mdlle. Mars, for example, accepted the character of Doña Sol, in *Hernani*, not because she liked it, but because she did not choose that a rival should play in it. Here is a specimen of her demeanour at rehearsal:—

'Pardon, mon ami,' she would say to Firmin or Joanny, 'I want to speak to the author.'

The actor paused with a nod of assent. Mdlle. Mars walked up to the footlights, put her hand up to her eyes, and although, of course, perfectly aware of the spot in the orchestra where Hugo sat, pretended to look for him.

'M Hugo; is he there?'

Hugo rose—'Here, madame.'

'Ah! very good; thanks…M Hugo, I have to say this verse—"Vous êtes mon lion superbe et généreux." Do you like that, M Hugo?'

'I wrote it, madame, so I must have thought it all right.'

'Then you stick to your lion.'

'Yes, and no, madame; find me something better, and I will substitute it.'

'It is not for me to do that; I am not the author.'

'In that case, madame, let us leave it as it is written.'

'The fact is, it sounds so droll to call Firmin *my lion*.'

'That is because you forget you are Doña Sol, and only remember you are Mdlle. Mars.'

'Well, since you must have your lion, no more need be said. I am here to speak what is written, and *my lion* is in the manuscript. I will say *my lion*—it is all the same to me. Come, Firmin—"Vous êtes mon lion superbe et généreux." '

On the following day the same scene recommenced. She asked him if he had reflected on his *lion*, and being informed that no thought had been given to it, asked if he did not think it dangerous.

'I don't know what you call dangerous.'

'I call that dangerous which may be hissed.'

'Madame, I never had the pretension of not being hissed.'

'Good; but one must be hissed as little as possible.'

'You think the lion will be hissed. In that case you will not have spoken it with your accustomed talent.'

'I will do my best. Nevertheless, I should prefer something else; for example—"Vous êtes monseigneur superbe et généreux." Does not *monseigneur* make out the verse as well as *mon lion*?'

'With this difference: *mon lion* is poetical, and *monseigneur* commonplace. I would rather be hissed for a good verse than applauded for a bad one.'

'Well, well, don't let us quarrel; I will speak your good verse. Allons, mon ami Firmin,—"Vous êtes mon lion superbe et généreux." '

Irritated by scenes like this, Victor Hugo threatened to give the part to another actress. 'Mdlle. Mars was no longer impertinent, but she was dumb. She protested against the piece by her icy manner. Her example chilled the others.'

It is difficult for one who has had no experience of the stage to understand the galling trials which the dramatist has to endure from the sullen, silent opposition of dissatisfied actors. I do not blame the actors; I only pity the author. In every play there must be characters of inferior effectiveness, yet sometimes requiring the aid of good actors. There are pieces which, either owing to the necessities of the story, or the defectiveness of its construction, allow of only one or two good parts. We can hardly expect an actor to throw himself heartily into a part which he knows will bring him no applause; and when, at the same time, he sees a rival in possession of a part which will be effective, and will overshadow him, we can hardly expect that he will stifle his *amour propre* and devote himself to the author's success. It is always a great difficulty to get actors to play up to each other, unless their own parts are thrown into strong relief by it. You can understand that if A. has some terrible announcement to make to B., the effect of this will be greatly heightened by B.'s face and manner showing terror or interest, and will be proportionately lessened if B. is looking away, or remains unmoved. When King John hints his designs to Hubert, part of the effect will depend on Hubert's playing up to the King. But actors can with difficulty be brought to assist each other thus; and hence the advantage of husband and wife or brother or sister playing together; they are interested in each other's success. Rivals will not assist each other; they often do their best quietly to thwart each other. A friend of mine once asked an actress why she did not get a celebrated actor to look at her, and express interest in the narrative she had to deliver. 'Oh! she replied, 'I can't expect Mr_____ to look at me; it's *my scene*, you know!'

This is a chronic difficulty; you can imagine how it is heightened when the actors are in a state of dissatisfaction with their parts, and consequently do not wish the play to succeed. Nor is this without its effect on the audience. Acting is an art which depends largely on a state of sympathy between the actors and the public; whatever chills the confidence of the one lessens the pleasure of the other. No one ever knows what piece will succeed or what character will be a hit; half the prosperity of the effect lies with the audience. In this state of uncertainty, unless the actor be encouraged to believe that he will produce an effect, he is very liable to fail. And his confidence may often be shaken at rehearsal by the conduct and remarks of others. I once read a piece to the principal actor and actress. Their unmistakeable interest, their applause, and her tears, convinced me that with them, at least, I might feel at ease; and as the other parts were comparatively insignificant, I thought in my innocence that my success was secured. At the reading in the green-room I observed, without surprise, the gloomy reserve of two or three who disapproved of their parts, and expected one at least to throw up his part. But no. Rehearsals began. I *felt* the discontent diffused through the theatre, silent, but unmistakeable. I was heedless of it—my principal actors remained firm. In a few days, however, the general depression began to affect them; they became uneasy, afraid of certain passages, which before had delighted them. I tried to inspirit them, but saw with each rehearsal that their doubts grew stronger. They knew what was the opinion current in the theatre; they knew that failure was confidently predicted, and they began to fear. At last one unlucky word was uttered respecting the principal part, which it was 'feared' might prove dangerous. From that day the struggle became hopeless. As a matter of self-preservation I withdrew the piece. You think I ought to have gone on? Well, it is possible that had the actor been somewhat less impress-ionable, or somewhat more self-confident, he might have resisted all this opposition, and made the piece a triumph; but it is far more likely that, troubled by misgivings, he would have played feebly, and then the failure would have been inevitable.

These troubles, you will observe, are not accidental, but essential; they will be active in every theatre, and in every country. I need not say how they become aggravated by the tyranny of 'stars', or by that still more vexatious tyranny which reigns in a theatre where the manager's wife, or *chère amie*, is an actress, and an indifferent one, to whom everything must give way. It is bad enough when the manager is also an actor; but the manager's wife! The novelist and poet happily know nothing of miseries like these.

Another immunity belongs to the novelist and poet from the fact that they require no medium between them and the public. The drama *represents*. Now there are many imaginative conceptions which cannot be represented on the stage without peril, and some that become positively ridiculous. In a novel or a poem the sudden opening of clouds and appearance of the moon looking down with silent solemnity on a murder which has just been committed in secrecy and darkness may thrill the murderer with horror and remorse; but when this comes to be represented on the stage, the parting of carpenters' clouds, and the appearance of a feeble stage-moon, will certainly produce no solemn impression, and will probably cause a titter. Then, again, there is the dangerous material of inferior actors. The author conceives a group of noblemen, or a party of young men of fashion; these have to be represented by 'supers', men engaged to 'go on' at a shilling a night. In a comedy written in my days of inexperience, there was a scene, the idea of which was droll enough, and taken from reality: the young hero, flushed with wine, had affectionately invited a number of strangers to breakfast with him next morning, went to bed, slept off the effects of the supper, and awoke forgetting all about it. Next morning one by one the guests arrive, and the confusion may be imagined! This scene the manager proved to me to be utterly impracticable, because the guests would necessarily have to represented by 'supers'; and how *they* would represent young Cantabs it is needless to say.

Some one has said: 'Supers are the small-pox of the drama; where they do not *kill*, they leave indelible *scars*.'

The exigencies of representation often inflict great pangs on the author by forcing him to cut out what he considers to be his finest passages. They may be fine; but a passage which in the reading would be universally admired, may, in the acting, cause the audience to yawn. It is difficult to persuade the author of this. Sheridan Knowles[4] never learned the simple relations of quantity; and although at rehearsal he was implored to shorten speeches, obstinately refused to cut out a line. After the first night he was the first to propose heroic slashing, because then he had felt how the length of speeches damaged certain scenes.

Apropos of 'cutting out the poetry', so much dreaded by poetic dramatists, I may tell a story of an author, now deceased. He was a regular writer for the theatres, but had not yet ventured on such high flights as tragedy. One day he said to his manager, 'I'm going to say something—I know you'll laugh, but I don't care. Well, I've written a tragedy, which I should like you to see.' He was asked to send it; did so; and thus the story proceeds in his own words: 'Well, sir, a few days afterwards I got this note from him: "My dear_____, Of all the preposterous things I ever read, your tragedy is the most stupendous. But come and dine with me to-morrow at six." Just like him: wounds your feelings in the tenderest point, and then tries to wipe it out with the dirty bribe of a dinner. However, I went. He told me to *cut out all the poetry*, and send it to Astley's.[5] I did; and it ran a hundred nights. So you see what a piece it must have been.'

I have not enumerated all the vexations which precede the First Night; but have named enough to prove my case. The day of publication to a novelist or poet is a supremely happy day; as the work lies before him, he fondles it, dips into it, imagines the effect it is going to produce, and writes the names of friends and big-wigs in the 'presentation copies' (never read, not always acknowledged), with a sense of drawing cheques on the bank of Fame. He thinks only of the vast public. If some 'envious critics' (all who do not praise a work are envious) and some stupid readers fail to detect his merit, he can appeal from them to that noble but mysterious entity, the General Reader, supposed capable of the most delicate and generous appreciation. Far otherwise feels the dramatist. He has horrible misgivings. The last rehearsal was anything but perfect. Some of the actors had not yet mastered 'the words'. It is to be all right at night; and he hopes it will be. Moreover, he knows that this night's publication is final. Unless he pleases the audience he has no chance of reaching the great public. The verdict is instantaneous, and admits of no appeal. The pit has no time to ponder; first impressions are final on the stage. So anxious is the trial of a first night, that some authors shirk the slow agony, and keep away from the theatre until the joyful news of success is brought them. I should have suffered more from apprehension, so I always braved the chances, seated at the back of a private box.

The house is slowly filling. You are on the stage, trying to encourage the actors by admiring their 'get up', and predicting what they will effect with certain scenes; looking through the hole in the curtain to see who has come, and whether there is a good pit; and trying to share the manager's confidence that 'B. is certain to be all right.' The overture begins. You see critics and friends scattered about the boxes; and the pit is rapidly filling. You are passed from the stage to your private box, and the curtain rises. A first-night audience is always good-natured; not only are there many friends of the author come to 'ensure a success', and really anxious that the piece should succeed; but the bulk of the indifferent public is only too willing to admire and be pleased. Any chance of applause is eagerly sought by friends and willingly accepted by the audience.

You are thrilled with the plaudits; but you sit in alternations of triumph and agony, for, although the piece may be 'going famously', you are but too painfully conscious of all its defects. You sit there condemned to endure poetry mangled, wit blunted, and conceptions distorted. The man who, at rehearsal, was 'letter perfect', is nervous, and makes havoc with the verse. The actress who was charming in one scene at rehearsal, is totally without charm to-night. Effects upon which you calculated fall flat; passages are suddenly revealed as perilous; too late you see a hundred errors, and you foresee rocks ahead. More than once an author thus frightened and enlightened has rushed behind the scenes, and arranged to omit a scene or passage because of the risk. The applause may keep up your sinking courage, but it does not protect you from these pangs.

Amid such fluctuations, the piece proceeds. At last the curtain falls to immense cheering. Vociferous shouts of 'Author! author!' burst out like rockets from all sides. This is a supreme moment. You bow from your box and love mankind. Every man and woman of that intelligent pit is your friend. You hurry behind the scenes to congratulate and be congratulated, to compliment and be complimented, to shake the leading actors warmly by the hand, and gratefully salute the cheek of the heroine—if she will let you. With generous, effusive insincerity you find yourself complimenting the very actors whose stupidity but a little while since evoked curses not loud but deep. One or two well-known dramatists and critics are on the stage, and perhaps a nobleman of theatrical tastes; to these you are presented, and by these you are congratulated. It is a wild, delirious moment. But the stage has to be cleared for the afterpiece. You make an appointment to be at the theatre to-morrow at eleven, 'to go over the piece'; and either, if you are wise, return to your home to gladden your wife with the news; or, if you are otherwise, join a few friends at supper.

'The supper after the play' might form a chapter by itself. Sometimes the author, confident of success, invites his guests beforehand, and if the success has been equivocal, this makes it rather awkward for the friends. Sometimes the manager provides supper. I remember one, given by a manager now dead, who was more hospitable than literate, and who had invited the chief actors, two dramatic critics (whom I saw writing their columns in the corners of his private room), and some 'literary friends', myself included, to rejoice over the successes of a drama called the *Broken Heart*. A jovial and joyous supper it was. At an early period the enthusiastic *impresario* rose, and lifting his champagne glass in the air, said, in a voice tremulous with nervousness (or drink), 'Ladies and gentlemen,—It is with feelings of very particular pleasure, and I may say gratification, that I rise to propose a toast, which I am sure you will agree with me is well deserved, and I am sure you will drink with all the honours: *"Here's to the Broken Art, and the And which guided it."* '

Of what followed, I have only a dim recollection of much noise, extravagant eulogies, a gradually increasing introduction of the name of Shakespeare, which at first was mentioned with timidity, and a sort of vinous conviction that the And had inaugurated a new era of dramatic art. I hope, for his own sake, that the author was sufficiently wise to accept all this eulogy with the necessary 'discount', or sufficiently heated with wine not to have understood it; otherwise he must have tumbled into bed that morning with an inflated sense of his greatness, and must have waked up with considerable astonishment to read in the morning papers that he was, after all, *not* a Shakespeare.

I shall not touch upon the dramatist in relation to the critics, because whatever he may have to endure on that score is not peculiar to him. There is, however, a source of vexation after the triumph which may be mentioned. I have said that the first-night audience is always good-natured; it is more, it is intelligent. The number of critics, old playgoers, and (if the author has a name in the world) of literary men present on a first night, leaven the audience in a surprising manner. But if this has its advantages, it has also its drawbacks. Many a passage which went brilliantly at first, passes unnoticed ever afterwards; and the disappointed author notices it with disgust. It was remarked that Douglas Jerrold's plays were always triumphant on the first night. The audience appreciated his wit; the laughter was incessant. Afterwards, the unadulterated public listened with stolid faces to those flashing repartees; for it is unhappily the fact that our audiences seldom laugh at any but the oldest jokes—the family Joe Millers—the Wandering Jews *d'esprit*—and if you offer them wit at all, it must be wit they already know.

On the supposition, then, that your comedy has really been witty and successful, there are great chances against its taking hold of the public unless it have other theatrical qualities. The same may be said of your tragedy: a first-night audience may applaud speeches which will afterwards be listened to with impatience. Hence it is that many a man has flattered himself that he has achieved a great dramatic success, and has perhaps incurred expenses on the strength of it, when, after a few nights' run, the work is withdrawn because the public would not come to see it. At one of those suppers just mentioned, a play was freely spoken of as destined 'to live in the literature of our country'. It was performed four nights.

Thus, if the applause received by the dramatist be more concentrated and intoxicating than the applause received by the novelist or poet, it is purchased by a far greater amount of vexation, and the failure is proportionately emphatic. Moreover, if, in rare exceptional cases, his work has the immense benefit of being presented to the public through the medium of fine acting, which of course intensifies its effect; on the other hand, this strong light can only be shed on one or two parts—bad acting will as much distort his work in the other parts. True it undoubtedly is that a fine actor will sometimes raise an insignificant part into one of surprising effect; but much oftener the actors rob their parts of all significance. Now, the dramatist is far less grateful to the fine actor for his aid (because not so conscious of it) than he is wrath with the bad actor for his failures. What is the most cherished hope of every author? That he may be understood; that his work may be fairly brought before the public. What, then, must be the misery of the dramatic author who has to see his work mutilated to fit it for the stage, and mangled when produced?

Charles Dickens

Pickwick Papers, Oliver Twist and *Sketches by Boz*
(December 1837)

It is a difficult thing to distinguish between popularity and fame; and the distinction, though it may be made during the present time, must still wait the corroboration of the future. Literature undergoes greater and more frequent changes than the geological view of the earth points out in our globe; strata after strata are embedded and lost amidst the rushing of new tides, both of popularity and caprice; and we see that men who were the idols of the day are scarcely mentioned in a succeeding age, and only known to the curious. This is ever the effect of popularity without true fame: the adventitious circumstances by which a man obtains popularity are no longer in action in a succeeding age; and if his popularity in the main depended on them, he is naturally forgotten.

People always like to have a *reason* for their likings or dislikings; and it becomes a fit subject of inquiry, whether Charles Dickens (Boz) has attained his astonishing and extensive popularity from the caprice of the moment, the patronage of the great, the puffing of booksellers, or from his own intrinsic merit; whether, in short, people have any reason (beyond the momentary impulse notoriety always creates) for their delight in perusing his works; and whether he has written that which catches the attention of the 'fleeting hour,' or that which the 'world will not willingly let die.' Two of the Quarterlies have taken up the subject, but not in our opinion with sufficient analytic power to settle the question, or to prevent our offering a few remarks. The *London and Westminster*'s was immeasurably superior to the *Quarterly*, (a blundering article, which made Boz's reputation to arise from his having 'struck out a new vein' in the common language of the Londoners! an assertion as false as it is ridiculous), but, as it seemed to us, very unequal in its criticism. Let us not be supposed to attempt supplying the deficiencies of these articles; all we would endeavour here is to examine some of the more prominent features in Mr Dickens' genius.

'Boz' has perhaps a wider popularity than any man has enjoyed for many years. Nor alone are his delightful works confined to the young and old, the grave and gay, the witty, the intellectual, the moralist, and the thoughtless of both sexes in the reading circles, from the peer and judge to the merchant's clerk; but even the common people, both in town and country, are equally intense in their admiration. Frequently have we seen the butcher-boy, with

57

his tray on his shoulder, reading with the greatest avidity the last *Pickwick*;
the footman, (whose fopperies are so inimitably laid bare,) the maid servant,
the chimney-sweep, all classes, in fact, read '*Boz*'. And how has this
surprising popularity been attained? Not a puff—with the exception of an
occasional extract in the newspapers, hardly a notice—no patronage heralded
his fame. He chose, perhaps, the worst possible medium for making his
entrée—the columns of a newspaper! Yet such was the delicacy of touch,
the fineness of observation, and the original, quiet humour of these papers,
that he was induced to collect and publish them in two volumes. When the
Sketches came out, 'Have you read Boz?' was the eternal question. We have
traced his popularity upwards, and have, in our limited way, done not a little
to make all we knew acquainted with them; but we own that we were fairly
astonished at the rapidly increasing popularity of his name. Byron used to
say, that he awoke one morning and found himself celebrated: Boz may say
the same; for never was a more rapid, more deserved a reputation made.

The *Sketches*, though distinguished by the same nicety of observation
that startles us with its fidelity, and a great fund of humour and sympathy,
are more evidently the first efforts of a strong genius, and stand, in comparison with the *Pickwick Papers*, and *Oliver Twist*, rather in the shade. In them
he certainly did approach nearer to Washington Irving[6] than any living writer;
but we think he now transcends his model. In his two last and most celebrated
works, we find qualities combined which no other writer ever had; to
compare him to Theodore Hook,[7] (who, with a certain talent of a certain sort,
has never written anything that will live), is absurd. Theodore Hook is all
extravagance and affectation—writing like a man who wishes to be thought
a gentleman and considers that a profound contempt for the *canaille* and
Bloomsbury Square are the requisite characteristics. 'Boz' should be compared to no one since no one has ever written like him—no one has ever
combined the nicety of observation, the fineness of tact, the exquisite
humour, the wit, heartiness, sympathy with all things good and beautiful in
human nature, the perception of character, the pathos, and accuracy of
description, with the same force that he has done. His works are volumes of
human nature, that have a deep and subtle philosophy in them, which those
who read only to laugh may not discover; but an attentive reading (and we
have read some of the numbers three or four times) will convince any one
that in nothing he has written has amusement been his only aim.

Boz has been accused of not giving individuality to his characters—an
accusation, we think, particularly unsound. We would beg the reader to bear
in mind that a character may be hit off by a master hand in a few lines, and
yet retain so perfect an individuality as never to be confounded. Again, a
character may be left to develop itself in the action of the work—a method
Scott always preferred; or, thirdly, it may be described at length, and with
great accuracy of detail. The two first methods have been adopted by Boz;
the latter (which we conceive as the worst, but which we think his reviewers

have mistaken for the only one) he has not attempted. We would ask, are Jingle, Pickwick, the two Wellers, Solomon Pell, the Medical Students, Old Wardle, Job Trotter, not individuals in the truest sense of the word? That they partake of generality is admitted; and they partake of it from the very fidelity to nature with which they are drawn; for, however different individuals may be, there are always certain generalities running through every class;—*if there were not, how should we class them?*—and of these generalities alone do Boz's more prominent characters partake. The fat boy we admit to be a caricature, yet it gives variety to the work, and is too palpable to admit of cause to criticise; he is very laughable, and his peculiarities, however exaggerated, in many situations give great drollery to the scenes. But what we have more to notice regarding him, is that which has been entirely overlooked by the critics. On a former occasion we pointed out a canon, which we think must be always applied to works of imagination, *viz.*, extravagance is *inconsistent imagination*; poetry is *consistent imagination*, i.e., *constant with itself*. Thus when Ovid, by a beautiful prosopopoeia, creates Echo, he so *sustains* the creation throughout, that, though absurd in point of nature, it is true to poetry. Let this be applied to the 'fat boy'. The creation of this character is not true to nature, (and it is immediately seen not to be), but it is consistent with itself throughout. It has also been said that no man ever uttered broken sentences like Jingle; this we deny, for we ourselves knew a man, who, long before the *Pickwick* came out, always spoke in that way. 'Glorious day, my dear sir—fished—caught plenty—dined—capital wine—good fellow,' and so forth.

If asked by what peculiar talent is Boz characterised, we find ourselves at a dead fault—if we feel inclined to say, startling fidelity of observation, his wit and humour rise before us, and compel us to pause; and we are obliged to answer that we cannot fairly say what we think he is greatest in, but that it is a combination of those qualities (before enumerated) that characterises him. Look, for instance, at the trial scene, the 'Swarry' at Bath, the Medical Students' supper, the scene with Editor Pott and his Wife, (with her throwing herself on the rug, and asking why she was born), the scene in the Fleet, the Christmas Party, the Review, the Sliding and Skating, (with Tupman scream-ing '*Fire*' when his leader fell into the water), the Election, Nupkins Mayor, the Temperance Meeting, the Madman's Manuscript, and the Stroller's Tale, or any of the admirable situations in this book, and then ask yourself to which quality do you give the preference? There is only one thing worthy of notice, because it speaks the kindliness of his heart and the sympathy of his nature; and that is the charm which he throws over every nature, making you love it in spite of yourself. As for Pickwick, he is the incorporation of benevolence, with a dash of the infirmities of humanity; the two Wellers gain every one's good word; so does Wardle; and even Jingle, scamp though he be, shows many of the better points of our nature, and we like him in spite of ourselves. There is also another thing which is remarkable. Although he takes us into scenes of the lowest description, (more particularly in *Oliver Twist*), and although he gives us the language of vagabond, thief, footman, ostler, and gentleman, catching their several idioms with the most surprising felicity, yet there is not a single coarse word, or one allusion that could call a blush into the cheek of the most fastidious; and it is this circumstance which has not unfrequently raised our bile, to hear affected, mincing girls (who would come admirably under Swift's definitions of a *nice* man, 'one with *nasty* ideas'), who utter all their indelicate words in *French*, say they cannot read 'Boz', he is *so low*! This disgusting affection alarms some people from mentioning 'Boz' (without exception the purest writer of the day) before them.

We have said 'Boz' was the purest writer of the day; not alone in his language, where, when one of his low characters has to utter an oath, he does not give us this expression, but adds, 'with a fearful oath', or some such phrase, which does not destroy the illusion by making blackguards gentlemen, neither does it offend with the expression no lady should read, but he is the purest also in his morality, and this is the most estimable purity. For the offence of the one is that it is dirty, of the other, that it is corrupting!

'Boz's' satire is the finest that we ever read, because it is generally satire by *implication*, not personality—we do not say that it cuts so deep as Voltaire or Swift, or that it crushes like Hobbes—but it is pointed enough for its purpose, and has none of the bitter, withering tincture which forms so large a portion of satire in general; and it is done in that style that one might easily suppose an individual under the lash laughing at it himself, and feeling its deep truth at the same time—an effect very different to the satire of the great writers above-mentioned. And this satire is also more powerful, for when a man makes us writhe, we are more apt, with roused feelings, to attack him than to think of reforming ourselves, as was the case with Cobbett;[8] he shocked the prejudices of people too abruptly—told them they were fools in too plain a manner, to make them feel so. The meeting of the 'Pickwickians', and the speeches on the occasion, the Lion Hunting, Mrs Leo Hunter, the Election, the Two Editors, and the Discussion of the Seventeen Foreign Learned Societies and the Seventeen Home Learned Societies on the stone, bearing 'Bill Stumps, his mark', are playful touches of satire, yet one or two of them containing startling truths.

One of the peculiar merits of 'Boz' is that of bringing before us things which we have all noticed hundreds of times, yet which we never thought of committing to paper, and they are written with such unaffected ease, that we feel convinced he has witnessed every thing of the kind, and laughed at them. Then, too, his language, even on the most trivial points, has from a peculiar collocation of the words, or some happy expression, a drollery which is spoiled by repeating or reading loud, because this drollery arises from so fine an association of idea that the sound of the voice destroys it. We cannot help remarking, however, in this respect, a continual straining after humorous things, and this straining gives a laboured air to the work, besides which, it gives a want of light and shade, which fatigues the mind, if reading much at a time. While we are finding fault, an ungrateful task, and one which we feel rather reluctant about, when it is with one from whom we have derived so much gratification—we would notice the incongruity (the more remarkable in one so true to nature) of which he has been guilty in the character of Oliver Twist. To say nothing of the language which this uneducated workhouse-boy ordinarily uses, there are many phrases which amount to positive absurdities in one of his standing, among which is his reply to Mr Bumble (when about five or six years old), that he feels as if the blood was rushing from his heart, or some such metaphor, to express his grief. These are sad blots in this otherwise surpassing work—a work pregnant with philosophy and feeling, such as a metaphysician would be proud to have developed, with the same nicety and fidelity of observation, the same admirable delineation of character, and the same wit and humour as the Pickwick. What characters are the artful Dodger, Grimwig, Nancy, and Mr Bumble! We feel we must conclude, although we have not said one half of what we wished, or what we ought to have said. We have, we hope, fulfilled in some measure our purpose, *viz.*, to show that Boz has hit fame, not popularity, or in other words, that the admiration with which he is almost universally regarded, is well founded.

The Spontaneous Combustion Controversy (December 1852-September 1853)

G.H. Lewes in the Leader *(11 December 1852)*

There has been not a little outcry raised against the concluding incident of the last number of *Bleak House*: the death of Krook by Spontaneous Combustion is certainly not an agreeable incident, but it has a graver fault than that of 'shocking' people with 'sensitive nerves'; it is a fault in Art, and a fault in Literature, overstepping the limits of Fiction, and giving currency to a vulgar error. We must be permitted a passing remark on both these faults.

It is allowable to introduce the Supernatural in Art, but not the Improbable; the reason is, that in the one case, Imagination and our mysterious sympathy with the Unknown are appealed to, without pretence of claiming more than imaginative credence; in the other, the Understanding is called upon to ratify as a truth what it rejects as falsehood. When Shakespeare introduces the Supernatural, it is enough for us that in those remote ages people believed in the existence of Ghosts and Fairies; but when Balzac and Dumas introduce Clairvoyance as a part of their machinery, and make the events depend thereon, doing so as if Clairvoyance were an undoubted element in our human life, then the rebellious Understanding rejects as impertinent what it recognises as false. Dickens, therefore, in employing Spontaneous Combustion as a part of his machinery, has committed this fault of raising the incredulity of his readers; because even supposing Clairvoyance and Spontaneous Combustion to be scientific truths, and not the errors of imperfect science, still the simple fact that they belong to the extremely questionable opinions held by a very small minority, is enough to render their introduction into Fiction a mistake. They are questions to be argued, not to be treated as ascertained truths.

In the second place, we assure Mr Dickens that Spontaneous Combustion is not only a scientific error, which we doubt if he can find one organic chemist of any authority to countenance now, but is absolutely *impossible*, according to all known laws of combustion, and to the constitution of the human body. As a novelist he is not to be called to the bar of science; he has doubtless picked up the idea among the curiosities of his reading from some credulous adherent to the old hypothesis, and has accepted it as not improbable. This is not the place to enter minutely into such a question, but we will endeavour to state a few fundamental objections in language sufficiently popular for general comprehension.

The hypothesis is, that ardent drinkers so steep the tissues of their bodies in alcohol, or induce so morbid a constitution, that a highly combustible gas is formed within their bodies, which either spontaneously, or by the accidental approach of a flame, kindles, and burns away the whole body, as a candle burns away when once lighted.

Now, if you consider this simple fact, that in the human body *three-fourths of it are water*, and that even gunpowder will not ignite if damp, you will understand one reason why the human body is not combustible. You may char it as you may char damp wood, but you cannot produce flames from it as long as it retains its fluids.

Suppose the body soaked in alcohol, and the alcohol to remain in the tissues *as* alcohol, even that will not make the tissues burn. This Christmas you will, at snapdragon,[9] see the proof; the raisins will be soaked in alcohol, the alcohol will burn, but *not* the raisins.

It has been said, indeed, that in certain morbid conditions of the tissues, there is a gas formed which will ignite on contact with the air; this gas, phosphuretted hydrogen, is unfortunately a gas that never has been detected in any living tissue, that *could not* exist there, and even if it could, would only consume itself, and not the incombustible moist tissues; for to burn the body you must first completely *dry* it, and when you have dried it, it is no longer a living body. With moistened fingers we snuff candles unhurt; with moistened hands Boutigny tossed about molten iron as if it had been snow. Unless, therefore, it is maintained that the effect of continued drinking is altogether to change the conditions of vitality, to remove the liquids from the body, and substitute alcohol in their place, Spontaneous Combustion is an impossibility; the body will not burn except by the continued application of intense heat furnished externally; and cannot be made to *flame*.

In one sense, Spontaneous Combustion is the incessant act of Life itself: the tissues are called into constant activity through constant oxidation; and Man is truly said to be ashes. But Spontaneous Combustion, as the dénouement of the drama with blue fire from the side scenes, is only admissible as a metaphor.

Captain Marryat, it may be remembered, employed the same equivocal incident in *Jacob Faithful*. One phrase deserves immortality for its cynicism; it ran somewhat thus, 'There was a puff of smoke up the chimney, and that was all I saw of my mother.'

From Bleak House, *chapter 33, January 1853*

Out of the court, and a long way out of it, there is considerable excitement too; for men of science and philosophy come to look, and carriages set down doctors at the corner who arrive with the same intent, and there is more learned talk about inflammable gases and phosphuretted hydrogen than the court has ever imagined. Some of these authorities (of course the wisest) hold with indignation that the deceased had no business to die in the alleged manner; and being reminded by other authorities of a certain inquiry into the evidence for such deaths, reprinted in the sixth volume of the *Philosophical Transactions*; and also of a book not quite unknown, on English Medical Jurisprudence; and likewise of the Italian case of the Countess Cornelia Baudi as set forth in detail by one Bianchini, prebendary of Verona, who wrote a scholarly work or so, and was occasionally heard of in his time as having gleams of reason in him; and also of the testimony of Messrs Foderé and Mere, two pestilent Frenchmen who *would* investigate the subject; and further, of the corroborative testimony of Monsieur Le Cat, a rather celebrated French surgeon once upon a time, who had the unpoliteness to live in a house where such a case occurred, and even to write an account of it;—still they regard the late Mr Krook's obstinacy, in going out of the world by any such by-way, as wholly unjustified and personally offensive.

G.H. Lewes in the Leader *(5 February 1853)*

My dear Dickens,—What you write is read wherever the English language is read. This magnificent popularity carries with it a serious responsibility. A vulgar error countenanced by you becomes, thereby, formidable. Therefore am I, in common with many of your admirers, grieved to see that an error exploded from science, but one peculiarly adapted to the avid credulity of unscientific minds, has been seriously taken up by you, and sent all over the world with your imprimatur—an act which will tend to perpetuate the error in spite of the labours of a thousand philosophers. No journal but the

Leader has taken up this matter; but I would fain hope that if the case can be clearly stated, and the error shown, on all sides, to be an error, the press of England will lend its aid towards the disabusing of the public mind, and that you yourself will make some qualifying statement in your Preface.

My object in these two letters will be to show, that the highest scientific authorities of the day distinctly disavow the notion of Spontaneous Combustion; that the evidence in favour of the notion is worthless; that the theories in explanation are absurd; and that, according to all known chemical and physiological laws, Spontaneous Combustion is an *impossibility*. In continuing this discussion, I withdraw the slight veil of the anonymous 'we', and address you openly, in order that criticism may be deprived of even the appearance of asperity.

Let me commence with an apology. When this subject was first briefly noticed in the *Leader*, I very much underrated its seriousness. Believing that it was an error long banished to the region of vulgar errors, and that you had picked it up among the curiosities of your reading, without thinking of verifying it, I fancied a few plain statements of a physiological nature would be sufficient to convince you and others. Herein lay my mistake. I have since become aware of a serious fact,—*viz.*, that the belief is very current among medical men, and has grave authorities to support it. This, while it excuses your adoption of the theory, renders that adoption still more dangerous, for the readers of *Bleak House*, startled at the incident of Krook's death, will turn to their medical adviser for confirmation or disproof.

Nor is there anything wonderful in this assent of medical men; for,—not to mention the text-books where they would see it gravely set forth as an established fact,—they are, *ex officio*, rather men of *art* than men of *science*. I allude to this distinction between art and science (more clearly seen, perhaps, in the distinction between navigation and astronomy), to make way for subsequent exposition of the ignorance—or forgetfulness, equivalent to ignorance—shown by the adherents to the theory of Spontaneous Combustion—forgetfulness which may, without presumption, be pointed out by one who never wrote a prescription, and cannot set a dislocated limb.

It is due to you that I should declare a large majority on your side. Works on medical jurisprudence, Dictionaries, and Encyclopaedias, lend the theory their authority. Medical men frequently adopt it. So that you, not specially engaged in any subjects of this nature, may well be excused for having adopted it.

On the other hand, it is necessary I should declare that these authorities are insignificant, beside the authorities ranged against them. What are medical dictionaries and works on jurisprudence compared with authorities of such commanding eminence as Liebig, Bischoff, Regnault, Graham, Hofmann, and Owen?[10] I only name those whom I *know* to have pronounced unequivocally on this point, but I believe you will find no one eminent organic chemist of our day who credits Spontaneous Combustion. When I mentioned the subject to Professor Graham, the other evening, he replied, *'There is no more completely exploded error in chemistry.* It has been carefully examined, and found to have no vestige of probability.' Dr Hofmann said the same, adding that, two years ago, on the occasion of the Görlitz murder, the subject was thoroughly investigated by Liebig and Bischoff, who proved in court, that all the alleged cases were no more credible than were the alleged cases of witchcraft. In the last edition of his *Letters on Chemistry*, Liebig devotes a chapter to this subject, from which I will borrow largely in the course of my argument. [Here Lewes quotes from Liebig.]

Thus, as a question of *authority*, it is decisively against you. Perhaps you refuse to accept authority in such a matter; you may say, 'men of science, even the best of them, often err, and they may be wrong here.' Nevertheless, when you consider the excessive complexity of this subject, the superficial acquaintance with organic chemistry so general among medical writers, and the eminence of the men I have just named, you must acknowledge that none of the authorities on your side can be allowed to have equivalent value. Your reply to my remarks was this: [quotes from Part XI, chapter 33, of *Bleak House* the passage beginning 'Out of court, and a long way out of it...'].

Humorous, but not convincing! The authority of the *Philosophical Transactions* of 1750 can be brought into no chemical court of 1853; Beck's *Medical Jurisprudence*, though an excellent work, is only a work of erudition, not of scientific authority; the same of Fodéré's *Médecine Légale*; the prebendary of Verona may have been a first-rate scholar, but you will not ask any one to accept his authority in chemistry—a man may be a giant among verbs 'in μ' yet a child among oxides and anhydrous acids. Then, as to Le Cat, the fact of his 'having lived in the house where such a case occurred' is evidence only to the fact of combustion, not at all to the fact of the combustion having been spontaneous. In the house where he lived a body was found burned. His residence in no way alters the value of his evidence. The persons who were in the château where the last Prince de Condé was found hanging were witnesses to the fact that he was found hanging, but could not testify on the point at issue—whether the Prince hanged himself or was murdered.

[Lewes continues with more paraphrase and quotation from Liebig to disprove the phenomenon.]

There is in the human mind an inherent and irresistible desire for *explanations*, and a naturally facile credulity springing from that desire. We cannot hold the mind in suspense; we hate to admit our ignorance. We insist on overarching the chasm, if it be but with a *word*. For every unusual phenomenon there is consequently an explanation at once desired and forthcoming. The man who boldly flings forth the word, and satisfies the intellectual craving by even the semblance of an explanation, at once gains facile credence. This is the origin of legends and myths. Man, the hungry logophagist, swallowed the phrase Spontaneous Combustion as soon as it was thrown out to explain certain unexplained deaths; and semi-science built up theories to accredit it. Science, when grown older and wiser, saw through it; and eliminated the testimony to certain facts from the additions unconsciously furnished by imagination.

I utterly reject the evidence, partly because it is bad evidence for anything, but mainly because it testifies to a physical impossibility.

Let us not deceive ourselves respecting the value of reported cases. You, Dickens, would not believe a whole neighbourhood of respectable witnesses who should declare that the lamp-post had been converted, by a flash of lightning, into an elm tree. No, not if they swore to having *seen* it. Why? Simply because you would rather believe these witnesses in error than disbelieve the millions of testimonies *implied* in the establishment of those scientific truths which contradict such a transmutation. Although the notion of Spontaneous Combustion may not be so *obviously* impossible as the change from a lamp-post into an elm tree, yet I believe it is *really* so; and if the testimony of reported cases be allowed to shake our faith in the simple laws of organic chemistry, hereafter to be adduced, on the same ground respectable testimony may shake our faith in the possibility of a lamp-post becoming an elm. But for the clear enunciation of these laws, and their application to Spontaneous Combustion, I shall require another letter.

Believe me, my dear Dickens,
Yours very faithfully,
G.H. Lewes.

From the Preface to the First Edition of Bleak House *(September 1853)*

The possibility of what is called Spontaneous Combustion has been denied since the death of Mr Krook; and my good friend Mr Lewes—(quite mistaken, as he soon found, in supposing the thing to have been abandoned by all authorities) published some ingenious letters to me at the time when that event was chronicled, arguing that Spontaneous Combustion could not possibly be. I have no need to observe that I do not wilfully or negligently mislead my readers, and that before I wrote that description I took pains to investigate the subject. There are about thirty cases on record, of which the most famous, that of the Countess Cornelia de Bandi Cesenate, was minutely investigated and described by Giuseppe Bianchini, a prebendary of Verona, otherwise distinguished in letters, who published an account of it at Verona, in 1731, which he afterwards republished at Rome. The appearances beyond all rational doubt observed in that case, are the appearances observed in Mr Krook's case. The next famous instance happened at Rheims, six years earlier; and the historian in that case is Le Cat, one of the most renowned surgeons produced by France. The subject was a woman, whose husband was ignorantly convicted of having murdered her; but, on solemn appeal to a higher court, he was acquitted, because it was shown upon the evidence that she had died the death to which the name of Spontaneous Combustion is given. I do not think it necessary to add to these notable facts, and that general reference to the authorities which will be found at page 329, the recorded opinions and experiences of distinguished medical professors, French, English, and Scotch, in more modern days; contenting myself with observing, that I shall not abandon the facts until there shall have been a considerable Spontaneous Combustion of the testimony on which human occurrences are usually received.

Dickens in Relation to Criticism (February 1872)

The old feud between authors and critics, a feud old as literature, has not arisen on the ground of chariness in praise, but rather on the ground of deficient sympathy, and the tendency to interpret an author's work according to some standard which is not his. Instead of placing themselves at his point of view, and seeing what he has attempted, how far he has achieved the aim, and whether the aim itself were worthy of achievement, critics have thrust between his work and the public some vague conception of what they required, and measured it by an academic or conventional standard derived from other works. Fond as an author necessarily is of praise, and pained as he must always be by blame, he is far more touched by a sympathetic recognition of his efforts, and far more hurt by a misrepresentation of them. No hyperbole of laudation gives a tithe of the delight which is given by sympathetic insight. Unhappily for the author, this can but sparingly be given by critics, who trust less to their emotions than to their standards of judgment; for the greater the originality of the writer, and the less inclination he has for familiar processes and already-trodden tracks, the greater must be the resistance he will meet with from minds accustomed to move in those tracks, and to consider excellence confined within them. It is in the nature of the critical mind to judge according to precedent; and few minds have flexibility enough to adopt at once a novelty which is destined in its turn to become a precedent.

There is another source of pain. Besides the very great difficulties of independent judgment, of adjusting the mental focus to new objects under new perspectives, and the various personal considerations which trammel even open minds—considerations of friendship, station, renown, rivalry, etc.—there is the immense difficulty which all men find in giving anything like an adequate expression to their judgments. It is easy for us to say that a book has stirred, or instructed us; but it is by no means easy to specify the grounds of our pleasure, or profit, except in a very general way; and when we attempt to do so we are apt to make ludicrous mistakes. Thus it is that the criticism which begins with a general expression of gratitude to the author, will often deeply pain him by misplaced praise, or blame misdirected.

Longinus declares that criticism is the last result of abundant experience;

he might have added that even the amplest experience is no safeguard against utter failure. For it is true in Art as in the commonest details of life, that our perceptions are mainly determined by our preperceptions, our conceptions by our preconceptions. Hence I have long maintained the desirability of preserving as far as possible the individual character of criticism. The artist in his work gives expression to his individual feelings and conceptions, telling us how Life and Nature are mirrored in his mind; we may fairly state how this affects us, whether it accords with our experience, whether it moves or instructs us; but we should be very chary of absolute judgments, and be quite sure of our ground before venturing to assume that the public will feel, or ought to feel, as we feel. Now it is the tendency of criticism to pronounce absolute verdicts, to speak for all; and the exasperation of the artist at finding individual impressions given forth as final judgments is the main cause of the outcry against criticism. The writer who would feel little irritation on hearing that A and B were unmoved by his pathos, dead to his humour, unenlightened by his philosophy, may be excused if he writhe under the authoritative announcement that his pathos is maudlin, his humour flat, his philosophy shallow. He may be convicted of bad grammar, bad drawing, bad logic; and if the critic advances reasons for particular objections, these reasons may be weighed, and perhaps accepted with resignation if not without pain; but no verdict which does not distinctly carry its evidence can be accepted as more than an individual judgment; and in matters of Art there is always a great difficulty, sometimes a sheer impossibility, in passing from the individual to the universal. It is impossible to resist feeling. If an author makes me laugh, he is humorous; if he makes me cry, he is pathetic. In vain will any one tell me that such a picture is not laughable, not pathetic; or that I am wrong in being moved.

While from these and other causes, especially from the tendency to exaggerate what is painful, authors have deeply resented 'the malevolence' of critics—a malevolence which has been mostly incompetence, or incon- siderateness—it is not less true that there has been much heartfelt gratitude given by authors to critics who have sympathised with and encouraged them; and many lasting friendships have been thus cemented. It was thus that the lifelong friendship of Dickens and his biographer began, and was sustained. Nor is it just to object to Mr Forster's enthusiasm on the ground of his friendship, since he may fairly answer, 'Dickens was my friend because I so greatly admired him.' One thing is certain: his admiration was expressed long before all the world had acknowledged Dickens' genius, and was continued through the long years when the majority of writers had ceased to express much fervour of admiration, preferring rather to dwell on his shortcomings and exaggerations.

And this brings me to the noticeable fact that there probably never was a writer of so vast a popularity whose genius was so little *appreciated* by the critics. The very splendour of his successes so deepened the shadow of his failures that to many eyes the shadows supplanted the splendour. Fastidious readers were loath to admit that a writer could be justly called great whose defects were so glaring. They admitted, because it was indisputable, that Dickens delighted thousands, that his admirers were found in all classes, and in all countries; that he stirred the sympathy of masses not easily reached through Literature, and always stirred healthy, generous emotions; that he impressed a new direction on popular writing, and modified the Literature of his age, in its spirit no less than in its form; but they nevertheless insisted on his defects as if these outweighed all positive qualities; and spoke of him either with condescending patronage, or with sneering irritation. Surely this is a fact worthy of investigation? Were the critics wrong, and if so, in what consisted their error? How are we to reconcile this immense popularity with this critical contempt? The private readers and the public critics who were eager to take up each successive number of his works as it appeared, whose very talk was seasoned with quotations from and allusions to these works, who, to my knowledge, were wont to lay aside books of which they could only speak in terms of eulogy, in order to bury themselves in the 'new number' when the well-known green cover made its appearance—were nevertheless at this very time niggard in their praise, and lavish in their scorn of the popular humorist. It is not long since I heard a very distinguished man express measureless contempt for Dickens, and a few minutes afterwards, in reply to some representations on the other side, admit that Dickens had 'entered into his life'.

Dickens has proved his power by a popularity almost unexampled, embracing all classes. Surely it is a task for criticism to exhibit the sources of that power? If everything that has ever been alleged against the works be admitted, there still remains an immense success to be accounted for. It was not by their defects that these works were carried over Europe and America. It was not their defects which made them the delight of grey heads on the bench, and the study of youngsters in the counting-house and school-room. Other writers have been exaggerated, untrue, fantastic, and melodramatic; but they have gained so little notice that no one thinks of pointing out their defects. It is clear, therefore, that Dickens had powers which enabled him to triumph in spite of the weaknesses which clogged them; and it is worth inquiring what those powers were, and their relation to his undeniable defects.

I am not about to attempt such an inquiry, but simply to indicate two or three general points of view. It will be enough merely to mention in passing the primary cause of his success, his overflowing fun, because even uncompromising opponents admit it. They may be ashamed of their laughter, but they laugh. A revulsion of feeling at the preposterousness or extravagance of the image may follow the burst of laughter, but the laughter is irresistible, whether rational or not, and there is no arguing away such a fact.

Great as Dickens is in fun, so great that Fielding and Smollett are small in comparison, he would have been only a passing amusement for the world had he not been gifted with an imagination of marvellous vividness, and an emotional, sympathetic nature capable of furnishing that imagination with elements of universal power. Of him it may be said with less exaggeration than of most poets, that he was of 'imagination all compact'; if the other higher faculties were singularly deficient in him, this faculty was imperial. He was a seer of visions; and his visions were of objects at once familiar and potent. Psychologists will understand both the extent and the limitation of the remark, when I say that in no other perfectly sane mind (Blake, I believe, was not perfectly sane) have I observed vividness of imagination approaching so closely to hallucination. Many who are not psychologists may have had some experience in themselves, or in others, of that abnormal condition in which a man hears voices, and sees objects, with the distinctness of direct perception, although silence and darkness are without him; these *revived* impressions, revived by an internal cause, have precisely the same force and clearness which the impressions originally had when produced by an external cause. In the same degree of vividness are the images *constructed* by his mind in explanation of the voices heard or objects seen: when he imagines that the voice proceeds from a personal friend, or from Satan tempting him, the friend or Satan stands before him with the distinctness of objective reality; when he imagines that he himself has been transformed into a bear, his hands are seen by him as paws. In vain you represent to him that the voices he hears have no external existence; he will answer, as a patient pertinently answered Lélut:[11] 'You believe that I am speaking to you because you hear me, is it not so? Very well, I believe that voices are speaking to me because I hear them.' There is no power of effacing such conviction by argument. You may get the patient to assent to any premises you please, he will not swerve from his conclusions. I once argued with a patient who believed he had been transformed into a bear; he was quite willing to admit that the idea of such a transformation was utterly at variance with all experience; but he always returned to his position that God being omnipotent there was no reason to doubt his power of transforming men into bears: what remained fixed in his mind was the image of himself under a bear's form.

The characteristic point in the hallucinations of the insane, that which distinguishes them from hallucinations equally vivid in the sane, is the coercion of the image in *suppressing comparison* and all control of experience. Belief always accompanies a vivid image, for a time; but in the sane this belief will not persist against rational control. If I see a stick partly under water, it is impossible for me not to have the same feeling which would be produced by a bent stick out of water—if I see two plane images in the stereoscope, it is impossible not to have the feeling of seeing one solid object. But these beliefs are rapidly displaced by reference to experience. I know the stick is not bent, and that it will not appear bent when removed from the water. I know the seeming solid is not an object in relief, but two plane pictures. It is by similar focal adjustment of the mind that sane people know that their hallucinations are unreal. The images may have the vividness of real objects, but they have not the properties of real objects, they do not preserve consistent relations with other facts, they appear in contradiction to other beliefs. Thus if I see a black cat on the chair opposite, yet on my approaching the chair feel no soft object, and if my terrier on the hearthrug looking in the direction of the chair shows none of the well-known agitation which the sight of a cat produces, I conclude, in spite of its distinctness, that the image is an hallucination.

Returning from this digression let me say that I am very far indeed from wishing to imply any agreement in the common notion that 'great wits to madness nearly are allied'; on the contrary, my studies have led to the conviction that nothing is less like genius than insanity, although some men of genius have had occasional attacks; and further, that I have never observed any trace of the insane temperament in Dickens' works, or life, they being indeed singularly free even from the eccentricities which often accompany exceptional powers; nevertheless, with all due limitations, it is true that there is considerable light shed upon his works by the action of the imagination in hallucination. To him also *revived* images have the vividness of sensations; to him also *created* images have the coercive force of realities, excluding all control, all contradiction. What seems preposterous, impossible to us, seemed to him simple fact of observation. When he imagined a street, a house, a room, a figure, he saw it not in the vague schematic way of ordinary imagination, but in the sharp definition of actual perception, all the salient details obtruding themselves on his attention. He, seeing it thus vividly, made us also see it; and believing in its reality however fantastic, he communicated something of his belief to us. He presented it in such relief that we ceased to think of it as a picture. So definite and insistent was the image, that even while knowing it was false we could not help, for a moment, being affected, as it were, by his hallucination.

This glorious energy of imagination is that which Dickens had in common with all great writers. It was this which made him a creator, and made his creations universally intelligible, no matter how fantastic and unreal. His types established themselves in the public mind like personal experiences. Their falsity was unnoticed in the blaze of their illumination. Every humbug seemed a Pecksniff, every nurse a Gamp, every jovial improvident a Micawber, every stinted serving-wench a Marchioness. Universal experiences became individualised in these types; an image and a name were given, and the image was so suggestive that it seemed to *express* all that it was found to *recall*, and Dickens was held to have depicted what his readers supplied. Against such power criticism was almost idle. In vain critical reflection showed these figures to be merely masks,—not characters, but personified characteristics, caricatures and distortions of human nature,—the vividness of their presentation triumphed over reflection: their creator managed to communicate to the public his own unhesitating belief. Unreal and impossible as these types were, speaking a language never heard in life, moving like pieces of simple mechanism always in one way (instead of moving with the infinite fluctuations of organisms, incalculable yet intelligible, surprising yet familiar), these unreal figures affected the uncritical reader with the force of reality; and they did so in virtue of their embodiment of some real characteristic vividly presented. The imagination of the author laid hold of some well-marked physical trait, some peculiarity of aspect, speech, or manner which every one recognised at once; and the force with which this was presented made it occupy the mind to the exclusion of all critical doubts: only reflection could detect the incongruity. Think of what this implies! Think how little the mass of men are given to reflect on their impressions, and how their minds are for the most part occupied with sensations rather than ideas, and you will see why Dickens held an undisputed sway. Give a child a wooden horse, with hair for mane and tail, and wafer-spots for colouring, he will never be disturbed by the fact that this horse does not move its legs, but runs on wheels—the general suggestion suffices for his belief; and this wooden horse, which he can handle and draw, is believed in more than a pictured horse by a Wouvermanns or an Ansdell. It may be said of Dickens' human figures that they too are wooden, and run on wheels; but these are details which scarcely disturb the belief of admirers. Just as the wooden horse is brought within the range of the child's emotions, and dramatising tendencies, when he can handle and draw it, so Dickens' figures are brought within the range of the reader's interests, and receive from these interests a sudden illumination, when they are the puppets of a drama every incident of which appeals to the sympathies. With a fine felicity of instinct he seized upon situations having an irresistible hold over the domestic affections and ordinary sympathies. He spoke in the mother-tongue of the heart, and was always sure of ready listeners. He painted the life he knew, the life every one knew; for if the scenes and manners were unlike those we were familiar with, the feelings and motives, the joys and griefs, the mistakes and efforts of the actors were universal, and therefore universally intelligible; so that even critical spectators who complained that these broadly painted pictures were artistic daubs, could not wholly resist their effective suggestiveness. He set in motion the secret springs of sympathy by touching the domestic affections. He painted nothing ideal, heroic; but all the resources of the bourgeois epic were in his grasp. The world of thought and passion lay beyond his horizon. But the joys and pains of childhood, the petty tyrannies of ignoble natures, the genial pleasantries of happy natures, the life of the poor, the struggles of the street and back parlour, the insolence of office, the sharp social contrasts, east-wind and Christmas jollity, hunger, misery, and hot punch—these he could deal with, so that we laughed and cried, were startled at the revelation of familiar facts hitherto unnoted, and felt our pulses quicken as we were hurried along with him in his fanciful flight.

Such were the sources of his power. To understand how it is that critics quite competent to recognise such power, and even so far amenable to it as to be moved and interested by the works in spite of all their drawbacks, should have forgotten this undenied power, and written or spoken of Dickens with mingled irritation and contempt, we must take into account two natural tendencies—the bias of opposition, and the bias of technical estimate.

The bias of opposition may be illustrated in a parallel case. Let us suppose a scientific book to be attracting the attention of Europe by the boldness, suggestiveness, and theoretic plausibility of its hypotheses; this work falls into the hands of a critic sufficiently grounded in the science treated to be aware that its writer, although gifted with great theoretic power and occasional insight into unexplored relations, is nevertheless pitiably ignorant of the elementary facts and principles of the science; the critic noticing the power, and the talent of lucid exposition, is yet perplexed and irritated at ignorance which is inexcusable, and a reckless twisting of known facts into impossible relations, which seems wilful; will he not pass from marvelling at this inextricable web of sense and nonsense, suggestive insight and mischievous error, so jumbled together that the combination of this sagacity with this glaring inefficiency is a paradox, and be driven by the anger of opposition into an emphatic assertion that the belauded philosopher is a charlatan and an ignoramus? A chorus of admirers proclaims the author to be a great teacher, before whom all contemporaries must bow; and the critic observes this teacher on one page throwing out a striking hypothesis of some geometric relations in the planetary movements, and on another assuming that the hypothenuse is equal to its perpendicular and base, because the square of the hypothenuse is equal to the square of its sides—in one chapter ridiculing the atomic theory, and in another arguing that carbonic acid is obtained from carbon and nitrogen—can this critic be expected to join in the chorus of admirers? and will he not rather be exasperated into an opposition which will lead him to undervalue the undeniable qualities in his insistence on the undeniable defects?

Something like this is the feeling produced by Dickens' works in many cultivated and critical readers. They see there human character and ordinary events portrayed with a mingled verisimilitude and falsity altogether un-exampled. The drawing is so vivid yet so incorrect, or else is so blurred and formless, with such excess of *effort* (as of a showman beating on the drum) that the doubt arises how an observer so remarkably keen could make observations so remarkably false, and miss such very obvious facts; how the rapid glance which could swoop down on a peculiarity with hawk-like precision, could overlook all that accompanied and was organically related to that peculiarity; how the eye for characteristics could be so blind to character, and the ear for dramatic idiom be so deaf to dramatic language; finally, how the writer's exquisite susceptibility to the grotesque could be insensible to the occasional grotesqueness of his own attitude. Michael

Angelo is intelligible, and Giotto is intelligible; but a critic is nonplussed at finding the invention of Angelo with the drawing of Giotto. It is indeed surprising that Dickens should have observed man, and not been impressed with the fact that man is, in the words of Montaigne, *un être ondoyant et diverse*. And the critic is distressed to observe the substitution of mechanisms for minds, puppets for characters. It is needless to dwell on such monstrous failures as Mantalini, Rosa Dartle, Lady Dedlock, Esther Summerson, Mr Dick, Arthur Gride, Edith Dombey, Mr Carker—needless, because if one studies the successful figures one finds even in them only touches of verisimilitude. When one thinks of Micawber always presenting himself in the same situation, moved with the same spring, and uttering the same sounds, always confident on something turning up, always crushed and rebounding, always making punch—and his wife always declaring she will never part from him, always referring to his talents and her family—when one thinks of the 'catchwords' personified as characters, one is reminded of the frogs whose brains have been taken out for physiological purposes, and whose actions henceforth want the distinctive peculiarity of organic action, that of fluctuating spontaneity. Place one of these brainless frogs on his back and he will at once recover the sitting posture; draw a leg from under him, and he will at once draw it back again; tickle or prick him and he will push away the object, or take *one* hop out of the way; stroke his back, and he will utter *one* croak. All these things resemble the actions of the unmutilated frog, but they differ in being *isolated* actions, and *always the same*: they are as uniform and calculable as the movements of a machine. The uninjured frog may or may not croak, may or may not hop away; the result is never calculable, and is rarely a single croak or a single hop. It is this complexity or the organism which Dickens wholly fails to conceive; his characters have nothing fluctuating and incalculable in them, even when they embody true observations; and very often they are creations so fantastic that one is at a loss to understand how he could, without hallucination, believe them to be like reality. There are dialogues bearing the traces of straining effort at effect, which in their incongruity painfully resemble the absurd and eager expositions which insane patients pour into the listener's ear when detailing their wrongs, or their schemes. Dickens once declared to me that every word said by his characters was distinctly *heard* by him; I was at first not a little puzzled to account for the fact that he could hear language so utterly unlike the language of real feeling, and not be aware of its preposterousness; but the surprise vanished when I thought of the phenomena of hallucination. And here it may be needful to remark in passing that it is not because the characters are badly drawn and their language unreal, that they are to be classed among the excesses of imagination; otherwise all the bad novelists and dramatists would be credited with that which they especially want—powerful imagination. His peculiarity is not the incorrectness of the drawing, but the vividness of the imagination which while rendering that incorrectness insensible to him, also renders it potent with multitudes of his fellowmen. For although his weakness comes from excess in one direction, the force which is in excess must not be overlooked; and it is overlooked or undervalued by critics who, with what I have called the bias of opposition, insist only on the weakness.

This leads me to the second point, the bias of technical estimate. The main purpose of Art is delight. Whatever influences may radiate from that centre,—and however it may elevate or modify,—the one primary condition of influence is stirred emotion. No Art can teach which does not move; no Art can move without teaching. Criticism has to consider Art under two aspects, that of emotional pleasure, and that of technical pleasure. We all—public and critics—are susceptible of the former, are capable of being moved, and are delighted with what stirs the emotions, filling the mind with images having emotional influence; but only the critics are much affected by technical skill, and the pleasure it creates. *What* is done, what is suggested, constitutes the first aspect; *how* it is done the second. We all delight in imitation, and in the skill which represents one object in another medium; but the refinements of skill can only be appreciated by study. To a savage there is so little suggestion of a human face and form in a painted portrait that it is not even recognised as the representation of a man; whereas the same savage would delight in a waxwork figure, or a wooden Scotchman at the door of a tobacconist. The educated eye sees exquisite skill in the portrait, a skill which gives exquisite delight; but this eye which traces and estimates the subtle effects of colour and distribution of light and shade in the portrait, turns with disgust from the wax figure, or the wooden Highlander. In the course of time the pleasure derived from the perception of difficulty overcome, leads to such a preponderance of the technical estimate, that the sweep of the brush, or the composition of lines, becomes of supreme importance, and the connoisseur no longer asks, What is painted? but How is it painted? The *what* may be a patch of meadow, the bend of a river, or a street boy munching bread and cheese, and yet give greater delight by its *how*, than another picture which represented the Andes, Niagara, or a Madonna and Child. When the critic observes technical skill in a picture, he pronounces the painter to be admirable, and is quite unmoved by any great subject badly painted. In like manner a great poet is estimated by the greatness of his execution of great conceptions, not by the greatness of his intention.

How easily the critic falls into the mistake of overvaluing technical skill, and not allowing for the primary condition, how easily he misjudges works by applying to them technical rules derived from the works of others, need not here be dwelt on. What I wish to indicate is the bias of technical estimate which, acting with that bias of opposition just noted, has caused the critics to overlook in Dickens the great artistic powers which are proved by his immense success; and to dwell only on those great artistic deficiencies which exclude him from the class of exquisite writers. He worked in delft, not in porcelain. But his prodigal imagination created in delft forms which delighted thousands. He only touched common life, but he touched it to 'fine issues'; and since we are all susceptible of being moved by pictures of children in droll and pathetic situations, and by pictures of common suffering and common joy, any writer who can paint such pictures with sufficient skill to awaken these emotions is powerful in proportion to the emotion stirred. That Dickens had this skill is undisputed; and if critical reflection shows that the means he employs are not such as will satisfy the technical estimate, and consequently that the pictures will not move the cultivated mind, nor give it the deep content which perfect Art continues to create, making the work a 'joy for ever', we must still remember that in the present state of Literature, with hundreds daily exerting their utmost efforts to paint such pictures, it requires prodigious force and rare skill to impress images that will stir the universal heart. Murders are perpetrated without stint, but the murder of Nancy is unforgettable. Children figure in numberless plays and novels, but the deaths of little Nell and little Paul were national griefs. Seduction is one of the commonest of tragedies, but the scene in Peggoty's boathouse burns itself into the memory. Captain Cuttle and Richard Swiveller, the Marchioness and Tilly Slowboy, Pecksniff and Micawber, Tiny Tim and Mrs Gamp, may be imperfect presentations of human character, but they are types which no one can forget. Dr Johnson explained the popularity of some writer by saying, 'Sir, *his* nonsense suited *their* nonsense'; let us add, 'and his sense suited their sense', and it will explain the popularity of Dickens. Readers to whom all the refinements of Art and Literature are as meaningless hieroglyphs, were at once laid hold of by the reproduction of their own feelings, their own experiences, their own prejudices, in the irradiating splendour of his imagination; while readers whose cultivated sensibilities were alive to the most delicate and evanescent touches were, by virtue of their common nature, ready to be moved and delighted at his pictures and suggestions. The cultivated and uncultivated were affected by his admirable *mise en scène*, his fertile invention, his striking selection of incident, his intense vision of physical details. Only the cultivated who are made fastidious by cultivation paused to consider the pervading commonness of the works, and remarked that they are wholly without glimpses of a nobler life; and that the writer presents an almost unique example of a mind of singular force in which, so to speak, sensations never passed into ideas. Dickens sees and feels, but the logic of feeling seems the only logic he can manage. Thought is strangely absent from his works. I do not suppose a single thoughtful remark on life or character could be found throughout the twenty volumes. Not only is there a marked absence of the reflective tendency, but one sees no indication of the past life of humanity having ever occupied him; keenly as he observes the objects before him, he never connects his observations into a general expression, never seems interested in general relations of things. Compared with that of Fielding or Thackeray, his was merely an *animal* intelligence, i.e., restricted to perceptions. On this ground his early education was more fruitful and less injurious than it would have been to a nature constructed on a more reflective and intellectual type. It furnished him with rare and valuable experience, early developed his sympathies with the lowly and struggling, and did not starve any intellectual ambition. He never was and never would have been a student.

My acquaintance with him began soon after the completion of 'Pickwick'. Something I had written on that book pleased him, and caused him to ask me to call on him. (It is pleasant for me to remember that I made Thackeray's acquaintance in a similar way.) He was then living in Doughty Street; and those who remember him at that period will understand the somewhat disturbing effect produced on my enthusiasm for the new author by the sight of his bookshelves, on which were ranged nothing but three-volume novels and books of travel, all obviously the presentation copies from authors and publishers, with none of the treasures of the bookstall, each of which has its history, and all giving the collection its individual physiognomy. A man's library expresses much of his hidden life. I did not expect to find a bookworm, nor even a student, in the marvellous 'Boz'; but nevertheless this collection of books was a shock. He shortly came in, and his sunny presence quickly dispelled all misgivings. He was then, as to the last, a delightful companion, full of sagacity as well as animal spirits; but I came away more impressed with the fulness of life and energy than with any sense of distinction. I believe I only saw him once more before I went to Germany,[12] and two years had elapsed when next we met. While waiting in his library (in Devonshire Terrace) I of course glanced at the books. The well-known paper boards of the three-volume novel no longer vulgarised the place; a goodly array of standard works, well-bound, showed a more respectable and conventional ambition; but there was no physiognomy in the collection. A greater change was visible in Dickens himself. In these two years he had remarkably developed. His conversation turned on graver subjects than theatres and actors, periodicals and London life. His interest in public affairs, especially in social questions, was keener. He still remained completely outside philosophy, science, and the higher literature, and was too unaffected a man to pretend to feel any interest in them. But the vivacity and sagacity which gave a charm to intercourse with him had become weighted with a seriousness which from that time forward became more and more prominent in his conversation and his writings. He had already learned to look upon the world as a scene where it was the duty of each man in his own way to make the lot of the miserable Many a little less miserable; and, having learned that his genius gave him great power, he was bent on using that power effectively. He was sometimes laughed at for the importance he seemed to attach to everything relating to himself, and the solemnity with which he spoke of his aims and affairs; but this belonged to his quality. *Il se prenait au sérieux*, and was admirable because he did so. Whatever faults he may have committed there were none attributable to carelessness. He gave us his best. If the effort were sometimes too strained, and the desire for effect too obtrusive, there was no lazy indulgence, no trading on a great renown, no 'scrumbling' in his work. 'Whatever I have tried to do in life,' he said, speaking through Copperfield, 'I have tried with all my heart to do well. Never to put one hand to anything on which I could throw my whole self, and never to affect depreciation of my work, whatever it was, I now find to have been my golden rules.'

Since I have been led in the course of argument to touch upon my personal acquaintance with Dickens, I may take advantage of the opening to introduce a point not mentioned in Mr Forster's memoir, though he most probably is familiar with it. Mr Forster has narrated Dickens' intense grief at the death of his sister-in-law, Mary—a grief which for two months interrupted the writing of 'Pickwick', and which five years afterwards thus moves him in a letter to Mr Forster on the death of her grandmother. The passage itself is in every way interesting, displaying a depth and delicacy of feeling, combined with a tenderness towards the sacredness due to the wishes of the dead, which is very noticeable:

It is a great trial to me to give up Mary's grave; greater than I can possibly express. I thought of moving her to the catacomb, and saying nothing about it; but then I remembered that the poor old lady is buried next her at her own desire, and could not find it in my heart directly she is laid in the earth to take her grandchild away. The desire to be buried next her is as strong upon me now as it was five years ago; and I *know* (for I don't think there ever was love like that I bear her) that it will never diminish. I cannot bear the thought of being excluded from her dust; and yet I feel that her brothers and sisters and her mother have a better right than I to be placed beside her. It is but an idea. I neither hope nor think (God forbid) that our spirits would ever mingle *there.* I ought to get the better of it, but it is very hard. I never contemplated this; and coming so suddenly, and after being ill, it disturbs me more than it ought. It seems like losing her a second time.

Again, when writing from America and describing his delight at the Niagara Falls, he says:

What would I give if you and Mac were here to share the sensations of this time! I was going to add, what would I give if the dear girl whose ashes lie in Kensal Green had lived to come so far along with us; but she has been here many times, I doubt not, since her sweet face faded from my earthly sight.

Several years afterwards, in the course of a quiet chat over a cigar, we got on a subject which always interested him, and on which he had stored many striking anecdotes—dreams. He then narrated, in his quietest and most impressive manner, that after Mary's death her image not only haunted him by day, but for twelve months visited his dreams every night. At first he had refrained from mentioning it to his wife; and after deferring this some time, felt unable to mention it to her. He had occasion to go to Liverpool, and as he went to bed that night there was a strong hope that the change of bed might break the spell of his dreams. It was not so however. That night as usual the old dream was dreamt. He resolved to unburthen his mind to his wife, and wrote that very morning a full account of his strange experience. From that time he ceased to dream of her. I forget whether he said he had never dreamt of her since; but I am certain of the fact that the spell had been broken then and there.

Here is another contribution to the subject of dreams, which I had from him shortly before his death. One night after one of his public readings, he dreamt that he was in a room where every one was dressed in scarlet. (The probable origin of this was the mass of scarlet opera-cloaks worn by the ladies among the audience, having left a short of *afterglow* on his retina.) He stumbled against a lady standing with her back towards him. As he apologised she turned her head and said, quite unprovoked, 'My name is Napier'. The face was one perfectly unknown to him, nor did he know any one named Napier. Two days after he had another reading in the same town, and before it began, a lady friend came into the waiting-room accompanied by an unknown lady in a scarlet opera-cloak, 'who,' said his friend, 'is very desirous of being introduced.' 'Not Miss Napier?' he jokingly inquired. 'Yes; Miss Napier.' Although the face of his dream-lady was not the face of this Miss Napier, the coincidence of the scarlet cloak and the name was striking.

In bringing these detached observations to a close, let me resume their drift by saying that while on the one hand the critics seem to me to have been fully justified in denying him the possession of many technical excellences, they have been thrown into unwise antagonism which has made them overlook or undervalue the great qualities which distinguished him; and that even on technical grounds their criticism has been so far defective that it failed to recognise the supreme powers which ensured his triumph in spite of all defects. For the reader of cultivated taste there is little in his works beyond the stirring of their emotions—but what a large exception! We do not turn over the pages in search of thought, delicate psychological observation, grace of style, charm of composition; but we enjoy them like children at a play, laughing and crying at the images which pass before us. And this illustration suggests the explanation of how learned and thoughtful men can have been almost as much delighted with the works as ignorant and juvenile readers; how Lord Jeffrey[13] could have been so affected by the presentation of Little Nell, which most critical readers pronounce maudlin and unreal. Persons unfamiliar with theatrical representations, consequently unable to criticise the acting, are stirred by the suggestions of the scenes presented; and hence a great philosopher, poet, or man of science, may be found applauding an actor whom every play-going apprentice despises as stagey and inartistic.

Charlotte Brontë and Mrs Gaskell

Jane Eyre (December 1847)

We wish to gossip about novels in general, and some new ones in particular. Novel readers are to be divided into three classes,—those who 'adore' them, who will read them, perhaps, in the course of a wet day, and whose tastes are as indiscriminating as their appetites are insatiable. They are the pillars on which repose the ponderous weights of the circulating-library—the Colburn caryatides![14] They are the innocent-minded, to whom *Reginald Delmar, Adalbert Montmorency*, and *Ida de Courcy* are heroes and heroines; by whom the characters, passions, incidents, and dialogue adopted by the clumsiest dramatists and novelists, are believed to represent life. They are the mysteriously generalised entity so often thus solemnly apostrophised: 'Gentle reader, such is the effect of unbridled passion!'

The second class is the antithesis of the first. Its members 'despise' all novels as 'frivolous' and 'grievous waste of time'. Hear them: *they* never read novels! This is uttered with the complacency which surrounds the expression of any fact of which a man thinks he has cause to be proud. Yet is it surprising how much of the 'circulating library trash' these supercilious readers manage to wade through, taking only their own confession as our guide. An odious and pretending class!

The third class is composed of those persons, and they are not few, who, unable to devour novels like the first—not having the necessary time, not having the requisite appetite—do, nevertheless, unlike the second, thoroughly enjoy and unhesitatingly proclaim the enjoyment they derive from a good novel. The great difficulty with them is, to get novels enough; but as the good are scarce, and their tastes cannot be tickled with the indifferent, they remain, in effect, limited in their enjoyment. Ourselves we place in the third class. We are somewhat fastidious in our tastes; we know that our standard is a high one; but if difficult to please, no schoolgirl is more delighted than we are when we meet with a novel we can read through. Our enjoyment is keen and hearty; perhaps made more so by the many disappointments we pass through before we reach the book that does delight us; and we then feel that novel-writing, or novel-reading, so far from being frivolous or injurious, is really a fine thing, and the novel rises into the first rank of literature. This is not the time and place for a defence of the novel, though few causes are easier to defend; we are now only preparing the reader's mind for the reception of a few remarks which a recent feast of novel-reading has

81

suggested, and which, if, like us, he knows how to relish a good book, will deserve his thanks, since the remarks will indicate to him where he may safely go for amusement.

To make ourselves still further intelligible, and to give our criticisms their just significance, we may make a brief confession of our peculiar tastes. What we most heartily enjoy and applaud, is truth in the delineation of life and character: incidents however wonderful, adventures however perilous, are almost as naught when compared with the deep and lasting interest excited by any thing like a correct representation of life. That, indeed, seems to us to be Art, and the only Art we care to applaud. To make our meaning precise, we should say that Fielding and Miss Austen are the greatest novelists in our language. Scott has greater invention, more varied powers, a more poetical and pictorial imagination; but although his delineation of character is generally true, as far as it goes, it is never deep; and his deficiencies are singularly apparent, when, as in *St Ronan's Well*, he ventures into the perilous sphere of contemporary life. We bid no one adopt our opinions on this point. If Scott is preferred to all others, we have no quarrel on that score; we have merely to record an individual opinion, that great—indeed, astonishing as Scott's powers of attraction are, we would rather have written *Pride and Prejudice*, or *Tom Jones*, than any of the Waverley Novels. Scott was the Ariosto of prose romance. Let no word savouring of depreciation fall from our lips; but if he was an Ariosto, he was not a Shakespeare: he had not that singular faculty of penetrating into the most secret recesses of the heart, and of shewing us a character in its inward and outward workings, in its involuntary self-betrayals and subtle self-sophistication; he had not, above all, those two Shakespearian qualities—tenderness and passion. We can never hear him likened to Shakespeare without a strange sense of the incongruity. The two minds had certainly some peculiarities in common, but they belonged altogether to a different species. Now Miss Austen has been called a prose Shakespeare; and, among others, by Macaulay. In spite of the sense of incongruity which besets us in the words *prose* Shakespeare, we confess the greatness of Miss Austen, her marvellous dramatic power, seems more than any thing in Scott akin to the greatest quality in Shakespeare.

Not to pursue this point further, we may repeat our confession of decided preference for true and artistic delineation of life and character to all the other ingredients supposed to be necessary for the success of a novel. Adventure will not replace it; eloquence will not atone for its absence; wit or humour will not conceal the deficiency. A novel may by the dashing brilliancy of its style create a momentary sensation; by some well-kept-up mystery, some rapid incidents, or some subject of horror dragged from the reeking shambles of civilisation, it may hurry the reader onward through its three volumes; but to produce a pleasant, satisfactory, and lasting impression, it must be true to nature. It will then live. It will bear reading and re-reading. It will create towards the author a feeling of regard in all his readers, to whom it will be a pleasant and thought-suggesting reminiscence. It will have fulfilled the real purpose of literature. [Here Lewes reviews Savage's novel, *The Bachelor of the Albany*.]

After laughing over the *Bachelor of the Albany*, we wept over *Jane Eyre*. This, indeed, is a book after our own heart; and, if its merits have not forced it into notice by the time this paper comes before our readers, let us, in all earnestness, bid them lose not a day in sending for it. The writer is evidently a woman, and, unless we are deceived, new in the world of literature. But, man or woman, young or old, be that as it may, no such book has gladdened our eyes for a long while. Almost all that we require in a novelist she has: perception of character, and power of delineating it; picturesqueness; passion; and knowledge of life. The story is not only of singular interest, naturally evolved, unflagging to the last, but it fastens itself upon your attention, and will not leave you. The book closed, the enchantment continues. With the disentanglement of the plot, and the final release of the heroine from her difficulties, your interest does not cease. You go back in memory to the various scenes in which she has figured; you linger on the way, and muse upon the several incidents in the life which has just been unrolled before you, affected by them as if they were the austere instructions drawn from a sorrowing existence, and not merely the cunning devices of an author's craft. Reality—deep, significant reality—is the great characteristic of the book. It *is* an autobiography,—not, perhaps, in the naked facts and circumstances, but in the actual suffering and experience. The form may be changed, and here and there some incidents invented; but the spirit remains such as it was. The machinery of the story may have been borrowed, but by means of this machinery the authoress is unquestionably setting forth her own experience. This gives the book its charm: it is soul speaking to soul; it is an utterance from the depths of struggling, suffering, much-enduring spirit: *suspiria de profundis!*

When we see a young writer exhibiting such remarkable power as there is in *Jane Eyre*, it is natural that we should ask, Is this experience drawn from an abundant source, or is it only the artistic mastery over small materials? Because, according as this question is answered, there are two suggestions to be made. Has the author seen much more and felt much more than what is here communicated? Then let new works continue to draw from that rich store-house. Has the author led a quiet, secluded life, uninvolved in the great vortex of the world, undisturbed by varied passions, untried by strange calamities? Then let new works be planned and executed with excessive circumspection; for, unless a novel be built out of real experience, it can have no real success. To have vitality, it must spring from vitality. All the craft in the circulating-library will not make that seem true which is not true—will not affect the reader after his curiosity is satisfied.

It is too often forgotten, that the most ignorant reader is a competent judge of truth in this sense, that he is always powerfully influenced by it, and always feels the absence of it. *Hamlet, Don Quixotte, Faust,* marvellous creations as they are, with roots diving deep into the profoundest regions, and with branches rising into the highest altitudes of thought, do, nevertheless, powerfully interest even the foolishest readers. There is a chord in the human breast which vibrates sympathetically whenever it be touched; and no artist need fear that, if he touch it with skill, his skill will be thrown away.

Quite true it is that the merest platitudes will also gain attention; true that a novelist, scorning all experience, may give such a representation of life as, while outraging every thing we know of life, while substituting the empty phantasmagoria of the library for breathing flesh and blood, shall, nevertheless, enchain the reader's attention, and create for the author a certain vogue. This may seem to militate against all we have said on the necessity for truth,—may *seem,* but does not. For, not to speak of the merited contempt with which all cultivated minds regard such an author and his works, it is very certain that the admiring readers themselves treat him no better than they would a conjuror; they are not his re-readers. No one, as Jean Paul[15] remarks, will look twice at a conjuring trick of which he knows the secret. No one will read one of these novels twice when he knows the plot. The curiosity in both cases is excited, and during that excitement the means are never attended to, only the end. Thus we often hear professed novel-readers declare, that however stupid, trashy, and absurd the novel, they must finish it, 'to see what becomes of the hero and heroine!' They are compelled to finish; but they never go back to it, never think of it afterwards. Whereas, if to that curiosity about the story there are added scenes which, being transcripts from the book of life, affect the reader as all truth of human nature must affect him, then the novel rises from the poor level of street-conjuring into the exalted region of art.

Of this kind is *Jane Eyre.* There are some defects in it—defects which the excellence of the rest only brings into stronger relief. There is, indeed, too much melodrama and improbability, which smack of the circulating-library,—we allude particularly to the mad wife and all that related to her, and to the wanderings of Jane when she quits Thornfield; yet even those parts are powerfully executed. But the earlier parts—all those relating to Jane's childhood and her residence at Lowood, with much of the strange love story—are written with remarkable beauty and truth. The characters are few; and drawn with unusual mastery: even those that are but sketched such as Mr Brocklehurst, Miss Temple, Mrs Fairfax, Rosamund, and Blanche—are sketched with a vividness which betrays the cunning hand: a few strokes, and the figure rises before you. Jane herself is a creation. The delicate handling of this figure alone implies a dramatic genius of no common order. We never lose sight of her plainness; no effort is made to throw romance about her—no extraordinary goodness or cleverness appeals to your admiration; but you admire, you love her,—love her for the strong will, honest mind, loving heart, and peculiar but fascinating person. A creature of flesh and blood, with very fleshy infirmities, and very mortal excellences; a woman, not a pattern: that is the Jane Eyre here represented. Mr Rochester is also well drawn, and from the life; but it is the portrait of a man drawn by a woman, and is not comparable to the portrait of Jane. The way in which the authoress contrives to keep our interest in this imperfect character is a lesson to novelists. St John Rivers, the missionary, has a touch of the circulating-library, but not enough to spoil the truth of delineation; there is both art and artifice in the handling, and, although true in the main, and very powerful in parts, one feels a certain misgiving about him: it is another example of the woman's pencil. Helen Burns is lovely and loveable; true, we believe, even in her exalted spirituality and her religious fervour: a character at once eminently ideal and accurately real.

The story is so simple in its outlines, yet so filled out—not spun out—with details, that we shall not do it the injustice of here setting down the mere plot. It is confined to few characters, and is easily, naturally evolved (with exceptions always of those melodramatic incidents before alluded to), carrying the reader on with it to the end. We have spoken of the reality stamped upon almost every part; and that reality is not confined to the characters and incidents, but is also striking in the descriptions of the various aspects of Nature, and of the houses, rooms, and furniture. The pictures stand out distinctly before you: they *are* pictures, and not mere bits of 'fine writing'. The writer is evidently painting by words a picture that she has in her mind, not 'making-up' from vague remembrances and with the consecrated phrases of 'poetical prose'. It would be exceedingly easy to quote many examples, but we will content ourselves with this very brief passage, strongly charac- terised by the reality we speak of. It occurs in the third page:-

> Folds of scarlet drapery shut in my view to the right hand; to the left were the clear panes of glass, protecting, but not separating, me from the drear November day. At intervals, while turning over the leaves of my book, I studied the aspect of that winter afternoon. Afar, it offered a pale blank of mist and cloud; near, a scene of wet lawn and storm-beat shrub, with ceaseless rain sweeping away wildly before a long and lamentable blast.

Is not that vivid, real, picturesque? It reads like a page out of one's own life; and so do many other pages in the book

In her delineation of country-houses and good society there is the ease and accuracy of one who has well known what she describes. We noticed but one slip of the pen, and that was giving to the door of Thornfield Hall a knocker; all the rest is not only accurate, but accurate in being represented from the governess point of view.

This faculty for objective representation is also united to a strange power of subjective representation. We do not simply mean the power over the

passions— the psychological intuition of the artist, but the power also of
connecting external appearances with internal effects—of representing the
psychological interpretation of material phenomena. This is shewn in many
a fine description; but we select that of the punished child shut up in the old
bed-room, because it exhibits at the same time the power we speak of, and
the power before-mentioned of representing the material aspect of things.
The passage about the looking-glass, towards the close, strikes us as singularly fine:

> The red room was a spare chamber, very seldom slept in; I might say
> never, indeed; unless when a chance influx of visitors at Gateshead
> Hall, rendered it necessary to turn to account all the accommodation
> it contained: yet it was one of the largest and stateliest chambers in the
> mansion. A bed, supported on massive pillars of mahogany, hung with
> curtains of deep red damask, stood out like a tabernacle in the centre;
> the two large windows, with their blinds always drawn down, were
> half-shrouded in festoons and falls in similar drapery; the carpet was
> red; the table at the foot of the bed was covered with a crimson cloth;
> the walls were a soft fawn colour, with a blush of pink in it, the
> wardrobe, the toilet-table, the chairs, were of darkly polished maho-
> gany. Out of these surrounding shades rose high, and glared white, the
> piled-up mattresses and pillows of the bed, spread with a snowy
> Marseilles counterpane. Scarcely less prominent was an ample, cu-
> shioned, easy chair, near the head of the bed, also white, with a
> footstool before it, and looking, as I thought, like a pale throne.
>
> This room was chill, because it seldom had a fire; it was silent,
> because remote from the nursery and kitchens; solemn, because it was
> known to be so seldom entered. The housemaid alone came here on
> Saturdays, to wipe from the mirrors and the furniture a week's quiet
> dust; and Mrs Reed herself, at far intervals, visited it to review the
> contents of a certain secret drawer in the wardrobe, where were stored
> divers parchments, her jewel-casket, and a miniature of her deceased
> husband; and in those last words lies the secret of the red room; the
> spell which kept it so lonely in spite of its grandeur.
>
> Mr Reed had been dead nine years; it was in this chamber he
> breathed his last; here he lay in state; hence his coffin was borne by
> the undertaker's men; and, since that day, a sense of dreary consec-
> ration had guarded it from frequent intrusion. My seat, to which Bessie
> and the bitter Miss Abbot had left me riveted, was a low ottoman near
> the marble chimneypiece; the bed rose before me; to my right hand
> there was the high, dark wardrobe, with subdued, broken reflexions
> varying the gloss of its panels; to my left were the muffled windows;
> a great looking-glass between them repeated the vacant majesty of the
> bed and room. I was not quite sure whether they had locked the door;

and, when I dared to move, I got up, and went to see. Alas! yes: no jail was ever more secure. Returning, I had to cross before the looking-glass; my fascinated glance involuntarily explored the depth it revealed. All looked colder and darker in that visionary hollow than in reality; and the strange little figure there gazing at me, with a white face and arms specking the gloom, and glittering eyes of fear moving where all else was still, had the effect of a real spirit. I thought it like one of those tiny phantoms, half fairy, half imp, Bessie's evening stories represented as coming up out of lone, ferny dells in moors, and appearing before the eyes of belated travellers. I returned to my stool.

We have no space to go on quoting charming passages, though our pencil has been freely employed in marking them. We have already given enough to make both the authoress and the reader understand what we mean by our praise. To her we emphatically say, Persevere; keep reality distinctly before you; and paint it as accurately as you can: invention will never equal the effect of truth.

The style of *Jane Eyre* is peculiar; but, except that she admits too many Scotch or North-country phrases, we have no objection to make to it, and for this reason: although by no means a fine style, it has the capital point of all great styles in being *personal*,—the written speech of an individual, not the artificial language made up from all sorts of books.

In philosophical remark she is sparing, and justly. It is what few women ever succeed in; as Göthe jocosely says:

Was die Weiber lieben und hassen,
Das wollen wir ihnen gelten lassen;
Wenn sie aber urtheilen and meinen,
Da will's oft wunderlich erscheinen.[16]

It is, therefore, a decided gain to the reader, this absence of aphoristic display; and many a writer, male and female, would be more agreeable if a similar absence were noticeable in their works. [Here Lewes goes on to review a French novel.]

Charlotte Brontë: Three Letters to G.H. Lewes (November 1847-January 1848)

6 November 1847

Dear Sir
Your letter reached me yesterday; I beg to assure you, that I appreciate fully the intention with which it was written, and I thank you sincerely both for its cheering commendation and valuable advice.

You warn me to beware of melodrama, and you exhort me to adhere to the real. When I first began to write, so impressed was I with the truth of the principles you advocate, that I determined to take Nature and Truth as my sole guides, and to follow in their footprints; I restrained imagination, eschewed romance, repressed excitement; over-bright colouring, too, I avoided, and sought to produce something which should be soft, grave, and true.

My work (a tale in one volume) being completed, I offered it to a publisher. He said it was original, faithful to nature, but he did not feel warranted in accepting it; such a work would not sell. I tried six publishers in succession; they all told me it was deficient in 'startling incident' and 'thrilling excitement', that it would never suit the circulating-libraries, and, as it was on those libraries the success of works of fiction mainly depended, they could not undertake to publish what would be overlooked there.

Jane Eyre was rather objected to at first, on the same grounds, but finally found acceptance.

I mention this to you, not with a view of pleading exemption from censure, but in order to direct your attention to the root of certain literary evils. If, in your forthcoming article in *Frazer*, you would bestow a few words of enlightenment on the public who support the circulating libraries, you might, with your powers, do some good.

You advise me, too, not to stray far from the ground of experience, as I become weak when I enter the region of fiction; and say, 'real experience is perenially interesting, and to all men.'

I feel that this also is true; but, dear Sir, is not the real experience of each individual very limited? And, if a writer dwells upon that solely or principally, is he not in danger of repeating himself, and also of becoming an egotist? Then, too, imagination is a strong, restless faculty, which claims to be heard and exercised: are we to be quite deaf to her cry, and insensate to her struggles? When she shows us bright pictures, are we never to look at them, and try to reproduce them? And when she is eloquent, and speaks rapidly and urgently in our ear, are we not to write to her dictation?

I shall anxiously search the next number of *Frazer* for your opinions on these points.—Believe me, dear Sir, yours gratefully,

C. Bell.

12 January 1848

Dear Sir

I thank you then sincerely for your generous review; and it is with the sense of double content I express my gratitude, because I am now sure the tribute is not superfluous or obtrusive. You were not very severe on my *Jane Eyre*; you were very lenient. I am glad you told me my faults plainly in private for in your public notice you touch on them so lightly, I should perhaps have passed them over, thus indicated, with too little reflection.

I mean to observe your warning about being careful how I undertake new works; my stock of materials is not abundant, but very slender; and, besides, neither my experience, my acquirements, nor my powers, are sufficiently varied to justify my ever becoming a frequent writer. I tell you this, because your article in *Frazer* left on me an uneasy impression that you were disposed to think better of the author of *Jane Eyre* than that individual deserved; and I would rather you had a correct than a flattering opinion of me, even though I should never see you.

If I ever *do* write another book, I think I will have nothing of what you call 'melodrama'; I *think* so, but I am not sure. I *think*, too, I will endeavour to follow the counsel which shines out of Miss Austen's 'mild eyes', 'to finish more and be more subdued'; but neither am I sure of that. When authors write best, or, at least, when they write most fluently, an influence seems to waken in them, which becomes their master—which will have its own way—putting out of view all behests but its own, dictating certain words, and insisting on their being used, whether vehement or measured in their nature; new-moulding characters, giving unthought-of turns to incidents, rejecting carefully-elaborated old ideas, and suddenly creating and adopting new ones.

Is it not so? And should we try to counteract this influence? Can we indeed counteract it?

I am glad that another work of yours will soon appear; most curious shall I be to see whether you will write up to your principles, and work out your own theories. You did not do it altogether in *Ranthorpe*—at least not in the latter part; but the first portion was, I think, nearly without fault; then it had a pith, truth, significance in it, which gave the book sterling value; but to write so, one must have seen and known a great deal, and I have seen and known very little.

Why do you like Miss Austen so very much? I am puzzled on that point. What induced you to say that you would have rather written *Pride and Prejudice*, or *Tom Jones*, than any of the Waverley Novels?

I had not seen *Pride and Prejudice* till I read that sentence of yours, and then I got the book. And what did I find? An accurate, daguerreotyped portrait of a commonplace face! a carefully-fenced, highly-cultivated garden, with neat borders and delicate flowers; but no glance of a bright, vivid physiognomy, no open country, no fresh air, no blue hill, no bonny beck. I should hardly like to live with her ladies and gentlemen, in their elegant but confined houses. These observations will probably irritate you, but I shall run the risk.

Now I can understand admiration of George Sand; for though I never saw any of her works which I admired throughout (even *Consuelo*, which is the best, or the best that I have read, appears to me to couple strange extravagance with wondrous excellence), yet she has a grasp of mind, which, if I cannot fully comprehend, I can very deeply respect; she is sagacious and profound; Miss Austen is only shrewd and observant.

Am I wrong—or were you hasty in what you said? If you have time, I should be glad to hear further on this subject; if not, or if you think the questions frivolous, do not trouble yourself to reply.—I am, yours respectfully.

C. Bell

18 January 1848

Dear Sir

I must write one more note, though I had not intended to trouble you again so soon. I have to agree with you, and to differ from you.

You correct my crude remarks on the subject of 'influence'; well, I accept your definition of what the effects of that influence should be; I recognise the wisdom of your rules for its regulation....

What a strange lecture comes next in your letter! You say I must familiarise my mind with the fact, that 'Miss Austen is not a poetess, has no "sentiment" (you scornfully enclose the word in inverted commas), no eloquence, none of the ravishing enthusiasm of poetry,'—and then you add, I *must* 'learn to acknowledge her as *one of the greatest artists, of the greatest painters of human character*, and one of the writers with the nicest sense of means to an end that ever lived'.

The last point only will I ever acknowledge.

Can there be a great artist without poetry?

What I call—what I will bend to, as a great artist then—cannot be destitute of the divine gift. But by *poetry*, I am sure, you understand something different to what I do, as you do by 'sentiment'. It is *poetry*, as I comprehend the word, which elevates that masculine George Sand, and makes out of something coarse, something godlike. It is 'sentiment', in my sense of the term—sentiment jealously hidden, but genuine, which extracts the venom from that formidable Thackeray, and converts what might be corrosive poison into purifying elixir.

If Thackeray did not cherish in his large heart deep feeling for his kind, he would delight to exterminate; as it is, I believe, he wishes only to reform. Miss Austen being, as you say, without 'sentiment', without *poetry*, maybe *is* sensible, real (more *real* than *true*), but she cannot be great.

I submit to your anger, which I have now excited (for have I not questioned the perfection of your darling?); the storm may pass over me. Nevertheless, I will, when I can (I do not know when that will be, as I have no access to a circulating-library), diligently peruse all Miss Austen's works, as you recommend...You must forgive me for not always being able to think as you do, and still believe me, yours gratefully,

C. Bell.

Charlotte Brontë's *Villette* and Mrs Gaskell's *Ruth* (April 1853)

Should a work of Art have a moral? In other words, must the Artist, during creation, keep the wandering caprices of his fancy within the limits of some didactic formula? The question has been often, but somewhat confusedly, debated. It has been seen, on the one hand, that the merely didactic tale frustrates, in a great measure, its own objects: the reader resents having his pill gilded—resents having the leaves of a religious tract slipped in between the pages of a novel; and in the spirit of reaction, it has been said that the Artist has nothing to do with morality. On the other hand, there are people whose first question is, What is the moral? What does this prove? Hegel has said very truly, that 'there is a moral in every work of art, but it depends on him that draws it.' George Sand, in the preface to her last novel, makes a decided stand against this moral requisition, and both in her own person, and vicariously for all other novelists, declares that 'art can prove nothing, nor should it be expected to prove anything.' She says that readers have always wished to see vice punished and virtue rewarded; and that, in this respect, she is one of the public. But poetical justice proves nothing either in a story or in a drama. When vice is not punished on the stage or in a book—as it very often is not in life—this does not prove that vice is unhateful and unworthy of punishment; for a narrative can prove nothing. If the vessel which carried 'Paul and Virginia' had not been wrecked, would it have proved that chaste love is always crowned with happiness? And because this vessel goes to the bottom with the interesting heroine, what does 'Paul and Virginia' prove? It proves that youth, friendship, love, and the tropics are beautiful things, when Bernardin de Saint Pierre describes them. If 'Faust' were not led away and vanquished by the devil, would it prove that the passions were weaker than reason? And because the devil is stronger than the philosopher, does it prove that philosophy can never vanquish the passions? What does 'Faust' prove? It proves that science, human life, fantastic images, profound, graceful or terrible ideas, are wonderful things, when Goethe makes out of them a sublime and moving picture. So far George Sand; but this does not meet the question. Although a *narrative* is not a *demonstration*, and cannot be made one; although, therefore, in the strict sense of the word, Art *proves* nothing; yet it is quite clear that the details of a narrative may be so grouped as to satisfy the mind like a sermon. It is an exhortation, if you like, not a demonstration, but it does not the less appeal to our moral sense. What does a sermon prove? And can a sermon prove anything? Yet, by appealing to the moral sense, it works its purpose. The debaters of this question seem to leave out of view the fact that in fiction as in real life, while our emotions are excited by the narrative, and, so to speak, by the physical accidents of the story, our moral sense requires to be gratified; and the meaning of poetical justice is, that the satisfaction required by this moral sense should be furnished in the conclusion of the story. If we hear of an actual injustice done upon earth, remaining unpunished, we are indignant and dissatisfied, and exclaim, 'Oh! I wish I could punish that fellow.' Precisely the same feeling is left in our minds when poetical justice is violated. In a fiction, we are angry with the author for not doing what our moral sense demands should be done. When the incidents of the story, besides exciting our interest, run along moral lines, and call up *tableaux vivans* of just retribution, and the happy terminations of worthy lives, then not only is that faculty gratified to which fiction more immediately appeals, but the moral sense is also gratified. The illustration of a sermon will help to make this clear. When we hear a beautiful discourse, we do not expect the preacher to prove anything before unproven, we only expect him to call up further illustrations of truth long since ratified by our consciences.

Now, in the question of the moral as respects fiction, it is quite clear, from French practice more than any other, that without formally inculcating any immoral *dogma*, the writer may very successfully produce an immoral *effect*. Who can mistake the immoral moral which breathes through the pages of Eugène Sue? Who can mistake the foregone conclusion employed in his selection of main incidents and characters? in his flattery of the people, which consists in making the virtuous poor, and the vicious rich; linking together, as in necessary connexion, virtue and dirty hands, maculate consciences and immaculate linen? On the other hand, there is no mistaking the moral influence of good novels; even when no specific formula can be appended to the closing chapter. The novel may carry its moral openly on its very title-page, through all its conclusions; or, it may carry within it, not one but many moral illustrations, naturally arising out of the way the incidents are grouped, and the way the characters express themselves.

These two forms of moral are illustrated in *Ruth*, and *Villette*, two works by our most popular authoresses. *Ruth* has a moral carried in the story; not preached, but manifested. It is a story of seduction—a subject of the most delicate nature that can well be taken up; being one which has rarely if ever been looked fairly in the face; and one on which, of all others, it is the rarest to hear a rational word spoken. The circulating-libraries have furnished, and will continue to furnish, abundance of sickly sentimentality on this subject, wherein heroines strive to atone by consumption and broken hearts, for their lapse from virtue; or, if they do not take this 'rose-pink' turn, present a frigid and barren morality, under which the luckless maiden, if her mind be very much set upon re-entering the Eden of Respectability, lingers through the remainder of her life under a deadly weight of patronage and encouragement, 'her sincere repentance and subsequent good conduct' being like a badge of infamy perpetuating the memory of her shame: a scarlet letter flaming upon her breast, attracting every eye; until one wonders how any being can be found able to live under such a restoration to social amnesty! In a very different spirit does the authoress of *Ruth* approach this delicate subject. She approaches it like a woman, and a truly delicate-minded woman; with a delicacy that is strong in truth, not influenced by conventions. In *Ruth* there is no confusing of right with wrong; no tampering with perilous sympathies, no attempt to make a new line of action such as the world's morality would refuse to warrant, but a clear insight into the nature of temptation, and wise words of exhortation to those who have fallen—showing them, that no matter what clouds of shame may have gathered around them, they may still redeem themselves if they will only rise and do honestly the work that still lies before them to be done, and that, in every position, however dark or degraded, there is always a certain right course which, if followed, will lead them once more into light. It is only women who can help women, and it is only women who can really raise those that have 'fallen'; not indeed by 'countenancing' them, but by appealing to their self-respect. As the world goes, a woman's fault is always painted irretrievable; and she is, in consequence, nailed up as a scare-crow on the barn-door of society, to protect the interests of female virtue! That ancient punishment of burying alive was surely less terrible than the pitiless finality which thus pronounces judgment.

Ruth is introduced to us as a beautiful girl, left an orphan in a singularly friendless condition. She is apprenticed to a milliner, and in this position is seduced; but under such 'extenuating circumstances', that the question of 'guilt' is reduced to a point of casuistry. We may observe in passing, that in using the words 'guilt', or 'crime', or 'sin', we are for the moment accepting what in reality we do not accept, the current language on this subject, and in her exposition we follow, as she has followed, ordinary notions. The guilt, then, of Ruth is accompanied by such entire ignorance of evil, and by such a combination of fatalities, that even the sternest of provincial moralists could hardly be harsh with her; and this we think a mistake on the part of the authoress. Her position would have been stronger had Ruth been older, and had she more clearly perceived the whole consequence of her transgression. We think, for the object Mrs Gaskell had in view, the guilt should not have had so many extenuating circumstances, because as it is, Ruth, although she has much to regret, cannot in her conscience have much to repent. But this by the way: Ruth is seduced, and therefore has practically incurred all the penalties of social reprobation. Her lover has fallen ill, and his mother is come to nurse him. Poor Ruth, who, till then, had been his nurse, must now slink out of the mother's virtuous presence; and very touching is the picture of her anxiety, crouching like a dog at his door, knowing what must be going on within the room, and yet not allowed to enter it. The scene of watching we must quote for its exquisite beauty.

It was summer; there was no black darkness in the twenty-four hours, only the light grew dusky, and colour disappeared from objects, of which the shape and form remained distinct. A soft grey oblong of barred light fell on the flat wall opposite to the windows, and deeper grey shadows marked out the tracery of the plants, more graceful thus than in reality. Ruth crouched where no light fell. She sat on the ground close by the door; her whole existence was absorbed in listening; all was still—it was only her heart beating with the strong, heavy, regular sound of a hammer. She wished she could stop its rushing, incessant clang. She heard a rustle of a silken gown, and knew it ought not to have been worn in a sick room; for her senses seemed to have passed into the keeping of the invalid, and to feel only as he felt. The noise was probably occasioned by some change of posture in the watcher inside, for it was once more dead-still. The soft wind outside sank with a low, long, distant moan among the windings of the hills, and lost itself there, and came no more again. But Ruth's heart beat loud; she rose with as little noise as if she were a vision, and crept to the open window to try and lose the nervous listening for the ever-recurring sound. Out beyond, under the calm sky, veiled with a mist rather than with a cloud, rose the high, dark outlines of the mountains, shutting in that village as if it lay in a nest. They stood, like giants, solemnly watching for the end of Earth and Time. Here and there a black round shadow reminded Ruth of some 'Cwm,' or hollow, where she and her lover had rambled in sun and in gladness. She then thought the land enchanted into everlasting brightness and happiness; she fancied, then, that into a region so lovely no bale or woe could enter, but would be charmed away, and disappear before the sight of the glorious guardian mountains. Now she knew the truth, that earth has no barrier which avails against agony. It comes, lightning-like, down from heaven, into the mountain house and the town garret; into the palace and into the cottage. The garden lay close under the house; a bright spot enough by day, for in that soil, whatever was planted grew and blossomed in spite of neglect. The white roses glimmered out in the dusk all the night through; the red were lost in shadow. Between the low boundary of the garden and the hills swept one or two green meadows; Ruth looked into the grey darkness till she traced each separate wave of outline. Then she heard a little restless bird chirp out its wakefulness from a nest in the ivy round the walls of the house. But the mother-bird spread her soft feathers, and hushed it into silence. Presently, however, many little birds began to scent the coming dawn, and rustled among the leaves, and chirruped loud and clear. Just above the horizon, too, the mist became a silvery grey cloud, hanging on the edge of the world; presently it turned shimmering white; and then, in an instant, it flushed into rose, and the mountain tops sprang into heaven, and bathed in the presence of the shadow of God. With a bound, the sun, of a molten fiery red, came above the horizon, and immediately thousands of little birds sang out for joy, and a soft chorus of mysterious, glad murmurs, came forth from the earth; the low whispering wind left its hiding-place among the clefts and hollows of the hills, and wandered among the rustling herbs and trees, waking the flower-buds to the life of another day. Ruth gave a sigh of relief that the night was over and gone; for she knew that soon suspense would be ended, and the verdict known, whether for life or for death. She grew faint and sick with anxiety; it almost seemed as if she must go into the room and learn the truth. Then she heard movements, but they were not sharp or rapid, as if prompted by any emergency; then, again, it was still. She sat curled up upon the floor, with her head clasped round her knees. She had yet to wait. Meanwhile, the invalid was slowly rousing himself from a long, deep, sound, health-giving sleep. His mother had sat by him the night through, and was now daring to change her position for the first time; she was even venturing to give directions, in a low voice, to the old nurse, who had dozed away in an arm-chair, ready to obey any summons of her mistress. Mrs Bellingham went on tiptoe towards the door, and chiding herself because her stiff, weary limbs, made some slight noise. She had an irrepressible longing for a few minutes' change of scene after her night of watching. She felt that the crisis was over; and the relief to her mind made her conscious of every bodily feeling and irritation, which had passed unheeded as long as she had been in suspense.

She slowly opened the door. Ruth sprang upright at the first sound of the creaking handle. Her very lips were stiff and unpliable with the force of the blood which rushed to her head. It seemed as if she could not form words. She stood right before Mrs Bellingham. 'How is he, madam?'

Mrs Bellingham was for a moment surprised at the white apparition which seemed to rise out of the ground. But her quick, proud mind, understood it all in an instant. This was the girl, then, whose profligacy had led her son astray, had raised up barriers in the way of her favourite scheme of his marriage with Miss Duncombe; nay, this was the real cause of his illness, his mortal danger at this present time, and her bitter, keen anxiety. If, under any circumstances, Mrs Bellingham could have been guilty of the ill-breeding of not answering a question, it was now; and for a moment she was tempted to pass on in silence. Ruth could not wait; she spoke again:

'For the love of God, madam, speak! How is he? Will he live?' If she did not answer her, she thought the creature was desperate enough to force her way into his room. So she spoke.

'He has slept well; he is better.'

'Oh! my God, I thank thee,' murmured Ruth, sinking back against the wall.

It was too much to hear this wretched girl thanking God for her son's life; as if, in fact, she had any lot or part in him, and to dare to speak to the Almighty on her son's behalf! Mrs Bellingham looked at her with cold, contemptuous eyes, whose glances were like icebolts, and made Ruth shiver up away from them.

'Young woman, if you have any propriety or decency left, I trust that you will not dare to force yourself into his room.'

Poor Ruth is abandoned, her lover is carried off; she has no resource but suicide. Succour comes, however, in the shape of the Bensons—a dissenting clergyman and his sister—who, pitying her forlorn condition, and believing in her real goodness, agree to adopt her into their own family till she be able to earn a living for herself.

In the midst of their unostentatious self-denying charity a touch of human weakness shows itself: partly from the desire to spare Ruth's feelings and save her from the terrible tongues of a provincial town, and partly to save themselves and make their task smoother and easier, they agree to pass her off as a distant relative—a widow. Admirable is the stroke of nature by which Ruth cannot be made to feel 'sorry' that she is to have a baby! This revelation, which so disturbs Miss Benson, and does so materially complicate Ruth's position, is to the young girl nothing but a source of joy. It is new life, new strength, new hope! Admirable also is Miss Benson's confession to her brother, that she cannot help enjoying the novelty of 'filling up the outline they had agreed upon, and inventing a few details of Ruth's widowhood.'

Yielding to the temptation of this piece of specious wordly wisdom is the one flaw in an otherwise perfect act of Christian charity, and its consequences are ably worked out. There is no strain to save the moral, all follows naturally upon one false step taken at the onset, which, at the time, seemed scarcely to be a dereliction from the straight path; but as all who have read John Bunyan know, 'By-path Meadow' leads to 'Doubting Castle, and Giant Despair.' It was Tom Paine who said that 'A lie is strength in the beginning, and weakness in the end,' and all find it to be so in this instance.

Ruth's baby is born under the Bensons' roof, and the mother's love is made the main influence which strengthens her to rise up under her load of shame, and begin her life afresh, endeavouring, with all her might, to be worthy of the blessing and the responsibility of a child.

The author has treated this phase of the history of a fallen woman with immense truth and delicacy. She has separated the consequences of an action from the action itself. The natural and pure relationship between a mother and her child ought not to be considered as poisoned and vitiated, because the antecedents of that relationship are to be regretted; it is an opportunity afforded to her of rehabilitating her life, by nobly and courageously accepting the responsibility she has incurred, and qualifying herself to discharge the trust committed to her. If women who have placed themselves in Ruth's position only could find the moral courage to accept the duties entailed upon them by their own conduct, it would much lessen the misery and social evil that now follows in the train of illicit connexions.

Under the influence of her new duties, and the instructions of Mr Benson, Ruth's character and talents develop themselves, and she becomes, in all respects, an educated gentlewoman. Nature had already made her a 'born lady'. We confess that, for the sake of the teaching, we should have preferred a more simple trust in the principle involved, and less attempt to interest and propitiate the reader by all manner of graceful accessories. Ruth, as the governess to the children of the ostentatious, hard-judging merchant, has won golden opinions, and been, in all respects, a most exemplary and valuable servant; in fact, her superiority to all around her has shone out bright and clear, when the fatal secret of her previous life is rumoured about, and comes to the ears of Mr Bradshaw, who, never having had any mercy on anybody in his life, but always piquing himself on being a Roman stoic, and trampling on his feelings, is, of course, prodigiously indignant at having been imposed upon by Mr Benson and his governess. His wrath flames out like the indignation of a fishwoman, and, after speaking his coarse mind, he turns Ruth out of doors, breaks off his friendship with Mr Benson, withdrawing from attendance at his chapel, and conducts himself, in all respects, like an angry and much-injured man. The gossip and scandal of the whole affair is very great, and the indignation against Mr Benson for his 'want of truth' is only equalled by horror at Ruth for her want of virtue, and the rage at having been so long defrauded of the facts is greater than all!

The bitterest portion of Ruth's punishment has now overtaken her, she has to tell the secret of her shame to her son, then eleven years old. However, this painful and sudden uprooting of all wordly prospects is the final perfecting of Ruth's character.

The following scene takes place immediately after she has spoken to her son:-

Ruth's hand was on the latch when Mr Benson came out. Her face was very white, except two red spots on each cheek—her eyes were deep sunk and hollow, but glittered with feverish lustre. 'Ruth,' exclaimed he. She moved her lips, but her throat and mouth were too dry for her to speak.

'Where are you going?' asked he, for she had all her walking things on; yet trembled so, even as she stood, that it was evident she could not walk far without falling. She hesitated; she looked up at him still with the same dry, glittering eyes. At last she whispered (for she could only speak in a whisper) 'To Helmsby—I am going to Helmsby!'

'Helmsby! my poor girl!—where is Helmsby?'

'I don't know—in Lincolnshire, I think.'

'Come here,' said he, authoritatively, drawing her into the study;

'sit down in that chair—I will come back directly.'...

He went for the cup of tea. 'Drink this,' he spoke as you would to a child, if desiring it to take medicine....

Mr Benson sat down by her. 'Now, Ruth, we must talk a little together. I want to understand what your plan was. Where is Helmsby? Why did you fix to go there?'

'It is where my mother lived,' she answered. 'Before she was married, she lived there, and wherever she lived the people loved her dearly; and I thought—I think that, for her sake, some one would give me work. I want to tell them the truth,' said she, dropping her eyes; 'but still they would, perhaps, give me some employment—I don't care what—for her sake.'...

Mr Benson's heart was very sore. 'Ruth, you must be still and quiet. I cannot have this. I want you to listen to me. Your thought of Helmsby would be a good one if it were right for you to leave Eccleston; but I do not think it is. I am certain of this, that it would be a great sin in you to separate yourself from Leonard. You have no right to sever the tie by which God has bound you together.'

'But if I am here, they will all know and remember the shame of his birth, and if I go away they may forget—'.

'And they may not.... No dread of shame, either for yourself or even for him, can ever make it right for you to shake off your responsibility.... Besides, Ruth,' he continued, 'we have gone on falsely, hitherto. It has been my doing, my mistake, my sin. I ought to have known better. Now, let us stand firm on the truth. You have no new fault to repent of. Be brave and faithful. It is to God you answer, not to men. The shame of making your sin known to the world should be as nothing to the shame you felt at having sinned. We have dreaded men too much, and God too little, in the course we have taken. But now be of good cheer. Perhaps you will find your work in the world very low,...nay, perhaps, Ruth, you may have to stand and wait for some time; no one may be willing to use the services you would gladly render; all may turn aside from you, and speak very harshly of you. Can you accept all this treatment meekly, as but the reasonable and just penance God has laid upon you—feeling no anger against those who slight you—no impatience for the time to come?—(I speak as having the word of God for what I say.) When He, having purified you even as by fire, will make a straight path for your feet? My child, it is Christ the Lord who has told us of the infinite mercy of God. Have you faith enough in it to be brave, and bear on, and do rightly in patience and in tribulation?'

Ruth had been hushed and very still until now, when the pleading earnestness of his question urged her to answer.

'Yes,' said she, 'I hope, I believe, I can be faithful for myself, for I have sinned and done wrong. But Leonard—' she looked up at him.

'But Leonard,' he echoed. 'Ah! there it is hard, Ruth. I own the world is hard and persecuting to such as he.'

He paused to think of the true comfort for this sting. He went on.

'The world is not everything, Ruth, nor is the want of men's good opinion and esteem the highest need which man has. Teach Leonard this. You would not wish his life to be one summer's day. You dared not make it so, if you had the power. Teach him to bid a noble Christian welcome to the trials which God sends, and this is one of them. Teach him not to look on a life of struggle, and perhaps of disappointment and incompleteness, as a sad and mournful end, but as the means permitted to the heroes and warriors in the army of Christ, by which to show their faithful following.... Oh, Ruth,' he exclaimed, 'when I look and see what you may be—what you *must* be to that boy, I cannot think how you could be coward enough for a moment to shrink from your work! But we have all been cowards hitherto,' he added, in bitter self-accusation; 'God help us to be so no longer!'

To those who 'are wearied with the greatness of their way,' meeting with this passage will be like the 'shadow of a great rock in a weary land.'

Ruth *does* bear her trial. For two years the offended virtue of the people of Eccleston keeps her excommunicated. At the end of that time a work seems opened to her; she goes out as sick nurse, for which office she has a decided vocation. Had she been a Catholic, she would have been a Sister of Charity. A terrible fever comes, sweeping away alike the nurses, the doctors, and the patients. The hospital of the town is left almost without attendants, so great is the fear; and yet not greater than the danger. Ruth comes forward, and offers herself at the fever ward, and stays there until the pestilence is abated. From an outcast she is now become a heroine; addresses, and votes of thanks, and testimonials pour in upon her. Her simple, childlike unconsciousness of any merit in what she has done, is beautifully indicated. But, just when all the difficulties and contradictions of her life are reconciled, the *end* comes. Her lover and betrayer, who has come down to Eccleston to see after his election, lies at the hotel in the town ill of the fever, with no one to nurse him; Ruth hears it, and insists upon going, (no one being aware of his identity except herself). Her old passion had been sternly burnt out of her; she had learned to see him in his true nature, which was simply worthless. Still, lying there, helpless and abandoned, something which—if not love, is yet more than compassion—impels her to go to him. He is delirious; there is no recognition; but he takes a favourable turn; and in the same hour Ruth is stricken down by the disease, and—dies! followed by the love and reverence of those who had once been the most bitter against her. The working up of the concluding scenes is beautiful, and yet they are so simple and unexaggerated, that they haunt the reader like a reality. The author has gone into no vituperation of Ruth's seducer, but he is so drawn as to suggest all that could be said; the interview between him and Mr Benson, by the side of Ruth's dead body, satisfies the requirements of poetical justice. He is none the less miserable and contemptible that he does not know himself to be so.

The moral, or morals of *Ruth* (for there are two), without being formally inculcated, are legible enough. The first is, that if women are to have their lives rehabilitated, it must be through the means of women, who, noble and pure in their own lives, can speak with authority, and tell them that in this world no action is final; and that, to set the seal of despair and reprobation upon any individual during any one point of his career, is to blot out the inner life by which we live. The second moral is suggested in the untruth by which the Bensons endeavoured to shield their protegée. They were willing in their own persons to disregard conventionalisms, to believe in the purity of one who had sinned, to take her to their hearts and to their homes, like a child of their own; but, what they could believe in for *themselves*, they could not believe in for *others*. *They* faced the truth, and yet were afraid lest others should face it! Had they confronted conventionalism, they would have awed and conquered it; their own high characters would have been a coat of mail against the sarcasms of virtuous indignation; and the comments of a gossiping town would have been powerless. The real goodness and purity of Ruth, which endeared her to their hearts, would have endeared her to all the hearts of Eccleston, slowly, indeed, but surely. The Bensons have but suffered for their want of reliance on truth, and the moral of the whole is plainly this,—however dark and difficult our course may seem, the straight path of truth is the only one to lead us through it into the light.

Ruth, then, besides being a beautiful novel, satisfies the highest moral sense by the pictures it suggests. It is a sermon, and of the wisest, but its teaching is unostentatious. We need only allude in passing, to the wonderful beauty of some of the descriptions; to the clear truthful portraiture of the characters, especially Sally, Bradshaw, his meek Wife, and the sensible Farquhar, and to the somewhat common-place incidents by which the novel is carried on. We have not space for lengthened criticism, but we must protest against one portion of the work, which strikes us as being conventional and unnatural: we allude to the intensity of grief with which Ruth's child is afflicted on hearing that his mother has not been married.

> Leonard threw his arms tight round her, and hid his face against her bosom. She felt him pant there like some hunted creature. She had no soothing comfort to give him. 'Oh, that she and he lay dead!'
>
> At last, exhausted, he lay so still and motionless, that she feared to look. She wanted him to speak, yet dreaded his first words. She kissed his hair, his head, his very clothes; murmuring low inarticulate moaning sounds.
>
> 'Leonard,' said she, 'Leonard, look up at me! Leonard, look up!'

But he only clung the closer, and hid his face the more. (p. 79)

> His health seemed shaken, he spoke half sentences in his sleep, which showed that in his dreams he was battling on his mother's behalf against an unkind and angry world. And then he would wail to himself, and utter sad words of shame, which they never thought had reached his ears. By day, he was in general grave and quiet; but his appetite varied, and he was evidently afraid of going into the streets, dreading to be pointed at as an object of remark. Each separately in their hearts longed to give him change of scene, but they were all silent, for where was the requisite money to come from?
>
> His temper became fitful and variable. At times he would be most sullen against his mother; and then give way to a passionate remorse. (pp. 120-1)

This language is sheerly impossible. No child would at once realise any such shame, even were it a fact, that illegitimacy in actual life *did* bring with it disgrace, so that the illegitimate child must 'go forth branded into the world, with his hand against every man's, and every man's hand against him'; the least reflection will tell Mrs Gaskell that in our day no such brand affects the illegitimate child. And as to Leonard's anticipating this social degradation, to render *that* intelligible to the reader there should have been scenes of insult and opprobrium from his companions and the world at large, to make him bitterly aware that the misfortune of his birth was regarded as a brand. We are, however, in no mood to point out the defects of so charming a work, and close this notice with the following little bit—we had almost said little poem—describing Ruth's feelings on the eve of her departure from that place where she has been so happy with her love, and where she has been so wretched under abandonment.

> When the black gown, at which she had stitched away incessantly, was finished—when nothing remained but to rest for the next day's journey—Ruth could not sit still. She wandered from window to window, learning off each rock and tree by heart. *Each had its tale, which it was agony to remember; but which it would have been worse agony to forget.* The sound of running waters she heard that quiet evening, was in her ears as she lay on her death-bed; so well had she learnt their tune.

Turning from *Ruth* to *Villette*, the contrasts meet us on all sides. Never were two women's books more unlike each other. There is a moral too in *Villette*, or rather many morals, but not so distinctly a *morale en action*. It is a work of astonishing power and passion. From its pages there issues an influence of truth as healthful as a mountain breeze. Contempt of conventions in all things, in style, in thought, even in the art of story-telling, here visibly springs from the independent originality of a strong mind nurtured in solitude. As a novel, in the ordinary sense of the word, *Villette* has few claims; as a *book*, it is one which, having read, you will not easily forget. It is quite true that the episode of Miss Marchmont, early in the first volume, is unnecessary, having no obvious connexion with the plot or the characters; but with what wonderful imagination is it painted! Where shall we find such writing as in that description of her last night, wherein the memories of bygone years come trooping in upon her with a vividness partaking of the last energy of life? It is true also that the visit to London is unnecessary, and has many unreal details. Much of the book seems to be brought in merely that the writer may express something which is in her mind; but at any rate she *has* something in her mind, and expresses it as no other can. We have objected to Mrs Gaskell's portraiture of a child's feelings as unnatural, and we have heard Currer Bell's portrait of little Polly also objected to, but we cannot agree in this latter objection. Polly's quaintness and primness are not more than the experience of many people will guarantee. Where the defect lies, is in an occasional 'over-ageing' of her feelings and emotions, such as at page 13, where her nurse says, 'Be a good child, missy,' and she replies, 'I am good, but I ache here,' putting her hand on her heart, and moaning, while she reiterated 'papa! papa!' Now that is not the language of a child of six years old; children have no such anatomical knowledge; and to make it credible, it would be necessary to surround it, and the other 'old-fashioned things', she says, with the prattle of childhood and nonsense which is best sense to it and to parents, in order that the reader might feel he had a child before him, and not a little idealism. The want of attention to reality is certainly not the complain we can make against Currer Bell, and therefore were we the more surprised to find her saying, for instance, that John Bretton was accustomed to take up the Greek dramatists, and read off a translation of them for the benefit of the family circle. To any one who has ever read a Greek dramatist, the supposition of this feat will be extremely amusing. It would be a large demand upon our credulity, to imagine a man reading off in that way a French or German dramatist, without terribly fatiguing his audience, but considering the difficulty of reading the Greek with all appurtenances, the idea of 'improvising' a translation is preposterous. In the same way Currer Bell makes M Paul read aloud novels and plays to the young ladies, and whenever he comes upon any passage not very well adapted to young ladies' reading, (which must be very often, one would think) we are told, that he improvised passages to supply their places, and that these were often better than the original. She gives us sufficient evidence of M Paul's vigour of intellect without having recourse to such a weak expedient. While we are thus hinting at defects in a book for which we can scarcely find measured language to express our admiration, let us further note the melodramatic character of Madame Beck, who passes into unreality simply from the want of a little light and shade, and the occasional indistinctness in the drawing of John Bretton.

Currer Bell has also the fault of running metaphors to death sometimes, and is oppressively fond of the allegorical expression of emotions; thus making passages look mechanical and forced, which if more directly put before us would be very powerful. The power with which she writes at times is marvellous: read this, for example, and read it slowly, not as you read it in the hurry of running through the volumes for the story.

At last a day and night of peculiarly agonizing depression were succeeded by physical illness, I took perforce to my bed. About this time the Indian summer closed, and the equinoctial storms began; and for nine dark and wet days, of which the Hours rushed on all turbulent, deaf, dishevelled, bewildered with sounding hurricane, I lay in a strange fever of the nerves and blood. Sleep went quite away. I used to rise in the night, look round for her, beseech her earnestly to return. A rattle of the window, a cry of the blast only replied—Sleep never came!

I err; she came once, but in anger. Impatient of my importunity she brought with her an avenging dream. By the clock of St Jean Baptiste, that dream remained scarce fifteen minutes—a brief space, but sufficing to wring my whole frame with unknown anguish; to confer a nameless experience that had the hue, the mien, the terror, the very tone of a visitation from eternity. Between twelve and one that night a cup was forced to my lips, black, strong, strange, drawn from no well, but filled up seething from a bottomless and boundless sea. Suffering, brewed in temporal or calculable measure, and mixed for mortal lips, tastes not as this suffering tasted. Having drank and woke, I thought all was over: the end come and past by. Trembling fearfully—as consciousness returned—ready to cry out on some fellow-creature to help me, only that I knew no fellow-creature was near enough to catch the wild summons—Goton, in her far distant attic, could not hear—I rose on my knees in bed. Some fearful hours went over me; indescribably was I torn, racked and oppressed in mind. Amidst the horrors of that dream I think the worse lay here. Methought the well-loved dead, who had loved *me* well in life, met me elsewhere, alienated; galled was my inmost spirit with an unutterable sense of despair about the future. Motive there was none why I should try to recover or wish to live; and yet quite unendurable was the pitiless and haughty voice in which Death challenged me to engage his unknown terrors. When I tried to pray, I could not utter these words:

'From my youth up Thy terrors have I suffered with a troubled mind.'

Most true was it.

On bringing me my tea next morning, Goton urged me to call in a doctor. I would not; I thought no doctor could cure me.

One evening—and I was not delirious—I was in my sane mind, I got up—I dressed myself, weak and shaking. The solitude and the stillness of the long dormitory could not be borne any longer; the ghastly white beds were turning into spectres—the coronal of each became a death's head, huge and sun-bleached—dead dreams of an elder world and mightier race lay frozen in their wide gaping eyeholes. That evening more firmly than ever fastened into my soul the conviction that Fate was of stone, and Hope a false idol—blind, bloodless, and of granite core. I felt, too, that the trial God had appointed me was gaining its climax, and must now be turned by my own hands, hot, feeble, trembling as they were. It rained still, and blew; but with more clemency, I thought, than it had poured and raged all day. Twilight was falling, and I deemed its influence pitiful; from the lattice I saw coming night-clouds trailing low like banners dropping. It seemed to me that at this hour there was affection and sorrow in Heaven above for all pain suffered on earth beneath; the weight of my dreadful dream became alleviated—that insufferable thought of being no more loved, no more owned, half-yielded to hope of the contrary—I was sure this hope would shine clearer if I got out from under this house roof, which was crushing as the slab of a tomb, and went outside the city to a certain quiet hill, a long way distant in the fields. Covered with a cloak (I could not be delirious, for I had sense and recollection to put on warm clothing), forth I set. The bells of a church arrested me in passing: they seemed to call me in to the *salut*, and I went in. Any solemn rite, any spectacle of sincere worship, any opening for appeal to God was as welcome to me then as bread to one in extremity of want. I knelt down with others on the stone pavement. It was an old solemn church, its pervading gloom not gilded but purpled by light shed through stained glass.

Or this—

The drug wrought. I know not whether Madame had over-charged or under-charged the dose; its result was not that she intended. Instead of stupor, came excitement. I became alive to new thought—to reverie peculiar in colouring. A gathering call ran among the faculties, their bugles sang, their trumpets rang an untimely summons. Imagination was roused from her rest, and she came forth impetuous and venturous. With scorn she looked on Matter, her mate—

'Rise!' she said. 'Sluggard! this night I will have *my* will; nor shalt thou prevail.'

'Look forth and view the night!' was her cry; and when I lifted the heavy blind from the casement close at hand—with her own royal gesture, she showed me a moon supreme, in an element deep and splendid.

To my gasping senses she made the glimmering gloom, the narrow limits, the oppressive heat of the dormitory, intolerable. She lured me to leave this den and follow her forth into dew, coolness, and glory. She brought upon me a strange vision of Villette at midnight. Especially she showed the park, the summer-park, with its long alleys all silent, one, and safe; among these lay a huge stone-basin—that basin I knew, and beside which I had often stood—deep-set in the tree-shadows, brimming with cool water, clear with a green, leafy, rushy bed. What of all this? The park-gates were shut up, locked, sentinelled; the place could not be entered.

Could it not? A point worth considering; and while revolving it, I mechanically dressed. Utterly incapable of sleeping or lying still—excited from head to foot—what could I do better than dress? (pp. 258-9).

Quiet Rue Fossette! I find on this pavement that wanderer-wooing summer night of which I mused; I see its moon over me; I feel its dew in the air. But here I cannot stay; I am still too near old haunts; so close under the dungeon, I can hear the prisoners moan. This solemn peace is not what I seek, it is not what I can bear; to me the face of that sky bears the aspect of a world's death. The park also will be calm—I know, a mortal serenity prevails everywhere—yet let me seek the park.

I took a route well-known, and went up towards the palatial and royal Haute-Ville; thence the music I had heard certainly floated; it was hushed now, but it might reawaken. I went on; neither band nor bell-music came to meet me; another sound replaced it, a sound like a strong tide, a great flow, deepening as I proceeded. Light broke, movement gathered, chimes pealed—to what was I coming? Entering on the level of a Grande Place, I found myself, with the suddenness of magic, plunged amidst a gay, living, joyous crowd.

Villette is one blaze, one broad illumination; the whole world seems abroad; moonlight and heaven are banished: the town, by her own flambeaux, beholds her own splendour—gay dresses, grand equipages, fine horses, and gallant riders, throng the bright streets. I see even scores of masks. It is a strange scene, stranger than dreams. But where is the park?—I ought to be near it. In the midst of this glare the park must be shadowy and calm—*there*, at least, are neither torches, lamps, nor crowd! (pp. 262-3).

We were speaking just now of standing by the truth—see what Currer Bell says of facing it:

I always, through my whole life, like to penetrate to the real truth; I like seeking the goddess in her temple, and handling the veil, and daring the dread glance. O Titaness amongst deities! The covered outline of thine aspect sickens often through its uncertainty, but define to us one trait, show us one lineament, clear in awful sincerity; we may gasp in untold terror, but with that gasp we drink in a breath of thy divinity: our heart shakes, and its currents sway like rivers lifted by earthquake, but we have swallowed strength. To see and know the worst is to take from Fear her main advantage. (pp. 209-10)

This is not the writing of fiction; it is prose poetry of the very highest order. Here, again, is a passage which has a rhythm and a cadence of its own, not surpassed by the march of verse:

Dim I should not say, for the beauty of moonlight—forgotten in the park—here once more flowed in upon perception. High she rode, and calm and stainlessly she shone. The music and the mirth of the fête, the fire and bright hues of those lamps had out-done and out-shone her for an hour, but now, again, her glory and her silence triumphed. The rival lamps were dying: *she held her course like a white fate.* Drum, trumpet, bugle, had uttered their clangour and were forgotten: with pencil-ray she wrote on heaven and on earth records for archives everlasting. She and those stars seemed to me at once the types and witnesses of truth all regnant. The night sky lit her reign: like its slow-wheeling progress, advanced her victory—that onward movement which has been, and is, and will be from eternity to eternity. (p. 297)

We could go on quoting and commenting through several pages, for indeed it is as a book that *Villette* most affects us, and every chapter contains or suggests matter for discourse. We say emphatically, a book; meaning by a book, the utterance of an original mind. In this world, as Goethe tells us, 'there are so few voices, and so many echoes'; there are so few books, and so many volumes—so few persons thinking and speaking for themselves, so many reverberating the vague noises of others. Among the few stands *Villette*. In it we read the actual thoughts and feelings of a strong, struggling soul; we hear the cry of pain from one who has loved passionately, and who has sorrowed sorely. Indeed, no more distinct characteristic of Currer Bell's genius can be named, than the depth of her capacity for all passionate emotions. Comparing *Villette* with *Ruth*, in this respect, we are comparing sunlight with moonlight, passion with affection; and there is no writer of our day, except George Sand, who possesses the glory and the power which light up the writings of Currer Bell. She has not the humour, so strong and so genial, of Mrs Gaskell. There are, occasionally, touches approaching to the comic in *Villette*, but they spring mostly from fierce sarcasm, not from genial laughter. Ginevra Fanshaw is 'shown up' in all her affectations and careless coquetry, but there is something contemptuous in the laugh, nothing sympathetic. Nor has Currer Bell any tendency towards the graceful, playful, or fanciful. There is more of Michael Angelo than of Raffaelle in her drawing; more of Backhuysen than of Cuyp; more of Salvator Rosa than of Claude. Very characteristic of her style is this little bit of scenery—

A new influence began to act upon my life, and sadness, for a certain space, was held at bay. Conceive a dell, deep-hollowed in forest secrecy; it lies in dimness and mist: its turf is dank, its herbage pale and humid. A storm or an axe makes a wide gap amongst the oak-trees; the breeze sweeps in; the sun looks down; the sad, cold dell, becomes a deep cup of lustre; high summer pours her blue glory and her golden light out of that beauteous sky, which till now the starved hollow never saw.

A new creed became mine—a belief in happiness.

Or, still more so, is this exquisite description of Paulina—

Her eyes were the eyes of one who can remember; one whose child-hood does not fade like a dream, or whose youth vanish like a sunbeam. She would not take life, loosely and incoherently, in parts and let one season slip as she entered on another: she would retain and add; often review from the commencement, and so grow in harmony and consistency as she grew in years.

Indeed, one may say of Currer Bell, what a contemporary has already said, that her genius finds its fittest illustration in her 'Rochesters' and 'Jane Eyres';

they are men and women of deep feeling, clear intellects, vehement tempers, bad manners, ungraceful, yet loveable persons. Their address is *brusque*, perhaps unpleasant, but at any rate, individual, direct, free from 'shams' and convention of all kinds. They outrage good taste, yet they fascinate. You dislike them at first, yet you learn to love them. The power that is in them makes its vehement way right to your heart. 'Propriety,' ideal outline, good features, good manners, ordinary thought, ordinary speech, are not to be demanded of them. They are the 'Mirabeaus of Romance'.

If, as critics, we have one thing to say with regard to the future, it is, that Currer Bell, in her next effort, should bestow more pains on her story. With so much passion, with so much power of transmuting experience into forms of enduring fiction, she only needs the vehicle of an interesting story to surpass the popularity of *Jane Eyre*.

W.M. Thackeray

Thackeray's Early Work (1848)

Thackeray is one of the foremost writers of the day; and considering the eminence to which he has risen of late, has very few detractors. In truth, his style of writing is so singularly winning, so easy, masculine, felicitous, humourous and pleasant, that unless to very obtuse perceptions, one sees not how he could fail of being attractive. He has no asperities; he presents no rough points against which the reader's mind is thrust with pain; his manner is unobtrusive, his mannerism is not obvious. He offends no one by the vehemence of his opinions, nor by dogmatism of manner. His wit is delicate, his pathos simple, and rather indicated than dwelt upon. He indulges in no false sentiment; disturbs you by no ambitious burst of rhetoric. There is no fustian in him, no glare from the footlights is thrown upon exaggerated distortions of human nature. Trusting to truth and humour, he is the quietest perhaps of all contemporary writers.

Thackeray is not a man to create partizans. He espouses no 'cause'; has no party. The applause he seeks is the legitimate applause bestowed on an artist; and he excites, therefore, admiration rather than passionate attachment. The absence of any strong 'purpose' is in some sense a drawback to his popularity, but in another sense it is an additional aid. He does not please a party, but he does not offend the opponents of that party. His popularity thus gains in extent what it loses in intensity.

We, for our own part, cannot but applaud this. The artist, unfettered by political or social theories, is better enabled to represent human nature in its truth, and his works thus leave a more permanent and satisfactory impression. *Ridentem dicere verum quid vetat?*[17] But many humourists, taking advantage of the cap and bells, seem to have adopted as their motto—'Ridentem dicere *falsum* quid vetat?' Because laughter is not serious, and what is laughingly spoken is not critically accepted, they have sacrificed the truth (as well as their friends) to the joke. Perhaps no advocate of a cause should be more scrupulously watched than he who laughing teaches. Against the dogmas of the politician, philosopher, or theologian we prepare ourselves. He comes in such a questionable shape that we *must* examine him. His seriousness alarms us. We scrutinise his proofs, we combat his conclusions. Not so with the jester. He is priviliged. He throws us off our guard, and storms conviction by enveloping it in laughter. A semblance of truth has more effect in a jest, because we do not look for it there, than a demonstration in a serious essay.

The laughter passes, but the idea remains: it has gained admittance in our unsuspecting minds, and is left there unsuspected.

Although, therefore, we by no means wish to restrict the sphere of the jester, and are willing enough to take ridicule in some cases as the test of truth, we think it is the duty of critics to watch very narrowly the doctrines which the jester desires to disseminate. With regard to ridicule as the test of truth, one simple rule will suffice to limit its efficiency: Whenever the ridicule is developed *ab intra*, and not cast upon the argument *ab extra*, then it is a test, and then only.

We are getting very serious; but it is surely no paradox to say that writers of Thackeray's stamp incline one to seriousness as much as to mirth? And while in this vein, while applauding him for his admirable judgment in steering clear of party questions, and didactic purposes, we must not let slip the occasion of remonstrance on two points—the only two—in which he seems to us reprehensible.

As a satirist, it is his business to tear away the mask from life, but as an artist and a teacher he grievously errs when he shows us *everywhere* corruption underneath the mask. His scepticism is pushed too far. While trampling on cant, while exposing what is base and mean, and despicable, he is not attentive enough to honour, and to paint what is high, and generous, and noble in human nature. Let us not be understood to say that he *fails* to honour the finer portion of our nature; but he does not honour it enough. He uses the good more as a condiment to relieve the exhausted palate. Touches here and there, exquisite though brief, show us that his heart responds to what is noble, and that his soul conceives it distinctly. But he almost seems ashamed of it, as if it were an unmanly weakness; and he turns it off with a laugh, like a man caught in tears at the theatre. In *Vanity Fair*, his greatest work, how little is there to love! The people are all scamps, scoundrels, or humbugs. The only persons who show paternal affection are Rawdon Crawley and old Osborne. Beautifully is it done, with exquisite truth and feeling; but by what bitter irony are this foolish blackleg[18] and this coarse brutal old wretch selected as the sole exhibitors of such an affection! Dobbin, whose heart is so noble—the only one in the book—is made ridiculous. We are perfectly aware of the *truth* of these portraits; we admit the use of contrasts in art; but we still think that in thus making the exception stand for the rule he has erred both against art and nature. Dickens has beautifully shown us the union of the noble and the ridiculous; but in his writings this union is by no means the rule. He has painted so many loveable people that people love him for it.

Thackeray laughs all round; his impartiality has something terrible in it; so complete is the irony that he turns it even upon himself. 'O brother wearers of motley!' he exclaims, 'are there not moments when one grows sick of grinning and tumbling and the jingling of cap and bells?' He feels that there is something sad in that perpetual laughter; sad indeed, for it is blasphemy against the divine beauty which is in life. Yet what is his object? He has told us—if for once we are to take even him at his word—'This, dear friends and companions, is my amiable object; to walk with you through the Fair, to examine the shops and shows there, and that we should all come home after the flare, and the noise, and the gaiety, and be *perfectly miserable in private!*' Said in jest, or said in earnest, that unhappily is the sentence which characterises his writings. Whether carelessness or scepticism we know not, but the moral of his books is that every one—reader and author included—is no more than a puny, miserable pretender; that most of our virtues are pretences, and when not pretences are only kept up because removed from temptation.

And this brings us by a natural transition to the second count in our charge against him. We refer to a detestable passage in *Vanity Fair*, wherein, after allowing Becky, with dramatic propriety, to sophisticate with herself, to the effect that it is only her poverty which makes her vicious, he adds from himself this remark:

> And who knows but Rebecca was right in her speculations, and that it was only a question of money and fortune which made the difference between her and an honest woman? If you take temptations into account, who is to say that he is better than his neighbour? A comfortable career of prosperity, if it does not make men honest, at least keeps them so. An alderman coming from a turtle feast, will not step out of his carriage to steal a leg of mutton; *but put him to starve, and see if he will not purloin a loaf.*

Was it carelessness, or a deep misanthropy, distorting that otherwise clear judgment, which allowed such a remark to fall? What, in the face of starving thousands, men who literally die for want of bread, yet who prefer death to stealing, shall it be said that honesty is only the virtue of abundance!

There are many criminals in our vast population, and the majority are doubtless urged by poverty. But on the one hand, how many of the poor are heroically honest—honest while starving with temptation horribly besetting them; and on the other hand, how many of the comparatively wealthy stand in the prisoner's dock! Of all falsehoods, that about honesty being a question of money is the most glaring and the most insidious. Blot it out, Thackeraay; let it no longer deface your delightful pages!

To quit this tone of serious remonstrance for one of more congenial admiration, let us notice how peculiarly his own is Thackeray's humour. It steals upon you in the quietest unpretending way, so that you seem to co-operate with him in producing the joke. He never frames and glazes his ideas. He never calls upon you to admire them by any trick of phrase or oddity of language. He does not insist upon your admiration—he wins it. The simplest words, and in the simplest manner, are used to bring out his meaning; and wit of the finest quality, as well as hearty humour, seem to spring from him without an effort. The ease of his writing is little less than marvellous; and to judge from the carelessness of his style in its idiomatic flow, we should suppose that it is really written with a facile, current pen.

Another peculiarity in Thackeray, which he has in common with all the great writers, and which distinguishes him from almost all his contemporaries, is the strong sense of reality pervading his writing—a reality never lost sight of even in his most extravagant bursts of humour. He has had experience; and he has done more—he has reflected on it, so as to be able to reflect in turn. Life, not the phantasmagoria of the stage and circulating library, is the storehouse from whence he draws. We said before that there was nothing theatrical in his matter; the same must be said of his people; they are all individuals (in the right sense of that word, and not in the loose sense which Archdeacon Hare so admirably ridicules, as current in modern writing),[19] having the unmistakeable characteristics of men, and not being abstract ideas nor traditional conceptions of character. While reading Thackeray you feel that he is painting 'after nature'; not that he is inventing figments, nor drawing from the *repertoire* of a worthless stage.

In the book before us, what a variety of characters, and how unmistakeable! *Snobs* perhaps they are not all; but are they not all real? And yet what a tempting subject to seduce a writer into farcical impossibilities—mere fancy pieces humorously drawn!

The impartiality with which he has laid on the lash, is one of the most amusing things in the book; he does not content himself with sneering at the rich and titled snobs, but turns round with equal severity on the poor and envious snob. Grub-street writing diatribes against Belgravia, yet overwhelmed with delighted pride if Belgravia should happen to notice its existence, is happily shown up. The reader laughing at some ludicrous picture of sycophantic snobbishness, is suddenly turned upon by this terrible satirist, and made to confess that he, the laughing reader, in spite of his scorn of all this snobbishness, would do the very same thing were he in the same place. We believe Thackeray stands alone in the art with which he achieves this. Other satirists flatter their readers, by implication at least,—but he ruthlessly arrests the complacent chuckle, and turns the laugh against the laugher.

There never was a humourist of high excellence without an accompanying power of pathos. In Thackeray we find repeated touches as exquisite as Sterne or Jean Paul; but they are seldom more than touches. He seems averse to grief, and dwells not on the 'luxury of woe'. There is one passage, however, in *Vanity Fair*, where he seems to have lingered with a mournful pen that would not quit the subject; we allude to the affecting parting between Amelia and her boy, whom she is forced to give up to his grandfather: one bit we must copy, though it is difficult to read it, our eyes are not dry enough.

That night Amelia made the boy read the story of Samuel to her, and how Hannah his mother, having weaned him, brought him to Eli the High Priest to minister before the Lord. And he read the song of gratitude which Hannah sang: and which says, who it is who maketh poor and maketh rich, and bringeth low and exalteth—how the poor shall be raised up out of the dust, and how, in his own might, no man shall be strong. Then he read how Samuel's mother made him a little coat, and brought it to him from year to year when she came up to offer the yearly sacrifice. And then, in her sweet simple way, George's mother made commentaries to the boy upon this affecting story. How Hannah, though she loved her son so much, yet gave him up because of her vow. And how she must always have thought of him as she sat at home, far away, making the little coat; and Samuel, she was sure, never forgot his mother; and how happy she must have been as the time came (and the years pass away very quickly) when she should see her boy, and how good and wise he had grown. This little sermon she spoke with a gentle solemn voice, and dry eyes, until she came to the account of their meeting—then the discourse broke off suddenly, the tender heart overflowed, and taking the boy to her breast, she rocked him in her arms, and wept silently over him in a sainted agony of tears.

And what a profound—almost savage—touch is that of the childlike selfishness with which Georgy receives the announcement of the approaching separation:

> The widow broke the matter to Georgy with great caution; she looked to see him very much affected by the intelligence. He was rather elated than otherwise, and the poor woman turned sadly away. He bragged about the news that day to the boys at school.

But if we venture into details we shall never conclude. To use the consecrated phrase—'Thackeray's writings will repay perusal'—and reperusal!

W.M. Thackeray: Letter to G.H. Lewes (6 March 1848)

My dear Sir,
I have just read your notice in the Chronicle (I conclude it is a friend who has penned it) and am much affected by the friendliness of the sympathy, and by the kindness of the reproof of the critic.
    That passage which you quote bears very hardly upon the poor alderman certainly: but I don't mean that the man deprived of turtle would as a consequence steal bread: only that he in the possession of luxuries and riding through life respectably in a gig, should be very chary of despising poor Lazarus on foot, and look very humbly and leniently upon the faults of his less fortunate brethren—If Becky had had 5000 a year I have no doubt in my mind that she would have been respectable; increased her fortune advanced

her family in the world: laid up treasures for herself in the shape of 3 per cents, social position, reputation etc.—like Louis Philippe let us say, or like many a person highly and comfortably placed in the world not guilty of many wrongs of commission, satisfied with himself, never doubting of his merit, and decorously angry at the errors of less lucky men. What satire is so awful as Lead us not into temptation? What is the gospel and life of our Lord (excuse me for mentioning it) but a tremendous Protest against pride and self-righteousness? God forgive us all, I pray, and deliver us from evil.

I am quite aware of the dismal roguery which goes all through the Vanity Fair story—and God forbid that the world should be like it altogether: though I fear it is more like it than we like to own. But my object is to make every body engaged, engaged in the pursuit of Vanity and I must carry my story through in this dreary minor key, with only occasional hints here and there of better things—of better things which it does not become me to preach.

I never scarcely write letters to critics and beg you to excuse me for sending you this. It is only because I have just laid down the paper, and am much moved by the sincere goodwill of my critic.

Very faithfully yours W.M. Thackeray.

Thackeray's *Pendennis* (21 December 1850)

'No age,' says Carlyle, 'is romantic to itself', and no age thinks its writers equal to those who have gone before—
    [Tis distance lends enchantment to the view;][20]
and we turn from the 'superficial trash' of our age to the grander thews and sinews of those who wrote the 'superficial trash' of their time. The history of Literature is full of such complaints. Old Nestor, speaking to the illustrious host before Troy could see nothing in Achilles, Ajax, Diomed, and the King of Men, equal to the heroes who had flourished in *his* youth. Tacitus, in the opening of his *Dialogue on the Orators* (if it be his) speaks of the sterile epoch when the name of orator could not be applied to any living man, 'for *our* men are dissertators, gabblers, lawyers, everything, in short, but orators—*horum autem temporum diserti causidici et advocati, et patroni et quidvis potius quam oratores vocantur.*'

That the men of our day should think slightingly of their contemporaries in comparison with the writers of former times, is no more than natural, and we are prepared for uplifted eyebrows when we gravely assert that England has at no time produced a writer of fiction with whom Thackeray may not stand in honourable comparison. Others have surpassed him in particular qualities, but taking the sum total of his powers, as the only fair means of comparison, we are prepared to maintain our position. But will he live as they have lived? That is another question, and one which no amount of present popularity can affect; for popularity, as Victor Hugo admirably says, is the vulgarisation of fame—

La popularité? C'est la gloire en gros sous.[21]

He has the two great qualities which embalm a reputation—truth and style. But he is to be separated from the great writers of other days by one peculiarity of our own, and one that endangers the durability of his renown— we mean a want of respect for his art, a want of respect for his public. In the care with which former writers, however, pressed by poverty, planned and executed their works, we see something wholly different from that nonchalance and easy confidence in his own powers, which makes Thackeray (nor is he alone in this) sacrifice the artist to the improvisatore. How greatly his writings suffer from this it is impossible to calculate; our marvel is that they are so remarkable in spite of it. To gossip with the reader, to wander from the path into pleasant digressions and sketches of society, is a facile method of discharging his monthly task; and with knowledge so abundant and a style so graceful and winning, the success is great enough to foster the temptation. But that which is written for the hour is apt to perish with the hour; and he is capable of enduring works.

Pendennis has, perhaps, even more of this fault than *Vanity Fair*, and it flags occasionally in consequence. But it is, nevertheless, a great, a masterly work, weighty with knowledge, luminous with beautiful thoughts, caustic, subtle, pathetic, varied with unrivalled pictures of human life and character, and incomparable in style. A loving spirit moves throughout the book, taking from its satire all the bitterness of misanthropy, making human nature loveable amidst all its infirmities. As everyone must have read or will read it, we need occupy no space by an exposition of its contents; a few remarks on his general characteristics, as therein exhibited, will suffice.

First let us mention the beauty of his style. For clearness, strength, idiomatic ease, delicacy, and variety, there is no one since Goldsmith to compare with him. It is not a style in the vulgar sense of the word; that is to say, it is not a *trick*. It is the flowing garment which robes his thoughts, and moves with every movement of his mind into different and appropriate shapes, simple in narrative, terse and glittering in epigram, playful in conversation or digression, rising into rhythmic periods when the mood is of more sustained seriousness, and becoming indescribably affecting in its simplicity when it utters pathetic or solemn thoughts. It is devoid of trick though not devoid of art. Somebody said of it that it was essentially the style of a gentleman. We wish gentlemen would write so.

Then as to knowledge. The endless charm of his writing for men and women who have experience cannot be divined by those who as yet know nothing (though their hairs be grey). It is the same with Horace. No schoolboy, no young poet cares a straw for Horace. Men who have lived like him better as they grow older. In Thackeray we see many resemblances to Horace: both have outlived their illusions, and yet look back with fondness on them, so that their laughter is rather sad than bitter. It seems as if most of the various scenes of the drama of life had been acted in Thackeray's breast, and he laughs as we laugh at our youthful follies, with a certain regret that those follies are past, and a respect for the ingenuousness which committed them. It is a great mistake to suppose Thackeray's experience to lie only on the surface, and that the life he depicts is merely the movement of society. Although he knows that better, and depicts it more truly than any one else, he is separated from the fashionable novelists by the power they have little claim to—the power of representing human life. Take Disraeli for example, and compare any sketch of fashionable life by him with one by Thackeray, and the difference is at once apparent. Disraeli sees society—not very clearly, but he sees it; Thackeray sees it, and sees through it, sees all the human feelings, all the motives, high and low, simple and complicated, which make it what it is. Observe Major Pendennis, Warrington, Laura, Blanche Amory, Old Costigan, or even one of the minor persons, and on examination you will find that he seizes *characters* where other writers seize only *characteristics;* he does not give you a peculiarity for the man, he places the man himself, that 'bundle of motives', before you. To test how true this is, you have only to ask yourself 'Can I describe one of his characters truly in a phrase?' Or you may test it thus: In Becky Sharp and in Blanche Amory he has drawn the same class of woman; did that ever strike you? did you ever think he was repeating himself? Is Blanche more like Becky than Iago is like Edmund? Yet the two women belong to one type, and so marvellously true to nature, so minutely and profoundly true, that we who know one who might have sat for the portraits (but did not) are puzzled to say which of the two is most like her. Blanche does not play the same important part in *Pendennis* that Becky does in *Vanity Fair*, but the Artist's power is equally apparent to a connoisseur. By knowledge then we mean not merely the familiarity with the modes of life from Gaunt House to the Back Kitchen, but familiarity also with the realities of life as they move in human breasts.

Another peculiarity he has, and one which makes critics remonstrant,— *viz.*, that of mercilessly pointing out the skeleton which is in every closet. He passes among illusions only to show them to be follies; he turns round upon you while the tears are standing in your eyes, only to laugh at your emotion; he stands at the feast only to declare its vanity; he recites a noble sentiment only to connect it with some ignoble motive. A mocking Mephistopheles, he will not suffer you to be deceived; he laughs at you, at everybody, at himself.

There is some truth in this; but, as respects *Pendennis*, it is overstated, and the cause, we take it, does not lie in his mocking spirit, but elsewhere. It lies—if we have read his nature aright—in a predominating tendency to *antithesis*. Other writers have this tendency; but in him it acquires peculiar force. He does not, as others do, manifest it in antitheses of diction. His writing, one may say, is remarkably free from that. Nor does he proceed with the false systematic method of Victor Hugo, in whom the love of antithesis amounts to a disease (to be sure, Hugo excuses himself on the plea that God is greater in that department than himself, God being *le plus grand faiseur d'antithèses!*—a modest and satisfactory exculpation!), but, nevertheless, the law of Thackeray's mind seems to be a conception of opposites, which makes him a perfect Janus Bifrons. No sooner does he think of poetic aspirations than his mind suddenly swerves to the other side to contemplate the foolish sentimentalism which apes those aspirations. If he were drawing Caesar, he would lift up the laurel wreath to expose his baldness. His own Warrington is seen 'drinking beer like a coalheaver, and yet you couldn't but perceive that he was a gentleman.' Miss Fotheringay is a splendid actress and as ignorant as a horse. Foker is a blackguard in his tastes, but a gentleman in feeling. We might run through the volumes and point out this constant antithesis, but the reader must know very well how characteristic it is. Enough if we have indicated the reason for its constant presence.

That it does not arise from a mocking spirit, may easily be shown by reference to the examples, in which he shows a soul of goodness in things evil, as well as the spot of evil in things good. Look at Old Costigan, the Major, Strong, Altamont, and see how characters which in ordinary hands would be simply contemptible or hateful from their selfishness and scoundrelism, are preserved from corruption by the salt of human virtues, and your very scorn is modified, human sympathy appealed to, and Charity made to own a brother in the sinner. The same tendency of his mind which makes him see that a hero has the gout, makes him perceive that a scamp is not all vice. The antithesis is the one case *may* proceed from a mocking spirit; it cannot in the latter; unless we are to suppose him destitute of all reverence for human worth, and wishing to revile even goodness by locating it in vile places: a supposition contradicted, we venture to say, by the whole temper of his writings. Thackeray is a man who loves all worth, and reverences whatever is true, though his scorn of pretence is uncompromising enough. It seemed to us while reading this work, as if he had drawn himself in Warrington—a sad, thoughful, kindly, yet sarcastic man, whose very scorn proceeds from love of what is high and noble; whose dislike of pretence is so great, that he is afraid of being suspected of pretence if he adopts a more serious manner.

Not a mocking spirit but a loving spirit has he; not a Mephisto but a Goethe sits at his elbow. Goethe, too, is often reproached for the same thing, and is pronounced 'cold' because he was not one-sided. Moreover, Thackeray's antitheses differ from those of Sue and Victor Hugo in arising out of the actual truth of nature, and not out of a systematic desire for contrast. You do not catch him selecting his type of Chastity from among young ladies at the *tapis franc*;[22] in depicting the paternal and maternal sentiment he does not seek a Triboulet or a Lucrèce Borgia;[23] to show the venerableness of age he does not exhibit a brutal bandit; to show the power of love he does not choose a courtesan. He takes the Contradictions offered him daily by Nature—such as they are in us and in those around us; and the difference between him and other novelists is that he sees these Contradictions, they do not.

In *Vanity Fair* we felt the scoundrelism and pretence oppressive. In *Pendennis* this is no longer the case. It abounds of course, for Thackeray is above all things a satirist; but in *Pendennis* we note a very decided advance upon *Vanity Fair* with respect to a broader and more generous view of humanity, a larger admixture of goodness with what is evil, and a more loving mellowed tone throughout. It brought the tears into our eyes at several passages of manly pathos, and revealed to us capabilities for more serious writing than is to be found in *Vanity Fair*. Nevertheless, it is not so popular; partly because it is not so new, but mostly because it wants the leading interest of a story: Pen is not so strong a thread to hang pearls on as Becky. Yet *Vanity Fair* has no such charming woman as Laura, no such noble fellow as Warrington. Old Bows, too, is very touching: his hopeless love of the Fotheringay, and then for Fanny, and the way he educates these two only to see others carry them off, are in the best manner of poor Balzac.

Miss Fotheringay has been pronounced a caricature—by those not very familiar with theatrical life. But it was a bold and a successful stroke thus to paint the truth and to show the public that success in acting implies no commensurate intelligence, or even sympathy with the passions depicted. There are exceptions, but, speaking generally, actors are certainly *below* par rather than above it in intellect. So much of acting is factitious, so much tradition, that a very mediocre person, with tolerable physique and mimetic powers, may 'take the town by storm'. You might as reasonably suppose the leading tragedians endowed with all the heroism of the parts they play, as capable of intellectual sympathy with them. If any one doubts this, let him listen to a green-room conversation for half an hour!

We find that we have said little or nothing of the faults of *Pendennis*; but, although we could have indulged in that *antithesis* without much expenditure of ingenuity through some columns, yet in truth we thought little of the faults while reading, and care not to be critical just now; they seem to us all resolvable into natural defects which no criticism can cure, or into that carelessness which, at the outset, we declared to constitute his one inferiority to the great writers of other days. But this we will say, that we do *not* count it as a fault when we see him holding up an unflattering picture to society; nor do we think the truth immoral. 'It must be bad, indeed,' says Goethe, 'if a book *has a more demoralizing effect than life itself*, which daily displays the most scandalous scenes in abundance, if not before our eyes, at least before our ears.'

Robert Browning

'Christmas Eve and Easter Day' (27 April 1850)

Robert Browning has one inestimable quality – originality. Whatever *other* qualities he may want, this one cannot be denied him. He is not simply an original poet, but perhaps the only original poet of the day; for Tennyson, though far more richly endowed in faculties, is obviously a product of Keats, Shelley, and Wordsworth. Browning sees for himself, thinks for himself, speaks for himself. You may quarrel with his manner, but you cannot say it belongs to another; it is *his*, every line of it. If you accept it you will probably delight in it, and place the poet on an exalted pedestal. Accordingly Browning's admirers are 'fit' and *not* 'few'; they swear by their master with an enthusiasm pleasant to witness, and not insignificant as a tribute to his power.

But with full recognition of what is excellent in Browning's poetry we are prevented from sharing all that enthusiasm by the serious deficiences we note in it. Our space admits of no detailed estimate of his genius; we cannot pause to enumerate the various grounds on which we take our stand; they may all be summed up in one sentence: he is not a Singer. That which distinguishes Poetry from Verse – that music, not of language only but of thought, which constitutes the grand peculiarity and enduring delight of poetry, forms but an insignificant element in his writings. With a command over language, and powers of easy movement in the fetters of rhyme greater than in almost any writer of the day, his poems want the one redeeming grace, the one perfection of art which no teaching can give: his verse is not 'full-sailed', borne onwards by the current of imperious sound, formed out of strange velocities of thought intermingling with emotion, and raising in the hearer a like mysterious agitation. We might turn the objection into another shape, and say that in Browning's poems we miss the element of Beauty.

It will be seen that we make a serious objection. Let us add that we are testing him severely, and according to a high standard. That is right, for his aims are high. Measure him by the standard of his contemporaries, or that of many whose names in days gone by have had resounding echoes, and he will seem a man of gigantic thews and sinews. Every thing he writes is worthy of attention – he has written nothing more worthy of it than 'Christmas Eve'. It is a great theme powerfully conceived, picturesquely, sometimes grotesquely handled. In distinctness of purpose, pregnancy of meaning, and power of illustration it shows the masterhand.

118

The poet is standing in the doorway of a Methodist chapel while the rain is drenching the desolate common; and as he stands there the strange congregation glare at him before entering:—

> Well, from the road, the lanes, or the common,
> In came the flock: the fat weary woman
> Panting and bewildered, down-clapping
> Her umbrella with a mighty report,
> Grounded it by me, wry and flapping,
> A wreck of whalebones.

You must not be disconcerted with the rough realism of this poem, and complain of the tone being unsuitable to the gravity of the subject; with a keen eye for the truth Browning never idealizes: this is at once the source of his strength and of his weakness.

The fat weary woman is thus followed:

> Prompt in the wake of her, up-pattered
> On broken clogs, the many-tattered
> Little old-faced, peaking sister-turned-mother
> Of the sickly babe she tried to smother
> Somehow up, with its spotted face,
> From the cold, on her breast, the one warm place;
> She too must stop, wring the poor suds dry
> Of a draggled shawl, and add thereby
> Her tribute to the door-mat, sopping
> Already from my own clothes' dropping,
> Which yet she seemed to grudge I should stand on;
> Then stooping down to take off her pattens,
> She bore them defiantly, in each hand one,
> Planted together before her breast
> And its babe, as good as a lance in rest.
> Close on her heels, the dingy satins
> Of a female something past me flitted,
> With lips as much too white, as a streak
> Lay far too red on each hollow cheek:
> And it seemed the very door-hinge pitied
> All that was left of a woman once,
> Holding at least its tongue for the nonce.

>   . . . .

> And, when the door's cry drowned their wonder,
> The draught, it always sent in shutting,

Made the flame of the single tallow candle
In the cracked square lanthorn I stood under,
Shoot its blue lip at me, rebutting
As it were, the luckless cause of scandal:
I verily thought the zealous light
(In the chapel's secret, too!) for spite,
Would shudder itself clean off the wick,
With the airs of a St. John's Candlestick.

Shamed by the reproachful looks of the faithful, and by the 'zealous light',
he resolves to enter the chapel:—

Accordingly, as a shoemaker's lad
With wizened face in want of soap,
And wet apron wound round his waist like a rope,
After stopping outside, for his cough was bad,
To get the fit over, poor gentle creature,
And so avoid disturbing the preacher,
Passed in, I sent my elbow spikewise
At the shutting door, and entered likewise,
Received the hinge's accustomed greeting,
Crossed the threshold's magic pentacle,
And found myself in full conventicle.

Admirable is the description of the interior of Zion Chapel, and the preacher
who there 'deals damnation round' while 'the old fat woman purred with
pleasure', and of the droning sermon which sent the poet to sleep. In that
sleep he dreams that he is once more out in the open air, beneath the sky,
subject to all the influences of nature, and he also dreams that there he meets
the Saviour:—

All at once I looked up with terror,
He was there.
He Himself with His human air,
On the narrow pathway just before.
I saw the back of Him, no more —
He had left the chapel, then, as I.
I forgot all about the sky.
No face: only the sight
Of a sweepy Garment, vast and white,
With a hem that I could recognise.
I felt terror, no surprise;
My mind filled with the cataract,
At one bound of the mighty fact.

I remembered, He did say
Doubtless, that to this world's end,
Where two or three should meet and pray,
He would be in their midst, their Friend:
Certainly He was there with them.
And my pulses leaped for joy
Of the golden thought without alloy,
That I saw His very Vesture's hem.

Holding by the sacred Garment he is wafted to Rome, and at St Peter's witnesses the Catholic celebration of Christmas Eve. The plan of this is striking. No contrast could be finer than that of squalid Methodism and gorgeous Romanism; but Browning, whose observant eye sees the one vividly enough, fails to do adequate justice to the other. The pomp, and splendour, and sensuous grandeur of Catholicism are indicated rather than painted. Having witnessed the two antipodes of worship, he next is carried to the centre of Scepticism. From Roman forms he passes to the inquisitor of all forms – he is at Göttingen listening to a mythical interpretation of Christianity by a 'hawknosed high-cheekboned professor':—

I felt at once as if there ran
A shoot of love from my heart to the man –
That sallow, virgin-minded, studious
Martyr to mild enthusiasm,
As he uttered a kind of cough preludious
That woke my sympathetic spasm,
(Beside some spitting that made me sorry)
And stood, surveying his auditory
With a wan pure look, wellnigh celestial
—Those blue eyes had survived so much!
While under the foot they could not smutch,
Lay all the fleshly and the bestial.
Over he bowed, and arranged his notes,
Till the auditory's clearing of throats
Was done with, died into a silence;
And, when each glance was upward sent,
Each bearded mouth composed intent,
And a pin might be heard drop half a mile hence,
He pushed back higher his spectacles,
Let the eyes stream out like lamps from cells,
And giving his head of hair – a hake
Of undressed tow, for colour and quantity –
One rapid and impatient shake,
(As our own young England adjusts a jaunty tie

When about to impart, on mature digestion,
Some thrilling view of the surplice-question)
—The Professor's grave voice, sweet though hoarse,
Broke into his Christmas-Eve's discourse.

We cannot quote the lecture, but it is not a very unfair version of the mythic
doctrine. Truly enough does he say:—

Unlearned love was safe from spurning—
Can't we respect your loveless learning!
Let us at least give learning to honour!
What laurels had we showered upon her,
Girding her loins up to perturb
Our theory of the Middle Verb;
Or Turklike brandishing a scimitar
O'er anapaests in comic trimeter;
Or curing the halt and maimed Iketides,
While we lounged on at our indebted ease:
Instead of which, a tricksy demon
Sets her a Titus or Philemon!
When Ignorance wags his ears of leather
And hates God's word, 'tis altogether;
Nor leaves he his congenial thistles
To go and browse on Paul's Epistles.

But he prefers the errors of Romanism or Methodism to those of
Hegelianism:—

Truth's atmosphere may grow mephitic
When Papist struggles with Dissenter,
Impregnating its pristine clarity,
– One, by his daily fare's vulgarity
Its gust of broken meat and garlic;
– One, by his soul's too-much presuming,
To turn the frankincense's fuming
And vapours of the candle starlike
Into the cloud her wings she buoys on:
And each, that sets the pure air seething,
Poisoning it for healthy breathing—
But the critic leaves no air to poison:
Pumps out by a ruthless ingenuity
Atom by atom and leaves you – vacuity.
Thus much of Christ, does he reject?
And what retain? His intellect?

What is it I must reverence duly?
Poor intellect for worship truly.
Which tells me simply what was told
(If mere mortality, bereft
Of the God in Christ, be all that's left)
Elsewhere by voices manifold.

He wakes in the little chapel again, taught some lessons by his dream; and the substance of what he has learned is given in the second poem – or division of the poem called 'Easter-day' – wherein, after setting forth the difficulties which beset the mind desirous of becoming truly Christian, he concludes by the orthodox-heterodoxy – or heterodox-orthodoxy, whichever you please – that Christianity is love.

On the theology of the poem we should have much to say did time and place serve; meanwhile we need only applaud in passing the sincere and earnest spirit which breathes through it. The sincerity of it will to many look like levity. Already we have heard strange objections to the 'tone', as not elevated enough. Do these critics imagine that an 'elevated' tone is difficult? Do they suppose that Browning could not have adopted it, had he thought fit? But he did *not* think fit. Instead of imitating Milton he spoke as Robert Browning; his keen sense of the ludicrous and grotesque fading into the background whenever the presence of more solemn themes overshadowed it. In the bold and artful mingling of the ludicrous with the intensely serious he reminds us of Carlyle. His style is swayed by the subject. It is a garment, not a mould; it takes the varying shapes of varied movement, and does not force its one monotony on all.

As a page out of the history of a life, the poetic confession of a troubled soul, 'Christmas Eve' has a significance and a value peculiarly its own. We have read it three times, and with increasing admiration. What it wants to make it an enduring work of art is that which the author cannot give it, has not to give – the magic and the mystery of Beauty. But of its kind it is really great. The luxury of rhyme – the marvellous facility playing with difficulties as an Indian juggler plays with balls, every one will have noticed. Since Butler no English poet has exhibited the same daring propensity and facility in rhyming. If the verse is sometimes rugged it is but the better exponent of the thought. Realism in Art has Truth as its Aim, Ugliness as a pitfall.

Alfred Tennyson

'In Memoriam' (22 June 1850)

Sacred to the memory of one long loved and early dead, this tablet bears neither the name of the deceased nor of the affectionate hand that raised it. Our readers have already been informed that it is erected by our greatest living poet – Alfred Tennyson – to the memory of Arthur Hallam. On first announcing the volume we stated our belief that it was unique in the annals of literature. The only poems that occurred to us as resembling it were the 'Lament of Bion', by Moschus; 'Lycidas', by Milton; and 'Adonais', by Shelley; but these are all distinguished from it both by structural peculiarities, and by the spirit which animates them. They may fitly be compared with each other, because they are all rather the products of sorrowing Fancy than of genuine sorrow. Herein note a fundamental difference from 'In Memoriam', which is the iterated chant of a bereaved soul always uttering one plaint, through all the varying moods of sorrow. There is iteration in Moschus, and it is effective; but this ever-recurring burden,

ἄρχετε Σικελικαὶ τῶ πένθεος, ἄρχετε Μοῖσαι,[24]

is not the 'trick of grief' but the trick of art. The unity and recurrence in Tennyson lie deeper – they are internal, not external. Tennyson does not, like Moschus, Milton, and Shelley, call upon the woods and streams, the nymphs and men, to weep for his lost Arthur; he weeps himself. He does not call upon his fancy for images of woe; he lets his own desolate heart break forth in sobs of music. The three great poets are superior to him in what the world vulgarly calls poetry, in the graceful arabesque of fancy, when the mind at ease plays with a grief that is just strong enough to stimulate it, not strong enough to sombre it; but they are all three immeasurably below him in strength, depth, and passion, consequently in the effect produced upon the minds of others. To read Moschus is a critical delight; beautiful conceits are so beautifully expressed, that our admiration at the poet's *skill* is intense; but who believes in the poet's grief? who is saddened by his mournfulness, or solaced by his hope? The first twelve lines are exquisite, and even the conceit,

> Now, Hyacinth, give all thy letters voice,
> And more than ever call 'Alas! alas!'

[Lewes quotes the Greek] is felt to be in proper keeping with the spirit of the whole; and so is the beautiful line wherein he says that Echo, hidden among the reeds, fed on Bion's songs: [Lewes quotes the Greek]. But from first to last you feel that he is playing with his subject, and *si vis me flere*, &c.[25] Milton, again, has nobly imitated his favourite classics, and drawn from the wealthier stores of his own capacious mind, images which will live for ever; but the only passage recurring to memories of friendship is that famous one,

> Together both, ere the high lawns appeared
> Under the opening eyelids of the morn,
> We drove afield, &c.

Every one knows the 'beauties' of this poem: the passage about Amaryllis in the shade, and that about Alpheus, set to noble music; but there is one passage we have not seen quoted, and as, in our estimation, it is the most beautiful in the poem, we will give it here:—

> There entertain him all the saints above
> In solemn troops and sweet societies,
> That sing, *and, singing in their glory move,*
> *And wipe the tears forever from his eyes.*

What potency of language, image, rhythm!

The reader sees it is not lightly, or irreverently to Milton's genius, that we have placed 'Lycidas' below 'In Memoriam'. The comparison is not here of genius, but of feeling. Tennyson sings a deeper sorrow, utters a more truthful passion, and, singing truly, gains the predominance of passion over mere sentiment.

In mere amplitude 'In Memoriam' differs from all its predecessors. It is not *one* expression of bereavement; it is the slow gathering of seventeen years, and bears within it the varying traces of those varying moods which a long-enduring sorrow would necessarily assume. Our criticism need not be long. The elegiac mournfulness bears the impress of genuine feeling; it is the musical utterance of a noble loving heart. Instead of criticising, let us suppose the reader has an observing pencil, and that we are looking over his shoulder exchanging remarks. We first bid him notice – perhaps we are fanciful, but the remark comes spontaneously – how exquisitely adapted the music of the poem is to its burden; the stanza chosen, with its mingling rhymes, and its slow yet not imposing march, seems to us the very perfection of stanzas for the purpose. We then bid him notice how free from 'conceits' (and what magazine poets call 'poetry') the whole volume is, and yet how abundant the felicities of diction and image, painting by one energetic word a picture which fills the mind, – as in this sea-burial

His *heavy-shotted* hammock-shroud
Drops in his vast and wandering grave.

Never was the wild, mysterious, indefinite idea of sea-burial more grandly
pictured than in the incomparable felicity of those words, 'vast and wandering grave', wherein the rhythm partakes of the feeling of the image, and
seems to bear away the corpse into infinity.
     Then, again,

Calm on the seas and silver sleep,
And waves that sway themselves in rest,
And dead calm in that noble breast
Which heaves but with the heaving deep.

Or such touches as

The rocks are *blown* about the skies.

Or as this of

Some dead lake
That holds the shadow of a lark
Hung in the shadow of a heaven.

Or this:—

And hush'd my deepest grief of all,
When fill'd with tears that cannot fall,
I brim with sorrow drowning song.

Or this:—

Her eyes are homes of silent prayer.

Or this larger landscape:—

Till now the doubtful dusk reveal'd
The knolls once more, where, couch'd at ease,
The white kine glimmer'd, and the trees
Laid their dark arms about the field.

And, suck'd from out the distant gloom,
A breeze began to tremble o'er
The large leaves of the sycamore,
And fluctuate all the still perfume.

And gathering freshlier overhead,
Rock'd the full-foliaged elms, and swung
The heavy-folded rose, and flung
The lilies to and fro, and said,

'The dawn, the dawn!' and died away;
And East and West, without a breath,
Mixt their dim lights, like life and death,
To broaden into boundless day.

While you, reader, are pencilling in this way with so much love, do not forget to place a mark of disapproval against the insufferable rhymes which three times mar the beauty of the page: *again*, to rhyme with *then*, must be vulgarised into *agen*; and *Christ*, to rhyme with *mist*, and elsewhere with Evange*list*, can only be accepted upon a total change in our pronunciation. Certain prosaisms and obscurities may be better defended; false rhymes admit of no defence.

But how beautiful, how simple, and how touching are the poems when you read them uncritically, giving full sway to the feelings which that music rouses in you! Who does not feel with him:—

I sometimes hold it half a sin
To put in words the grief I feel;
For words, like nature, half reveal
And half conceal the Soul within.

[Lewes quotes several more verses here.]

From the specimens already given you may estimate the beauty of the volume. We shall be surprised if it does not become the solace and delight of every house where poetry is loved. A true and hopeful spirit breathes from its pages. Sorrow has purified him. Its lessons are no ungenerous or repining thoughts; and truly does he say,

I hold it true, whate'er befal;
I feel it, when I sorrow most
'Tis better to have loved and lost,
Than never to have loved at all.

Sorrow is the deepest teacher; it opens the portals of worlds which otherwise were unexplored; it mingles with our life, enlarges our capacity of feeling, deepens our sympathy, corrects the egotisms of our nature, and raises our moral development. All who have sorrowed will listen with delight to the chastened strains here poured forth 'In Memoriam'.

Elizabeth Barrett Browning

Poems (30 November 1850)

We have a grudge against Mrs. Browning's critics for having, by their praises, kept us so long in ignorance of her beauties. We cannot, at this distance of time, specify where certain critiques appeared, nor what was the peculiar imbecility they expressed; but we are distinctly conscious of the general impression left by them, which was such as to destroy all curiosity to see the poems they so clumsily bepraised: the impression was that Mrs Browning, then Miss Barrett, belonged to the least-amiable section of the modern school of affectation and verbosity – an impression some sonnets she published in *Blackwood* seemed fully to bear out.

Mrs Browning, in our hearts we make you the *amende honorable*! The loss has been ours; but we have wronged you in our thoughts, – wronged you and scorned you, – when we should have honoured you and loved you, had not your critics deluded us with hyperboles of nonsense. To be saved from one's friends has been an ancient prayer; when the friends are critics and noodles the prayer receives a triple intensification!

Probably some of our readers are in the same mood that we were, and from the same causes. If so, we conjure them to rush to the first shop, and carry off the two caskets of jewels bearing the name of Elizabeth Barrett Browning – *paying* for them if finances permit, but *stealing* them if necessary; for to possess them is imperative on all lovers of 'numerous verse'. By fair means or foul, they must be had. 'Steal? *convey*, the wise it call.' Any jury – having read the volumes – would give a verdict of 'extenuating circumstances.'

We cannot pretend, in the novelty of our admiration, to utter a final verdict on Mrs Browning's claims; no real poet is fathomed by the first cast of a sounding line, be the caster never so skilful. What we propose at present is merely to jot down rough notes towards the final elaboration of a judgment.

And, first, we note the quality – which takes precedence of all other excellences, without which no affluence of imagery or experience can avail – the quality of song. Poetry differs from prose as song differs from speech. The orator may be great, powerful, impassioned; but the highest sublimation of his qualities will never raise him into a singer. The singer may be feeble, his song scarce worth the hearing; but, nevertheless, he remains distinguished from all other men by this one gift of song. Mrs Browning is a born singer – a poet by the irresistible decree of Nature. Herein she is distinguished from

128

her husband, who, with a far greater reach of intellect, is a poet *made* by culture – a poet because other poets have lived before him, and spurred his ambitious horse till its paces made him fancy it was Pegasus. There is music in her mind, and that music becomes resonant in verse. Except Tennyson, there is no living writer of whom this is so essential a characteristic. Except Tennyson, there is no living writer to whom we should sooner point as an example of a *born poet*.

Connected with this primary quality of song there is also a singular magnificence of diction, such as recalls the prodigality of Shelley and Keats. She plays tricks with our noble language, occasionally ; but this arises from the very indulgence of power unrestrained by taste; and these tricks look ugly in extracts. She is somewhat overlearned, also, in her diction; yet not pedantically so. The severe strength of simplicity is not in the nature of her genius, which is affluent, redundant, and lyrical, rather than collective, suggestive, and proportional: the *emotions* rule her genius, not the *intellect*.

This leads us to the primary defect of her writings – want of substantive wealth. Partly, we suspect because of her position, isolated in its womanhood from the great experiences which enrich a man (for it is only your unhappy or *extra*ordinary women, such as George Sand or De Staël, whose lives furnish them with the material open to men), but still more owing to the natural tendency of her nature, she has allowed her phantasy to move amidst the reveries and unrealities of a silent life, instead of seeking to rebaptize in beauty the thoughts and sufferings of our work-day world.[26] There are exceptions to this charge, and we shall notice them anon; but, taking a broad survey of her writings, this one fact continually forces itself upon us. She does not image forth the world. She does not, with the solemn introspection of egotism, make her own life the image wherein we are to recognise ourselves. Her works are works of pure imagination, or say, rather, of pure phantasy; not the utterances of a deliciously over-burdened soul speaking to our souls. Hence her great admirers will be found among feminine minds of both sexes; among the youthful who are still inhabitants of the realms of fancy, not dragged earthward by sorrowing realities or stern necessities; and among critics and poets, who will consider form, and form only. But, as George Sand so finely says: 'La poesie n'est qu'une forme, une expression de la vie en nous, et là ou elle n'exprime ni voeux, ni convictions, elle n'est qu'un ornement frivole, un instrument sonore.'

The very choice of subjects implies – to our apprehension – the want of real poetic material. 'A man can only coin guineas', said Johnson, 'in proportion to his gold'; but the poet, whether he has gold or not, will persist in coining, and *invents* or borrows his material to satisfy the craving of his desire to create, just as the hen, though widowed, will lay eggs, to fulfil her function in the universe, even if housewives scorn her eggs as worthless: they *look* as good as other eggs, and gratify her maternal pride, but you cannot hatch them into chickens!

Open these volumes, and you find, first, 'The Drama of Exile' – the old fable of *Paradise Lost*, treated not as Milton treated it, with human nature for his constant theme, and theological argument itself made human; but as Shelley would have treated it, had he been orthodox – with fanciful choruses of earth spirits, flower spirits, angels, and all the supernatural company vexing the reader with the sense of its being 'all imagination'. We do not deny the beauty of many passages – the paradisaical glow that lights up the whole; but we say the poem is a caprice: it is not hewn out of experience; it does not appeal to human sympathies. It is a work produced by mere delight in production. Then comes a still more remote and fanciful drama – 'The Seraphim' – in the reading of which we fairly broke down. Years ago we should have gloried in it, and, doubtless, have straightway proceeded to spoil foolscap with an imitation of it! but 'years which bring the philosophic mind'[27] have brought the natural distaste for unrealities. And by unrealities we do not mean the things which have no actual existence in the outward world; we mean the things which do not really exist anywhere – which have no vitality. The *Arabian Nights* are intensely real and true; so are Fairy Tales when good. Puck, Titania, Caliban, and Ariel are as real as Hamlet or Falstaff. But Mrs Browning's Seraphim – Ador and Zerah – are unreal in every acceptation of the term.

Following the 'Seraphim' come translations of the 'Prometheus Bound' (of which more in detail hereafter) and the 'Lament for Adonis' of Bion: subjects which, as exercises in translation, might be chosen by any poet, but which confirm the view we take of her natural tendency to *avoid* mingling with the moving currents of life, and to choose the realm of phantasy. That noble Greek drama lay open to her; why did not the human interests of the Antigone, the Oedipus, the Philoctetes, the Ajax, or the Iphigenia attract her, and why were they foregone for the mythologic grandeur of the Prometheus? To our minds the answer is simple. The remoteness of a subject from human interest (and there is very little human interest in the Prometheus – it ends with the first scenes) was to her a fascination.

After these there come 'A Vision of Poets' – 'The Poet's Vow' – two ballads, and some sonnets. In the second volume the ballads occupy a foremost place, and miscellaneous poems fill the remainder. We will not pause here to criticise these ballads and romaunts; our present purpose is to indicate the subjects chosen, and to suggest how they are those which a poet would select when moved by *reading* and reverie rather than by the *oestrus* of experience. And what the mere choice indicates the treatment confirms. The poems want substance. The form of the vase is beautiful, and its arabesque tracery flatters the eye; but the material is fragile or indifferent. The true regal *stamp* of the guinea is visible; but unfortunately the coin is not gold.

Enough on this point. Next week we will narrow our criticism to particulars, and tie up a nosegay of lovely flowers culled from her garden; for the present we will lighten the prosing we have just remorselessly flung upon your patience by the quotation of two sonnets, which will show how she can write when her own experience is the fuel of her flame:

TEARS

Thank God, bless God, all ye who suffer not
More grief than ye can weep for. That is well –
That is light grieving! lighter none befel
Since Adam forfeited the primal lot.
Tears! what are tears? the babe weeps in its cot,
The mother singing; at her marriage bell
The Bride weeps; and before the oracle
Of high-faned hills the poet hath forgot
That moisture on his cheeks. Thank God for grace
Whoever weep; albeit as some have done,
Ye grope tear-blinded in a desert place,
And touch but tombs – look up! Those tears will run
Soon in long rivers down the lifted face,
And leave the vision clear for stars and sun.

Noble writing that; true, musical, and potent. Hear her again on

GRIEF

I tell you hopeless grief is passionless –
That only men incredulous of despair,
Half taught in anguish, through the midnight air
Beat upward to God's throne in loud access
Of shrieking and reproach. Full desertness
In souls, as countries, lieth silent, bare
Under the blenching, vertical eye-glare
Of the absolute heavens. Deep-hearted man, express
Grief for thy dead in silence like to death;
Most like a monumental statue set
In everlasting watch and moveless woe
Till itself crumble to the dust beneath.
Touch it: the marble eyelids are not wet,
If it could weep it could arise and go.

Matthew Arnold

Schools of Poetry (26 November 1853)

It is with individuals as with nations, the baffled turbulence if Youth subsides into the calm acquiescence of Age, but in both the ideal is placed beyond the Present. Jean Paul has said, 'Keiner ist mit der Zeit zufrieden: das heisst die Jünglinge halten die Künftige für idealer als die Gegenwärtige, die Alten die Vergangene', (None are content with the age: the young believe the Future, the old the Past to be the ideal era.) And with this we may connect what Goethe says of all men being Radicals in their youth, and Conservatives in their old age. We see a Goethe and a Schiller escaping from the notoriety of the 'storm and stress period' which they had created, into Grecian classicality, just as we see the unrestrained and 'chartered libertinism' of the Elizabethan period changing to the classicality of Charles and Anne, which in its turn was to be set aside by a 'new school'; and that new school, now old, will perhaps have to give place to another revival of the classical: indications whereof may be read in the vehement protests against Tennyson and Alexander Smith,[28] as also in the artistic strivings of some poets, Arnold among the number. Scorn of the past we hold to be as unwise as scorn of 'our wondrous Mother-Age'; but with whatever reverence and retrospective longing the Past is regarded, it should always be regarded as *past*: it should have historical, not absolute significance: it is our Ancestry, and not our Life. And as the retention in our organism of the elements which *have lived* is in itself a fatal source of destruction, poisoning the very life these elements once served, so in the onward progression of Humanity the old elements must pass away, transmitting to successors the work they had to perform: 'Et quasi cursores vitae lampada tradunt!'[29]

Matthew Arnold, in the Preface to this new edition of his poems, defends himself against those critics who bid him 'leave the exhausted past, and fix his thoughts upon the present'. It seems to him that his critics know very little of what they are talking about. Whatever he may once have thought of 'Our Age', it is clear he does not now regard it as so fruitful in poetry as the olden time; and all he says on this point is worthy of attention:

> What are the eternal objects of Poetry, among all nations, and at all times? They are actions; human actions; possessing an inherent interest in themselves, and which are to be communicated in an interesting manner by the art of the Poet. Vainly will the latter imagine that he has

132

everything in his own power; that he can make an intrinsically inferior action equally delightful with a more excellent one by his treatment of it: he may indeed compel us to admire his skill, but his work will possess, within itself, an incurable defect.

The Poet, then, has in the first place to select an excellent action; and what actions are the most excellent? Those, certainly, which most powerfully appeal to the great primary human affections: to those elementary feelings which subsist permanently in the race, and which are independent of time. These feelings are permanent and the same; that which interests them is permanent and the same also. The modernness or antiquity of an action, therefore, has nothing to do with its fitness for poetical representation; this depends upon its inherent qualities. To the elementary part of our nature, to our passions, that which is great and passionate is eternally interesting; and interesting solely in proportion to its greatness and to its passion. A great human action of a thousand years ago is more interesting to it than a smaller human action to-day, even though upon the representation of this last the most consummate skill may have been expended, and though it has the advantage of appealing by its modern language, familiar manners, and contemporary allusions, to all our transient feelings and interests. These, however, have no right to demand of a poetical work that it shall satisfy them; their claims are to be directed elsewhere. Poetical works belong to the domain of our permanent passions: let them interest these, and the voice of all subordinate claims upon them is at once silenced.

Achilles, Prometheus, Clytemnestra, Dido—what modern poem presents personages as interesting, even to us moderns, as these personages of an 'exhausted past'? We have the domestic epic dealing with the details of modern life which pass daily under our eyes; we have poems representing modern personages in contact with the problems of modern life, moral, intellectual, and social; these works have been produced by poets the most distinguished of their nation and time; yet I fearlessly assert that Hermann and Dorothea, Childe Harold, Jocelyn, The Excursion, leave the reader cold in comparison with the effect produced upon him by the latter books of the *Iliad*, by the *Orestea*, or by the episode of Dido. And why is this? Simply because in the three latter cases the action is greater, the personages nobler, the situations more intense; and this is the true basis of the interest in a poetical work, and this alone.

It may be urged, however, that past actions may be interesting in themselves, but that they are not to be adopted by the modern Poet, because it is impossible for him to have them clearly present to his own mind, and he cannot therefore feel them deeply, nor represent them forcibly. But this is not necessarily the case. The externals of a past action, indeed, he cannot know with the precision of a contemporary;

but his business is with its essentials. The outward man of Oedipus or
of Macbeth, the houses in which they lived, the ceremonies of their
courts, he cannot accurately figure to himself; but neither do they
essentially concern him. His business is with their inward man; with
their feelings and behaviour in certain tragic situations, which engage
their passions as men; these have in them nothing local and casual:
they are as accessible to the modern Poet as to a contemporary.

The date of an action, then, signifies nothing: the action itself, its
selection and construction, this is what is all-important. This the
Greeks understood far more clearly than we do. The radical difference
between their poetical theory and ours consists, as it appears to me, in
this: that, with them, the poetical character of the action in itself, and
the conduct of it, was the first consideration; with us, attention is fixed
mainly on the value of the separate thoughts and images which occur
in the treatment of an action. They regarded the whole; we regard the
parts. With them, the action predominates over the expression of it;
with us, the expression predominates over the action. Not that they
failed in expression, or were inattentive to it; on the contrary, they are
the highest models of expression, the unapproached masters of the
grand style: but their expression is so excellent because it is so
admirably kept in its right dregree of prominence; because it is so
simple and so well subordinated; because it draws its force directly
from the pregnancy of the matter which it conveys.

There is excellent matter amid some that is questionable here. We remark,
in passing, that he maintains opinions respecting the Greek and Latin poets,
which are *traditional*, but which, to our experience, are very far removed
from the truth. We will not, however, encumber the argument by questioning
his illustrations; let us grant for a moment that the Greeks *are* what he
describes, and quote his criticism on the contrasted defects of modern poets:–

We have poems which seem to exist merely for the sake of single lines
and passages; not for the sake of producing any total-impression. We
have critics who seem to direct their attention merely to detached
expressions, to the language about the action, not to the action itself. I
verily think that the majority of them do not in their hearts believe that
there is such a thing as a total-impression to be derived from a poem
at all, or to be demanded from a poet; they think the term a common-
place of metaphysical criticism. They will permit the Poet to select any
action he pleases, and to suffer that action to go as it will, provided he
gratifies them with occasional bursts of fine writing, and with a shower
of isolated thoughts and images. That is, they permit him to leave their
poetical sense ungratified, provided that he gratifies their rhetorical
sense and their curiosity. Of his neglecting to gratify these, there is

little danger; he needs rather to be warned against the danger of attempting to gratify these alone; he needs rather to be perpetually reminded to prefer his action to everything else; so to treat this, as to permit its inherent excellences to develop themselves, without inter-ruption from the intrusion of his personal peculiarities: most fortunate, when he most entirely succeeds in effacing himself, and in enabling a noble action to subsist as it did in nature.

True, most true, and needful to be said. But when he lays it down as a canon that the 'highest problem of an art is to imitate actions', he seems to us either to employ an abusive extension of the term 'action', or else to misconceive the problem and the function of Art. Indeed, one may say that Art is only an imitation of actions in its earliest and rudest forms. He himself is forced to admit that according to this canon *Faust* is not a great work of Art:–

> Wonderful passages as it contains, and in spite of the unsurpassed beauty of the scenes which relate to Margaret, Faust itself, judged as a whole, and judged strictly as a poetical work is defective: its illust-rious author, the greatest poet of modern times, the greatest critic of all times, would have been the first to acknowledge it; he only defended his work, indeed, by asserting it to be 'something incommensurable.'

A canon which excludes *Faust*, must *ipso facto* be suspicious. But Mr Arnold's friends, the Ancients, will also fare badly if this rule be applied to them; even among the dramatists, in spite of action being the *principium et fons*[30] of the drama, one meets with a *Philoctetes* for example, of which no one will say that the interest or beauty lies in the action; and if we turn to the *Divine Comedy* we shall find it as defective as *Faust* according to this rule. Actions are not ends in Art, but means to an end; they are not for their own sake, but for the sake of the thoughts and emotions they excite in us. Admirable as means, they are still only means. If the poet can read his end through other means we do not tell him he has sinned against Art.

Turn to the other forms of Art, and the incorrectness of the canon will be obvious: it is not through action that Music reaches its effect; it is not through the representation of any story that Sculpture necessarily excites in us the emotions proper to it. Titian's portrait of a 'Young Man with a Glove' is a finer work of Art than Haydon's 'Judgment of Solomon':[31] althouh one has no story, no action, the other a nobler story, and a situation of deep interest. It may be answered that Haydon has ill-executed his idea; but this draws the question from the 'choice of a subject', to that of 'representation'; and while it is a truism to assert that execution being equal, rank will depend on the greatness of the thing represented, it is a falsism to assert the rank of a work of Art depends on its *idea*—its conception. Not that Mr Arnold asserts this, but others do who start from the same point.

It is to the classics Mr Arnold would have our poets turn for guidance. Dissatisfied with the Present, and having no vision of it as an ideal life, he is also dissatisfied with its utterances in Art:

Ah! how unlike
To that large utterance of the early gods!

Overlooking the fact that if a man has something of his age to say or sing, some expression by which he can make articulate what is inarticulate in the mass or class of which he is one, he will imperiously say or sing it without much regard to 'models' at all, Mr Arnold tells us:

The confusion of the present times is great, the multitude of voices counselling different things bewildering, the number of existing works capable of attracting a young writer's attention and of becoming his models, immense: all he wants is a hand to guide him through the confusion, a voice to prescribe to him the aim which he should keep in view, and to explain to him that the value of the literary works which offer themselves to his attention is relative to their power of helping him on his road towards this aim. Such a guide the English writer at the present day will nowhere find.

Shakespeare he considers a dangerous model (but indeed all models are dangerous to minds that 'copy' them), and he prefers the Greeks. If his counsel is rightly interpreted, it will be useful to that large class of Amateurs who write verse but who are not 'born Singers'; but, if rigidly interpreted, it will lead the despairing classicists to exclaim with Charles Lamb, 'Hang the critics, *I'll write for antiquity!*'

Our own belief is, that schools of poetry are the changing fashions of one eternal spirit; and that good poetry is everywhere the same in its essential conditions, everywhere fluctuating with the fluctuating modes of thought and language. Further our belief is, that all conscious imitation is weakness, and that 'models' produce no real good, though little harm, because the servile mind is one which if emancipated would not be strong. To study models with a view to *emulate* them is not the same as to study them with a view to *imitate* them; the one is an invigorating—the other an enervating study.

We have tarried so long over Mr Arnold's preface that we must defer till next week all attempt to characterise his poems.

Arnold's Poems (3 December 1853)

Having in a previous article discussed the propositions of Mr Arnold's preface, and tried to come to an understanding on the subject of his critical precepts, we have now to consider his practice, and to read his poems in the light of his precepts.

Study the Classics, and beware of the syren-charms which enervate the Moderns! that is the text from which he preaches. The logical consequence is Imitation.

Study the Classics, and the Moderns too, but beware of the rudeness and baldness of the one, no less than of the rhetoric and glitter of the other! That is our text. For we believe the Ancients to have had every virtue and every vice conspicuous in the Moderns, over and above the *remoteness* of their ideas and feelings, which to us moderns becomes a vice. When the Classics are good, they are so by virtue of qualities essential in all excellent works of Art; when they are bad, which is mostly the case, they are so by vice of qualities noticeable in every age—rudeness, incongruity, untruth, greater regard for manner than for matter, and for the mere fopperies of manner. Homer, with all his fine qualities, is as rude as hemp; Aeschylus is often as fantastic, obscure, and incongruous, and Virgil as feeble, affected, and unpictorial as the very worst specimens which can be selected from eminent poets of Modern times. To deny this would be to deny evidence. It is the traditional belief, but it is a fact.

Such being our critical faith, instead of Imitation we counsel Emulation; instead of following the mere fashions of Greek Art, follow no fashions but those which bear the general verdict of your age, and while learning from the Greeks the lessons they and all great artists have to teach, beware, above all things, of imitating them.

Mr Arnold, as a scholar, and one of poetical tendencies rather than of poetical genius, a man of culture, reflection, and sensibility, but not forming one of that small band of Singers who 'sing as the birds sing', naturally looks towards Greece for inspiration. His poems will delight scholars, who will with curious pleasure follow him in his undisguised imitations of works which long have been their ideals; they will note his curiosities of verse, and his Graecism of imagery. Nor will the larger public read without delight. Poems such as there are not common. Some of the qualities most easily appreciable these poems possess, and they will secure an audience. But the fit audience is that of the cultured few. The longest poem in the volume, *Sohrab and Rustum*, will be the greatest favourite, for it tells an intelligible and interesting story, and the story moves through pictures and pathos such as we rarely meet in 'volumes of poetry'. It has its Graecisms, but they are little more than ornaments of questionable taste; the real attractiveness lies in the qualities just named. Let a brief analysis make this apparent.

Sohrab, who is Rustum's son, unknown to Rustum, is everywhere seeking his father and the place most certain to find Rustum is a battlefield. In order that his fame may reach his father's ear, Sohrab entreats to be allowed to challenge, in single combat, a champion from the Persian ranks. The request is granted. In the following graphic description of the filing hosts, the reader will have no difficulty in tracing Homer and Milton:–

> The sun by this had risen, and cleared the fog
> From the broad Oxus and the glittering sands.
> And from their tents the Tartar horsemen filed
> Into the open plain; so Haman bade—
> Haman, who next to Peran-Wisa ruled
> The host, and still was in his lusty prime.
> From their black tents, long files of horse, they
>   streamed;
> As when some grey November morn the files,
> In marching order spread, of long-necked cranes
> Stream over Casbin and the southern slopes
> Of Elburz, from the Aralian estuaries,
> Or some frore Caspian reed-bed, southward bound
> For the warm Persian sea-board—so they streamed.[32]

The imitation mars this for all except scholars. But to continue. The Persians accept the challenge, and then go to Rustum's tent, as the Greeks did to that of Achilles, and implore his arm:

[Lewes paraphrases and quotes extensively from the poem.]

It will be confessed that this is far from ordinary writing. The poem, indeed, is not an ordinary production; but we should have an easy task to show that its excellencies are not derived from the Greek, although most of its defects are. More than this, its defects are often the mere defects of rude art, which are copied from Homer; such, for example, as the practice of conducting the narrative through lengthy similies, elaborately circumstantial, positively retarding and encumbering what they are meant to accelerate and lighten. If Homer lived in our days he would not write like Homer's imitators. In fact the mistake of all imitation is that it naturally fastens on the fleeting modes, and not on the eternal spirit.

Criticism might also have something to say in other directions, if this poem were to be closely scrutinised. We point, in passing, to such prosaisms as 'fate' treading something or other down, with an 'iron heel', and to such mistaken familiarities of illustration as those at p. 20 and p. 47. But we need not dwell on them. Our purpose is gained if we have directed the reader's attention to an unequal but delightful volume of poems, and if we have, at the same time, indicated the real position which the poet is to hold, with respect to both Ancients and Moderns.

Charles Lamb

Charles Lamb: His Genius and Writings (May 1848)

Early in the present century, there was, every Wednesday evening, in very humble quarters in the Temple, a snug little *réunion*, to which one would rather have been admitted than to any dozen brilliant conversaziones which London could offer. Nothing could be simpler than the entertainment; it had none of the attractions of wealth, of fashion, or of celebrity. It was never chronicled in the *Morning Post*. What was said and done there, afforded no food to idle *on dits*. No magnificent flunkies lined the staircase, and roared your name from one to the other, trumpeting your arrival. You were not ushered into a blaze of light, amidst jewels, plumes, and rustling dresses, crowding beneath chandeliers. It was a very small room, dimly lighted, modest in appearance, the walls graced with an engraving or two, and a famous head of Milton, the possessor's pride. A quiet rubber, the solemnity of which was from time to time relieved by quaint 'quips, and cranks, and wanton wiles'; a plain clay pipe; a crust of bread and cheese—perhaps oysters; a foaming tankard of porter; a glass of ginger wine, and a glass or so of grog: these were all that hospitality could offer, but they were offered hospitably. The champagne was in the talk,—and to hear them was worth the sacrifice of any entertainment. The guests were various, but all 'choice spirits'. There you might see gentle George Dyer, as scholarly and simple as Parson Adams. There also Manning, with his burning ardour, and great mathematical science. There Leigh Hunt, with overflowing animal spirits, quoting, misquoting, punning, and criticising—bold, yet timid; his audacity in speculation always restrained by constitutional timidity, which made him do away (in a parenthesis) with the very purpose of his opinion. There his fierce, irascible, dogmatic, acute, honest-hating, honest-loving, paradoxical friend Hazlitt, by turns giving vent to some political vehemence, and to some delicate criticism on painting—describing with gusto, and analysing with startling acuteness. There also Coleridge, fat, florid, indolent, dreaming, silver-haired, and silver-tongued, pouring forth rivers of talk, on the banks of which grew lovely wild flowers of all kinds; discoursing blandly and poetically on all the 'high arguments' which can interest mankind, but coming to no definite conclusion on any one of them; always intending to accomplish great works, never writing them; weak, selfish, and dreamy; his fascinating talents somewhat tinged with moral *cant*; a great powerless power, an amorphous genius. There Wordsworth, rough in manner, stern in

139

morals, cold, prosing, didactic, but surrounded by a halo of poetic glory;
having left his mountains for a few weeks of London fog and sociality. There
Godwin, the audacious theorist, dreaming of perfectibility and political
justice: cold, grave, and oracular; uttering paradoxes with the passionless air
of deliberative wisdom; rigid at the whist table; admitting no aristocracy but
that of letters; receiving all opinions opposed to his own with silent scorn
and exasperating superiority; unmoved by the convulsions of society; 'a ruler
of the spirits'—'the central calm at the heart of all agitation'. There Talfourd,
then a struggling barrister and flowery essayist, soon to become an eminent
barrister and flowery poet. There also Holcroft, the author of the 'Road to
Ruin', having risen from the bottom of the social scale to an eminent position
in the world of letters—having passed the strangest and most chequered of
lives; the son of a hawking pedlar, always roaming, always changing his
means of livelihood; now employed as an infant to lead a donkey to the coal
pit, there to get it loaded, and then conduct it home; now taken as a stable
boy at a trainer's, there to store up materials for 'Goldfinch'; now setting up
a school with one scholar; now trying to be a cobbler; now joining strolling
players, and at last succeeding as a dramatic author; marrying four wives;
indicted for high treason on the most frivolous grounds, owing to the arbitrary
measures 'when George the Third was king'; acquitted, but ever afterwards
damaged in reputation, being looked upon as an 'acquitted felon'; and now
finally having passed through all these vicissitudes, and settled into old age,
still writing feeble comedies, translating from the German, and dabbling in
pictures.

The central figure of this group—the host, who numbered all these
various men of genius and talent as his friends, and who differing from all,
yet sympathised with all, was Charles Lamb, perhaps, on the whole, the most
interesting of the set.

> Charles Lamb, to those who know thee justly dear
> For rarest genius, for sterling worth,
> Unchanging friendship, warmth of heart sincere,
> And wit that never gave an ill thought birth.

So sang Robert Southey, with more truth than felicity; and so would every
heart respond. As a writer, whose place is for ever conquered in our literature;
and as a character, full of piquant contrast and matter for study, we shall not
be blamed, we trust, for occupying the reader's time for a brief while, in
endeavouring to present some of the characteristics of his genius.

'*Die Gestalt des Menschen,*' says Göthe, '*ist der Text zu allem was sich
über ihn empfinden und sagen lässt.*'[33] This is peculiarly applicable to
Charles Lamb. The contrasts of his organisation were reflected in his mind.
He was an oddity in appearance and in manner; uniting contrasts in the
subtlest way imaginable. He had a head worthy of Aristotle, but it was placed

upon a *shadowy stem*, (to use Talfourd's happy description), so fragile, so puny was the body which sustained it. His features were strongly, yet delicately cut. Over an expanded forehead black hair crisply curled. His dark eyes twinkled with varying expression, though the prevalent feeling was sadness. His nose was of the Jewish cut; indeed, clad in his clerk-like black, with his oriental style of feature, his delicate organisation, and sweetness of demeanour, he presented an appearance very much like what he describes Braham's to be, 'a compound of the Jew, the gentleman, and the angel'.

Hitherto we have taken only the favourable view of him—the painter's view. But, besides what the artist transfers to his canvass, there is always an indefinite something which he cannot transfer; and hence the reason why painters are said to flatter, and also why they always fail in representing wholly those whom we greatly admire or greatly love. Charles Lamb is only half portrayed as yet. To the above must be added a certain oddity of look and manner—a something tantamount to his stammering. It was not disagreeable; rather let us call it quaint—individual.

Good simple King Duncan says—

'There is no art
To read the mind's construction in the face,' etc.

It is a subtle touch of Shakespeare's to make the man just deceived by one he trusted, draw a general conclusion from a particular instance, such as the above; but no one could look in Charles Lamb's face without reading there the lineaments of the 'mind's construction'. The mixture of intellect and feeling; of reasoning and sensibility; of wit, humour, and sadness; of innocence and knowingness; of gentleness and brusquerie, stamped itself legibly upon his features.

The affection he inspired, together with the real unobtrusive kindness of his nature, has led his friends and critics into an oversight which it is necessary we should notice. So much stress has been laid upon his 'gentleness', that the other part of his character—his recklesness and brusquerie—has been overlaid.

My gentle-hearted Charles! is the apostrophe of Coleridge, in one of his poems; and to show how deserved was the epithet, let us recall the testimony of his school-fellow, Mr Le Grice, who says, 'I never heard his name mentioned without the addition of Charles, although, as there was no other boy of the name of Lamb, the addition was unnecessary; but there was an implied kindness in it, and it was a proof that his gentle manners excited kindness.' Gentle he undoubtedly was; and a gentle spirit lends its grace to all his writings. But there was also a whimsical recklessness which would occasionally beset him. To give an instance: he dined one day at the house of a friend of ours,[34] and on entering the drawing-room, after dinner, saw a gentleman standing in the middle of the room, whose bent shoulders, in

schoolboy leapfrog phrase, 'made a back'; the temptation was too great for
Lamb, he placed his hands on the unconscious victim, and 'flew' over his
head, to the astonished indignation of many, and amusement of the few. This,
perhaps, may be called a mere disregard to the proprieties of time and place;
but Lamb was at times less excusably aggressive. He was fond of startling
people on sacred subjects; though really religious himself, he liked to play
with the religious scruples of others. In the same way he reversed the process
on those who held sceptical opinions. We have heard a friend of his say, that
whenever Godwin broached any infidel doctrines in Lamb's room, Lamb
would check him by pointing to a volume of sermons on the shelf, which
Godwin had written early in life. But to return to his aggressiveness: his love
of practical joking is surely a strong proof. His jokes were more ludicrous
than malicious, and in this they differ from ordinary practical jokes; nor do
we wish much stress to be laid on them, but they indicate, as we said, a certain
aggressive tendency, which must be taken as a set-off against his gentleness.
While on this subject, and because, like the former anecdotes, it has not been
made public, we may relate the story of his first meeting with Thomas
Carlyle. Lamb was never partial to the Scotch,[35] and on this evening he was
more than usually offensive in his remarks on their character; but when
supper appeared, and a bowl of porridge was placed before Carlyle, Lamb's
jokes and remarks upon it were so insulting, as almost to lead to an open
quarrel. Even Lamb's friend, from whom we had the story, could say nothing
in his justification; his behaviour was wantonly offensive.

The epithet 'gentle' was not the less merited because of these occasional
outbreaks; and we should be sorry if our endeavour to represent more
accurately the man, should lead anyone to suppose that he was not as kind
and gentle as his writings. Even in his writings there are outbreaks:

And as round mountain-tops the lightning plays,
Thus innocently sported, breaking forth
As from a cloud of some grave sympathy,
Humour and wild instinctive wit, and all
The vivid flashes of his spoken words.[36]

So Wordsworth. Leigh Hunt gives another and truer explanation:–'His
sensibility to strong contrasts is the foundation of his humour, which is that
of a wit at once melancholy and willing to be pleased. He will beard a
superstition, and shudder at the old phantasm while he does it. One could
imagine him cracking a jest in the teeth of a ghost, and melting into thin air
himself out of sympathy with the awful.'

Lamb was heart and soul a Londoner. Dr Johnson himself was not more
so. Although he passed the greater part of his life as clerk in the India
House—doomed to the desk in murky Leadenhall-street, yet had he no
yearnings for the country. He was not the man to sing—

I care not, fortune, what you me deny,
You cannot rob me of sweet Nature's face.

Johnson said, 'When you have seen one green field, you have seen all green fields. Sir, I like to look upon mankind: let us walk down Fleet-street.' Lamb said the same; he was, as Talfourd prettily says of him, 'formed to nestle rather than to roam.' In a letter to Southey, he says:

I have a timid imagination, I am afraid. I do not willingly admit of strange beliefs, or out-of-the-way creeds or places. I never read books of travels, at least, not farther than Paris or Rome. I can just endure Moors, because of their connexion as foes with Christians; but Abyssinians, Ethiops, Esquimaux, Dervises, and all that tribe, I hate. I believe I fear them in some manner. A Mahometan turban on the stage, though enveloping some well-known face, (Mr Cook or Mr Maddox, whom I see another day good Christian and English waiters, innkeepers, etc.) does not give me pleasure unalloyed. I am a Christian, Englishman, Londoner, *Templar*.

And again, in a letter from Enfield to Wordsworth:

Here we have nothing to do with our victuals but to eat them; with the garden but to see it grow; with the tax-gatherer but to hear him knock; with the maid but to hear her scolded. Scot and lot, butcher, baker, are things unknown to us, save as spectators of the pageant. We are fed we know not how; quietists,—*confiding ravens*. We have the *otium pro dignitate*, a respectable insignificance. Yet in the self-condemned obliviousness, in the stagnation, some molesting yearnings of life, not quite killed, rise, prompting me that there was London, and that I was of that old Jerusalem. In dreams I am in Fleet Market, but I wake and cry to sleep again. I die hard, a stubborn Eloisa in this detestable Paraclete. What have I gained by health?—Intolerable dulness. What by early hours and moderate meals?—A total blank. O! never let they lying poets be believed, who 'tice men from the cheerful haunts of streets, or think they mean it not of a country village. In the ruins of Palmyra I could gird myself up to solitude, or muse to the snorings of the Seven Sleepers; but to have a little teasing image of a town about one; country folks that do not look like country folks; shops two yards square, half a dozen apples and two penn'orths of overlooked gingerbread for the lofty fruiterers of Oxford Street; and for the immortal book and print stalls, a circulating library that stands still, where the show picture is a last year's valentine, and whither the fame of the last ten scotch novels has not yet travelled,—(marry, they just begin to be

conscious of Redgauntlet;) to have a new plastered flat church, and to
be wishing that it was but a cathedral! The very blackguards here are
degenerate; the topping gentry stock-brokers; the passengers too many
to insure your quiet, or let you go about whistling or gaping; too few
to be the fine indifferent pageants of Fleet Street. Confining, room
keeping, thickest winter, is yet more bearable here than the gaudy
months. Among one's books at one's fire, by candle, one is soothed
into an oblivion that one is not in the country; but with the light the
green fields return, till I gaze, and in a calenture can plunge myself into
St Giles's. O! let no native Londoner imagine that health, and rest, and
innocent occupation, interchange of converse sweet, and recreative
study, can make the country anything better than altogether odious and
detestable. A garden was the primitive prison, till man, with Promethe-
an felicity and boldness, luckily sinned himself out of it. Thence
followed Babylon, Nineveh, Venice, London, Haberdashers, goldsmiths, taverns, playhouses, satires, epigrams, puns,—these all came
in on the town part, and the thither side of innocence.

Nor was this the feeling of a moment; it was his taste through life. He had
no eye for the picturesque. Human nature, in its miseries, infirmities, its
virtues and socialities, was what lovingly attracted him; and he liked towns
because they spoke of man. In the same way he loved books. Mere descriptive
passages, mere caprices of fancy, except in the authors he loved, were lost
upon him. He cared nothing for theories; speculations on the great questions
of philosophy and religion never troubled him, and he humorously describes
Proclus (Coleridge having asked him to procure a copy) as one of those books
the lid of which he shut faster than he opened it. But the dramatists were his
especial favourites. He saw no flaws in them. To his guileless mind their
reckless disregard of the boundaries of morality and decency was nothing
but the sportive freedom of imagination. He has written a most elaborate and
ingenious defence of the comic dramatists of the Restoration, upon the
ground that they were dealing with the fictitious world of wit, and ought not
to be measured by the ordinary standards of morality, because they treated
not of actual life. No one but himself could have written this; no one but
himself could believe it. Besides the dramatists, he also loved the old
humourists and moralists; was fond of quaker folios, because they led him
into a quaint honest world; and had an especial regard to all *old* books. He
had the spirit of an antiquary, not the grubbing patience, not the inordinate
appreciation of minute points, which accompanies the antiquarian spirit. He
was not a Cockletop; he was not a Ritson.[37] To discover that some obscure
man was born on the 16th of May, and not, as generally supposed, on the
18th, inspired him with no thrill of delight, nor did it make him assume
contemptuous airs towards the ignorant rest of mankind.

A book was not better in his eyes than all other books, because it was older and more illegible; but in that affectionate regard for the mysterious past, in that lingering over the fragments of the ruined edifice, in that endeavour to reanimate in his mind the times which had been, and were no more, he showed the antiquarian spirit in its true aspect. He loved to recall the scenes of his boyhood, to live over again the emotions which had agitated his youthful heart; and in the same backward-looking spirit he threw himself into the bygone years of his country's life. It was no affectation in him; it was the bias of his mind. Without the strong pulse of hope, without the forward-looking speculations of philosophy, he was more prone to recall than to prophesy.[38] His very style was tinged with an archaic hue; and this, not as a matter of literary artifice, but because his thoughts themselves had that colour. His careless letters show it quite as plainly as his studied essays.

A great reader, he cared little for modern books; the only contemporary writings which interested him were those of his personal friends. Scott's novels had no attraction for him; but Fielding, Smollett, and Richardson he read over and over again. Shelley could not win a word from him. Byron moved him not. But how he fondled an old folio! how he hugged some time-hallowed quarto! Wisdom only spoke to him authoritatively when grey hairs gave it authority.

The feeling which lies at the bottom of our great admiration for old books, and which causes us to exaggerate their merits, has yet to be analysed. There cannot be a doubt that we are more struck by a shrewd remark in an ancient writer, than by a profound remark in a modern. Is not this the effect of *unconscious surprise?* Do we not, in reading an old treatise, sit down prepared to make all sorts of allowances, which we never accord to a modern? The modern writer speaks, or ought to speak, from the fulness of all time; his predecessors ought to have enriched him by the legacy of their wealth, and this makes us critical in our demands. But the ancient writer we read *as* ancient: his prosiness we forgive, his mistakes seem excusable, his very infirmities have something of the veneration due to age, while his beauties not only stand out prominent from the dull background, but surprise us with their existence. The other day we were looking over our Plato, and the passages marked by an approving pencil, though certainly often happy, and sometimes remarkable, were assuredly passages which in a modern author few pencils would have paused to indicate; moreover, compared with the quantity of unmarked passages, and its small *intrinsic* value, (apart from the charm of language and the *historical* value of these remnants of antiquity), it seemed to us that the passages admired owed no little to the effect of contrast.[39] This led us into the train of thought expressed above. If it be just—if we do read ancient authors with a secret understanding that they had not the same advantages as moderns, we shall easily understand how the detection of great beauties in an old book leads the reader into an exaggerated estimate of its superiority. And this was Charles Lamb's feeling. He liked old books because he forgave their faults and admired their beauties; and he liked them because they were old. He liked the nonsense of Sir Thomas Browne (set off as it was by glorious glimpses of wisdom) better than any modern sense; it was old, quaint, and had a perfume of antiquity about it. This feeling is amusingly exhibited in a letter to Bernard Barton—the charming quaker poet—who wrote to him about a proposed edition of *The Pilgrim's Progress*, illustrated by Martin:–

'A splendid edition of Bunyan's Pilgrim!' he exclaims; 'why, the thought is enough to turn one's moral stomach. His cocked hat and staff transformed to a smart cocked beaver and a jemmy cane; his amice grey to the last Regent Street cut; and his painful palmer's pace to the modern swagger. Stop thy friend's sacrilegious hand. Nothing can be done for B. but to reprint the old cuts in as homely, but good a style as possible. The Vanity Fair and the Pilgrims there—the lily-smoothness in his setting out countenance—the Christian idiocy (in a good sense) of his admiration of the shepherds on the Delectable Mountains; the Lions *so truly allegorical and remote from any similitude to Pidcock's.*

Here the unintentional imperfections of the old book are transmuted by affection into absolute merits; and so we may say of all other drawbacks which an unprejudiced eye might detect. It is worth noting that this thorough-going partisanship was carried by Lamb into his friendships. He did not love his friends in spite of their faults—he loved them, faults and all. While on the subject of his antiquarianism, we cannot resist one witticism he uttered, when his sonnet was rejected as not sufficiently delicate for Annual readers: 'Hang the age!' he exclaimed, *'I will write for antiquity!'* As a wind-up of this subject, let us give what he says on Burnet's History:

I am reading '*Burnet's Own Times*'. Did you ever read that garrulous, pleasant history? He tells his story like an old man past political service, bragging to his sons on winter evenings of the part he took in public transactions, when his 'old cap was new'. Full of scandal, which all true history is. No palliatives; but all the stark wickedness that actually gives the *momentum* to national actors. Quite the prattle of age and outlived importance. Truth and sincerity staring out upon you perpetually in *alto relievo*. Himself a party man, he makes you a party man. None of the cursed philosophical Humeian indifference, so cold and unnatural and inhuman! None of the cursed Gibbonian fine writing, so fine and composite. None of Dr Robertson's periods with three members. None of Mr Roscoe's sage remarks, all so apposite, and coming in so clever, lest the reader should have had the trouble of drawing an inference. Burnet's good old prattle I can bring present to my mind; I can make the revolution present to me—the French revolution, by a converse perversity in my nature, I fling as far *from* me.

As a humorist, Lamb takes a high place. His humour was essentially his own—the quaint, ludicrous expression of his own strange nature. It is not necessary to refer to his works in illustration, because his letters teem with it. Here is a passage we just stumbled on in a letter to Bernard Barton, in which the humour runs riot:–

I have not a thing to say; nothing is of more importance than another; I am *flatter than a denial or a pancake; emptier than Judge _____'s wig when the head is in it;* duller than a country stage when the actors are off it; a cipher—an O! I acknowledge life at all, only by an occasional convulsional cough, and a permanent phlegmatic pain in the chest. I am weary of the world, and the world is weary of me. My day is gone into twilight, and I don't think it worth the expense of candles. My wick hath a thief in it, but I can't muster courage to snuff it. I inhale suffocation; I can't distinguish veal from mutton; nothing interests me. 'Tis twelve o'clock, and Thurtell is just now coming out upon the New Drop, Jack Ketch alertly tucking up his greasy sleeves to do the last office of mortality, yet cannot I elicit a groan or a moral reflection. If you told me the world will be at an end to-morrow, I should just say, 'Will it?' I have not *volition enough left to dot my i's,* much less to comb my eyebrows; my eyes are set in my head; my brains are gone out to see a poor relation in Moorfields, and they did not say when they'd come back again; my skull is a Grub Street attic to let—not so much as a joint stool left in it; my hand writes, not I; *just as chickens run about a little, when their heads are off.* O for a vigorous fit of gout, of cholic, toothache!—an earwig in my auditory, a fly in my visual organs; pain is life—the sharper, the more evidence of life; but this apathy, this death! Did you ever have an obstinate cold,—a six or seven weeks' unintermitting chill and suspension of hope, fear, conscience, and everything? Yet do I try all I can to cure it; I try wine, and spirits, and smoking, and snuff in unsparing quantities, but they all only seem to make me worse instead of better. *I sleep in a damp room, but it does me no good;* I come home late o'nights, *but do not find any visible amendment!*

The passages to which we have given the emphasis of italics are in the richest style of Lamb's quiet humour—a twinkling laugh peering through the sober gravity of style. Of his grave humour there is an example in his letters which inexpressibly delights us. It is where, speaking of the Persian ambassador, who was then in London, the great 'lion' of the day, he says—'I sent some people to see him worship the sun on Primrose Hill, at half-past six in the morning, 28th November; but he did not come, which makes me think the old fire-worshippers are a sect almost extinct in Persia.' The splendid hoax of sending people out, on a dull, foggy November morning, to see the Persian worship the sun, and the droll seriousness of the conclusion he draws respecting the extinction of the race of fire-worshippers, are irresistibly ludicrous. Lamb did not jest merely with his intellect—his whole heart was in the joke. His perception of the ludicrous was not purely an intellectual perception, but carried with it the whole of his feelings. Thus, when his farce was hissed at Drury Lane, he joined in the hiss, and was among the loudest; and it was always a standing joke with him ever afterwards. He congratulated himself upon the fact of being free of the house, though the house had been pretty free with him.

> Hang 'em!' he wrote, 'how they hissed. It was not a hiss neither, it was a sort of frantic yell, like a congregation of mad geese, with roaring something like bears, mows and mops like apes, sometimes snakes that hissed me into madness. 'Twas like St Anthony's temptations. Mercy on us! that God should give his favourite children mouths to speak with, to discourse rationally, to praise smoothly, to flatter agreeably, to encourage warmly, to counsel wisely, to sing with, to drink with, and to kiss with, and that they should turn them into mouths of adders, bears, wolves, hyaenas, and whistle like tempests, and emit breath through them like distillations of aspic poison, to asperse and vilify the innocent labours of their fellow-creatures desirous to please them.

It was the same thorough-going enjoyment of a joke which made him submit to have his personal identity merged into that of the persecuted Guy Fawkes. One evening, it was the 5th of November, he was with some old friends, who, particularly struck with the large flapping brim of his round hat, pinned up the sides. Lamb made no objection, but stuck it on his head, and sauntered towards his home in the Temple. On his way, he was met by a party of young men, 'flushed with insolence and wine', who exclaimed, 'a Guy! a veritable Guy! no man of straw!' and making a chair of their hands, carried him in triumph into St Paul's Church-yard, where they seated him on a post and left him, there to await the fagots of traditionary patriotism and juvenile anti-catholicism. Lamb quietly enjoyed the proceedings. It was an *historical* joke; it threw him, by a humorous identification, back into the past he loved so well, and he always told the story with immense relish.

There was not only heart in Lamb's wit, there was also imagination; and hence its exquisite perfection. The wits and wordcatchers of the present day are, unhappily, too *mechanical* in their efforts; they bring together ideas remote enough to raise a laugh by the suddenness of the collision; but these ideas have only remoteness as the primary quality for wit, and the juxtaposition is a mechanical process. Sydney Smith's famous witticisms have almost always some exquisite flavour of imagination or sterling wisdom, beyond the mere felicity of expression and juxtaposition of antagonistic ideas. Thus, descanting on the prodigies of railway travelling, he said, 'the early Scotchman, scratching himself in the mist of his mountain tops, may that very afternoon dine in Pall Mall.' There is a fine pictorial feeling in this joke which gives it an immense value; had he merely said, 'the Scotchman scratching himself in the morning may dine in London that very afternoon,' what a poor joke it would have been! One of Lamb's most imaginative touches of humour is where deploring that being no longer a clerk, he has no gratis pens and paper. The comparison of his banishment from the plenty of the India House with that of Adam from paradise—the ludicrous assimilation of ideas connected with Adam and the apple-stall 'in Mesopotamia', are so wonderfully represented, that we scarcely know of any witticism to surpass it, while the delicate manner in which any irreverence is avoided, has made even strict persons enjoy its humour without misgivings. It would have made Sydney Smith roll with delight. Since his name has again been mentioned, let us notice Lamb's anticipation of the famous joke which Sydney Smith made to the Bishop of New Zealand, with respect to the civilities he would receive from his new parishoners, who would offer him luncheon, adding, 'there is *cold clergyman* on the *sideboard*'. Lamb, dissuading Manning from going to China, adds 'some say they are cannibals, and then conceive a Tartar fellow *eating* my friend, and adding the *cool malignity* of mustard and vinegar!…'Tis terrible to be *weighed out at fivepence the pound.*'

Lamb's repartees were often brilliant, and were greatly heightened in effect by his stammer, which delayed and kept the mind in suspense for the joke which the eye plainly told you was coming. Many of them have been quoted; but they want the aid of his manner, as well as that of the circumstances which called them forth. Here is a story which has not yet been printed. On one occasion he was very inconsiderately invited to a party where the room was crowded with children. Their noise and tricks plagued him not a little, and at supper, when toasts were flying to and fro, he rose to propose the health 'of the m-m-much ca-ca-calumniated g-g-*good* King Herod!'

In the letters we are constantly stumbling upon passages of grave humour, which we can imagine him uttering, as where he says, 'I sometimes think the lower notes of my voice resemble those of Mrs Bland'; or where quoting a pretended passage in German, he erases it and says:–

the English meaning is, 'Avoid to approach an animal suspected of madness, as you would avoid a fire or a precipice,' which I think is a sensible observation. *The Germans are certainly profounder than we.*

His writings are full of such sly hits. Here is a very ludicrous opening of a letter (it relates to a dog, to whom for some time he had been a perfect slave, and was forced at last to consign to the care of a friend):–

Excuse my anxiety, but how is Dash? I should have asked if Mrs P_____e kept her rules, and was improving; but Dash came uppermost. The order of our thoughts should be the order of our writing. Goes he muzzled, or *aperto ore?* Are his intellects sound, or does he wander a little in *his* conversation? You cannot be too careful to watch the first symptoms of incoherence. The first illogical snarl he makes, to St Luke's with him. All the dogs here are going mad, if you believe the overseers; but I protest they seem to me very rational and collected. But nothing is so deceitful as mad people, to those who are not used to them. Try him with hot water: if he won't lick it up, it is a sign—he does not like it. Does his tail wag horizontally, or perpendicularly? That has decided the fate of many dogs in Enfield. Is his general deportment cheerful? I mean when he is pleased—for otherwise there is no judging. You can't be too careful. Has he bit any of the children yet? If he has have them shot; and keep *him* for curiosity, to see if it was hydrophobia. They say all our army in India had it at one time; but that was in *Hyder*-Ally's time. Do you get paunch for him? Take care the sheep was sane. You might pull out his teeth, (if he would let you,) and then you need not mind if he were as mad as Bedlamite. It would be rather fun to see his odd ways.

The touch about shooting the children, and keeping the dog for scientific purposes, is admirable. Indeed, it is the peculiarity of all real humour, that it does not arise from words alone, but has intense meanings underneath the grotesque sound, and therefore the more we ponder on it the more we are amused. How different is the humour now current in our comic writers! Perhaps there never was before so much joking at any one period of our literary history, and yet how little of it is above worthlessness! Joking has become a trade. The cap and bells are assumed with deliberate calculation. Wit is manufactured, like Sheffield hardware, at a fixed tariff. With dismal jocosity men drudge at jokes. Shall we wonder at the produce? Shall we wonder that men called upon to be facetious at so much per sheet, pestered by impatient editors for comic 'copy', should, in the dearth of spontaneous humour, resort to any artifice to supply 'the demand'? When subjects do not suggest themselves, they must be invented. What invention is easier than to turn into ridicule everything which men hold sacred? It is not wit, it is parody, and of the vulgarest kind.

Charles Lamb, like most other wits, the most religious men included, was prone to play with sacred subjects: his very seriousness gave intensity to his perception of the contrast. But there was an implied reverence in his sportiveness which never shocked any but the most fastidious. You felt all the while that there was earnestness in him. He did not manufacture his jokes. On another point he is in striking contrast to the jokers of our day. He did not think it necessary to prowl about the disreputable haunts of London dissipation, nor to enter into the shambles of London civilisation, to seek subjects for his mirth. He did not breathe the hot air of casinos and masked balls, nor the fetid air of 'back slums' and pothouses, to move our mirth. On his pages there are no stains of beer, no cinders of cigars, no distorted humour of slang. He cared only for London, yet as delicate a breath rises from his page as from a bank of violets. He neither herded with the fashionable nor with the reprobate. From human life in its eternal truth, and not its conventional vulgarities, he drew his pictures, and they are painted 'for all time'. Thus he excels his successors not less in the healthy pleasant tone of his writings than in the depth of wit and felicity of expression.

He was eminently a *genial* writer: Dickens is not more so. Amidst all the quips and sports of humour—all the exaggerations of fun—all the licensed riot of wit, you never lose sight of the kindly, loving, honest, enjoying nature of the writer. So distinctly is this personality impressed, and so loveable the personality, that few have read his works without forming an attachment to the man: in this also resembling Dickens. But who ever formed any attachment (on the mere grounds of their writings) to the writers we are contrasting him with? These writers, as far as the mere readers can judge, have no personality; they are joke manufacturers, having no sympathy with anything—no pity for anything—no *hearty* laugh at anything. They use the poor because of their dirt, rags and misery; they *use* them as contrasts.

Lamb, in truth, belonged to the highest class of humorists: Cervantes, Molière, Sterne, and Jean Paul would have called him brother; and, like them all, he made humour the safety-valve of a sad, earnest heart. It has been said that all true humour rests upon melancholy, and that without a keen sense of the contradictions and the wrongs which disturb the stream of life, no real humour is possible. Humour is not levity—not inane laughter. It does not result from a fortuitous juxtaposition of words or ideas, but from deep sense of the contrasts of life, and the subtle harmony which may unite the jarring discords. Thus is pathos inseparable from humour. There are tears in its smile; in its laughter there are convulsive sobs.

Charles Lamb was by nature of a serious and reflective turn; and the accidents of his life, acting upon a sensitive organisation, made him peculiarly alive to the tragic under-currents which flowed beneath the grotesque and farcical incidents and characters passing before him. Little did the majority of those who saw this social, punning, gentle, frolicsome, stammering, quaint humorist, imagine the awful shadow which for ever rested upon his spirit, mingling with and deepening by contrast the brightness of its sunshine. Yes, in that queer-looking clerk—in the gentle-hearted Charles—in the delicate Elia, underneath the lightsome wit and playful fancy, there was shrouded a dark tragedy, such as would have broken many a robust spirit. The story is known but to few, and those few have hitherto, from obvious motives of delicacy, refrained from speaking of it. The time has now come, we believe, when the grave having closed over all whom it may concern, the story ought to be told as a noble example of unobtrusive heroism.

Lamb's parents were very poor. Lamb himself, at the time we speak of, being a mere clerk, and unable to afford them much assistance, the weight of their maintenance fell upon his sister, the well-known Mary Lamb. By her needle she contrived to support them. She had taken a young girl into the house as an apprentice, and things went on smoothly enough till the increasing infirmities of the old lady, and the incessant watching thereby rendered necessary, made great inroads upon Mary Lamb's health. Having in the earlier part of her life suffered temporary insanity from harassment, Mary's present state was alarming, and her brother went to Dr Pitcairn in the morning to consult about her, but unhappily did not find him at home. On that very afternoon—it was the 22nd Sept. 1796—while the family were preparing for dinner, Mary seized a knife which lay on the table, and making a rush at her little apprentice, pursued her round the room with fearful menaces. Her infirm old mother, with eager and terrified calls upon her to desist, attempted to interfere. With wild shrieks Mary turned upon her mother, and stabbed her to the heart! She then madly hurled the knives and forks about the room, one of which struck her helpless old father on the forehead. The shrieks of the girl, and her own wild cries, brought up the landlord of the house; but it was too late; he stood aghast at the terrible spectacle of the old woman lifeless on the chair, her daughter fiercely standing over her with the fatal knife still in her hand; her father bleeding at the forehead, and weeping by the side of his murdered wife; the girl cowering in the corner!

An inquest was held the next day, at which the jury, without hesitation, brought in the verdict of lunacy. Here there is a blank in our narrative. We do not know whether Mary Lamb was confined for any period in an asylum, and released on being pronounced sane, or whether Charles from the first undertook that watchful care of her which formed the heroism of his subsequent life. It is difficult to get at the details of an event which occurred fifty years ago, and which even at the time seems to have been carefully hushed up; for in the account of the inquest reported in the 'Annual Register' of that year, from some inexplicable cause, *no name whatever is mentioned,* except that of Dr Pitcairn. It merely says, 'the coroner's jury sat on the body of an *old lady,* in the *neighbourhood* of Holborn'. But that the matter was not wholly unknown is proved by the curious fact of the name being mentioned in the *index* to the 'Annual Register', (compiled in 1826—that is to say, thirty years after the account was originally published), where it stands thus—'Murder of Mrs Lamb by her insane daughter'.

This ghastly incident gave a new shape to all Lamb's subsequent career. At that time he was in love—the only time he ever felt the passion—and it inspired 'a few sonnets of very delicate feeling and exquisite music'; but he felt that his sister demanded all his care, and to her he sacrificed love, marriage, everything. Like a brave, suffering unselfish man, he, at twenty-one, renounced the dream of love for the stern austerity of duty:–

> And let him grieve who cannot choose but grieve
> That he hath been an Elm without his Vine,
> And her bright dower of clustering charities,
> That round his trunk and branches might have clung
> Enriching and adorning. Unto thee,
> Not so enriched, not so adorned, to thee
> Was given a sister...
> In whom thy reason and intelligent heart
> Found—for all interests, hopes and tender cares,
> All softening, humanizing, hallowing powers—
> More than sufficient recompence.[40]

If singleness of heart, and unshaken constancy of affection, could make a recompence for all he had renounced, then truly did Charles Lamb reap his reward. But we have only to put it to the reader's consideration, and he will at once acknowledge how noble a sacrifice it was which Lamb performed. We do not mean the mere renouncement of his hopes—it is not any one act—it is his whole life which we call heroic. To his sister he devoted himself, in the most absolute sense of the term; and that, in spite of recurring fits of insanity. Curiously enough, Mary Lamb was, as a friend of hers once said to us, 'the last woman in the world whom you could have suspected, under any circumstance, of becoming insane, so calm, so judicious, so rational was she'; and Hazlitt used to say, 'Mary Lamb is the only truly sensible woman I ever met with'. Nevertheless, she was at no time free from the danger of a relapse, and they never left home without her brother's taking a strait waistcoat with him!

No one will read this story without an increased tenderness towards Lamb, upon whose life and writings it sheds a flood of light. Perhaps the very extremity of his suffering, the very intensity of passion which had been revealed to him in this unhappy incident, may have led him to enter with such relish into the reckless horrors of our old English drama. Unquestionably, it must have led him to those deep reflections upon our moral nature, of which from time to time his writings give us glimpses. That he was somewhat morbid in self-scrutiny cannot be denied—perhaps this also was a result of that great moral shock he had received; and a curious instance of his self-condemnation is given in a letter to Bernard Barton:–

There is Southey, whom I ought to have thanked a fortnight ago for a present of the 'Church Book'. I have never had courage to buckle myself in earnest to acknowledge it: yet I am accounted by some people a good man! How cheap that character is acquired! Pay your debts, don't borrow money, nor twist your kitten's neck off, nor disturb a congregation, etc., and the business is done. I know things (for thoughts *are* things) of myself which would make every friend I have fly me as a plague patient. I once set a dog upon a crab's leg that was shoved out under a mass of sea-weeds—a pretty little feeler! Oh, pah! how sick I am of that. And a lie, a mean one, I once told. I stink in the midst of respect.

How well he felt the 'uses of adversity', the eloquent preaching of sorrow, may be seen in various passages, in none better than in *John Woodvil*—

My spirits turn to fire, they mount so fast.
My joys are turbulent, my hopes show like fruition
These high and gusty relishes of life, sure
Have no allayings of mortality in them.
I am too hot now and o'ercapable
For the tedious processes and creeping wisdom
Of human acts and enterprises of man.
I want some seasonings of adversity—
Some strokes of the old mortifier, Calamity,
To take those swellings down divines call Vanity.

From what has gone before, it will be apparent that the serious side of human nature was not shut against Lamb's penetrating gaze, and that his pathos springs from the depths of real feeling. Hence his works will be enduring.

Another most important elements in a writer's vitality, is style, and Lamb possessed it. Unlike that of all his predecessors, contemporaries, and successors, it is perculiarly his own: quaint, delicately picked, with a sweet simplicity, joined to an archaic and artificial air, which, however, only *seemed* artificial; singularly easy and idiomatic in its flow, and unencumbered by superfluous words—never rising to the height of eloquence, but never turbid with ambitious rhetoric; felicitous in illustration and in potent words; sounding the very depths of pathos with the simplest phrase, and seldom breaking up a sentence for the sake of antithesis or epigram. It has not force—it has not rapidity—it has not heat—but it is always luminous, always suited to the subject, and in tenderness and delicate gusto, has never perhaps been surpassed. As a sample of the gusto which he could infuse into language, we may recommend our readers to his famous *Dissertation on Roast Pig*.

If, from considering the general characteristics of the man, we descend to his particular works, we shall find no less matter for comment and applause. The single volume which contains these is, altogether, perhaps one of the most charming we could stand upon our shelves; it is a casket of gems of small size, but of the first water. It is not a book profoundly to influence the mind; it will make no epoch in a man's intellectual history; it will teach him nothing respecting his destiny, give him no clue wherewith to thread the labyrinth of doubt, furnish him with no great principles of action, open for him no tracks of thought on which discoveries can be made. But it is, nevertheless, a book to be studied with profit, to be read, and loved. In the whole range of our literature, we can point to no book so purely charming. Lamb is the first of all our humorists, and the one most deserving of a place in our regard. Others may excel him in particular points, but, taken as a whole, he is incomparable. [Lewes continues with two pages on Lamb's poetry.]

Benjamin Disraeli

From *British Quarterly Review* (August 1849)

Coningsby has reached a fifth edition, and its author has almost achieved the ambition of his life, and secured his position as the leader of a party and a place in the Cabinet.

Is it the disgrace of our literature, or the disgrace of our Parliament, that the only man who has risen into political eminence through literary ability is that clever, sarcastic, extravagant, reckless, disrespectable and disrespected person who formerly styled himself D'Israeli the Younger? In France, men point with some degree of pride to a Guizot, a Thiers, a Lamartine, a Villemain—not to mention numerous lesser names—as men in whom the aristocracy of intelligence has achieved its due political recognition. In England we must be content to point to the author of 'Coningsby'—a fact which the present writer contents himself with stating, leaving to others the task of moralising on it.

There is, we believe, a point of view from which D'Israeli's career may be examined with considerable interest. As a man of letters or as a statesman, he has small if any intrinsic value; but the combination is curious, and his success is a lesson. His position in the political world is analogous to his position in the literary world, with this enormous difference—that in the House of Commons he is in competition with a set of men for the most part greatly his inferiors in ability, and hampered by all sorts of routiniary prejudices; whereas in the world of literature he has rivals in the Past and in the Present, and is deficient in every quality which could sustain that rivalry with effect. The genesis of a statesman from an author is, however, here rendered doubly piquant as a subject of study, no less from his deficiences than from the serious defects in our political world which his success implies.

As an author, in spite of a certain notoriety and undeniable talents, his value is null. He has written books, and these books have been immensely successful; but they have no place in our literature—they are indubitable failures or fleeting ephemerides. He has taken many leaps, but has gained no footing. He has written a quarto epic; he has written a tragedy; he has written novels, pamphlets, and a political treatise on the Constitution; but all these works are as dead as the last week's newspaper. The most significant niche in the temple is denied them. If anybody looks at them, it is not on their account, but on his account. The noise they made has passed away like the vacuous enthusiasm of afterdinner friendships. They have achieved notoriety

156

for their author, oblivion for themselves. Let him write a novel, and 'all the world' will read it, quote it, laugh over it, talk about it; and among its hundreds of readers not one will have felt his heart stirred, his soul expanded, his experience deepened, his hopes exalted, his moral nature strengthened, or his taste refined; for not one single passage will have gone direct to any serious purpose. Personalities, sarcasms, and the piquancy of political scandal, will create a 'sensation'; but other qualities are needed to create a work. 'Coningsby' may reach a fifth edition, but 'Coningsby' has no place in out literature, for it has no enduring qualities. Place Mrs Gore's or Mrs Trollope's name upon the title page, and the factitious value of the book vanishes at once. Looked at calmly, what is all this display of wit and cleverness which glitters through the many novels of the author of 'Vivian Grey'? what is all their oriental gorgeousness of diction, their ambitious rhythm, sonorous and weighty words, which elsewhere have meanings in them? Verbiage—nothing else. There is no heart pulsing beneath that eloquence; there is no earnest soul looking through those grand words. It is all a show 'got up' for the occasion; and the showman, having no belief in his marionnettes, you have no belief in them. The bitter satirist of Grecian infidelity—Lucian—makes Timon the Misanthropist tell Jupiter that all the godlike epithets with which the poets dignify him, are not the utterances of reverent belief but the necessities of rhythm, not what their souls pour forth, but what the halting verse requires—τοτε γαρ αντοιϖ πολνωνυμοϖ γινομενοϖ μπερειδειϖ το πιπτον του μετρον και αναπληροιϖ το χεχηνος του ρυθμου. Just the same lip-worship of great principles covering practical disregard of all principles, do we meet with in D'Israeli's writings. This renders them null. He writes solely for effect, and no man who writes for effect can be permanently effective.

Earnestness always commands respect. No qualities will compensate for its absence. Without it, nothing can be done well, nothing can gain the tribute of mankind. Believe it a lie, and if you *believe* it you will be respected; but repeat a Gospel truth, if you only repeat it, and pretend to believe in it, no honest man will open his heart to you. For we all feel that in this life it is not the *rightness* but the *uprightness* of our views which distinguishes the honest man. *Humanum est errare.*

Now, in D'Israeli's works, we note as a decided characteristic the absence of all earnestness—a want of truthfulness. There is no gratitude in our admiration. An invincible feeling of distrust poisons our enjoyment. Knowing nothing of the author, you nevertheless pronounce him to be a charlatan, and one who has not even the grace to believe in his own charlatanerie. This it is which has damaged Benjamin D'Israeli; this feeling accompanies us in our estimate of him as a public man, and makes us all regard him as an adventurer in politics, no less than as an acrobat in literature. This and only this. Many persons suppose that it was his sudden conversion from radicalism to toryism which made his public career equivocal. But other men have changed, and yet survived the suspicion excited by the change. There is nothing really equivocal in a change of party; it may be very sudden and perfectly honest, and the world, which loves fair play and tolerably well discriminates honesty of purpose, is willing enough to credit such things. Moreover, in D'Israeli's case, we believe there never was a change, for he never was a radical. All that can fairly be brought against him is, that he allowed himself to be mistaken for a radical; allowed the false appearance of his enmity to the Whigs to be interpreted as radicalism. The dandy adventurer, Vivian Grey, never was or could have been a radical. He would if he could have entered Parliament through the radical interest, for he wanted a seat, and was unscrupulous *how* he attained it. Burning with the desire of political distinction, and firmly convinced that he had only to take his seat, to astonish Europe with his eloquence, all means were good which secured so great an end. There was a want of straightforwardness in this; but political morality is not *collet monté*,[41] and he might easily have lived that down, if his whole career, the whole tone of his mind, had not confirmed the impression. That impression indelibly is, that D'Israeli is an adventurer. It is not very easy to define the varied minutiae which go to form the impression which men make upon us; but we may, perhaps, convey our meaning by an illustration.

We all know what is meant by the 'look of a gentleman'; yet who shall define it? The man before us is far from handsome, nothing less than graceful, and is dressed so as to drive tailors to despair; yet he impresses everyone, high and low, with the indisputable fact that he is a 'gentleman'. Compare such a man with one of those 'striking' specimens of modern society, who, with radiant waistcoat, resplendent jewellery, and well-oiled whiskers, lounges through the public promenades 'the observed of all observers'; *him* you do not mistake for a gentleman. The waistcoat may be of the newest fashion, the jewellery genuine, and the whiskers perfectly oiled; nevertheless, the impression created is not, perhaps, one of great sympathy and respect.

There are minds of analogous contrast. Some there are which, even in their negligence and awkwardness, have still this 'look of a gentleman'. They produce works, sinning, it may be, against the rules of the craft—heavy, digressive, pedantic, perhaps, or feebly vivacious—works which act but slightly as levers towards helping the world forwards, and yet they impress you as being the products of manly, truthful minds; preferring to be dull rather than to be false; if they cannot be brilliant, not choosing to be flashy. There are others of the opposite kind; minds without grace or dignity in their splendour, without heartiness in their mirth, without charm in their familiarity. These produce works of beggarly magnificence, in which the jewelled ring sparkles on a dirty finger; here glitter is mistaken for light, paradox and mysticism for philosophy, rant for passion, sarcasm for humour. As a critic you cannot but admit the brilliancy of the glitter, the cleverness of the paradox, or the pungency of the sarcasm; but what is the sum total of the impression made upon you? do you sympathise with or greatly respect those works? No: they may amuse you, they may arrest you for a moment, but they want the substantial excellence of truth.

D'Israeli's mind has not this indefinable something which we have been trying to describe. He has not the 'look of a gentleman'. His talents fail to win respect. His coxcombry is without grace; his seriousness without conviction. He has an active fancy, surprising command of language, no inconsiderable knowledge, especially of history, powers of massing facts into a symmetrical appearance of generalisation, and a keen sense of the ludicrous and humbug in others; he is a shrewd observer of men and things, but he has neither the eye to see nor the soul to comprehend anything much below the surface. There is little depth in him of any kind—thought or feeling. Hence the want of vitality in all he does. He cannot paint, for he cannot grasp, a character; his sole power in that line consists in hitting off the obtrusive peculiarities, the juttings out of an individuality. In his books you meet with nothing noble, nothing generous, nothing tender, nothing impassioned. His passion is mere sensuality, as his eloquence is mere diction; the splendour of words, not the lustre of thoughts. Imagination, in the large and noble sense, he has none, for his sensibility is sustained by no warmth. Humour he has none, for humour is deep.

It is something to say for him that he has realised the ideal of his youth. By dint of indomitable perseverance and confidence in himself, unshaken by failure, he has trodden with considerable success the path which his imagination sketched. He early conceived the idea of a political adventurer rising into eminence through literary ability, and leading a party by means of dashing rhetoric and polished sarcasms. Vivian Grey was the hero of his youthful soul; the ideal to attain which his life has been given. What a hero, and what an ideal! If there is anything in his career which touches us with a feeling of pitiful sadness, it is to think that here was a young man, richly gifted, who at a time when, if ever, the soul is stung with resistless longings for high and noble things; at a time when, if ever, the soul is caressed by dreams which, even in their extravagance, have the redeeming grace of purity, and that exaltation which the love of the True and Noble inspires; at a time when conceptions err in their unwordliness, and our ideals are only extravagant because *above* the exigences of practical life; at such a time this man forms no other ideal of human nature, than that of a clever, sarcastic, unscrupulous adventurer, using men as tools wherewith to construct the miserable edifice of his notoriety! *That*, we say, is a sadder spectacle than any subsequent part of his career. If this be the youthful ideal, what will be the worked-out manhood? There is a problem for the moralist to solve; with Vivian Grey as an ideal, how may a man work out this life of ours?

We return to our old position, and say that it is the absence of earnestness which lies at the root of all D'Israeli's failures, positive and comparative, and

which has destroyed the impression his talents would otherwise have made.
People talk much of his coxcombry and conceit; but his conceit, though
colossal, is injurious to him, not through its greatness, but through its want
of basis. It is not because he has an *over* estimate of himself, but because he
has an entirely *false* estimate. We believe, that without intense self-
confidence no man would achieve greatness. It seems clear that all great men,
from Shakespeare to Napoleon, were perfectly aware of their superiority, and
could speak of it at times with unhesitating laudation. It is also true that very
small men have fancied and proclaimed themselves to be Shakespeares and
Napoleons. In the one case, we accept even a boast as the indication of
conscious power; in the other, we laugh at the strange hallucination of fatuity.
The origin of our laughter is in the recognition of the discrepancy between
the pretensions and the performance; the origin of the hallucination is in the
confusion of a *desire* for distinction with the *power* of distinguishing oneself.
When a man judges himself with some degree of accuracy, we allow him to
use a liberal measure; we admit his *over* estimate of himself as natural,
inevitable. But we are pitiless towards every *false* estimation he makes of
himself. Now D'Israeli is in this case. His notion of his own powers is not
simply inordinate, it is preposterous. He lives in an eternal Fool's Paradise.
One great weakness of his—the inability of so adjusting the focus of mental
vision as to distinguish the real proportions of things—arises, we believe,
from his fundamental deficiency, the want of truthfulness. He cannot appreciate the truth. He neither rightly sees what is within him, nor what is
around him. He fancies that the world can be made plastic to his wishes; that
he has only to wish to do something great, and to do it. To write epics, to
revive a fallen drama, to rule states—these may be accomplished *at once*,
and by a mere exertion of the will to do it! This is laughably shown in his
early attempts. An inhabitant of Bedlam never had less misgivings respecting
his right to the throne of England, than D'Israeli had to his power of assuming
the position of *the* great English poet. No one remembers, because no one
ever read, his 'Revolutionary Epick'; but many remember with a smile, the
magniloquence of its Preface. He who has laughed so much at others, has
there afforded a more than equivalent return; he has never made others half
so ridiculous by his satire, as he has made himself by his seriousness.

   Open this epic: it is worth the trouble. The very title-page of this quarto
volume has such an exquisite disregard of the 'eternal fitness of things'—
such a compound of puppyism and pomposity, that it deserves a place among
the facetiae of literature:–

THE REVOLUTIONARY EPICK.
THE WORK OF
D'ISRAELI THE YOUNGER.

No wonder it was received with a shout of derision; especially when the

Preface heralded the poem in this magnificent style:

> It was on the plains of Troy that I first conceived the idea of this work. Wandering over that illustrious scene, surrounded by the tombs of heroes and by the confluence of poetic streams, my musing thoughts clustered round the memory of that immortal song to which all creeds and countries alike respond, which has vanquished Chance and defies Time.
>
> Deeming myself, perchance too rashly, in that excited hour, a Poet, I cursed the destiny that had placed me in an age that boasted of being antipoetical. And while my Fancy thus struggled with my Reason, *it flashed across my mind like the lightning which was then playing over Ida*, that in those great poems which rise the pyramids of poetic art, amid the falling and the fading splendour of less creations, the Poet hath ever embodied the spirit of his Time. Thus the most heroic incident of an heroic age produced in the 'Iliad' an Heroic Epick; thus the consolidation of the most superb of Empires produced in the Aeneid a Political Epick; the revival of Learning and the birth of vernacular genius presented us in the Divine Comedy with a National Epick; and the Reformation and its consequences called from the rapt Lyre of Milton a Religious Epick;
>
> And the spirit of my Time, shall it alone be uncelebrated?

This home-thrust of a question has all the force of an epigram. What! shall Greece boast of a Homer, Rome of a Virgil, Italy of a Dante, and shall England, in her nineteenth century, big with events more glorious than any by-gone era, be uncelebrated while D'Israeli the Younger lives, who can embody the spirit of his Time? The age, indeed, is unpoetical—as all ages are to unpoetical minds; but the spirit of the Time demands embodiment, and when the lightning plays round Mount Ida, and a D'Israeli the Younger is watching it, something considerable *must* result.

> *Standing upon Asia*, [continues the inspired rhapsodist,] *and gazing upon Europe*, with the broad Hellespont alone between us, and the Shadow of Night descending on the mountains, these mighty continents appeared to me as it were the Rival Principles of Government that at present contend for the mastery of the world. 'What!' I exclaimed, 'is the Revolution of France a less important event than the siege of Troy? Is Napoleon a less interesting character than Achilles?
> *For me remains the Revolutionary Epick!'*

It was quite supererogatory to read a dozen lines of a poem thus prefaced; the man whose taste and judgment could have written, printed, and corrected proofs of such prose as that without any misgivings as to its exquisite absurdity, was assuredly the last man to write a poem of any worth whatever, much less a poem which was to rank beside Homer, Virgil, Dante, and Milton. Accordingly, this 'Dardanian reverie', as he styles it, which proposed to 'teach wisdom both to monarchs and multitudes', was received by the ungrateful age which it was to render illustrious, with such contempt and derision, that the poet broke his lyre, and forbore to sing again. It is, indeed, a pitiable performance; it is worthy of its Preface! Convinced that there was but little chance of his taking his place as the epic poet of his age, he made one gallant dash at the dramatic laurel wreath, feeling himself called upon to 'revive English tragedy'. 'Count Alarcos' is many degrees better than the 'Revolutionary Epick', because less fatuous and presumptuous; but it is in nowise better than the hundreds of unreadable, unactable tragedies which fatigue the press every season, as if to demonstrate the dearth of our dramatic genius. The preface to 'Alarcos' is also in better taste, though there are reminiscences of the old puppyism, as when he tell us:

Years have flown away since, rambling in the sierras of Andalusia, beneath the clear light of a Spanish moon, and freshened by the sea-breeze that had wandered up a river from the coast, I first listened to the chaunt of that terrible tale, (the ballad of 'Alarcos'). It seemed to me rife with all the materials of the tragic drama; and I planned, as I rode along, the scenes and characters of which it appeared to me susceptible.

That was the season of life, when the heart is quick with emotion and the brain with creative fire; when the eye is haunted with beautiful sights and the ear with sweet sounds; when we live in reveries of magnificent performance, and the future seems only a perennial flow of poetic invention—[the season in which we write 'Vivian Greys!']

Dreams of fantastic youth! Amid the stern realities of existence, I have unexpectedly achieved a long lost purpose.

All this was very unpromising in a dramatic poet; and again an ungrateful age refused to be delighted. D'Israeli does the age the justice, however, of saying that it is 'full of poetry, for it is full of passion'. Indeed, the common cry about the time being unpoetical, is only the cry of incapacity, and forces one to remember Gibbon's strange assertion, that the age of history was past—an assertion uttered on the eve of the French Revolution!

These two attempts are, we believe, the only attempts D'Israeli has made to win for himself a name amongst our poets; they are evidences of that want of self-knowledge, and of due estimate of his powers, which meet us at every turn in his career. The man who could so easily delude himself into the idea that he was a Homer might very easily persuade himself he was a Pericles, or, at the least, a Canning. And as he thought to reach the heights of Parnassus at one bound, and make himself immortal without toil, so did he fancy that he had only to get a seat in Parliamant to sway with his impassioned oratory the destinies of the nation. He had always hankered after political distinction. During the political excitement of the Reform agitation, he was wandering over the plains of Troy, watching the lightning playing over Ida, standing upon Asia, and gazing upon Europe, and being looked down upon by forty centuries from the heights of the pyramids. But he came back in 1832, prepared to astonish Europe as a poet and a statesman. The want of the age was a Great Man and lo! from the Pyramids came D'Israeli the Younger. Historians will note with surprise that his return did not perceptibly affect the funds.

Readers would not read the 'Revolutionary Epick', constituents would not elect the great statesman. He was forced to bide his time. Novels, pamphlets, and newspaper squabbles, kept him before the public. At last, he did secure a seat. Now, assuredly, Europe, will be astonished; now, if ever, the house will shake. The great orator has taken his seat. The Tories have their Orlando; a tottering cause has its Mirabeau. He rose, he spoke, and the house *did* shake—but it was with laughter. The failure was as signal as that of his 'Epick'; and from a similar cause. The utter want of discrimination which prevented his seeing the mistake he committed in his poetic grandilo-quence, prevented him from estimating aright the means by which an audience could be moved. He meant to be eloquent, and was ludicrous; his ornate periods only made men titter; instead of being warned, he proceeded in the same strain, until the laughter was so uproarious, that, breaking through all the courtesies which usually surround a maiden speech, it forced him to sit down, uttering an energetic prophecy, that the time would come when they should listen to him! We remember one passage which created great mirth at the time: he was alluding to Mr Hudson's having gone to Rome, to bring back Sir Robert Peel, and that simple matter was spoken of as 'when the *hurried Hudson swept into the chambers of the Vatican*'. This was the 'Revolutionary Epick' over again.

He has fulfilled his prophecy, however: they *have* listened to him, and now they listen to few men with more attention. He has learned to adapt himself to the tastes and temper of the house. He indulges in little of that oriental magnificence of style which amused them before. He knows his power lies in sarcasm, and he is sarcastic. Homer has broken his lyre, and changed places with Thersites. People yawn or sneer when he begins to unroll the panorama of his political philosophy; but they brighten up when they see by the twinkle of his eye that he is preparing one of his 'hits'.

D'Israeli conceives himself to be a man of genius; in truth he is only the *prospectus of a genius*. He has magnificent plans, but he writes prefaces instead of books. All the promise which allures in a prospectus arrests attention in him; but he does not perform what he promises. He has aspiration, but no inspiration; ambition, but no creative power. In his poems, in his novels, and in his speeches you see that he means something great, but has not the force to originate it. If epics could spring up out of the mere desire to embody the spirit of the time, then would he be the great national poet; if grandiloquence were eloquence, then would he stir the hearts of thousands and 'teach wisdom to monarchs and to multitudes'. So if statesmanship were only the perception of the incapacity of others, and the recognition of the necessity for a statesman to have large and distinct views, then would he be the 'Coming Man' whose advent he proclaims. But it is not so. Prospectuses will not do the work of books. They may serve to gull a list of subscribers and gain a fleeting notoriety: that is the utmost they can do. They have done that for D'Israeli.

We remarked before that his position in literature was analogous to his position in politics, modified by the enormous difference of the arena, and his combatants in that arena. Now in literature this prospectus-brilliancy counts for really very little; accordingly those works in which he has trusted to his intrinsic value have been lamentable failures. No one would accept his 'Revolutionary Epick'; no one would act his 'Alarcos'. The prose run mad of 'Alroy' was too extravagant even for the Minerva press. The philosophico-poetico-'psychological Romance' of 'Contarini Fleming' was unendurable to men and boys. 'Henrietta Temple' and 'Venetia' could not stand even beside Mrs Gore and Mr James. We all saw what was *meant* in these works; but we also saw what was *done*. 'Vivian Grey' and the 'Young Duke' amused by their portraits of public men, and by a certain dashing coxcombry and vivacity. 'Coningsby', 'Sybil', and 'Tancred' were political manifestoes spiced with personalities, and had the facile success such things achieve. But if you look into any of these works you will be struck with their utter worthlessness, which no cleverness of the author can disguise. They are adroitly 'got up' for effect; but they remain prospectuses. Examine them, and you will see a complete absence of all sterling excellence. They are written with astonishing command of language, and yet the style is ungrammatical, inelegant, inaccurate. In descriptions splendid words are made to stand for distinct pictures. In characterisation the mere outside is presented: insight into character, analysis of motives, the dynamic operation of passions, are not to be met with. The development of a plot is unattempted. Sketchy chapters changing from discussion to satire, from idle dialogues to grandiloquent rhapsodies, fill up the three volumes through which they have hurried the reader.

Whoever is at all conversant with our lighter literature will understand how, with the majority of readers, this prospectus-prodigality succeeds for a time. People see a sketch of social life, and accepts it as true. They see the author means to be eloquent and witty, and they take the will for the deed. They see he means to be profound and sagacious, and they believe in him. Who stops to think during a hand gallop through three volumes? It all *looks* very brilliant, and very solid. Whether it be gilt or gold, troubles them not. It is only readers of another class who see through the pretension.

In politics is it otherwise? Is he not the prospectus of a statesman? He sees clearly enough the necessity for ideas, and pretends to have them, though he has only the idea that there *ought* to be ideas. This is something: nay, in opposition, it is considerable. Owing to the state of political knowledge, any man who only *seems* to have ideas has power. There are two classes of politicians. One accepts the traditionary policy handed down by predecessors, 'the wisdom of our ancestors', or the policy painfully shaped out by the irresistible progress of events. These are men without political ideas, working upon established formulas. They cannot, even in theory, construct a policy which shall in any way embrace the life of a nation; but shroud their incapacity under delusive metaphors, such as—'The institutions of a country must grow': as if, because a man must grow, his career must also be one, not of *intelligent action*, but of derived *vegetation*. The aphorism may be set aside by a continuation of the metaphor: if they must grow, they must also decay, and thus the 'wisdom of our ancestors' becomes the decrepitude of our times! These men, the best of them, seem incapable of looking beyond the step they are to take next. Instead of viewing political life as a whole, they read only pages of history, and propose measures in place of comprehensive schemes. They are not leaders, but subalterns; the captains, not the generals of the army. Take, as a striking example, our present ruler, and our present terrible problem—Lord John Russell and Ireland. The Whig minister over and over again declares that Ireland *cannot* be treated by any scheme, but only by measures from time to time applicable to the occasion. This is a confession of incapacity. Specific application is the philosophy of quacks: general treatment, the practice of physicians. Lord John is a man who has read history, written history, and lived history; but he has not understood history. He can pick out authorities and precedents, and apply them with admirable ingenuity, but with what effect? He will quote a passage from Burke to settle a question of our day, not discriminating between eternal principles and the transient plans and incidents of an age. Burke is a great writer, and the page is luminous; but there has been a *context* added to it since the French Revolution, which strangely alters its significance. Quote Burke by all means: but to overlook the context!...

There is another class, which looks upon history as the life of a nation, which regards polity as the dynamics of national progression, which takes into view the action of one nation upon another, and which, *inducting* the future, attempts to construct large schemes that are national in their scope, and historic in their basis. This class is small in numbers—at least, in the House—and D'Israeli is of them. But here also he is only a prospectus. He is aware of the necessity for such views, but has himself only figments. Realities are reflected in a mirage to him. If ever he attempted to execute his prospectus, he would doubtless make a failure as egregious as the 'Revolutionary Epick'. Meanwhile, he has this much of strength—he does see beyond *Bills*. His prospectus is not humdrum. As an antagonist to the humdrum spirit, he is decidedly powerful; but we have no desire to see him placed in a position where he may experiment. His great notion of reviving a paternal aristocracy, with a cherished pleasantry dancing round May-poles—this Young-Englandism, about which so much discussion and pleasantry arose, to be forgotten so quickly—was pretty enough as a white-waistcoat philosophy to adorn novels and historic fancies, but as a political idea, it partook of D'Israeli's besetting sin, the fantastic. It was worse than an anachronism. It overlooked, as D'Israeli is apt to overlook, the influence of surrounding conditions.

He reasons with his imagination. Thus also in his interpretation of Venetian polity, which is ingenious, and quite in the spirit of Venetian history and its most characteristic statesman, even back to Dandolo, we see the same oversight of determining influences. Content with grouping and classifying the facts of history, assigning to each group or class its *function*, he neglects to inquire into its origin. He does not see how the strict aristocracy of Venice was aided by the lackland condition of its nobles, the absence of primogeniture, and other things which repaid the proud nobles for merging the individual in the class: a condition that could scarcely exist beyond the Lagoons.

Fanciful or sound, he has larger views of statesmanship than the vast majority of the Commons, and this gives him a position of superiority. It is the bitterest sarcasm on the House and its efficiency, that D'Israeli should have succeeded more by its viciousness than by his own powers. For no one will deny that he owes his success partly to this semblance of statesmanship, but principally to his satirical recklessness and pungency. He has always been attacking somebody, but Peel was the antagonist who elevated him. He began by a tilt against the Whigs in general, but he showed more animus than power. He attacked O'Connell, but was scornfully told by the arch-agitator that he was descended from the *impenitent* thief who died upon the cross—an elegance of invective in which O'Connell alone could indulge. But his attack on Peel was so timed as to raise him into instant importance.

Let us glance at his political history. After his splendid failure as an orator, he saw that the House was not to be swayed by picturesque sentences, and set himself to work at a specific object. He paid great attention to foreign affairs, to which his disposition to view things in broad masses naturally inclined him, and at this period he bestowed great pains on displaying a minute knowledge of social and personal matters abroad. It was manifest that he was aiming at a diplomatic appointment of some sort. It is generally understood that he applied to Peel for official employment, which was refused. Peel was not the man to tolerate what he probably considered as the aping emptiness of D'Israeli; but in his refusal he turned a very useful ally into a formidable, because bitter enemy. It is but right to state that D'Israeli in one of his attacks, asserted that he had never made any application to Peel for official employment; and this assertion Peel left uncontradicted. This would seem to be conclusive, were it not known that Peel can, if he choose, preserve unbroken silence against any amount of temptation or exasperation; so that the general impression still is that the cause of the sudden rupture was this refusal. But whatever the motive, the attacks upon Peel were exquisitely relished by the House, and those who despised the assailant cheered him on, for some of them disliked the minister, and all enjoyed seeing him baited. There is an ignoble tendency in the mass of men, which causes them to rejoice at every degradation of one who has proved himself their superior; and whoever panders to this tendency is sure of a disgraceful success. Hence the success of 'slashing' articles. The 'Quarterly Review' owed its prodigious influence to its reckless disregard of all the decencies of honour coupled with the high religious and moral tone which it assumed. In the great 'Rigby' days, it was a moot point whether a political adversary were better crushed by the accusation of atheistical principles, or of having pimples on his face; and no logic seemed so conclusive as that which, insinuating that a man lived unhappily with his wife, or that a woman wore a wig, proved triumphantly that a poem must be worthless, and that an argument was false. This evil has happily cured itself. We have revolted against such literature as worthy only of the kennel. Those critics are shamed into silence. But the coarse, ungenerous feeling which permitted such an evil, is not extinct. We still love to see a man baited, as our forefathers loved to bait a bear. The astonishing effect of D'Israeli's attacks on Peel sprang from this feeling. Not that he ever outraged the sense of decency. We will do him the justice to say that his sarcasm was exquisitely polished: there was no virulence, no coarseness, no Billingsgate. The point of his sarcasm, like the sting of the wasp, was never seen, never suspected, till the writhings of the victim betrayed its presence.

It is still a question whether this quarrel has not been unfortunate for both. It certainly damaged Peel; it assuredly damaged D'Israeli. Had Peel been less supercilious, had he managed himself so as to have overcome his personal distaste for the author of 'Coningsby', he might have attached a valuable partisan. Had D'Israeli been to him what he was to Lord George Bentinck, he would have facilitated and adorned with gaiety Peel's course. His own brilliant qualities would have shone with increased splendour attached to the solidity of Peel; and might have been as the gilding on the long enduring walls of some fine cathedral, instead of being thrown away upon some transitory pageant. This is one view; but there is another. Perhaps the quarrel gave D'Israeli an eminence which he never could otherwise have attained. It is the adventurer's old trick, that of attacking an eminent man, who is feared and hated by a powerful body; and the fact that D'Israeli's position was enormously increased by his assault on Peel, is beyond question.

For one thing it threw him into the protectionist party; which he had never heartily espoused before. Free Trade became an entity when Peel adopted it; and because Peel adopted it, D'Israeli attacked it. Left to himself, he doubtless would have taken the enlightened Conservative view of Free Trade. But he had to reconcile his own tendencies that way with his antagonism to Peel, and his mode of doing it was adroit. Free Trade, he said, was the policy of the Tories as paternal rulers of the people—those great families who had always cared more for the humble, the poor, &c., than Whigs or middle-class Liberals ever did. Peel was a deserter from the Tories to the hard-hearted Liberals of Manchester—those cotton lords who are supercilious without being magnanimous. Therefore, Peel was not the man who had the *right* to decree Free Trade. He was doing it badly, inopportunely, and ineffectively; and therefore his proposition was altogether bad, dishonest, unwarranted, and untimely.

The Protectionists are a compact band brought out by Peel's Free Trade policy, which they refused to follow. But, though compact, the band is feeble. For what do the Rutlands, Richmonds, Buckinghams, and their followers count? Really for very little. The party wants *men*. They have Lord Ashley, but he has more honesty than ability, and George Smyth, who has more ability than honesty; Augustus Stafford, well informed, adroit, witty, but deficient in weight, and power of sustained thought—a drawing-room statesman of the smartest and most agreeable gentlemanly kind—but more brilliant over a dessert table than in the house; Lord George Bentinck is gone; Lord Yarborough, who has grown feebler since his elevation to the peerage; Herries, and a few superannuated officials, protectionists by habit; Stanley alone remains to be named—an overrated man, but a man of power. In such a party D'Israeli really is a man of mark and likelihood. His effective powers of sarcasm, his statesmanlike sense of the necessity for large views, his historical knowledge, and his power of massing details, give him a strength which, though derivable rather from the weakness of his colleagues than from any positive greatness of his own, does nevertheless mark him out for a minister, if Stanley should come in.

Vivian Grey a minister! That would be a sight to make the most frivolous ponder; but it is a sight which we may not improbably see. Why not? Do not the Jews rule the world? Is not the unmixed Caucasian race entitled to rule it? Sidonia will demonstrate to you that the Jews are the greatest and grandest specimens of the human race, and, by prescriptive right divine, must and will rule it.

'Do you think that the quiet, humdrum persecution of a decorous representative of an English university can crush those who have successively baffled the Pharaohs, Nebuchadnezzar, Rome, and the feudal ages? The fact is, you cannot destroy a pure race of the Caucasian organisation. It is a physiological fact, a simple law of nature, which has baffled Egyptian and Assyrian Kings, Roman Emperors, and Christian Inquisitors. No penal laws, no physical tortures, can effect that a superior race should be absorbed in an inferior, or be destroyed by it. The mixed persecuting races disappear; the pure persecuted race remains. And at this moment, in spite of centuries, of tens of centuries, of degradation, the Jewish mind exercises a vast influence on the affairs of Europe. I speak not of their laws, which you still obey; of their literature, with which your minds are saturated; but of the living Hebrew intellect.

You never observe a great intellectual movement in Europe in which the Jews do not greatly participate. The first Jesuits were Jews; that mysterious Russian diplomacy which so alarms Western Europe, is organised and principally carried out by Jews, that mighty revolution which is at this moment preparing in Germany, and which will be, in fact, a second and greater Reformation, and of which so little is as yet known in England, is entirely developing under the auspices of Jews, who almost monopolise the professional chairs of Germany. Neander, the founder of spiritual Christianity, and who is Regius Professor of Divinity in the University of Berlin, is a Jew. Benary, equally famous, and in the same University, is a Jew. Wehl, the Arabic Professor of Heidelberg, is a Jew. Years ago, when I was in Palestine, I met a German Student who was accumulating materials for the History of Christianity, and studying the genius of the place—a modest and learned man. It was Wehl; then unknown, since become the first Arabic scholar of the day, and the author of the life of Mahomet. But for the German professors of this race, their name is Legion. I think there are more than ten in Berlin alone.

I told you just now that I was going up town to-morrow, because I always made it a rule to interpose when affairs of State were on the carpet. Otherwise, I never interfere. I hear of peace, of war in news-papers, but I am never alarmed, except when I am informed that the sovereigns want treasure, then I know that monarchs are serious. A few years back we were applied to by Russia. Now, there has been no friendship between the Court of St Petersburg and my family. It has Dutch connexions which have generally supplied it, and our repre-sentations in favour of the Polish Hebrews, a numerous race, but the most suffering and degraded of all the tribes, have not been very agreeable to the Czar. However, circumstances drew to an approxima-tion between the Romanoffs and the Sidonias. I resolved to go myself to St Petersburg. I had, on my arrival, an interview with the Russian Minister of Finance, Count Cancrin; I beheld the son of a Lithuanian Jew. The loan was connected with the affairs of Spain; I resolved on repairing to Spain from Russia. I travelled without intermission. I had an audience immediately on my arrival with the Spanish Minister, Senor Mendizabel; I beheld one like myself, the son of a Nuevo Christiano, a Jew of Arragon. In consequence of what transpired in Madrid, I went straight to Paris to consult the President of the French Council; I beheld the son of a French Jew, a hero, an imperial marshal,

and very properly so, for who should be military heroes if not those
who worship the Lord of Hosts?'

'And is Soult a Hebrew?'

'Yes, and others of the French Marshals, and the most famous;
Massena, for example, his real name was Manasseh: but to my anecdote. The consequence of our consultations was, that some Northern
power should be applied to in a friendly and mediative capacity. We
fixed on Prussia, and the President of the Council made an application
to the Prussian Minister, who attended a few days after our conference.
Count Arnim entered the cabinet, and I beheld a Prussian Jew. So you
see, my dear Coningsby, that the world is governed by very different
personages to what is imagined by those who are not behind the
scenes.'

'You startle, and deeply interest me.'

'You must study physiology, my dear child. Pure races of Caucasus
may be persecuted, but they cannot be despised, except by the brutal
ignorance of some mongrel breed, that brandishes fagots and howls
extermination, but is itself exterminated without persecution by that
irresistible law of nature which is fatal to curs.'

'But I come also from Caucasus,' said Coningsby.

'Verily; and thank your Creator for such a destiny: and your race is
sufficiently pure. You come from the shores of the Northern Sea, land
of the blue eye, and the golden hair, and the frank brow; 'tis a famous
breed, with whom we Arabs have contended long; from whom we have
much suffered; but these Goths, and Saxons, and Normans, were
doubtless great men.'

'But so favoured by Nature, why has not your race produced great
poets, great orators, great writers?'

'Favoured by Nature and by Nature's God, we produced the lyre of
David; we gave you Isaiah and Ezekiel; they are our Olynthians, our
Philippics. Favoured by Nature we still remain; but in exact proportion
as we have been favoured by Nature, we have been persecuted by Man.
After a thousand struggles; after acts of heroic courage that Rome has
never equalled; deeds of divine patriotism that Athens, and Sparta, and
Carthage, have never excelled; we have endured fifteen hundred years
of supernatural slavery, during which, every device that can degrade
or destroy man has been the destiny that we have sustained and baffled.
The Hebrew child has entered adolescence only to learn that he was
the Pariah of that ungrateful Europe that owes to him the best part of
its laws, a fine portion of its literature, all its religion. Great poets
require a public; we have been content with the immortal melodies that
we sung more than two thousand years ago by the waters of Babylon,
and wept. They record our triumphs; they solace our affliction. Great
orators are the creatures of popular assemblies; we were permitted only

by stealth to meet even in our temples. And as for great writers, the catalogue is not blank. What are all the schoolmen, Aquinas himself, to Maimonides? and as for modern philosophy, all springs from Spinoza.

But the passionate and creative genius, that is the nearest link to divinity, and which no human tyranny can destroy, though it can divert it; that should have stirred the hearts of nations by its inspired sympathy, or governed senates by its burning eloquence, has found a medium for its expression, to which, in spite of your prejudices and your evil passions, you have been obliged to bow. The ear, the voice, the fancy teeming with combinations, the imagination fervent with picture and emotion, that came from Caucasus, and which we have preserved unpolluted, have endowed us with almost the exclusive privilege of Music; that science of harmonious sounds which the ancients recognised as most divine, and deified in the person of their most beautiful creation. I speak not of the past, though, were I to enter into the history of the lords of melody, you would find it the annals of Hebrew genius. But at this moment even, musical Europe is ours. There is not a company of singers, not an orchestra in a single capital, that is not crowded with our children, under the feigned names which they adopt to conciliate the dark aversion which your posterity will some day disclaim with shame and disgust. Almost every great composer, skilled musician, almost every voice that ravishes you with its transporting strains, spring from our tribes. The catalogue is too vast to enumerate; too illustrious to dwell for a moment on secondary names, however eminent. Enough for us that the three great creative minds to whose exquisite inventions all nations at this moment yield; Rossini, Meyerbeer, Mendelssohn, are of Hebrew race; and little do your men of fashion, your 'muscadins' of Paris, and your dandies of London, as they thrill into raptures at the notes of a Pasta or a Grisi, little do they suspect that they are offering their homage to the sweet singers of Israel.'

This *plaidoyer* in favour of his race, and, by implication, in favour of his own pretensions to be minister, has excited so much laughter, not on account of its shallowness as a theory of races, as of its amusing personal pretension. Of this we are assured, that if the Jewish race is the finest in the world, Vivian Grey is a poor specimen of his race; and if Europe is to be governed by Jews, we would rather see another specimen governing England. For although we will say in his favour that he would not govern us upon those *parish principles* which assume that 'Bills' are the things needful, we confess that such is our invincible distrust in his capacity for anything like serious, sustained thought, that we would rather submit to the 'experiments' of the Socialists than to his.

Besides his Caucasian qualification he has another, and, according to him, indispensable qualification—youth. Plato, somewhere in the 'Republic', says that great works are only accomplished in youth: νεωνδε παντες οι μεγαλα και οι πολλοι πονοι; but he did not write his 'Republic' or his 'Laws' in youth, and Sophocles was ninety when he produced the master-piece of Athenian tragedy. There is, however, a good deal of truth in what D'Israeli says:

'Nay,' said the stranger; 'for life in general there is but one decree. Youth is a blunder; manhood a struggle; old age a regret. Do not suppose,' he added, smiling, 'that I hold that youth is genius; all that I say is, that genius, when young, is divine. Why the greatest captains of ancient and modern times both conquered Italy at five-and-twenty! Youth, extreme youth, overthrew the Persian empire. Don John of Austria won Lepanto at twenty-five—the greatest battle of modern times; had it not been for the jealousy of Philip, the next year he would have been Emperor of Mauritania. Gaston de Foix was only twenty-two when he stood a victor on the plain of Ravenna. Every one remembers Condé and Rocroy at the same age. Gustavus Adolphus died at thirty-eight. Look at his captains; that wonderful Duke of Weimar; only thirty-six when he died. Banier himself, after all his miracles, died at forty-five. Cortes was little more than thirty when he gazed upon the golden cupolas of Mexico. When Maurice of Saxony died at thirty-two, all Europe acknowledged the loss of the greatest captain and the profoundest statesman of the age. Then there is Nelson, Clive—but these are warriors, and perhaps you may think there are greater things than war—I do not: I worship the Lord of Hosts. But take the most illustrious achievements of civil prudence. Innocent III, the greatest of the popes, was the despot of Christendom, at thirty-seven. John de Medici was a cardinal at fifteen, and, Guicciardini tells us, baffled with his statescraft Ferdinand of Arragon himself. He was pope, as Leo X, at thirty-seven. Luther robbed even him of his richest province at thirty-five. Take Ignatius Loyola and John Wesley, they worked with young brains. Ignatius was only thirty when he made his pilgrimage, and wrote the 'Spiritual Exercises'. Pascal wrote a great work at sixteen, the greatest of Frenchmen, and died at thirty-seven!

Ah! that fatal thirty-seven, which reminds me of Byron, greater even as a man than a writer. Was it experience that guided the pencil of Raphael when he painted the palaces of Rome? He died, too, at thirty-seven. Richelieu was secretary of state at thirty-one. Well, then, there are Bolingbroke and Pitt, both ministers before other men leave off cricket. Grotius was in great practice at seventeen, and attorney-general at twenty-four. And Acquaviva—Acquaviva was general of the Jesuits, ruled every cabinet in Europe, and colonised America, before he was thirty-seven. What a career!' exclaimed the stranger, rising from his chair, and walking up and down the room; 'the secret sway of Europe! That was indeed a position! But it is needless to multiply instances. The history of heroes is the history of youth.'

Youth is then a great qualification for a political leader. True, 'Vivian Grey' is no longer at that divine period; but if not youthful himself he has youthful followers—he leads the New Generation! Besides, Genius is always young. Let the 'old fogies' sneer at me, and call me an adventurer if they will; I am of an unmixed race, I am a genius, I am the leader of youthful ardent spirits who believe me to be a profound and imaginative (oh! above all imaginative!) statesman; I will show the humdrums that it is not Reason but Imagination which rules the world!

We have been speaking hitherto in general terms because it is rather embarrassing to descend to particulars in a case where the particulars do not in any way seem to bear out the general result. Notoriety has been gained—a position has been gained. The general causes of this are not recondite; but if you look closely to examine the basis of this success you are astonished at its apparent discrepancy. If there is one quality which everyone would at once award D'Israeli, it is, perhaps, wit; yet we defy the most ardent admirer to bring good specimens. In his writings and in his speeches there is great vivacity, occasional felicity of expression, and some happy illustrations; but wit there is scarcely any. In the house it is notorious that his 'hits' produce an effect which no one who reads the speech can form an idea of; and this because there is more manner than wit. The wittiest thing, to our apprehension, he ever uttered, was his speaking of the 'American *language*'. His famous joke about Peel having caught the Whigs bathing, and stolen their clothes, is really a very feeble effort; though it amused the house more perhaps than a better joke would have amused it. From his forgotten pamphlet, 'The Crises Examined', we extract an illustration which created great mirth at the time, and is really humorous:–

The truth is, that this famous reform ministry, this great 'united' cabinet had degenerated into a grotesque and Hudibrastic faction, the very lees of ministerial existence, the offal of official life. They were a ragged regiment compared with which Falstaff's crew was a band of regulars. The king would not march with them through Coventry—that was flat. *The* reform ministry, indeed! Why scarcely an original member of that celebrated cabinet remained. I dare say now some of you have heard of Mr Ducrow, that celebrated gentleman who rides upon six horses. What a prodigious achievement! It seems impossible, but you have confidence in Ducrow! You fly to witness it. Unfortunately one of the horses is ill, and a donkey is substituted in its place. But Ducrow is still admirable; there he is, bounding along in a spangled jacket and cork slippers. The whole town is mad to see Ducrow riding at the same time on six horses. But now two more of the steeds are seized with the staggers, and lo! three jackasses in their stead! Still Ducrow persists, and still announces to the public that he will ride round his circus every night on six horses. At last all the horses are knocked up, and now there are half a dozen donkeys, while Mr Merryman, who like the Chancellor (Brougham), was once the very life of the ring, now lies in despairing length in the middle of the stage with his jokes exhausted and his bottle empty.

As to his literary pretensions we have before intimated that we think them frivolous. He has a certain artistic tendency, which makes him give to everything he handles whether literary or political, a symmetry and artistic effect; but he has none of the deeper qualities of an artist. We express his deficiency in one phrase when we say that his eloquence is grandiloquence. He does not work from *inwards*, but contents himself with externals; and as splendid words are the externals of eloquence, they suffice him. This gives a disagreeable hollowness to all his serious and more particularly to his impassioned passages; and it not unfrequently leads him into bathos. Of this bathos the reader may see samples in the passages previously quoted from his two prefaces. We have just opened 'Coningsby', and this strikes our eye:–

At school, friendship is a passion. *It entrances the being; it tears the soul.* All loves of after-life can never bring its rapture, or its wretchedness; *no bliss so absorbing, no pangs of jealousy or despair so crushing and so keen!* What tenderness and what devotion; what illimitable confidence; *infinite revelations of inmost thoughts;* what ecstatic present and romantic future; what bitter estrangements and what melting reconciliations; what scenes of wild recrimination, agitating explanations, passionate correspondence; *what insane sensitiveness and what frantic sensibility; what earthquakes of the heart and whirlwinds of the soul* are confined in that simple phrase—a schoolboy's friendship!

Does the Minerva Press groan under the weight of trash more intolerable than these 'earthquakes of the heart and whirlwinds of the soul'? Is this the sort of language which we are to hear from a minister, the serious reflections which are to adorn a work? The man who could write such sentences, not staggering under two bottles of champagne, must be pronounced either dead to all sense of the true meaning of words, or reckless and shameless in his use of them; either he has no just sense of expression, or he thinks that any fine words will serve his turn if they gull the indolent reader. Nor is this by any means an exceptional passage. His writings abound with similar instances of tawdry falsehood. They are thrown in probably out of that love of ornament, which is characteristic of his race: they are the mosaic chains and rings with which the young 'gentlemen of the Hebrew persuasion' adorn their persons, to give a *faux air de gentilhomme* to that which no adornment can disguise. We may seem to insist upon a trifle in thus insisting on such false eloquence; but trifles like these reveal a trivial mind, and when characteristic of a serious defect should not escape criticism. It shows that his eloquence like his imagination, like his poetry, like his philosophy, like his statesmanship, is the Prospectus, not the Work!

T.B. Macaulay

The Art of History (April 1856)

Monday, the 17th of December, 1855, was a great day in the annals of Paternoster-row. Twenty-five thousand copies of the third and fourth volumes of Macaulay were to be delivered to eager purchasers. The book had been bought to that extent before it appeared; so confident were booksellers of an unprecedented demand. Mudie, the enterprising librarian, had taken a house next to his premises to contain the five thousand five hundred volumes which fell to his share in the great literary scramble. The counters of retail booksellers, generally quiet, and seldom startled by the appearance of even one quite new work, this day groaned beneath a pile of purple volumes. As to the expectant public—although really far less agitated and eager than was anticipated—it manifested, in certain circles, a determination to enjoy the work, such as perhaps has not been felt since the Waverley novels appeared. To judge from a single instance: we happened to call on the greatest anatomist of our day,[42] and found him already halfway through the first volume, promising himself to sit up all that night to finish it; neither the charms of the Ant-eater he was then engaged in dissecting, nor the attractions of fossil remains of the Musk ox, could draw him from Macaulay's page. And the book which the great philosopher sat up all night to read, was read with scarcely less avidity in boudoirs by very fine ladies, and by perfectly stupid gentlemen in clubs.

Not a century ago, that is in 1776, the first volume of the *Decline and Fall of the Roman Empire* met with a success which was as enormous, *toute proportion gardée*. 'I am at a loss,' said Gibbon in after years,

> how to describe the success of the work without betraying the vanity of the writer. The first impression was exhausted in a few days; a second and third edition were scarcely adequate to the demand; and a bookseller's property was twice invaded by the pirates of Dublin. My book was on every table, and almost on every toilette; the historian was crowned by the taste or fashion of the day.

What was the number of copies in each edition? Unhappily he has not specified. The first was one thousand copies; five hundred having been originally agreed on, but 'the number having been doubled by the prophetic taste' of the printer; what the second and third editions were we are left to guess; but we may be certain that they made a very small approach to Macaulay's twenty-five thousand, the readers of those days bearing but a small proportion to the readers of our day. The *Decline and Fall* (which, for the consolation of struggling authors, we may add was refused by one publisher) certainly had a success as great as the *History of England* at the time of its appearance; and we must leave to our grandchildren to compute whether eight years hence Macaulay will have maintained an equal share of reputation. Time has in many respects only sanctioned Gibbon's fame; and the labours of successive scholars working in his track have only made his merit still more eminent. The conceptions of men respecting History have been modified, yet Gibbon still maintains his rank, while Hume and Robertson decline every year. Will Macaulay bear this test of time? To answer such a question we must examine his work with reference to certain indisputable principles. Instead therefore of reviewing it in the ordinary way, which would be altogether superfluous with a work already so well-known, we propose to consider it as a specimen of historical writing which commands the widest popularity, and shall endeavour to ascertain in what respect it fulfils, and in what it falls short of that standard of historical composition which the nineteenth century must apply. We hope to be misled into no unfairness in so doing. Our purpose is not that of applying an *ideal* standard which must necessarily dwarf all real performances. Nor do we intend to pursue the negative, and futile, method of applying an abstract and theoretic standard of our own which Macaulay could hardly be expected to come up to, for the simple reason that he could never have heard of it. We will try the honester, if less easy, plan of judging him by standards he himself acknowledges, by standards which the generality of his readers will accept.

History is a form of literature which has gone through many changes, and is still too far from anything like the definite settled condition which would admit of absolute dicta respecting it. Some regard it as a science, others as a ponderous mode of pamphleteering; some employ it for philosophical instruction, others for artistic representation; some to show how erudite they are, others to serve the party-questions of the day. Who is right? Are they all wrong? Time was when the present writer would have pronounced very decidedly on this matter; *fuit tempus!* and 'years which bring' (not always) 'the philosophic mind', have made him waver in those confident opinions, and feel that to set forth the full requirements and conditions of History, is not easier than to set forth the requirements and conditions of any other story. Indeed, if we consider it, History may justly subserve *any* purpose it is made to subserve. Why may not the pamphleteer employ it if he can? Why not the theologian, if he can? Why not the doctrinaire, if he can? Why not the antiquary, the scholar, the artist, if they can? History is the story of a nation's life. Like the story of a man's life it may be well told or ill-told, according to the talent and the temper of the narrator; we are not bound to read it, not bound to be amused by it; we may tell it better, if we will, and can; all that our criticism has to do in the matter is to pronounce whether it be good of its kind; whether its philosophy be sound, or shallow; its erudition honest, or sham; its temper truthful, or the reverse; and whether its 'stability of dates and punctuality of citation' would please critics like Dr Johnson. There is no absolute standard. No one can say: 'This is History, and this only.' He can only say: 'This History has such and such qualities.'

The only perfect History at present possible, or rather the only subjects which admit of treatment on rigidly defined principles, are Science and Philosophy; and a glance at what constitutes a History of Science may enable us to come to a distinct, if only approximative, conception of History in general. The history of a science would be that record of the successive stages of Speculation, Experiment, and Discovery through which the laws now forming the body of doctrine have been ascertained. It would include the failures and mistakes, the absurdities and guesses, of various thinkers; in a word, all the retarding causes, as well as the accelerating causes—the movement, the oscillation, and the final progress of each truth. Any art of presentation by which the writer could vividly set this story before us, would be legitimate means towards his end. He might be picturesque, anecdotical, discursive, reflective, polemical, anything but dull. His object being to make us follow the gradual development of true ideas amid the mass of absurdities, we may allow him to choose the method he thinks most suitable to achieve his object and not trouble him by reflections on the 'dignity of History', and so forth.

If this is an accurate conception of what the history of a science should be, it may help us to form a conception of what the history of a nation should be. What a body of doctrine is to Science that is Civilization to the Nation: the solid deposit left us by the retiring waves of Time. The real purpose of the grave historian, when writing history for history's sake, and not for the sake of some collateral purpose, is, and must be, to trace the story of the nation's growth, to select from the mass of records those typical incidents, grave or trifling, which, when skilfully marshalled in order, shall present, as in a panorama, the successive stages of social and political development through which the nation passed in its progress towards those final results civilization had reached at the period when the historian ceases. He must set forth the hopes and the despairs, the wild schemes and sullen acquiescences, the terrible moments of enthusiam and the still more terrible moments of lassitude, the heroisms and the infamies, which acted as accelerating and retarding causes of the movement, of the oscillating sweep, and the final advance in the direction of progress; *how* he must set them forth, criticism dare not prescribe; it can only judge whether he has done so effectively or ineffectively.

Here then, without having recourse to any abstract ideal standard, we seem to have reached a point of view from which criticism may regard Macaulay. The first question to be asked is—Has he told the story of the

Nation's growth? Has he written History for History's sake, or made History subservient to purposes of momentary influence, or of personal display? The answer cannot be dubious. He has written History, and written it worthily. He has traced for us the various episodes through which moves the story of our English civilization, and he has done so with a fulness of detail and general impartiality such as no predecessor has equalled. What shortcomings, both in matter and manner, a severe scrutiny may detect, will be of quite minor importance beside the general excellence of his work. Let them be stated with all frankness; let him be corrected even to his commas; but do not let us in our critical pride forget the good service he has done. Critics are apt to be very intolerant, and, in their haste to give prominence to errors they detect, forget that the substantial excellence of a book is the test alone by which it can live, the test alone by which it ought fairly to be estimated. The crime of mistaking a date, and declaring A to be the second cousin of B, when 'every well informed student knows' that he was only B's cousin by marriage, is, after all, a crime for which exile is scarcely the proper punishment. A minister may have pimples on his face, and yet serve his country efficiently. It would be better for him, and pleasanter for his associates, if his face were wholesome and radiant; but pimples will not hinder his work, and it is the work he does for which we are to be grateful.

Among the broad palpable excellences of Macaulay's History we reckon the emphatic lesson it presents implicitly in every chapter, and explicitly in many a sentence, of the slow but steady progress which England has made in moral, social, and political life. Better than pages of elegant declamation is the silent but irresistible force of historical demonstration. The growth is vividly depicted; the facts are irresistibly eloquent. Carlyle and Kingsley, the Puseyites, and the young gentlemen of a mediaeval turn, who vapour about the degeneracy of our age, the decay of public spirit, and the greatness of our ancestors, may have served a good purpose, inasmuch as they opposed the senseless declamation of men equally one-sided, and always clamorous on the claims of 'our wondrous mother-age', as if earnestness, honesty, and desire for progress had never been known before. But although useful as a corrective reaction, this idolatry of the past is essentially vicious in philosophy. It cannot withstand the confrontation of facts. In what were our ancestors superior to us? In health and physical strength? The simple fact of enormous decrease in the rate of mortality answers, No. If we live longer, it is because we live more wisely. In material prosperity, which results from a more complete subjugation of nature to our wants, no one pretends that we are not greatly superior: to deny material progress would be to deny the sun at noon. Does our inferiority lie in the moral life? And if so, where?

The declaimers whom we are now combating are forced to stake their arguments on the moral superiority of our ancestors, who, they affirm, were more earnest, more religious, more simple than we. What are all 'the steamships, and the railways, and the thoughts, which sway mankind?' What are our splendid cities, our palaces, our Birmingham and Sheffield produce, our Manchester goods, our cheap press, cheap clothes, and cheap conveyances; what our industrial triumphs, and our political freedom, but the poor prosperity of shopkeepers forgetful of their souls? Where is the martyr-spirit,—where is the heroism of our sturdy forefathers? Where is their deep religious earnestness, and their rude but homely virtues? We rot in wealth. Our prosperity is a fiction based upon a cheat. Our morality is commercial, obeying no law but that of the 'higgling of the market'. Our food is poisoned; our drugs are poisoned; our literature is poisoned; our religion is a mockery and pretence.

As long as declamation supplies the place of argument, he who is blessed with the stoutest lungs will generally prevail. But if one of these assertions comes to be tested, its ludicrous want of basis will be at once disclosed. To examine them *seriatim* would lead us far beyond our limits; we will content ourselves with a slight examination of only one, and for that purpose we will select the strongest and most generally accredited one, Religion. The devout earnestness of the Puritans and Covenanters, to which so many look back with a fondness which breeds a despair over our degeneracy, may be compared with the religious spirit of to-day. Every one must see that in this case we have chosen the point on which our antagonists are strongest. The Puritans were devout, showing the spirit of believers and martyrs, ready to sacrifice everything to the object they deemed sacred, and displaying the utmost alacrity in sacrificing everyone else. As no one gainsays the earnestness, sincerity, and heroism of the Puritans, we need occupy no space with circumstantial details. Let all that is claimed be granted to the full; what does it prove? A superficial glance at the England and Scotland of that period will detect one fact which our antagonists seem utterly to ignore, namely, that Puritans and Covenanters formed a small minority in a nation assuredly not blessed with heroic earnestness in religious matters. The sincere and devout formed an extremely small element in the indifferent mass. Even counting all who took up the garb of piety as belonging to the party, it was still a small one; and if intellectual scepticism was then far less frequent than it is in the nineteenth century, moral scepticism and indifference, as the times of the Restoration show, were abundant enough. Now, that which was certainly the case in the seventeenth century, and before it, namely, the existence of a sincere minority amid an indifferent majority, is unmistakeably the case in the nineteenth century; but with this difference:—the minority, although perhaps relatively less numerous, is absolutely far more numerous; it may be opposed by a greater mass of indifference and scepticism, but it consists of a far larger number of human souls, and its sincerity is not only as earnest as that of the Puritans, it is also more tempered by Christian spirit, more religious in all senses. To talk of heroism and marytrdom being extinct, in the presence of our missionaries wandering all over the globe; to talk of earnestness being extinct, in the presence of the deep and active influence of religious men and religious bodies, is the idlest disregard of palpable facts. Our sects, with their schisms, their bigotries, and their hypocrisies, may not seem so devout and so heroic to our eyes, as the Puritans and Covenanters seem through the gloaming of the past. But if earnest belief is to be taken as the sign of a higher moral condition, it cannot be denied that such earnestness is far more frequent in our day than it was in the sixteenth and seventeenth centuries; if there is less superstition there is assuredly more religion.

As a question of fact, and limiting it to the simple case of *earnestness* in belief, we assert that the present age exhibits decided progress; precisely because men are more moral, are they more in earnest. The intellectual propositions to which they assent may be different, but the earnestness with which they assent to, and try to work out, the propositions, is more common. That the standard of moral conduct is everywhere raised, scarcely admits of dispute. The chiefs of our parties, the heads of our churches, although not by any means realising the ideal we may form, would be utterly and for ever disgraced in every mind, if, in one weak moment, they consented to the basenesses which were of everyday occurrence in the reigns of Charles, James, and William. We talk, indeed, in lax railway talk, and in laxer leading articles, of ministers being in the 'pay of Russia', and 'conniving with our enemies'; but who seriously *believes* this? And if any idiot believes it, what miserable shred of evidence has ever appeared to justify the belief? Imagine such events as the Bloody Circuit or the massacre of Glencoe in our day! They belong to the nightmares of romance; no man can fairly realise them to his mind as truths. William Penn is probably held to be a more illustrious example of the Society of Friends than John Bright; and William Penn was one of the purest men of his day; yet no antagonist, in the most acrid moments of hustings oratory, would for one instant be betrayed into hinting that Bright's conduct could be stained with the infamy of Penn's. Macaulay shall here be laid under contribution for one of his striking and characteristic summaries of parliamentary corruption:–

The history of the rise, progress, and decline of parliamentary corruption in England still remains to be written. No subject has called forth a greater quantity of eloquent vituperation and stinging sarcasm. Three generations of serious and of sportive writers wept and laughed over the venality of the senate. That venality was denounced on the hustings, anathematised from the pulpit, and burlesqued on the stage; was attacked by Pope in brilliant verse, and by Bolingbroke in stately prose, by Swift with savage hatred, and by Gay with festive malice. The voices of Tories and Whigs, of Johnson and Akenside, of Smollett and Fielding, contributed to swell the cry. But none of those who railed or of those who jested took the trouble to verify the phenomena, or to trace them to the real causes.

Sometimes the evil was imputed to the depravity of a particular minister: but, when he had been driven from power, and when those who had most loudly accused him governed in his stead, it was found that the change of men had produced no change of system. Sometimes the evil was imputed to the degeneracy of the national character. Luxury and cupidity, it was said, had produced in our country the same effect which they had produced of old in the Roman republic. The modern Englishman was to the Englishman of the sixteenth century what Verres and Curio were to Dentatus and Fabricius. Those who held this language were as ignorant and shallow as people generally are who extol the past at the expense of the present. A man of sense would have perceived that, if the English of the time of George the Second had really been more sordid and dishonest than their forefathers, the deterioration would not have shown itself in one place alone. The progress of judicial venality and of official venality would have kept pace with the progress of parliamentary venality. But nothing is more certain than that, while the legislature was becoming more and more venal, the courts of law and the public offices were becoming purer and purer. The representatives of the people were undoubtedly more mercenary in the days of Hardwicke and Pelham than in the days of the Tudors. But the Chancellors of the Tudors took plate and jewels from suitors without scruple or shame; and Hardwicke would have committed for contempt any suitor who had dared to bring him a present. The Treasurers of the Tudors raised princely fortunes by the sales of places, titles, and pardons; and Pelham would have ordered his servants to turn out of his house any man who had offered him money for a peerage or a commissionership of customs. It is evident, therefore, that the prevalence of corruption in the Parliament cannot be ascribed to a general depravation of morals. The taint was local: we must look for some local cause; and such a cause will without difficulty be found.

Under our ancient sovereigns the House of Commons rarely interfered with the executive administration. The Speaker was charged not to let the members meddle with matters of State. If any gentleman was very troublesome he was cited before the Privy Council, interrogated, reprimanded, and sent to meditate on his undutiful conduct in the Tower. The Commons did their best to protect themselves by keeping their deliberations secret, by excluding strangers, by making it a crime to repeat out of doors what had passed within doors. But these precautions were of small avail. In so large an assembly there were always talebearers ready to carry the evil report of their brethren to the palace. To oppose the Court was therefore a service of serious danger. In those days, of course, there was little or no buying of votes. For an honest man was not to be bought; and it was much cheaper to intimidate or to coerce a knave than to buy him.

For a very different reason there has been no direct buying of votes within the memory of the present generation. The House of Commons is now supreme in the State, but is accountable to the nation. Even those members who are not chosen by large constituent bodies are kept in awe by public opinion. Everything is printed: everything is discussed: every material word uttered in debate is read by a million people on the morrow. Within a few hours after an important division, the lists of the majority and the minority are scanned and analysed in every town from Plymouth to Inverness. If a name be found where it ought not to be, the apostate is certain to be reminded in sharp language of the promises which he has broken and of the professions which he has belied. At present, therefore, the best way in which a government can secure the support of a majority of the representative body is by gaining the confidence of the nation.

But between the time when our Parliaments ceased to be controlled by royal prerogative and the time when they began to be constantly and effectually controlled by public opinion there was a long interval. After the Restoration, no government ventured to return to those methods by which, before the civil war, the freedom of deliberation had been restrained. A member could no longer be called to account for his harangues or his votes. He might obstruct the passing of bills of supply: he might arraign the whole foreign policy of the country; he might lay on the table articles of impeachment against all the chief ministers; and he ran not the smallest risk of being treated as Morrice had been treated by Elizabeth, or Eliot by Charles the First. The senator now stood in no awe of the Court. Nevertheless all the defences behind which the feeble Parliaments of the sixteenth century had entrenched themselves against the attacks of prerogative were not only still kept up, but were extended and strengthened. No politician seems to have been aware that these defences were no longer needed for their original purpose, and had begun to serve a purpose very different. The rules which had originally designed to secure faithful representatives against the displeasure of the sovereign, now operated to secure unfaithful representatives against the displeasure of the people, and proved much more effectual for the latter end than they had ever been for the former. It was natural, it was inevitable, that, in a legislative body emancipated from the restraints of the sixteenth century, and not yet subjected to the restraints of the nineteenth century, in a legislative body which feared neither the king nor the public, there should be corruption.

The plague spot began to be visible and palpable in the days of the Cabal. Clifford, the boldest and fiercest of the wicked Five, had the merit of discovering that a noisy patriot, whom it was no longer possible to send to prison, might be turned into a courtier by a goldsmith's note. Clifford's example was followed by his successors. It soon became a proverb that a Parliament resembled a pump. Often, the wits said, when a pump appears to be dry, if a very small quantity of water is poured in, a great quantity of water gushes out: and so, when a Parliament appears to be niggardly, ten thousand pounds judiciously given in bribes will often produce a million in supplies. The evil was not diminished, nay, it was aggravated, by that Revolution which freed our country from so many other evils. The House of Commons was now more powerful than ever as against the Crown, and yet was more strictly responsible than formerly to the nation. The Government had a new motive for buying the members; and the members had no new motive for refusing to sell themselves. William, indeed, had an aversion to bribery: he resolved to abstain from it; and, during the first year of his reign, he kept his resolution. Unhappily the events of that year did not encourage him to persevere in his good intentions. As soon as Caermarthen was placed at the head of the internal administration of the realm, a complete change took place. He was in truth no novice in the art of purchasing votes. He had, sixteen years before, succeeded Clifford at the Treasury, had inherited Clifford's tactics, had improved upon them, and had employed them to an extent which would have amazed the inventor. From the day on which Caermarthen was called a second time to the chief direction of affairs, parliamentary corruption continued to be practised, with scarcely any intermission, by a long succession of statesman, till the close of the American war. Neither of the great English parties can justly charge the other with any peculiar guilt on this account. The Tories were the first who introduced the system and the last who clung to it: but it attained its greatest vigour in the time of Whig ascendency. The extent to which parliamentary support was bartered for money cannot be with any precision ascertained. But it seems probable that the number of hirelings was greatly exaggerated by vulgar report, and was never large, though often sufficient to turn the scale on important divisions. An unprincipled minister eagerly accepted the services of these mercenaries. An honest minister reluctantly submitted, for the sake of the commonwealth, to what he considered as a shameful and odious extortion. But during many years every minister, whatever his personal character might be, consented, willingly or unwillingly, to manage the Parliament in the only way in which the Parliament could then be managed. (pp. 541-6)

The truth is, the whole moral nature of man has been elevated. He is less and less of an animal, more and more of a human being. The triumph of civilization is seen in the gradual predominance of the *moral* over the *animal* tendencies, t   sympathetic social instincts over the egoistic instincts; and this growth i   ntimately allied with industrial progress, enfranchisement from manual .abour, and the extension of conquest over physical resources. It is an error to isolate our progress, industrial and social, from our moral progress, as if manufacturers, steam-engines, and commerce could advance, without at the same time inducing a corresponding advance in intellectual and moral culture.

The progress which has been made in every department, industrial and moral, may be gathered from Macaulay's vivid narrative, of which, indeed, this may be called the ultimate aim. Such an aim was necessarily unthought of by ancient historians, for the conception of progress is modern. Even in the seventeenth century History had no other purpose, when its purpose was philosophic, than that of presenting a moral or religious lesson, such as we see in Bossuet's grand panorama, the *Discours sur l'Histoire Universelle*, written to prove the axiom—*l' homme s' agit, Dieu le mène*. History when not thus used, was only thought of as a repertory wherein erudition could discover political analogues, or the ancient forms of contemporary speculations. Pascal had, it is true, given utterance to that new and noble thought which connected the life of individuals and nations with the continuous life of Humanity; but no historian attempted to demonstrate the connexion. In the eighteenth century it was even worse with History. The eyes of men were fixed on the future; and the past, when not spoken of with contempt, was seldom studied in any philosophic spirit. The past was ransacked for examples of the tyranny of rulers and the villany of priests, for the crimes of the great and the superstitions of the many. If Greece and Rome, as the classic nations, were still revered, they were ill understood, and only prized as centres of liberty, of literature, and of art. A few potent voices were raised in favour of a nobler conception. Vico and Herder, Lessing and Condorcet, in ever-memorable accents, spoke of Humanity as one continuous life, of which History was the story; but they were not historians. Voltaire, Gibbon, and Hume are the three types of the epoch, and the three most illustrious historians; to all three such a conception of History as the one we are alluding to would have seemed no better than an idle play of fancy. It is probable, indeed, that Macaulay would side with them on this point. He is not what is called a philosophic historian, nor is he specially a philosophic thinker. We remember no passage in all his writings which would lead us to suppose that he had ever considered History in this light, and we could cite passages which imply the contrary. Let us not therefore palm upon him an intention which he might reject. Let us only note that he unconsciously submits to the influence of his age, and helps the spread of a doctrine which he has never perhaps seriously considered.

Another excellence in his volumes is the lesson they teach of the importance to a nation, no less than to an individual, of adhering conscientiously to justice. As an axiom, this is of commonplace vulgarity. No one disputes the abstract truth of the proposition that 'It is wiser, as well as ʒ̃ 𝑒𝑡̃ler, to forego seeming advantages when they can only be purchased b̧ ː ː violation of justice'. Yet, in the conduct of both men and of masses, the axiom is incessantly disregarded. This history is full of striking examples both of the evils which follow the neglect, and the advantages which follow the observance of the principle. And if England is greater than any other nation, her greatness can be shown to arise from the simple fact, that in the great crises of her history she has adhered more to justice, and obeyed more implicitly the established law, than any other nation. The respect with which Englishmen surround and sanctify Law lies in the best part of their character. It has often been a source of ludicrous folly and serious obstruction. It generates an adherence to the letter, which every on-looker can perceive to be a direct violation of the spirit; and thus injustice is perpetrated out of the very bigotry of justice. But the fault implies a virtue. The bigotry is belief run to seed. Better that notorious malefactors should escape through a rigid adherence to the letter of the law, than that the law itself should be made elastic to suit the interpretations of the moment. Tennyson has finely said of England that it is the land—

> Where freedom broadens slowly down
> From precedent to precedent.[43]

We may laugh, or we may sneer, at the ludicrous formality which adheres so religiously to precedent, but we cannot shut our eyes to the fact that Freedom *does* broaden slowly down, and if slowly, with a certain constancy of progress not visible in other nations. Macaulay abounds in illustrations. We will quote only one, and that shall be a ludicrous instance. When Schomberg, about to set out for Ireland, expressed his gratitude to the House of Commons for the munificent reward given to his services, Macaulay observes:–

> The precedent set on this interesting occasion was followed with the utmost minuteness, a hundred and twenty-five years later, on an occasion more interesting still. Exactly on the same spot on which, in July, 1689, Schomberg had acknowledged the liberality of the nation, a chair was set, in July, 1814, for a still more illustrious warrior, who came to return thanks for a still more splendid mark of public gratitude. Few things illustrate more strikingly the peculiar character of the English government and people than the circumstance that the House of Commons, a popular assembly, should, even in a moment of joyous enthusiasm, have adhered to ancient forms with the punctilious accuracy of a College of Heralds; that the sitting and rising, the covering and the uncovering, should have been regulated by exactly the same etiquette in the nineteenth century as in the seventeenth; and that the same mace which had been held at the right hand of Schomberg should have been held in the same position at the right hand of Wellington. (Vol. iii, p. 414)

Passing from generalities to particulars, we have now to inquire how Macaulay has accomplished the task which he has undertaken. That he has accomplished it with a success such as no other historian of England ever approached, is the general verdict every impartial reader will pronounce. That he has a rare combination of faculties peculiarly suited to such a task, and has employed those faculties conscientiously, even loud detractors will admit. Whatever faults they may espy, and whatever emphasis they may give to their blame, they cannot point to any work which better fulfils their requirements, or which deserves to be preferred to it as a narrative of English History. Or course the reader does not expect to find the work free from faults, nor expect that the critics should pass faults over. Let every latitude be given to criticism, so that recognition be generously given to merits which the work displays.

Some seven years ago[44] we attempted in this journal to sketch the characteristics of Macaulay's mind, with such estimate of his excellences and defects as we had been able to arrive at. If we may venture to refer the readers to that article it will save us from many pages of repetition, for our opinions have not altered since that article was written; and the space at our disposal may be more fitly occupied with some illustrations of the manner in which Macaulay writes History.

That he has made History even more attractive than a three volume novel, is, in our eyes, no crime at all, but an eminent virtue. We have but a quite mediocre admiration of the 'dignity of History'. Life itself is careless of such dignity, and no story is called upon to be more magnificant than the life it depicts. The first object is to tell the story truly; the second is to tell it so that men shall read and remember it. Macaulay has told it as truly as he could, and as effectively. He has not spared pains, nor has he wanted talent. If he does not always represent characters and actions with that fidelity which commands assent, the fault lies in the deficiencies of his materials or the peculiarities of his intellect, never in any negligence of research, never in any disregard of truth. He does not lie, even for the Whigs. He often falsifies for the sake of effect, but this is a transparent falsification which can deceive no careful reader. Words have sometimes to him the force of things; an antithesis coerces his mind, and prevents its perceiving anything beyond the points juxtaposed. We may say of him what Johnson said of Shakespeare's fondness for conceits—'Antithesis was the Cleopatra for which he lost the world, and was content to lose it.' This antithesis is often a very powerful artifice of rhetoric: it clenches a sentence, and assists the memory in retaining an idea; but it becomes fatiguing, as every artifice does, when prodigally employed; and to the writer it is a snare. Just as the ruling desire to preserve the dignity of History caused his predecessors to eliminate from their narrative all those details to which no dignity could be lent, so does the ruling desire to cast History in the mould of antithesis cause Macaulay to pass over the inconvenient facts, which would disturb, and often destroy the symmetry of a sentence, and the startling effect of unforeseen juxtaposition. Among the very

best and most characteristic specimens of Macaulay's use of this artifice is
the following passage, which occurs after the description of the battle of
Landen:–

> Never, perhaps, was the change which the progress of civilization has
> produced in the art of war more strikingly illustrated than on that day.
> Ajax beating down the Trojan leader with a rock which two ordinary
> men could scarcely lift, Horatius defending the bridge against an army,
> Richard the Lionhearted spurring along the whole Saracen line without
> finding an enemy to stand his assault, Robert Bruce crushing with one
> blow the helmet and head of Sir Henry Bohun in sight of the whole
> array of England and Scotland, such are the heroes of a dark age. In
> such an age bodily vigour is the most indispensable qualification of a
> warrior. At Landen, two poor sickly beings, who, in a rude state of
> society, would have been regarded as too puny to bear any part in
> combats, were the souls of two great armies. In some heathen countries
> they would have been exposed while infants. In Christendom they
> would, six hundred years earlier, have been sent to some quiet cloister.
> But their lot had fallen on a time when men had discovered that the
> strength of the muscles is far inferior in value to the strength of the
> mind. It is probable that, among the hundred and twenty thousand
> soldiers what were marshalled round Neerwinden under all the stand-
> ards of Western Europe, the two feeblest in body were the
> hunchbacked dwarf who urged forward the fiery onset of France, and
> the asthmatic skeleton who covered the slow retreat of England. (Vol.
> iv, pp. 409-10)

With what a glow he must have written the last sentence. The germ of the
whole passage is an antithesis, and it bursts into a flower at the close.

Among the worst cases are those in which *character* is sacrificed to
antithesis. Indeed, if we are to speak frankly on this point, we must declare
that we cannot echo the general applause of Macaulay's powers of portrait-
painting. His portraits, in our eyes, have, all of them, two fundamental
faults—they are neither true as portraits of the individuals, nor true as
portraits of human beings. We sometimes see hanging on the walls of the
Academy 'a portrait of a gentleman', which is the portrait of no living being,
and yet has a certain superficial linear resemblance to the Mr Smith who sat
for it. There are portraits such as Titian's 'Young Man with a Glove', in the
Louvre, which may be very unlike the men they represent (at any rate, we
have no means of ascertaining the closeness of the resemblance), but which
nevertheless speak irresistibly to all spectators as marvellous representations
of human beings. The bad painter may succeed in fixing on his canvas with
great accuracy Mr Smith's Roman nose and faltering chin; he may copy the
mole with some exactness, and indicate the cut of the whisker to perfection;

but we all resolutely aver that the portrait is *not* of a man, and consequently only a linear likeness of Mr Smith. The fine painter may have been careless in hitting off such linear details, but we feel that he has represented the man. Macaulay, to our apprehensions, fails in both these merits. He paints by means of sentence and antithesis, which fall agreeably on the ear, but either call up no image to the mind, or call up one which is a caricature of human nature. Sometimes they are trivial in their vagueness, sometimes ludicrous in their exaggeration. We are constantly informed that a man's temper was bland, his manners engaging, his diction elegant, his private life vicious, and his principles lax; and not only are these phrases vague, but in nine cases out of ten they are wholly superfluous; since, whether the person's diction were elegant or clumsy, and his temper bland or vehement, the scenes in which he figures as an actor would in nowise have been varied. But vagueness is the least of Macaulay's sins in portrait-painting, and exaggeration is the greatest. He paints in black and white: he cares nothing for intermediate shades. He paints by antithesis, without any apparent recognition of the excessive complexity of character, and without any of the philosopher's or the poet's delight in unravelling and depicting these complexities. He is a rhetorician; and rhetoric delights in startling contrasts, clear definite points which carry the easy conviction of the audience, because they present no perplexities. Hence it is that we see him pounce upon an apparent contradiction with an eagerness which expresses itself in ingenious terms, and which serves to increase instead of to resolve the contradiction. This defect was noticed at some length in the article to which reference has already been made; and we must notice it again in speaking of the characters presented in this history. Our limits do not permit an examination of these portraits, which we leave to the leisure of the reader, contenting ourselves with the remark that James, William, and Marlborough—the three leading figures—by no means impress us with a sense of *vraisemblance*; we refer our readers for a further illustration to his description of Lord Wharton (Vol. iv, pp. 456-60); the passage is too long for extract.

Honest Tom had assuredly his faults; but even his own party would not have called him Honest Tom had he been the man Macaulay paints. He had probably a religion of his own, which made him contemptuous towards the religion of his family. His devotion to a political party, which Macaulay represents as purely disinterested, suggests an integrity of character which renders perfectly ludicrous the antithesis that 'the falsest of mankind in all relations but one, he was the truest of Whigs'. Of this portrait of Lord Wharton we simply assert that, on the face of it, it is a caricature.

His remarks on character are often so trite as to excite surprise, and sometimes so superficial that only the haste of composition could excuse them. We will cite but two examples, for we wish rather to indicate than to dwell on the points which criticism will note in these volumes. Of Montague he says: 'It is a remarkable proof of his self-knowledge that, from the moment at which he began to distinguish himself in public life, he ceased to be a versifier.' If no proof more remarkable than that existed, Montague's reputation would scarcely have descended to our days. Had he persisted in writing bad verses, *invita Minerva*, after a great public career was opened to him; had neglected the work in which his power was recognised, for the scribbling which even friends could not warmly praise, we might perhaps have called *that* a proof of his wanting self- knowledge; but his neglect of a feeble talent when opportunities incessantly claimed all his power, is the sort of self-knowledge exhibited every year by thousands of bad poets who become good citizens and efficient common-councilmen, who make fortunes or reputations in other regions, leaving Parnassus to all who covet the laurel with intenser desire.

The Duke of Devonshire, when the Lords were discussing the question of Fenwick's attainder, had voted against Fenwick, hoping that fear would induce Fenwick to make a frank confession; but when the hope was at an end, the Duke refused to go further: the question being, whether a man should be put to death by an Act of Parliament, Devonshire said that he must answer, 'Not content'. Upon this Macaulay remarks: 'It is not easy to understand on what principle he can have thought himself justified in threatening to do what he did not think himself justified in doing.' As Macaulay finds something not easy to understand in this, we must presume there is a difficulty; but to our minds the great difficulty is to conceive *what* he considers to be difficult in the matter.

The triteness of many remarks is less disagreeable, because less obtrusive, than the elaboration with which he delights through several pages to demonstrate a truism. Whenever he says 'the reason of this is obvious', and he says it frequently, be sure that you are about to undergo several paragraphs of illustration and argument, meant to *prove* the obvious. We have learned where to skip by this signal. As a single specimen of this kind of moralising take the following:–

The enthusiasm with which the men of all classes had welcomed William to London at Christmas had greatly abated before the close of February. The new king had, at the very moment at which his fame and fortune reached the highest point, predicted the coming reaction. That reaction might, indeed, have been predicted by a less sagacious observer of human affairs. For it is to be chiefly ascribed to a law as certain as the laws which regulate the succession of the seasons and the course of the trade winds. It is the nature of man to overrate present evil, and to underrate present good; to long for what he has not, and to be dissatisfied with what he has. This propensity, as it appears in individuals, has often been noticed both by laughing and weeping philosophers. It was a favourite theme of Horace and of Pascal, of Voltaire and of Johnson. To its influence on the fate of great communities may be ascribed most of the revolutions and counter-revolutions recorded in history. A hundred generations have elapsed since the first great national emancipation, of which an account has come down to us. We read in the most ancient of books that a people bowed to the dust under a cruel yoke, scourged to toil by hard taskmasters, not supplied with straw, yet compelled to furnish the daily tale of bricks, became sick of life, and raised such a cry of misery as pierced the heavens. The slaves were wonderfully set free: at the moment of their liberation they raised a song of gratitude and triumph: but, in a few hours, they began to regret their slavery, and to murmur against the leader who had decoyed them away from the savoury fare of the house of bondage to the dreary waste which still separated them from the land flowing with milk and honey. Since that time the history of every great deliverer has been the history of Moses retold. Down to the present hour rejoicings like those on the shore of the Red Sea have ever been speedily followed by murmurings like those at the Waters of Strife. The most just and salutary revolution must produce much suffering. The most just and salutary revolution cannot produce all the good that had been expected from it by men of uninstructed minds and sanguine tempers. Even the wisest cannot, while it is still recent, weigh quite fairly the evils which it has caused against the evils which it has removed. For the evils which it has caused are felt; and the evils which it has removed are felt no longer. (Vol. iii, pp. 5-7)

Pages 411 to 450 are devoted to a recapitulation of those arguments for and against non-resistance which he never seems tired of repeating, but which we are excessively tired of skipping. Indeed, a not very fastidious pen might strike out so many pages of mere surplusage from these volumes, that their bulk would be sensibly decreased, and the reader much benefited.

While we are thus finding fault in detail with a work which, on the whole, we greatly admire, let us not omit to allude to the many brilliant and specious passages which captivate the unwary and astonish the few. The best example for the historian we can think of at this moment, is the much quoted passage about the scenery of the Highlands. It is eminently characteristic:–

It is not easy for a modern Englishman, who can pass in a day from his club in St James's-street to his shooting-box among the Grampians, and who finds in his shooting-box all the comforts and luxuries of his club, to believe that, in the time of his greatgrandfathers, St James's-street had as little connection with the Grampians as with the Andes. Yet so it was. In the south of our island scarcely anything was known about the Celtic part of Scotland; and what was known excited no feeling but contempt and loathing. The crags and the glens, the woods and the waters, were indeed the same that now swarm every autumn with admiring gazers and sketchers. The Trosachs wound as now between gigantic walls of rock tapestried with broom and wild roses: Foyers came headlong down through the birchwood with the same leap and the same roar with which he still rushes to Loch Ness; and, in defiance of the sun of June, the snowy scalp of Ben Cruachan rose, as it still rises, over the willowy islets of Loch Awe. Yet none of these sights had power, till a recent period, to attract a single poet or painter from more opulent and more tranquil regions. Indeed, law and police, trade and industry, have done far more than people of romantic dispositions will readily admit, to develop in our minds a sense of the wilder beauties of nature. A traveller must be freed from all apprehension of being murdered or starved before he can be charmed by the bold outlines and rich tints of the hills. He is not likely to be thrown into ecstasies by the abruptness of a precipice from which he is in imminent danger of falling two thousand feet perpendicular; by the boiling waves of a torrent which suddenly whirls away his baggage and forces him to run for his life; by the gloomy grandeur of a pass where he finds a corpse which marauders have just stripped and mangled; or by the screams of those eagles whose next meal may probably be on his own eyes. About the year 1730, Captain Burt, one of the first Englishmen who caught a glimpse of the spots which now allure tourists from every part of the civilised world, wrote an account of his wanderings. He was evidently a man of a quick, an observant, and a cultivated mind, and would doubtless, had he lived in our age, have looked with mingled awe and delight on the mountains of Inverness-shire. But, writing with the feeling which was universal in his own age, he pronounced those mountains monstrous excrescences. Their deformity, he said, was such that the most sterile plains seemed lovely by comparison. Fine weather, he complained, only made bad worse; for, the clearer the day, the more disagreeably did those misshapen masses of gloomy brown and dirty purple affect the eye. What a contrast, he exclaimed, between these horrible prospects and the beauties of Richmond Hill! Some persons may think that Burt was a man of vulgar and prosaical mind: but they will scarcely venture to pass a similar judgment on Oliver Goldsmith. Goldsmith was one of the very few Saxons who, more than a century ago, ventured to explore the Highlands. He was disgusted by the hideous wilderness, and declared that he greatly preferred the charming country round Leyden, the vast expanse of verdant meadow, and the villas with their statues and grottoes, trim flower beds, and rectilinear avenues. Yet it is difficult to believe that the author of the *Traveller* and of the *Deserted Village* was naturally inferior in taste and sensibility to the thousands of clerks and milliners who are now thrown into raptures by the sight of Loch Katrine and Loch Lomond. His feelings may easily be explained. It was not till roads had been cut out of the rocks, till bridges had been flung over the courses of the rivulets, till inns had succeeded to dens of robbers, till there was as little danger of being slain or plundered in the wildest defile of Badenoch or Lochaber as in Cornhill, that strangers could be enchanted by the blue dimples of the lakes and by the rainbows which overhung the waterfalls, and could derive a solemn pleasure even from the clouds and tempests which lowered on the mountain tops. (Vol. iii, pp. 300-2)

With what gusto he must have brought Goldsmith into contrast with the thousands of clerks and milliners! Yet if he had meditated the passage a little longer, we believe he would have seen a fallacy running through his argument. It is a fact that the feeling with which scenery affects most persons of sensibility in our day is a modern development. But this feeling had quite another origin than the mere sense of security. It belongs to the history of culture. The Greeks knew it not; the Romans never thought of scenery as a predominant poetical element; the great Italians, much as they may have loved the Alps, never went into modern raptures about them. French literature was dead to all scenic influences until Rousseau came to open that inexhaustible source. This is no place to write the history of the development, but we can answer Macaulay with a very simple reference to fact. He maintains that the traveller must be freed from apprehension before he can be charmed by bold outlines and rich hints of the hills. The traveller in Spain and Albania,—not to mention the more venturous excursions into Central Africa and so forth—is every day and night in very great apprehension of being robbed or murdered; does he not enjoy the beauty of the scenes through which he ventures? and will not his enjoyment of the Trosachs be proportionately less, than of any similar scene *away* from the improvements of civilization? We will not answer for the clerks and milliners, who may perhaps prefer Ben Lomond to Monte Rosa because it is reached with more ease, with less expense, and calls for no greater linguistic accomplishment than understanding broad vowels and monotonous intonations. But every real lover of scenery will confess, that the less it reminds him of law, police, and industry, the stronger the thrill it produces in him. The great master of poetical scenery, William Wordsworth, was so far from Macaulay's way of thinking on this point, that the project of 'vulgarizing' the lake scenery by bringing a railway into its neighbourhood, drew from him a very indignant, though not very wise, sonnet.

The style of these volumes strikes us as less finished than Macaulay's previous writings. It has the old excellences, but the old defects are even more apparent, and the diction is sometimes negligent to a fault. The trick of iteration is carried beyond the needs of clearness into wearisome tautology. Something of his influence on the mass of readers springs from a peculiarity which is the cause of many weak passages, namely, the care with which he elaborates a sentence, the sort of framing and glazing he gives to every little picture. The image which another writer, if he used it at all, would be content to place in the middle of a passage, there to contribute to the general effect, Macaulay throws into relief, gives it one, two, or three sentences to itself, frames and glazes it, and forces the reader to contemplate it for some moments. By this means an economical writer will produce more effect than the prodigal who casts his illustrations into the current of his text; and Macaulay is at once prodigal in illustration and economical in his method of distribution. He has a large account open at his bankers, yet makes every farthing purchase its full value. Two examples of this style may be cited, which will be read with interest by all critics. At the close of the justly celebrated chapter on Manners, there is an allusion to the tendency of men to be dissatisfied with the present, and to look lovingly back on the past, or hopingly forward to the future.

> In truth, [he adds] we are under a deception similar to that which misleads the traveller in the Arabian desert. Beneath the caravan all is dry and bare; but far in advance, and far in the rear, is the semblance of refreshing waters. The pilgrims hasten forward, and find nothing but sand where, an hour before, they had seen a lake. They turn their eyes, and see a lake, where, an hour before, they were toiling through the sand.

We have always considered this as one of the most characteristic specimens of Macaulay's happiest style. Nothing can be more common-place than the comparison; few good writers would venture to employ again so well-worn an ornament; and, if they did venture, would do so parenthetically, and say,—'the illusion of the past and future is like the mirage seen in the desert',—whereby the whole effect would be lost. But Macaulay takes the old image, pictures it to his mind, and paints it for the reader. He makes as much of the old comparison as if it were a novelty of his own. He frames and glazes it; the reader is detained, and made to admire.

Our second example is equally characteristic, but not equally felicitous; the comparison is old, and is not improved by the framing and glazing process:–

> It has long been usual to represent the imagination under the figure of a wing, and to call the successful exertions of the imagination flights. One poet is the eagle: another is the swan: a third modestly compares himself to the bee. But none of these types would have suited Montague. His genius may be compared to that pinion which, though it is too weak to lift the ostrich into the air, enables her, while she remains on the earth, to outrun hound, horse, and dromedary. If the man who possesses this kind of genius attempts to ascend the heaven of inven-

tion, his awkward and unsuccessful efforts expose him to derision. But if he will be content to stay in the terrestrial region of business, he will find that the faculties which would not enable him to soar into a higher sphere will enable him to distance all his competitors in the lower. (Vol. iv, p. 453)

Nevertheless, make what deductions you will, it becomes evident that a writer who thus elaborates his illustrations must produce a great effect on the mass of readers. He saves all effort of imagination. He prevents our hurrying past a picture with a careless casual glance. He detains us before it, not long enough to weary us, but long enough to let us see what in our haste we might possibly overlook. If 'True wit is Nature to advantage drest, Oft thought before, yet n'er so well expressed', Macaulay is the truest of wits, for he expresses what every one has thought, expresses it better than anyone else, and rarely attempts to think what no one has thought before him.

Even critics fastidious in style must cordially admire the breadth, clearness, rapidity, and picturesqueness of his expositions. As a specimen of his manner at once rapid and picturesque, read this brief passage describing the Irish when they rose at the call of Tyrconnel.

Never in modern Europe has there been such a rising up of a whole people. The habits of the Celtic peasant were such that he made no sacrifice in quitting his potatoe ground for the camp. He loved excitement and adventure. He feared work far more than danger. His national and religious feelings had, during three years, been exasperated by the constant application of stimulants. At every fair and market he had heard that a good time was at hand, that the tyrants who spoke Saxon and lived in slated houses were about to be swept away, and that the land would again belong to its own children. By the peat fires of a hundred thousand cabins had nightly been sung rude ballads which predicted the deliverance of the oppressed race. The priests, most of whom belonged to those old families which the Act of Settlement had ruined, but which were still revered by the native population, had, from a thousand altars, charged every Catholic to show his zeal for the true Church by providing weapons against the day when it might be necessary to try the chances of battle in her cause. (Vol. iii, pp. 154-5)

Or we might quote the whole of the massacre of Glencoe did not space fail us. Here is one passage:–

In the Gaelic tongue Glencoe signifies the Glen of Weeping; and in truth that pass is the most dreary and melancholy of all the Scottish passes, the very Valley of the Shadow of Death. Mists and storms brood over it through the greater part of the finest summer; and even on those rare days when the sun is bright, and when there is no cloud in the sky, the impression made by the landscape is sad and awful. The path lies along a stream which issues from the most sullen and gloomy of mountain pools. Huge precipices of naked stone frown on both sides. Even in July the streaks of snow may often be discerned in the rifts near the summits. All down the sides of the crags heaps of ruin mark the headlong paths of the torrents. Mile after mile the traveller looks in vain for the smoke of one hut, for one human form wrapped in a plaid, and listens in vain for the bark of a shepherd's dog or the bleat of a lamb. Mile after mile the only sound that indicates life is the faint cry of a bird of prey from some storm-beaten pinnacle of rock. The progress of civilisation, which has turned so many wastes into fields yellow with harvests or gay with apple blossoms, has only made Glencoe more desolate. All the science and industry of a peaceful age can extract nothing valuable from that wilderness: but, in an age of violence and rapine, the wilderness itself was valued on account of the shelter which it afforded to the plunderer and his plunder. Nothing could be more natural than that the clan to which this rugged desert belonged should have been noted for predatory habits. For, among the Highlanders generally, to rob was thought at least as honourable an employment as to cultivate the soil; and, of all the Highlanders, the Macdonalds of Glencoe had the least productive soil, and the most convenient and secure den of robbers. (Vol. iv, pp. 191-2)

How admirable the details, and how artfully introduced!

One noticeable characteristic of this history is the marvellous care with which it has been composed. The historian never flags. He has no passages which betray a weary pen. If the language is sometimes careless, the matter has always been arranged with care. All the documents have been consulted; the distribution of the matter has been duly considered. Even episodical details are treated as if they were of primary importance; a digression is an essay; a sketch is not sketchily touched; if the pages occupied are few, we see that the learning employed has been exhausted. Macaulay 'paints out' every corner of his picture; he does not 'scumble in'. The knowledge implied and employed in these volumes is equal to that of Gibbon, and surpasses that of every other historian with whom we are acquainted. Inconsiderate people grumble at the enormous space devoted to the transactions of only eight years. We may safely assert that many of these very people would have grumbled at his omissions, if he had told the story in less detail. For our own parts, we confess that nothing would so much have pleased us as a History of England told with the spirit and brevity of his preliminary sketch; but since his purpose was quite different, since he meant to tell his story in detail, we cannot venture to blame him for doing thoroughly what he sat down to do.

Although never professing to write the 'philosophy of history', Macaulay tells his story too thoroughly not to furnish the philosopher with ample material. A great deal of healthy political wisdom may be drawn from his pages; seldom in the way of direct inculcation, generally implied in the very tone of his narrative. A good example, from many, may be cited, because its practical application is still not quite obsolete:–

Some weak men had imagined that religion and morality stood in need of the protection of the licenser. The event signally proved that they were in error. In truth the censorship has scarcely put any restraint on licentiousness or profaneness. The *Paradise Lost* had narrowly escaped mutilation: for the *Paradise Lost* was the work of a man whose politics were hateful to the ruling powers. But Etherege's *She Would If She Could*, Wycherley's *Country Wife*, Dryden's *Translations from the Fourth Book of Lucretius*, obtained the Imprimatur without difficulty: for Dryden, Etherege, and Wycherley were courtiers. From the day on which the emancipation of our literature was accomplished, the purification of our literature began. That purification was effected, not by the intervention of senates or magistrates, but by the opinion of the great body of educated Englishmen, before whom good and evil were set, and who were left free to make their choice. During a hundred and sixty years the liberty of our press has been constantly becoming more and more entire; and during those hundred and sixty years the restraint imposed on writers by the general feeling of readers has been constantly becoming more and more strict. At length even that class of works in which it was formerly thought that a voluptuous imagination was privileged to disport itself, love songs, comedies, novels, have become more decorous than the sermons of the seventeenth century. At this day foreigners, who dare not print a word reflecting on the government under which they live, are at a loss to understand how it happens that the freest press in Europe is the most prudish. (Vol. iv, pp. 606-7)

In another way, and as a hint to legislators, we may quote the remarks with which he concludes his account of the passing of the Mutiny Bill:–

Thus was made, without one dissentient voice in Parliament, without one murmur in the nation, the first step towards a change which had become necessary to the safety of the State, yet which every party in the State then regarded with extreme dread and aversion. Six months passed; and still the public danger continued. The power necessary to the maintenance of military discipline was a second time entrusted to the crown for a short term. The trust again expired, and was again renewed. By slow degrees familiarity reconciled the public mind to the names, once so odious, of standing army and court martial. It was proved by experience that, in a well constituted society, professional soldiers may be terrible to a foreign enemy, and yet submissive to the civil power. What had been at first tolerated as the exception began to be considered as the rule. Not a session passed without a Mutiny Bill. When at length it became evident that a political change of the highest importance was taking place in such a manner as almost to escape notice, a clamour was raised by some factious men desirous to weaken the hands of the Government, and by some respectable men who felt an honest but injudicious reverence for every old constitutional tradition, and who were unable to understand that what at one stage in the progress of society is pernicious may at another stage be indispensable. This clamour, however, as years rolled on, became fainter and fainter. The debate which recurred every spring on the Mutiny Bill came to be regarded merely as an occasion on which hopeful young orators fresh from Christchurch were to deliver maiden speeches, setting forth how the guards of Pisistratus seized the citadel of Athens, and how the Praetorian cohorts sold the Roman empire to Didius. At length these declamations became too ridiculous to be repeated. The most old-fashioned, the most eccentric, politician could hardly, in the reign of George the Third, contend that there ought to be no regular soldiers, or that the ordinary law, administered by the ordinary courts, would effectually maintain discipline among such soldiers. All parties being agreed as to the general principle, a long succession of Mutiny Bills passed without any discussion, except when some particular article of the military code appeared to require amendment. It is perhaps because the army became thus gradually, and almost imperceptibly, one of the institutions of England, that it has acted in such perfect harmony with all her other institutions, has never once, during a hundred and sixty years, been untrue to the throne or disobedient to the law, has never once defied the tribunals or overawed the constituent bodies. To this day, however, the Estates of the Realm continue to set up periodically, with laudable jealousy, a landmark on the frontier which was traced at the time of the Revolution. They solemnly reassert every year the doctrine laid down in the Declaration of Rights; and they then grant to the sovereign an extraordinary power to govern a certain number of soldiers according to certain rules during twelve months more. (Vol. iii, pp. 46-7)

The rise of the national debt is another example:

During the interval between the Restoration and the Revolution the riches of the nation had been rapidly increasing. Thousands of busy men found every Christmas that, after the expenses of the year's house-keeping had been defrayed out of the year's income, a surplus remained; and how that surplus was to be employed was a question of some difficulty. In our time, to invest such a surplus, at something more than three per cent., on the best security that has ever been known in the world, is the work of a few minutes. But in the seventeenth century a lawyer, a physician, a retired merchant, who had saved some thousands and who wished to place them safely and profitably, was often greatly embarrassed. Three generations earlier, a man who had accumulated wealth in a profession generally purchased real property or lent his savings on mortgage. But the number of acres in the kingdom had remained the same; and the value of those acres, though it had greatly increased, had by no means increased so fast as the quantity of capital which was seeking for employment. Many too wished to put their money where they could find it at an hour's notice, and looked about for some species of property which could be more readily transferred than a house or a field. A capitalist might lend on bottomry or on personal security: but, if he did so, he ran a great risk of losing interest and principal. There were a few joint stock companies, among which the East India Company held the foremost place: but the demand for the stock of such companies was far greater than the supply. Indeed the cry for a new East India Company was chiefly raised by persons who had found difficulty in placing their savings at interest on good security. So great was that difficulty that the practice of hoarding was common. We are told that the father of Pope the poet, who retired from business in the City about the time of the Revolution, carried to a retreat in the country a strong box containing near twenty thousand pounds, and took out from time to time what was required for household expenses; and it is highly probable that this was not a solitary case. At present the quantity of coin which is hoarded by private persons is so small what it would, if brought forth, make no perceptible addition to the circulation. But, in the earlier part of the reign of William the Third, all the greatest writers on currency were of opinion that a very considerable mass of gold and silver was hidden in secret drawers and behind wainscots.

The natural effect of this state of things was that a crowd of projectors, ingenious and absurd, honest and knavish, employed themselves in devising new schemes for the employment of redundant capital. It was about the year 1688 that the world stockjobber was first heard in London. In the short space of four years a crowd of companies, every one of which confidently held out to subscribers the hope of immense gains, sprang into existence: the Insurance Company, the Paper Company, the Lutestring Company, the Pearl Fishery Company, the Glass Bottle Company, the Alum Company, the Blythe Coal Company, the Swordblade Company. There was a Tapestry Company which would soon furnish pretty hangings for all the parlours of the

middle class and for all the bedchambers of the higher. There was a
Copper Company which proposed to explore the mines of England,
and held out a hope that they would prove not less valuable than those
of Potosi. There was a Diving Company which undertook to bring up
precious effects from shipwrecked vessels, and which announced that
it had laid in a stock of wonderful machines resembling complete suits
of armour. In front of the helmet was a huge glass eye like that of a
cyclop; and out of the crest went a pipe through which the air was to
be admitted. The whole process was exhibited on the Thames. Fine
gentlemen and fine ladies were invited to the show, were hospitably
regaled, and were delighted by seeing the divers in their panoply
descend into the river and return laden with old iron and ship's tackle.
There was a Greenland Fishing Company which could not fail to drive
the Dutch whalers and herring busses out of the Northern Ocean. There
was a Tanning Company which promised to furnish leather superior
to the best that was brought from Turkey or Russia. There was a society
which undertook the office of giving gentlemen a liberal education on
low terms, and which assumed the sounding name of the Royal
Academies Company. In a pompous advertisement it was announced
that the directors of the Royal Academies Company had engaged the
best masters in every branch of knowledge, and were about to issue
twenty thousand tickets at twenty shillings each. There was to be a
lottery: two thousand prizes were to be drawn; and the fortunate
holders of the prizes were to be taught, at the charge of the Company,
Latin, Greek, Hebrew, French, Spanish, conic sections, trigonometry,
heraldry, japanning, fortification, bookkeeping and the art of playing
the theorbo. Some of these companies took large mansions and printed
their advertisements in gilded letters. Others, less ostentatious, were
content with ink, and met at coffeehouses in the neighbourhood of the
Royal Exchange. Jonathan's and Garraway's were in constant ferment
with brokers, buyers, sellers, meetings of directors, meetings of pro-
prietors. Time bargains soon came into fashion. Extensive
combinations were formed, and monstrous fables were circulated, for
the purpose of raising or depressing the price of shares. Our country
witnessed for the first time those phenomena with which a long
experience has made us familiar. A mania of which the symptoms were
essentially the same with those of the mania of 1720, of the mania of
1825, of the mania of 1845, seized the public mind. An impatience to
be rich, a contempt for those slow but sure gains which are the proper
reward of industry, patience, and thrift, spread through society. The
spirit of the cogging dicers of Whitefriars took possession of the grave
Senators of the City, Wardens of Trade, Deputies, Aldermen. It was
much easier and much more lucrative to put forth a lying prospectus
announcing a new stock, to persuade the ignorant people that the

dividends could not fall short of twenty per cent., and to part with five thousand pounds of this imaginary wealth for ten thousand solid guineas, than to load a ship with a well chosen cargo for Virginia or the Levant. Every day some new bubble was puffed into existence, rose buoyant, shone bright, burst, and was forgotten. (Vol. iv, pp. 319-22)

We cannot find room for the excellent remarks with which he disposes of the outcry against the national debt, and answers all the predictions of ruin by a triumphant appeal to facts, which show that when the debt was fifty millions, and croakers were certain of our immediate ruin, trade flourished, the nation became richer and richer, and when the increase rose to eighty millions, to a hundred and forty millions, to two hundred and forty millions, and to eight hundred millions, still the ruined nation grew richer and richer, till now there is no one who doubts that the England of 1856 is better able to pay her eight hundred millions than the England of 1692 was to pay fifty millions.

From what has been here rapidly said, it will be gathered that we greatly admire Macaulay's work, and consider it immeasurably our best English history for its period, and as likely to preserve its pre-eminence. The freedom with which we have criticised certain details of the execution is an earnest of our sincerity. It is but the opinion of an individual we have expressed, but it is a genuine opinion; and we should be doing ourselves an injustice if we closed this notice without the most explicit acknowledgment of our admiration of the work considered in its totality. We confess not to have yet reached that eminence from which certain critics look down upon Macaulay, and peremptorily declare his work 'is not history'. If it is not history, we should be grateful to learn whose work is history. Are we to consider Herodotus, Thucydides, Tacitus, Sallust, Voltaire, Gibbon, and Hume historians, and, if so, in what respect does Macaulay fall short of the conditions these writers have fulfilled? Or is it solely because Macaulay is brilliant, and very readable, whereas the historian ought to be, as indeed he mostly is, opaque and heavy? If the 'dull dogs' are to bear away the palm, let it be explicitly proclaimed in all quarters. Let us respect Guicciardini, Thuanus, Mr Roscoe, and Mr Prescott, as the grandest priests of the historic muse. Let us declare that the dignity of history lies in dulness, and that to be readable is to be historically contemptible. If Macaulay's charm of narrative is to make us despise his laborious erudition, and if, because he makes history readable as a novel, we are to tell him with supercilious brevity that he has completely failed, and that what he, poor man, imagines to be history is 'really nothing of the kind'; it is desirable that we, the ignorant, the reading, and the fascinated public, should know the precise grounds of such a judgment. When we are told *why* Macaulay has not written history, and what history really is, we can then make up our minds—to read Macaulay, and leave history to his critics.

Alexandre Dumas

The Art of Historical Romance (February 1848)

Alexandre Dumas is a fine specimen of the negro blood, and exhibits, in an almost equal degree, the qualities of the indefatigable slave and the brilliant Frenchman. With an insatiable lust for notoriety, he contrives that his sayings and doings shall occupy the gossips of France. Not only as a writer—not simply as *le roi du feuilleton*, the *facile princeps* of the circulating library, but also as a '*gentilhomme*', as a '*grand seigneur*', and as a man, must he always 'astonish' the public. If not noble himself, he at least assumes a noble name, Marquis Davy de la Pailleterie; and talks with easy familiarity of his friends the princes. If not an accomplished duellist, he is, at least, very great on the theory of duelling. His pen is the inheritance which enables him to give banquets, rivalling in splendour the oriental lavishness of his own Monte Christo. He has not 'smelt powder', but to see him on a grand review day, at the head of a company of national guards, you would fancy him the very Caesar, Alexander, Attila, Napoleon, and Wellington of private life—his breast is a blaze of orders. The objects of his existence seem to be two: firstly, to make enormous sums of money to spend with princely prodigality; secondly, incessantly to astonish the world. Above all things, he courts notoriety, scandal, and the power to set men wondering. He began life as a daring innovator, as a romanticist. Racine, and the whole traditional style of French art, he attempted to replace by effective melodramas, which he audaciously asserted were modelled after Shakespeare—his audacity was crowned with a loud but fugitive success. Since then his restless activity has exhibited itself in many ways, and of late, the *author* has almost been eclipsed by the *éclat* attached to the *man*.

Two celebrated trials have recently enabled him to gratify his craving for notoriety in a very striking manner. One of these was that strange revelation of corruption: the trial of Beauvallon for killing Dujarrier in a duel—a trial which, while its details scandalized all Europe, and showed them that the fearful pictures of French life painted by Balzac, in his *Grand Homme de Province à Paris*, were not exaggerations, also enabled Dumas, who was called as a witness, to display his science in the duellist's code, his delicate sense of '*gentilhommerie*', and his unquellable love of display. There was a buffoonery about his manner during this very serious trial of one man for the murder of another, which called forth general indignation. Aping the orators of the Chamber of Deputies, he said one or twice, '*M. le President, je demande la parole*'; and with a beautiful touch of French bombast affecting modesty, when asked his profession, he said: '*Monsieur, je dirais auteur dramatique, si je n'étais dans la patrie de Corneille.*' Whereupon the president, a man of true French wit, replied, '*Oh, Monsieur, il y a des degrés.*'[45]

The second occasion on which *le Marquis Nègre*, as the *National* called him, was enabled to display himself was in an action brought against him by a publisher for not fulfilling his contract, or rather, for dishonourably violating the terms thereof. It was a grand scene, colossal in its buffoonery. Dumas had engaged to furnish a specific number of volumes to certain newspapers, and to no others. He received the money in advance; and the action brought against him was brought, not simply for having failed in his engagements, but also for having written in other journals, all the time declaring he had 'no copy' to furnish his engagements. Dumas defended his own cause. It was too fine an opportunity of display for him to think of letting it slip. And how did he defend himself? By proving the nullity of the charges? by exculpating or even by extenuating himself? Not at all. That would have been a plain, vulgar course, a course wholly destitute of *éclat*. He chose another. His defence was a masterpiece of effrontery and vanity. Evading or disdaining the charges brought against him, he detailed at great length the history of the preceding months of his life, and detailed it with the pomp and veracity of one of his own romances. He let the audience pleasantly into the secret of his intimacy with the princes—jauntily alluded to the government having placed a steamer at his disposal—sketched his Spanish expedition—launched into Morocco—recounted how he saved the lives of several Frenchmen about to be butchered by savages—spoke with becoming immodesty of his own writings, and how he kept two express trains and couriers awaiting 'copy', which was dispatched piecemeal as it was written; and concluded with the magnificent boast, that although the Academy of France reckoned forty literary men as its members, yet he, Alexandre Dumas, had accomplished what those forty collectively could not have accomplished! 'Alone he did it!' Never, perhaps, did French sublimity transcend this: it was finer than the celebrated *Moi!* in Corneille.

Having 'astonished' his audience, instead of replying to the charges, Dumas left the court, and in presence of a gaping crowd, mounted a richly caparisoned Arabian horse, which stood waiting for him at the door, and rode off in triumph. He lost the action, of course; but he gained his object—he had produced a sensation.

We have given a specimen of the man in public; now let us give one of the man in private; not in that privacy of home which only impertinent curiosity has the conscience to penetrate; not in that sanctuary where the author retires behind the man. Such privacy, if Dumas ever knows it, is beyond our ken—beyond our curiosity; our glance is at that semi-publicity which may be spoken of without offence. When his dramatic arrangement of his own novel, *Les Trois Mousquetaires*, was finished, he invited all the performers to his house near Versailles, which he has christened the Chateau de Monte Christo, and sent carriages to convey them. The proposed object was to read the play to the performers. Arrived, they were shown over the grounds, and then seated before a splendid *dejeuner*. Having done honour to it, they imagined the reading of the play was to commence; but no: time passed in gay conversation; a magnificent dinner followed; then came the reading; then a supper, and finally, the whole party was conducted back again to Paris. The expense of such a *fête* we leave others to estimate. No wonder that couriers, ready saddled, and express trains are necessary, when 'copy' is to furnish the proceeds for such prodigality.

But now comes the mystery: how does any mortal's *pen* (we use the cant phrase advisedly, for there is much hidden meaning in saying that such and such works have 'proceeded from the prolific pen of Mr—')—how, then, we repeat, does any mortal's pen traverse the vast regions of space—those reams, not realms, of fancy and invention which bear the signature of Alexandre Dumas? We have had rapid writers before now, and prodigies; but whose rapidity ever approached that of *Alexandre le Grand?* what prodigy ever surpassed this friend of princes? Mr James has a pen which one can scarcely call slow; Mrs Gore is not a tortoise; Mr Warren has recently written a novel of five hundred pages in one-and-twenty days; and Lope de Vega, the personification of celerity, who took only three days to write a three-act comedy in verse, is credited by marvel-loving chroniclers with having accomplished twenty-one million three hundred thousand lines of printed verse in his not very long career. But Dumas distances them all. His rapidity is something so fabulous, that all sorts of suppositions are put forward to explain it; and one virulent pamphlet undertakes to prove that he has a regular manufactory where numbers of young men work, he only putting his name to their productions.

There is, however, one very strong objection to the current theory that Dumas sells under his own name the works of others; and in justice to the literary curiosity of the case, we must adduce it. It is this: if a number of men were employed writing novels, which Dumas had only to retouch, or if he only gave them a plot which they had to work out, Dumas would never be at a loss for 'copy' to satisfy the demands of those journals to which he is engaged. But in the trial before mentioned, it came out that not only had the journals great difficulty in getting from him the promised 'copy', but that having printed one or more volumes, they were, much to their disadvantage, compelled to publish volumes by other writers, because Dumas had not furnished them with continuation; thus considerable periods were allowed to elapse between the delivery of one volume and its successor. When we know that Dumas is in the habit of publishing several works simultaneously, and at this moment, has no less than six unfinished, and in course of piecemeal publication, we can understand the delay. He has not six hands to write six works at once; so his must finish volume three of this novel, volume three of that, volume six of another, volume ten of another and volume one of another—in this way he has, volume by volume, to satisfy the claims upon him; and on the supposition that he, in conjunction with Auguste Maquet, and, perhaps, also his son, really does wrote the works published under his name, the *delay* becomes intelligible. On the supposition of a manufactory, the delay is inexplicable; and we must also add in opposition to the idea of a manufactory, that all the works sold by Dumas are bound to be in his *own* handwriting; otherwise the publishers would be easy dupes. Now it is absurd to suppose Dumas undertakes the task of copying the works of his young workmen: absurd, because every one knows that a man who writes with ordinary celerity, will compose much quicker than he can copy anything—and it is the question of time which in Dumas' case forms the difficulty. On the whole, we believe this to be the truth: Dumas, in conjunction with Auguste Maquet, invents and dictates the novels, which young Dumas, whose handwriting is very like his father's, copies.

Should this be so, the fertility and rapidity of Dumas are really marvellous. Think of a man who binds himself, in consideration of a large retaining fee, not to publish *more* than five-and-thirty volumes in the course of the year—one more volume and it would be exactly three volumes a month! To accomplish such a feat for one month would be remarkable enough; but here is a man who is paid not to exceed that every month in the year!

And note, moreover, that these rapidly-written novels, like Lope de Vega's rapidly-written plays, are immensely successful—perhaps the most successful of all French books—eagerly read in France, drafted over into Spain, into Italy, reprinted, translated, and devoured in Germany and England, as if there were the works of a Scott. Whatever opinion may be formed of them as works—and we shall presently state our own with great explicitness—their enormous success is a fact, which in this portion of our article we wish to insist upon. We happen to know, that not only our aristocracy and our middle classes read these works with eagerness, but that even the highest person in this realm is impatient for the continuations of these endless romances in eighteen volumes. Into the palace Alexandre Dumas penetrates immediately; into the poor man's lodging he is not long in penetrating, by means of cheap translations. It is the same in Germany; and this fact forces us to write the present article: we cannot affect to ignore the presence and popularity of such works.

Rien ne réussit comme le succès, says Jules Janin, with his usual wit; and amply has Dumas illustrated the remark. He keeps the public in a fever of excitement and suspense; and the public having wondered at him in the café in the morning, are held breathless in the theatre in the evening by some comedy or drama from the indefatigable, inexhaustible, incessant, startling, sparkling, *grand Dumas*. Wherever he walks, Pactolus flows. He writes with a golden pen, and makes the fortunes of journals and theatres. Success enables him to do anything and everything with impunity. The ordinary rules of composition he violates, and turns his violation into a merit. Most persons agree in thinking that nothing can be more injurious than making three yards do the work of ten; every one objects to 'spinning out', as tedious. Dumas reverses the axiom, and makes tediousness a condition of success. Instead of a novel in three volumes, he gives you one in eighteen. You are forced to read it; 'everybody does'. Having closed the eighteenth volume—that is the third novel of the series—you find the story is not finished yet, and you see no reason why it should not continue for eighteen more.

Success smiles upon all his efforts. He has recently built a theatre, which, with an unintentional irony, he has entitled the *Théâtre Historique*, and there he produces dramas made up from his own novels, and they—yes, they succeed! We have, à propos to his managerial and dramatic career, one more beautiful specimen which, inasmuch as it relates to Shakespeare, and exhibits the French interpretation of our great poet, has more than a passing interest. Shakespeare has a great reputation in France, as may be seen by the frequent quotation of '*voilà la question, comme dit Hamlet*', as also by the exquisite apostrophe of Eugène Sue: 'O great Williams!' in which a Frenchman's well-known accuracy is gracefully exhibited. Well, it appeared to Dumas that a play by the 'great Williams', if properly adapted, might create a sensation. He chose one for his *Théâtre Historique*; of course it was Hamlet.

But 'Williams', great as he may be considered, is, after all, not a poet to present to a French audience without considerable alteration. It is one article of a Frenchman's faith, that in point of taste he gives the law to Europe—we beg pardon—to the Universe! A French critic always understands a work of art so much better than the artist, and is at no loss to see where it might be 'improved'. Thus Shakespeare, whose works we in England, as well as our brothers in Germany, believe to be, in spite of imperfections, singularly profound in their conception, and felicitous in their development—even Shakespeare was not able to conclude his Hamlet logically and effectively; at least Dumas and his admirers think so. Shakespeare must be 'improved'— made more 'effective'—passages cut out—passages thrust in—above all, a new dénouement is required, for the present is singularly weak. Dumas takes up his pen and in a few hours of that '*travail rapide et foudroyant*' (the phrase is an admiring critic's!) of which he alone possesses the secret, enriches the poem with a dénouement at once grand and poetic, logical and effective. The reader may imagine our curiosity to see this famous alteration, which critics pronounced so 'logical', and he may imagine the feelings with which we read it. Here it is: instead of Hamlet killing Laertes and the king, he calls upon the Ghost to appear:–

Hamlet. L'ombre! l'ombre!
Viens voir tes meurtriers mourir, fantôme sombre!
Le Roi. (Sous la main d'Hamlet.) A l'aide!

Hamlet. (*Aux courtisans sur un signe de l'Ombre.*) Laissez-nous.
(*Hésitation des courtisans.*)
                              Qu'un de vous fasse un pas,
Il n'en ferait pas deux! Je suis roi, n'est-ce pas?
Roi de votre existence et de votre agonie?
Il sied qu'entre nous cinq la pièce soit finie.
Sortez tous! (*Tous intimidés sortent lentement.*)
A présent, vous trois, le voyez-vous?
Laërte. Dieu puissant! le roi mort!
Le Roi. Mon frère!
Gertrude. Mon époux!
Laërte. Grâce!
L'Ombre. Oui, ton sang trop prompt t'entraîna vers l'abime,
Laërte, et le Seigneur t'a puni pour ton crime;
Mais tu le trouveras, car il sonde les coeurs,
Moins sévère là-haut. Laërte, prie et meurs! (*Laërte meurt.*)
Gertrude. Pitié! pitié!
L'Ombre. Ta faute était ton amour même,
Pauvre femme!
Va, ton coeur a lavé ta honte avec tes pleurs;
Femme ici, reine au ciel, Gertrude, espère et meurs! (*Gertrude meurt.*)
Le Roi. Pardon!
L'Ombre. Pas de pardon! va, meurtrier infâme,
Va; pour ton crime affreux, dans leurs cercles de flamme.
Satan et les enfers n'ont pas trop de douleurs;
Va, traître, incestueux, va, désespère et meurs! (*Le Roi meurt.*)
Hamlet. Et moi, vais-je rester, triste orphelin sur terre,
A respirer cet air imprégné de misere?
Tragédien choisi par le courroux de Dieu,
Si j'ai mal pris mon rôle et mal saisi mon jeu;
Si, tremblant de mon oeuvre, et lassé sans combattre,
Pour un que tu voulais j'en ai fait mourir quatre,
Oh! parle, est-ce que Dieu ne pardonnera pas,
Pére, et quel châtiment m'attend donc?...
L'Ombre. Tu vivras!

To dwell upon the poetic value of this would be invidious, but since the critics have set up a claim for it as being so very 'logical', let us ask: if the Ghost has this avenging power in his own hands—if, at his awful bidding, Laertes, the King, and Gertrude die,—what is the meaning of his former appearances, wherein he so sternly urges Hamlet to avenge him? If the Ghost was like a perturbed spirit, condemned to wander nightly till his murder was avenged, why did he not wander straight to the palace of the King, and breathe away his murderer's guilty soul? This would have finished the piece in the first act, it is true, but it would at least have been 'logical'. In M. Dumas's version, the Ghost is powerless till the last act; and then, like the dumb men in melodramas who recover their speech in time to accuse the villain, he suddenly appears armed with all the terrors of the ghostly world, and becomes his own avenger.

This, then, is the man who is the Historical Romancist of our times. Our rapid survey of his activity and his mode of life will have prepared the reader for the style of the novels which, under the presence of being historical, and therefore 'instructive', are read by those who could not otherwise read them. He is a man utterly without a literary conscience, so that conscientious works must not be expected from him. He chooses historical subjects, because it is the easiest style of fiction; in that department, a writer only requires a reasonable fund of historical ignorance, and, with a dashing pen, he is sure to succeed; if he unhappily knows anything about the period he has selected, he is in great danger of being troubled by misgivings, and his facile progress will be stopped.

But if we cannot accept Dumas as 'instructive', we must, at least, do him the justice of saying that his writings, for the most art, are free from two of the vices which deform the generality of French novels: he does not often stain his works with disgusting subjects, nor with the modern cant of gilding rags and dirt. Curious it is to observe the modern Frenchmen, having escaped from their old servilities, and no longer proclaiming the divine right of kings and kingly virtues, rushing to the opposite extreme, and deifying the lowest classes. The Romanticists proclaim that *le vrai beau c' est le laid*, and the new school of novelists proclaim that the seat of kingly grandeur and sublime virtue is not on the throne, but in the kennel. The wealthy classes have an incurable sin: their hands are white. This does not arise from the fact of their having no occupation which would dirty them, but from their inherent infamy and egotism. The people, on the contrary, have dirty hands: they are dirty and virtuous. They are great, moral, chivalric, disinterested, Christian—all by virtue of dirty hands and questionable linen. The People! Does not the very name exalt your soul? 'The People' is not only a name, it is an *Idea*![46]

Dumas indulges in no such rodomontade. He is not 'philosophical', he is not 'earnest', he has no 'theory of society', he cares very little for the People, and still less for Ideas spelled with a capital *I*. He leaves to Eugène Sue and Company the whole realm of filth and rags, of sentiment and social regeneration. He loves to deal more with velvet doublets and slashed satins, with 'amiable' roués, and ladies who rogue and coquet. There is not much to be said for the moral worth of the persons whom he clothes in velvet and satin; but it is some comfort to find that he does not imitate his contemporaries, who treat the reader as Raleigh treated Queen Bess—throwing the rich velvet cloak upon the ground, that her feet might not be soiled by the mud. They take you into very bad company, but your pockets are in no danger; they take you into very dirty places, but you have no occasion to hold your nose: the morals of the library and the perfumes of fancy are provided for the occasion. That young girl you see in yon 'boozing ken', with brandy before her, and strange language in her mouth, is not what you might suppose; in fact, she is a type of Innocence, the incarnation of Purity: while associating with cut-throats (who are, after all, no more than 'victims of society') and ladies of *un*easy virtue, her thoughts are with babbling brooks and flowery meadows. She will marry a great prince, who, strange to say, is virtuous, although a prince: to be sure, he is a German prince![47]

Dumas has not this sort of vice to answer for, but we should, nevertheless, be sorry to be understood as defending him. The tone of his morals is decidedly low, if not worse. If he has no cant, on the other hand, he has no apparent respect for moral worth. His heroes and heroines are often more than questionable. He seems more at home in the atmosphere of *la Régence* than in any other: its gaiety, easy morals, and love of adventure quite charm him. Hear him on the subject:–

> Moreover, the spirit of the times was not one of melancholy: this is a modern sentiment, caused by the overthrow of fortunes and the weakness of men. In the eighteenth century, it was a rare occurrence for any one to think of abstractions and aspire to the ideal; every one pursued pleasure, fame, or fortune; and, provided he was handsome, brave, or intriguing, was sure to succeed. It was an epoch when no one was ashamed of his own happiness. Now, mind is too much exalted over matter for any one to venture to own that he is happy.
>
> Besides, it must be confessed, the wind set in for gaiety, and France seemed in full sail in search of one of those enchanted islands which are to be found in the golden map of Arabian Nights. After the long, dreary winter of Louis XIV's old age, suddenly appeared the joyous and brilliant spring of a young reign; every one basked in that new sun, so radiant and beneficent, and went about humming and careless like bees and butterflies in the first days of summer. Pleasure, which had been absent and proscribed, once more returned; it was hailed like a friend never expected to be seen again: it was received with open heart and arms, lest it should escape anew. Every moment was made of use.

This is from *Le Chevalier D'Harmental*, and refers to the period when the orgies of the Regent were in unblushing career, when two royal princesses quarrelled for that reprobate, the Duke de Richelieu, and Mesdames de Nesle and de Polignac fought for him with pistols: a charming period, as every one knows who has read Duclos, or any of the French Memoirs!

Dumas has, in truth, a strong partiality for that period; he likes its manners and morals, and belongs to the set of men now in Paris, who think it a fine thing to revive the orgies of *la Régence*; and we are sorry to say, the gloss he gives to the vices of that epoch—the brilliant colours in which he paints

it—the absence of anything like reprobation of its worthlessness and frivolity, have a very immoral tendency. The Regent, Philip of Orleans,
himself—one of the most reprobate of rulers, in whom history can detect
scarcely any good qualities beyond an easy temper—is painted by Dumas as
a loving father, a careless, good-natured, easy sovereign, and an excellent
companion.

This is among the objections reasonably raised against History perverted
to the purposes of Fiction: the romance writer abuses the licence allowed
him, and goes far to undo the very purposes of History. It is thought, we
know, that inasmuch as novels are entertaining and many persons will read
them who will not read more serious works, to make them the medium of
historical instruction is to 'do the state some service', and to convert a
necessary evil into an advantage. This is a very popular notion, and is
entertained by parents who would not suffer their children to read novels,
were it not for the supposed advantage of 'giving a taste for history'.

We must be permitted to disturb this notion. Whether novels should be
read or not, is a question we leave each family to settle for itself: there are
very strong arguments on both sides—arguments which cannot be refuted—
and according as education and temperament determine the question, the
arguments have their weight. But when it is maintained that the historical
matter in novels is of itself a sufficient excuse to warrant their being admitted
into our families, then, indeed, the argument seems to us absurdly feeble and
rickety. With the greatest respect for Scott, for his manly, healthy tone, his
genial spirit, his astonishing powers, and gratitude for the delight he has
scattered over Europe, we cannot shut our eyes to the fact, that as far as the
historical portion of his novels is concerned, they have been of very questionable utility.

Not to mention their inaccuracies, which, after all, were not important,
inasmuch as for the most part they were what may be called external
inaccuracies—matters of chronology and *couleur locale*—the picture being
in the main accurate, being true as to essentials—it is scarcely to be denied
that he has damaged the study of history in two ways: Firstly, in his influence
on readers; secondly, in his influence on writers.

In his influence on readers, because his entertaining style has made them
impatient at the more laborious and conscientious study of History, causing
them to regard a serious work as 'dry', making them careless of facts, and
more solicitous of pictures than of ideas; in his influence on writers, because
it has made them desirous of feeding this awakened taste, and led them to
sacrifice the more honourable portion of their office to the vain attempt of
rivalling him in picturesque effect.

It would be unjust to deny, on the other hand, that Scott has done some
service to historical art, in making men aware of the picturesqueness of
history, as well as in indicating certain historical views with great sagacity.
Thierry, a great authority, and an accomplished historian, who is certainly

not open to the reproach of having shirked the labours of study and research, has deliberately pronounced Scott to be the greatest of all historical divinators. Had he employed his varied erudition and keen historical sense in essays, rather than in romances, the good would have been unalloyed; as it is, we cannot acquit him of having encouraged, if he did not originate, the evils above mentioned.

But if Scott, with his minute and abundant knowledge, has damaged history by his employment of it in fiction, what are we to say to his imitators? They have the worst of his vices, with none of his merits. They falsify history, they confuse the simplest notions, they fill the reader's mind with a mass of rubbish which it is very difficult to eject by a course of serious study, even if they have not enervated the mind, and made it averse to study. For observe, the error of a grave historian—and the gravest and acutest often err—nay, in so difficult a matter, it is difficult to avoid error—is, nevertheless, easily replaced by the mere presentation of the truth; but if once the novelist has succeeded in filling your mind with a false but brilliant picture, it will resist a long assault of evidence the most conclusive. The historian appeals to the judgment; the novelist enlists the sympathies and feeling; and when once he succeeds in forcing his conception of a character upon you, the most striking appeal to your judgment will scarcely destroy that impression. It has been said that 'no-knowledge is better than mis-knowledge; and the scraps of history picked up from the novel are just sufficient to mislead the indolent into the idea of their possessing "information". Either history is worth knowing, or it is not: if worth knowing, then worth studying in proper sources'. Who that has ever opened the imitators of Scott can for a moment suppose that they understood anything of history?

Alexandre Dumas is the great manufacturer of this contraband ware, and from these introductory pages the reader will be enabled to form some idea of his fitness for an historian. Scott had at least abundant knowledge; but Dumas, who travels over the whole history of France from the thirteenth to the nineteenth century—not to mention Italy, Spain, and England—has, perhaps, less knowledge than even our lady novelists. His falsifications are perpetual, and of all kinds. He not only fails to present a picture of the epoch—its beliefs, its feelings, and its manners—he also carelessly misrepresents almost every personage. We forgive him his magnificent mistakes about England. Frenchmen seem to have a prescriptive right to blunder on the smallest detail of that subject; but what are we to say to his miserable failures with regard to French characters, whom he misrepresents apparently *de gaieté de coeur?* If any persons ought to be accurately painted, surely Mademoiselle de Launay—the charming Madame de Staal—and Jean Jacques Rousseau, are the persons: they have left us minute and ample details of themselves, in works with which every one professing to know anything of French literature must be familiar; yet how has Dumas drawn them in *Le Chevalier d' Harmental* and in *Les Mémoires d' un Médecin?* The first named is an agreeable romance on the subject of the Cellemare conspiracy; the memoirs of that period are abundant and explicit in materials, and give us full-length portraits of all the principal actors; but if any one has the curiosity to compare these portraits with those painted by Dumas, he will know what to think of the value of historical romance!

Then, again, such portraits as Dumas presents us with of Cardinal Dubois in *La Fille du Régent*, and of Catherine de Medicis in *La Reine Margot*! The Cardinal was a man of whom impartial history can say little that is good, either as to his aims or his means; but to make him the mere pimp and pander, the mere police spy of a Surrey melodrama, incarnate selfishness, pettiness, and intrigue, is to fix an idea in the reader's mind which will distort the whole career and character of the ambitious Abbé. Catherine de Medicis is, it is true, a traditional bugbear; but even she was not so black as she is painted. She was at any rate a woman, and Dumas has made her the fiend of a puppet-show. This is not historical, but hysterical romance!

The falsifications, of which these are only specimens, may be said to run through his works; in all we have read, we have met with no single historical character correctly drawn, with no single event accurately presented. As to blunders of detail, they are as thick as leaves in Vallambrosa. Here is a specimen: in *Le Bâtard de Mauléon*, he makes Blanche of Castile, the wife of Don Pedro, in love with Don Henri de Trastamarra. This is a double blunder: the innocence of Blanche is so well established, that only fabulists and scandalmongers pretend to doubt it; moreover, the person with whom she was suspected of having been guilty was not Don Henri at all, but a very different person, Don Fadrique.

Mistakes, however, in periods so remote are, perhaps, excusable, in one who has never taken the trouble to study it; but Dumas is equally blundering when he comes down to comparatively recent times. In *Les Mémoires d'un Médecin*, he gives us society just before the breaking out of the French Revolution, and on one occasion he jauntily says, 'Il n'y a pas d'érudition à faire à propos d'une époque si bien connue de nos jours, qu'on pourrait presque la dire contemporaine, et que la plupart de nos lecteurs savent aussi bien que nous.' If the majority of his readers know it no better than he does, they cannot be complimented on their erudition, for the work abounds in errors, great and small. He cannot even speak of Zamore, the governor of the Chateau de Luciennes, a negro servant of La Dubarry, but he must make him a child, occupied with eating sugarplums and rolling his eyes, instead of the astute, servile, ungrateful man he was: and Dumas also makes him hideous, when it is notorious he was handsome—he was always styled *le beau nègre*.

Perhaps it is unfair, pedantic, to allude thus to the inaccuracies of a writer whose existence, instead of being passed in the solitudes of spacious libraries, ransacking the treasures there contained, is passed in scampering over Europe, and writing 'impressions'—in lounging with princes—patronising the Emperor of Morrocco—saving the lives of *les braves des braves*—glittering at Spanish marriages—giving splendid fêtes—and keeping couriers, ready saddled, as well as express trains, to convey his manuscripts. To expect erudition from such a man is to expect a greater marvel than all the rest. We do not expect it; we will not harshly blame him for the deficiency; but we may be permitted to express a doubt whether the 'instruction' derivable from such works as he produces be really sufficient to give a taste for history.

Before quitting this part of our article, let us call attention to the evil effect likely to be produced by these works upon an excitable and unsettled population such as that of France, by the very frequent employment of conspiracy as the subject-matter. The French are but too much disposed to revolutions,[48] and when their ingenious youth see Dumas' heroes constantly plunged into some romantic conspiracy to overturn the government, it is natural they should regard a conspirator as a hero; the more so, as the author never drops a hint that conspiracy is either criminal or objectionable. Whatever the cause, be it even such a frivolous affair as that headed by the Duchesse de Maine, the romance of the thing is insisted upon, and the reader's sympathies are wholly enlisted on the side of the conspirator.

Whatever we may think of Dumas, his immense popularity requires some explanation. Mere rapidity, mere voluminousness will not account for it—for who reads James or Mrs Gore? But in all Europe Dumas is read, and in all classes. His faults are very striking; nay, we are inclined to assert that his worthlessness is complete, unless some value is to be attached to the power of producing a transitory amusement. No one ever re-reads him. No one ever ponders on what he has written. He has added nothing to our intellectual stores; he has hung no fresh pictures in our gallery of imaginative portraits. What, then, has he done? He has amused thousands. How has he done it? To answer this question, it is necessary to take a survey of his qualities.

Dumas has gained loud popularity in three distinct departments of literature, and gained it by the same merits. He began as a dramatist, attacking the traditional form of French art, and substituting for it that hybrid species called *le drame*: the great conquest of the Romanticists in their assaults against Racine. He succeeded in creating a noise. Three *drames* were performed to furious acclamations. As works of art they were worthless, but they made an uproar: their novelty, audacity, and clever use of stage effect attracted attention. But the novelty wore off, and his succeeding efforts grew feebler and feebler, till they ended in the astounding dulness of 'Caligula'.

He next succeeded as a traveller, and his *Impressions de Voyages* are certainly the most amusing, impudent, and reckless works ever published under the pretence of travels. His light, careless pen skims over the surface— his admirable power to telling a story is called into play, and with it his audacious disregard of truth or probability; you read with a smile, and close the volume without a yawn; but there can be no misgiving as to the value of what you have read.

Novels succeeded; at first they were poor enough, but by practice he learned the art of telling a story with such rapidity and precision, with such a complication of incidents, yet such clearness in their conduct, and with characters so clearly represented, that it is difficult to open a volume and not proceed with it to the end. True it is that if once you set down the volume unfinished, you have little temptation to take it up again; and we found the reading necessary for this article rather tiresome work. But there is no disguising the fact that he possesses some of the qualities which command success, though none of those which render success enduring.

Style he has none; but he has an easy, agreeable, off-hand manner, destitute of pretension, and possessing in an extraordinary degree the excellent union of minute detail with rapidity. His dialogue, unless when the passions are called into play, or when the more ideal characteristics of man are touched on, is very life-like, gay, sparkling, and rapid. His characters are always happily presented, though never deeply conceived, or minutely analysed. They have somewhat the merit of Scott's portraits, only more superficial. Passion he has none; nor has he much humour; but considerable gaiety and a good eye for the picturesque. Such men as the Captain Roquefinette, in *Le Chevalier D'Harmental*, or the old copyist, in the same novel, who thinks it never too early to begin a child's education, and accordingly sets it a copy of *straight strokes* before it is a year old!—such men as Chicot and Gorenflot, in *La Dame de Monsoreau*; as Coconnas, in *La Reine Margot*; or as Porthos, in *Les Trois Mousquetaires*, are characters he draws with great felicity. Some of the incidental personages, such as Caderousse, la Carconte, and Benedetto, in *Le Comte de Monte Christo*, are also powerfully sketched. But his great art lies in the power of minutely yet vividly painting a long scene of adventure or of intrigue, so that it stands before you with almost unrivalled precision.

Probability is a thing he utterly sets at nought; and this is the great defect and drawback of *Monte Christo*, where the *incredulus odi* rises in the reader's mind at every chapter. This improbability is the more unpardonable as it is accompanied with great power of accurate delineation of the situations thus improbably brought about; but when we reflect upon the rapidity with which he writes, and on the gross indifference of his multitude of readers to anything beyond the sensation of the moment, we are not to wonder at this defect. People who read simply for amusement, who want their sluggish imaginations to be gratified without being called into active co-operation, whose indolent minds crave an excitement which they are unwilling to take the trouble of inducing by any activity of their own, find immense delight in a writer who, like Dumas, does everything for them, leaves nothing to their imaginations, and does not trouble them with explanations or with probabilities. Dumas never ruffles their repose. No reflection disturbs the even current of his narrative. No felicity of style causes them for an instant to pause and admire; no trait of human nature rouses a train of thought in their minds; no subtle glimpse into the complex world of character—no searching analysis of motive—no moral indignation bursting forth from the preacher drawing a lesson from the examples he has given—none of the *instruction* which it is in the novelist's power so felicitously to convey, ever retards the breath-suspended interest of his tale. The reader is hurried onwards to the end, impatient to see how the hero will extricate himself from the difficulties he is in. To express our condemnation, and to characterise his writings in one sentence, we should say: Dumas stimulates the vulgarest curiosity, but never stimulates the mind.

'Waste of time' the reading of his works assuredly is, except to those who want to fill the vacant hours of their worthless lives with a little amusement; or to those who after the fatigues of a laborious day are unable to bear any greater mental stimulus; yet no one who knows the frivolous public will wonder at the enormous success of these works: written rapidly, read rapidly, and as rapidly forgotten. It was wittily said by that acute critic, Gustave Planche, that 'l'art dramatique aux mains de M Hugo n'est plus qu'un escamotage de place publique': a sentence which applies with tenfold force to Alexandre Dumas, since gaping crowds do really gather together to wonder at his 'escamotage', and having seen him perform his tricks of legerdemain, lounge further on to gape at the next adroit audacious charlatan whose lusty voice bids them behold and wonder.

We are at no pains to conceal the contempt which we feel for Dumas, in spite of an undeniable cleverness and adroitness displayed in his works; but neither are we desirous of fulminating critical thunders against him for the absence of qualities to the possession of which he makes no pretence. Our object is to characterise him as briefly and as distinctly as we are able. He is not an artist, and cannot be criticised as such. He has no literary conscience; little literary merit. He is not a teacher; has no moral influence for good or for bad; if he does not proclaim truths, he abstains from dressing up sophisms. Amusement, and that of the lowest kind—the mere stimulus of the curiosity—is his object and his only object; and regarded as a sort of literary pyrotechnist, he is the most remarkable man of his time.

With deep sorrow and unspeakable bitterness might one regard this desecration of literature, this fantastic misemployment of a God-given life, were one to look seriously at it. For it is a truth that literature, which is the mental life of mankind—the incomplete, incoherent utterances of the thoughts which surge within the minds of men, struggling for distinct recognition—is *not* represented at all by ten volumes of incident and intrigue—and that our spiritual culture is in no degree fostered, purified, or strengthened by marvellous narratives of escapes, duels, murders, feastings, love-makings, processions, conspiracies, and executions; nor was any man ever endowed with reason, imagination, feeling, energy, and a perception of the incongruous, for the purpose of employing these on *Monte Christos, Trois Mousquetaires*, or *Reines Margot*. A truth, however, it seems pedantic to insist upon in reference to Dumas. We cannot be serious with him. We feel none of the sorrow for a fallen angel; none of the deep, painful pity for a misguided mind. No touch of the divinity of mind awakens our misgivings and compassion. The specific levity of the man forbids it. He is so light, so worthless, so reckless, so untroubled by any earnestness, that to speak a serious word to him would seem as misplaced as to preach sermons to drunkards, or demonstrate the problems of mathematics to idiots. We should speak in language unintelligible to him; and he would answer us with a new romance in thirty volumes. [The article continues with detailed accounts of more of Dumas' works.]

Johann Wolfgang von Goethe

Wilhelm Meister (1855)

A Frenchman, an Englishman, and a German were commissioned, it is said, to give the world the benefit of their views on that interesting animal the Camel. Away went the Frenchman to the *Jardin des Plantes*, spent an hour there in rapid investigation, returned and wrote a *feuilleton*, in which there was no phrase which added to the general knowledge. He was perfectly satisfied, however, and said, *Le voilà, le chameau!* The Englishman packed up his tea-caddy and a magazine of comforts; pitched his tent in the East; remained there two years studying the Camel in its habits; and returned with a thick volume of facts, arranged without order, expounded without philosophy, but serving as valuable materials for all who came after him. The German, despising the frivolity of the Frenchman, and the unphilosophic matter-of-factness of the Englishman, retired to his study, there *to construct the Idea of a Camel from out of the depths of his Moral Consciousness.* And he is still at it.

With this myth the reader is introduced into the very heart of that species of criticism which, flourishing in Germany, is also admired in some English circles, under the guise of Philosophical Criticism, and which has been exercised upon *Wilhelm Meister* as mercilessly as upon *Faust*.

My readers, it is hoped, will not generalise this remark so as to include within it all German critics and men of culture: such an extension of the remark would be almost as unfair in Germany as in England. There are many excellent critics in Germany, and excellent judges who are not critics; it would be too bad if our laughter at pedants and pretenders were to extend to these. But no one acquainted with Germany and German literature can fail to recognise the wide-spread and pernicious influence of a mistaken application of Philosophy to Art: an application which becomes a tyranny on the part of real thinkers, and a hideous absurdity on the part of those who merely echo the jargon of the schools. It is this criticism which has stifled Art in Germany, and ruined many a young artist who showed promise. It is a fundamental mistake to translate Art into the formulas of Philosophy, and then christen the translation the Philosophy of Art. This kind of critic is never easy until he has shifted his ground. He is not content with the work as it presents itself. He endeavours to get *behind* it, beneath it, into the depths of the soul which produced it. He is not satisfied with what the artist has *given*, he wants to know what he *meant*. He guesses at the meaning; the more remote the meaning lies on the wandering tracks of thought, the better pleased is he with the discovery, and he sturdily rejects every simple explanation in favour of this exegetical Idea. Thus the phantom of Philosophy hovers mistily before Art, concealing Art from our eyes. It is true the Idea said to underlie the work was never conceived by any one before, least of all by the Artist; but *that* is the glory of the critic: he is proud of having plunged into the depths. Of all horrors to the German of this school there is no horror like that of the surface—it is more terrible to him than cold water.

Wilhelm Meister has been the occasion of so many ideas constructed out of the depths of moral consciousness, it has been made to *mean* such wondrous (and contradictory) things, that its author must have been astonished at his unsuspecting depth. There is some obvious symbolism in the latter part, which I have little doubt was introduced to flatter the German tendency; as I have no sort of doubt that its introduction has spoiled a masterpiece. The obvious want of unity in the work has given free play to the interpreting imagination of critics. Hillebrand boldly says that the 'Idea of *Wilhelm Meister* is precisely this—that it has no Idea',—which does not greatly further our comprehension.

Instead of trying to discover the Idea, let us stand fast by historical criticism, and see what light may be derived from a consideration of the origin and progress of the work, which, from first to last, occupied him during twenty years. The first six books—beyond all comparison the best and most important—were written before the journey to Italy—they were written during the active theatrical period when Goethe was manager, poet, and actor. The contents of these books point very clearly to his intention of representing in them the whole nature, aims, and art of the comedian; and in a letter to Merck he expressly states that it is his intention to portray the actor's life. Whether at the same time he meant the actor's life to be symbolical, cannot be positively determined. That may, or may not, have been a *secondary* intention. The primary intention is very clear. Nor had he, at this time, yielded to the seduction of attempting the symbolical in Art. He sang as the birds sing; his delight was in healthy objective fact; he had not yet donned the robes of an Egyptian priest, or learned to write in hieroglyphs. He was seriously interested in acting, and the actor's art. He thought the life of a player a good framework for certain pictures, and he chose it. Afterwards, the idea of making these pictures symbolical certainly did occur to him, and he concluded the romance upon this after-thought.

Gervinus emphatically records his disbelief of the opinion that Goethe originally intended to make Wilhelm *unfit* for success as an actor; and I think a careful perusal of the novel, even in its present state, will convince the reader that Gervinus is right. Instead of Wilhelm's career being represented as the development of a false tendency—the obstinate cultivation of an imperfect talent, such as was displayed in Goethe's own case with respect to plastic Art—one sees, in spite of some subsequent additions thrown in to modify the work according to an after-thought, that Wilhelm has a true inborn tendency, a talent which ripens through practice. With the performance of *Hamlet* the apogee is reached; and here ends the first plan. Having written so far, Goethe went to Italy. We have seen the changes which came over his views. After a lapse of ten years he resumes the novel; and having in that period lived through the experience of a false tendency—having seen the vanity of cultivating an imperfect talent—he *alters* the plan of his novel, makes it symbolical of the erroneous striving of youth toward culture; invents the cumbrous machinery of a Mysterious Family, whose watchful love has guided all his steps, and who have encouraged him in error that they might lead him through error unto truth. This is what in his old age he declared—in the *Tag und Jahres Hefte*, and in his letters to Schiller—to have been the plan upon which it was composed. 'It sprang,' he says, 'from a dim feeling of the great truth that Man often seeks that which Nature has rendered impossible to him. All dilettantism and false tendency is of this kind. Yet is it possible that every false step should lead to an inestimable good, and some intimation of this is given in Meister.' To Eckermann he said: 'The work is one of the most incalculable productions; I *myself can scarcely be said to have the key to it.* People seek a central point, and that is difficult to find; nor is it even right. I should think a *rich manifold life brought close to our eyes would be enough in itself without any express tendency*, which, after all, is only for the intellect.' This is piercing to the very kernel. The origin of the symbolical matter, however, lies in the demands of the German intellect for such food. 'But,' he continues, 'if anything of the kind is insisted upon, it will, perhaps, be found in the words which Frederick at the end addresses to the hero, when he says, "Thou seem'st to me like Saul, the son of Kish, who went out to seek his father's asses, and found a kingdom." Keep only to this, for, in fact the whole work seems to say nothing more than that man, despite all his follies and errors, being led by a higher hand, reaches some happy goal at last.'

Schiller, who knew only the *second* plan, objected, and with justice, to the disproportionate space allotted to the players. 'It looks occasionally,' he wrote, 'as if you were writing *for* players, whereas your purpose is only to write *of* them. The care you bestow on certain little details of this subject and individual excellences of the art, which, although important to the player and manager, are not so to the public, give to your representation the false appearance of a particular design; and even one who does not infer such a design, might accuse you of being too much under the influence of a private preference for these subjects.' If we accept the latter plan, we must point out the inartistic composition, which allows five books of Introduction, one of disconnected Episode, and only two of Development. This is against all proportion. Yet Frederick Schlegel expressly says that the two last books are properly speaking the whole work; the others are but preparations.[49]

The purpose, or rather purposes, of *Wilhelm Meister* seem first, the rehabilitation of Dramatic Art; and secondly the theory of Education. The last two books are full of Education. Very wise and profound thoughts are expressed, and these thoughts redeem the triviality of the machinery. But otherwise these books are lamentably inferior to the first six books in style, in character, in interest. On the whole, *Wilhelm Meister* is, indeed, 'an incalculable work'. Several readings have intensified my admiration (which at first was tepid), and intensified also my sense of its defects. The beauties are ever new, ever wonderful; the faults press themselves upon notice more sharply than they did at first.

The story opens with great dramatic vivacity. Mariana and old Barbara stand before us, sketched with Shakespearian sharpness of outline and truth of detail. The whole episode is admirable, if we except the lengthy narrative in which Wilhelm details his early passion for the Marionnettes, which has probably made some readers as drowsy as it made Mariana. There is something painfully trivial in this long narrative; and it is an artistic error as a digression. The contrast between Wilhelm and the prosaic Werner is felicitously touched. But the happiest traits are those which show Wilhelm's want of decision, and incapacity of finishing the work he has begun; traits which indicate his peculiar temperament. Indeed throughout the novel Wilhelm is not the hero, but a creature of the incidents. He is a mere nose-of-wax. And this is artfully designed. Egmont and Goetz are heroes: living in stormy times, they remain altogether uninfluenced by the times. The poet represents noble characters, and he represents them in their strong, clear individuality, superior to circumstance. With Wilhelm, he shows how some characters change obedient to every external influence. The metamorphoses of Wilhelm would have been impossible with a character such as Egmont. This seems so obvious, that one is surprised to find critics objecting to the vacillating character of Wilhelm, as if it were a fault in art. It would be as reasonable to object to the vacillations of Hamlet. Wilhelm is not only led with ease from one thing to another, but is alwaays oscillating in his views of himself. Even his emotions are not persistent. He passes from love of the passionate Mariana to an inclination for the coquettish Philina; from Philina to the Countess, whom he immediately forgets for the Amazon; he is about to marry Theresa, but relinquishes her as soon as he is accepted, and offers himself to Natalie.

There is in this novel evidence of sufficient humour to have made a decidedly humorous writer, had that faculty not been kept in abeyance by other faculties. Wilhelm's unconscious pedantry, and his predominant desire to see the drama illustrated in ordinary life, and to arrange life into a theatre;[50] the Count and his eccentricities; the adventures of the players in the castle where they arrive, and find all the urgent necessaries wanting; the costume in which Wilhelm decks himself; the whole character of Philina and that of Frederic—are instances of this humorous power.

To tell the story of this novel would be too great an injustice to it; the reader has, therefore, it must be presupposed, already some acquaintance with it; in default thereof, let him at once make its acquaintance.[51] The narrative being presupposed as known, my task is easy. I have only to refer to the marvellous art with which the characters unfold themselves. We see them and see through them. They are never described, they exhibit themselves. Philina, for example, one of the most bewitching and original creations in fiction, whom we know as well as if she had flirted with us and jilted us, is never once described. Even her person is made present to us through the impression it makes on others, not by any direct information. We are not told that she was a strange mixture of carelessness, generosity, caprice, wilfulness, affectionateness, and gaiety; a lively girl, of French disposition, with the smallest possible regard for decorum but with a true decorum of her own; snapping her fingers at the world, disliking conventions, tediousness, and pedantry; without any ideal aspirations, yet also without any affectations; coquetting with all the men, disliked by all the women, turning every one round her finger, yet ready to oblige and befriend even those who had injured her: we are not told this: but as such she lives before us. She is so genuine, and so charming a sinner, that we forgive all her trespasses. On the whole, she is the most original and most difficult creation in the book. Mignon, the great poetical creation, was perhaps less difficult to draw, when once conceived. All the other characters serve as contrasts to Philina. She moves among them and throws them into relief, as they do her. The sentimental sickly Aurelia, and the sentimental Madame Melina, have an earnestness Philina does not comprehend; but they have the faults of their qualities, and she has neither. She has no more sense of earnestness than a bird. With bird-like gaiety and bird-like enjoyment of existence she chirrups through sunshine and rain. One never thinks of demanding morality from her. Morality? she knows it not, nay, has not even a bowing acquaintance with it. Nor can she be called immoral. Contrasting her with Mignon, we see her in contrast with Innocence, Earnestness, Devotion, and vague yearnings for a distant home; for Philina was never innocent; she is as quick and clever as a kitten; she cannot be serious: if she does not laugh she must yawn or cry; devoted she cannot be, although affectionate; and for a distant home, how can that trouble one who knows how to nestle everywhere? It is possible to say very hard words of Philina; but like many a naughty child, she disarms severity by her grace.

Of Mignon, and her songs, I need say nothing. Painters have tried to give an image of that strange creation which lures the imagination and the heart of every reader; but she defies the power of the pencil. The old Harper is a wild weird figure, bearing a mystery about with him, which his story at the close finely clears up. He not only adds to the variety of the figures in the novel, but by his unforgettable songs gives a depth of passion and suffering to the work which would otherwise move too exclusively in familiar regions. These two poetic figures, rising from the prosaic background, suggest an out-lying world of beauty; they have the effect of a rainbow in the London streets. Serlo, Laertes, the selfish Melina and his sentimental wife, are less developed characters, yet drawn with a masterly skill.

But when we quit their company—that is, when we quit the parts which were written before the journey to Italy, and before the plan was altered—we arrive at characters such as Lothario, the Abbé, the Doctor, Theresa, and Natalie, and feel that a totally new style is present. We have quitted the fresh air of Nature, and entered the philosopher's study; life is displaced by abstractions. Not only does the interest of the story seriously fall off, but the handling of the characters is entirely changed. The characters are described; they do not live. The incidents are crowded, have little vraisemblance and less interest. The diction has become weak—sometimes positively bad. As the men and women are without passion, so is the style without colour. Schiller, writing of the first book, says: 'The bold poetic passages, which flash up from the calm current of the whole, have an excellent effect; they elevate and fill the soul.' But the style of the last two books, with the exception of the exquisite Harper's story, is such that in England the novel is almost universally pronounced tedious, in spite of the wonderful truth and variety of character, and the beauty of so many parts. In these later books the narrative is slow, and carries incidents trivial and improbable. The Mysterious Family in the Tower is an absurd mystification; without the redeeming interest which Mrs Radcliffe would have thrown into it. With respect to the style, it is enough to open at random, and you are tolerably certain to alight upon a passage which it is difficult to conceive how an artist could have allowed it to pass. The iteration of certain set forms of phrase, and the abstractness of the diction, are very noticeable. Here is a sentence! 'Sie können aber hieraus die unglaubliche Toleranz jener Männer sehen, dass sie eben auch mich auf meinem *Wege* gerade *deswegen*, weil es mein *Weg* ist, keines*wegs* stören.'

One great peculiarity in this work is that which probably made Novalis call it 'artistic Atheism'.[52] Such a phrase is easily uttered, sounds well, is open to many interpretations, and is therefore sure to find echoes. I take it to mean that in *Wilhelm Meister* there is a complete absence of all *moral verdict* on the part of the author. Characters tread the stage, events pass before our eyes, things are done and thoughts are expressed: but no word comes from the author respecting the moral bearing of these things. Life forgets in activity all moral verdict. The good is beneficent, but no one praises it; the bad works evil, but no one anathematises it. It is a world in which we see no trace of the preacher, not a glimpse even of his surplice. To many readers this absence is like the absence of salt at dinner. They feel towards such simple objective delineation something of the repugnance felt in Evangelical circles to Miss Edgeworth's Tales. It puts them out. Robert Hall confessed that reading Miss Edgeworth hindered him for a week in his clerical functions; he was completely disturbed by her pictures of a world of happy active people *without* any visible interference of religion—a sensible, and on the whole, healthy world, yet without warnings, without exhortations, without any apparent terrors concerning the state of souls.

Much has been said about the immorality of *Wilhelm Meister* which need not be repeated here. Schiller hits the mark in his reply to what Jacobi said on this point:

> The criticism of Jacobi has not at all surprised me; for it is as inevitable that an individual like him should be offended by the unsparing truth of your pictures, as it is that a mind like yours should give him cause to be so. Jacobi is one of those who seek only their own ideas in the representation of poets, and prize more what *should be* than *what is*; the contest therefore begins in first principles. So soon as a man lets me see that there is anything in poetical representations that interests him more than internal necessity and truth, I give him up. If he could show you that the immorality of your picture does not proceed from the nature of the subject but from the manner in which you treat it, then indeed would you be accountable, not because you had sinned against moral laws, but against critical laws.

Wilhelm Meister is not a moral story—that is to say, not a story written with the express purpose of illustrating some obvious maxim. The consequence is that it is frequently pronounced immoral; which I conceive to be an absurd judgment; for if it have no express moral purpose, guiding and animating all the scenes, neither has it an immoral purpose. It may not be written for the edification of virtue; assuredly it is not written for the propagation of vice. If its author is nowhere a preacher, he cannot by his sternest critics be called a pander. All that can be said is that the Artist has been content to paint scenes of life, *without comment*; and that some of these scenes belong to an extensive class of subjects, familiar indeed to the experience of all but children, yet by general consent not much talked of in society. If any reader can be morally injured by reading such scenes in this novel rather than in the newspaper, his moral constitution is so alarmingly delicate, and so susceptible of injury, that he is truly pitiable. Let us hope the world is peopled with robuster natures; a robuster nature need not be alarmed.

But while asserting *Wilhelm Meister* to be in no respect a Moral Tale, I am bound to declare that deep and healthy moral meaning lies in it, pulses through it, speaking in many tones to him who hath ears to hear it. As Wordsworth says of *Tam o' Shanter*, 'I pity him who cannot perceive that in all this, though there was no moral purpose, there is a moral effect.' What each reader will see in it, will depend on his insight and experience. Sometimes this meaning results from the whole course of the narrative; such, for example, as the influence of life upon Wilhelm in moulding and modifying his character, raising it from mere impulse to the subordination of reason, from dreaming self-indulgence to practical duty, from self-culture to sympathy; but the way this lesson is taught is the artist's, not the preacher's way, and therefore may be missed by those who wait for the moral to be pointed before they are awake to its significance.

The 'Confessions of a Beautiful Soul,' which occupy the Sixth Book, have, in some circles, embalmed what was pronounced the corruption of the other books. Stolberg burned all the rest of the work, and kept these chapters as a treasure. Curious indeed is the picture presented of a quiet mystic, who is at the same time an original and strongly marked character; and the effect of religious convictions on life is subtly delineated in the gradual encroachment and final predominance of mysticism on the mind of one who seemed every way so well fitted for the world. Nevertheless, while duly appreciating the picture, I regret that it was not published separately, for it interrupts the story in a most inartistic manner, and has really nothing to do with the rest of the work.

The criticism on *Hamlet*, which Wilhelm makes, still remains the best criticism we have on that wonderful play. Very artfully is *Hamlet* made as it were a part of the novel; and Rosenkrantz praises its introduction not only because it illustrates the affinity between Hamlet and Wilhelm, both of whom are reflective, vacillating characters, but because Hamlet is further allied to Wilhelm in making the Play a touchstone, whereby to detect the truth, and determine his own actions.

Were space at disposal, the whole of Schiller's criticism on this work might fitly be given here from his enthusiastic letter; but I must content myself with one extract, which is quite delightful to read:

> I account it the most fortunate incident in my existence, that I have lived to see the completion of this work; that it has taken place while my faculties are still capable of improvement; that I can yet draw from this pure spring; and the beautiful relation there is between us makes it a kind of religion with me to feel towards what is yours as if it were my own, and so to purify and elevate my nature that my mind may be a clear mirror, and that I may thus deserve, in a higher sense, the name of your friend. How strongly have I felt on this occasion that the Excellent is a power; that by selfish natures it can be felt only as a power; and that only where there is disinterested love can it be enjoyed. I cannot describe to you how deeply the truth, the beautiful vitality, the simple fulness of this work has affected me. The excitement into which it has thrown my mind will subside when I shall have perfectly mastered it, and that will be an important crisis in my being. This excitement is the effect of the beautiful, and only the beautiful, and proceeds from the fact that my intellect is not yet entirely in accordance with my feelings. I understand now perfectly what you mean when you say that it is strictly the beautiful, the true, that can move you even to tears. Tranquil and deep, clear, and yet, like nature, unintelligible, is

this work; and all, even the most trivial collateral incident, shows the clearness, the equanimity of the mind whence it flowed.

The Principles of Success in Literature

Of Vision in Art (July 1865)

There are many who will admit, without hesitation, that in Philosophy what I have called the Principle of Vision holds an important rank, because the mind must necessarily err in its speculations unless it clearly sees facts and relations; but there are some who will hesitate before admitting the principle to a similiar rank in Art, because, as they conceive, Art is independent of the truth of facts, and is swayed by the autocratic power of Imagination.

It is on this power that our attention should first be arrested; the more so because it is usually spoken of in vague rhapsodical language, with intimations of its being something peculiarly mysterious. There are few words more abused. The artist is called a creator, which in one sense he is: and his creations are said to be produced by processes wholly unallied to the creations of Philosophy, which they are not. Hence it is a paradox to speak of the 'Principia', as a creation demanding severe and continuous exercise of the imagination; but it is only a paradox to those who have never analysed the processes of artistic and philosophic creation.

I am far from desiring to innovate in language, or to raise interminable discussions respecting the terms in general use. Nevertheless we have here to deal with questions that lie deeper than mere names. We have to examine processes, and trace, if possible, the methods of intellectual activity pursued in all branches of Literature; and we must not suffer our course to be obstructed by any confusion in terms that can be cleared up. We may respect the demarcations established by usage, but we must ascertain, if possible, the fundamental affinities. There is, for instance, a broad distinction between Science and Art, which, so far from requiring to be effaced, requires to be emphasised: it is that in Science the paramount appeal is to the Intellect—its purpose being instruction; in Art, the paramount appeal is to the Emotions—its purpose being pleasure. A work of Art must of course indirectly appeal to the Intellect, and a work of Science will also indirectly appeal to the Feelings; nevertheless a poem on the stars and a treatise on astronomy have distinct aims and distinct methods. But having recognised the broadly-marked differences, we are called upon to ascertain the underlying resemblances. Logic and Imagination belong equally to both. It is only because men have been attracted by the differences that they have overlooked the not less important affinities. Imagination is an intellectual process common to Philosophy and Art; but in each it is allied with different processes, and directed to different ends; and hence, although the 'Principia' demanded an imagination of not less vivid and sustained power than was demanded by 'Othello', it would be very false psychology to infer that the mind of Newton was competent to the creation of 'Othello', or the mind of Shakespeare capable of producing the 'Principia'. They were specifically different minds; their works were specifically different. But in both the imagination was intensely active. Newton had a mind predominantly ratiocinative: its movement was spontaneously towards the abstract relations of things. Shakespeare had a mind predominantly emotive, the intellect always moving in alliance with the feelings, and spontaneously fastening upon the concrete facts in preference to their abstract relations. Their mental Vision was turned towards images of different orders, and it moved in alliance with different faculties; but this Vision was the cardinal quality of both. Dr Johnson was guilty of a surprising fallacy in saying that a great mathematician might also be a great poet: 'Sir, a man can walk east as far as he can walk west.' True, but mathematics and poetry do not differ as east and west; and he would hardly assert that a man who could walk twenty miles could therefore swim that distance.

The real state of the case is somewhat obscured by our observing that many men of science, and some even eminent as teachers and reporters, display but slender claims to any unusual vigour of imagination. It must be owned that they are often slightly dull; and in matters of Art are not unfreqently blockheads. Nay, they would themselves repel it as a slight if the epithet 'imaginative' were applied to them; it would seem to impugn their gravity, to cast doubts upon their accuracy. But such men are the cisterns, not the fountains,[53] of Science. They rely upon the knowledge already organised; they do not bring accessions to the common stock. They are not investigators, but imitators; they are not discoverers—inventors. No man ever made a discovery (he may have stumbled on one) without the exercise of as much imagination as, employed in another direction and in alliance with other faculties, would have gone to the creation of a poem. Every one who has seriously investigated a novel question, who has really interrogated Nature with a view to a distinct answer, will bear me out in saying that it requires intense and sustained effort of imagination. The relations of sequence among the phenomena must be seen; they are hidden; they can only be seen mentally; a thousand suggestions rise before the mind, but they are recognised as old suggestions, or as inadequate to reveal what is sought; the experiments by which the problem may be solved have to be imagined; and to imagine a good experiment is as difficult as to invent a good fable, for we must have distinctly *present*—in clear mental vision—the known qualities and relations of all the objects, and must *see* what will be the effect of introducing some new qualifying agent. If any one thinks this is easy, let him try it: the trial will teach him a lesson respecting the methods of intellectual activity not without its use. Easy enough, indeed, is the ordinary practice of experiments already devised (as ordinary story-tellers re-tell the stories of others), or else a haphazard, blundering way of bringing phenomena together, to see what will happen. To invent is another process. The discoverer and the poet are inventors; and they are so because their mental vision detects the unapparent, unsuspected facts, almost as vividly as ocular vision rests on the apparent and familiar.

It is the special aim of Philosophy to discover and systematise the abstract *relations* of things; and for this purpose it is forced to allow the things themselves to drop out of sight, fixing attention solely on the quality immediately investigated, to the neglect of all other qualities. Thus the philosopher, having to appreciate the mass, density, refracting power, or chemical constitution of some object, finds he can best appreciate this by isolating it from every other detail. He abstracts this one quality from the complex bundle of qualities which constitute the object, and he makes this one stand for the whole. This is a necessary simplification. If all the qualities were equally present to his mind, his vision would be perplexed by their multiple suggestions. He may follow out the relations of each in turn, but he cannot follow them out together.

The aim of the poet is very different. He wishes to kindle the emotions by the suggestion of objects themselves; and for this purpose he must present images of the objects rather than of any single quality. It is true that he also must exercise a power of abstraction and selection. He cannot without confusion present all the details. And it is here that the fine selective instinct of the true artist shows itself, in knowing what details to present and what to omit. Observe this: the abstraction of the philosopher is meant to keep the object itself, with its perturbing suggestions, out of sight, allowing only one quality to fill the field of vision; whereas the abstraction of the poet is meant to bring the object itself into more vivid relief, to make it visible by means of the selected qualities. In other words, the one aims at abstract symbols, the other at picturesque effects. The one can carry on his deductions by the aid of colourless signs, x or y. The other appeals to the emotions through the symbols which will most vividly express the real objects in their relations to our sensibilities.

Imagination is obviously active in both. From known facts the philosopher infers the facts that are unapparent. He does so by an effort of imagination (hypothesis) which has to be subjected to verification: he makes a mental picture of the unapparent fact, and then sets about to prove that his picture does in some way correspond with the reality. The correctness of his hypothesis and verification must depend on the clearness of his vision. Were all the qualities of things apparent to Sense, there would be no longer any mystery. A glance would be Science. But only some of the facts are visible; and it is because we see little, that we have to imagine much. We see a feather rising in the air, and a quill, from the same bird, sinking to the ground: these contradictory reports of sense lead the mind astray; or perhaps excite a desire to know the reason. We cannot see,—we must imagine,—the unapparent facts. Many mental pictures may be formed, but to form the one which corresponds with the reality requires great sagacity and a very clear vision of known facts. In trying to form this mental picture we remember that when the air is removed the feather falls as rapidly as the quill, and thus we *see* that the air is the cause of the feather's rising; we mentally see the air pushing under the feather, and see it almost as plainly as if the air were a visible mass thrusting the feather upwards.

From a mistaken appreciation of the real process this would by few be called an effort of Imagination. On the contrary some 'wild hypothesis' would be lauded as imaginative in proportion as it departed from all suggestion of experience, i.e., real mental vision. To have imagined that the feather rose owing to its 'specific lightness' and that the quill fell owing to its 'heaviness', would to many appear a more decided effort of the imaginative faculty. Whereas it is no effort of that faculty at all; it is simply naming differently the facts it pretends to explain. To imagine—to form an image— we must have the numerous relations of things present to the mind, and see the objects in their actual order. In this we are of course greatly aided by the mass of organised experience, which allows us rapidly to estimate the relations of gravity or affinity just as we remember that fire burns and that heated bodies expand. But be the aid great or small, and the result victorious or disastrous, the imaginative process is always the same.

There is a slighter strain on the imagination of the poet, because of his greater freedom. He is not, like the philosopher, limited to the things which are, or were. His vision includes things which might be, and things which never were. The philosopher is not entitled to assume that Nature sympathises with man; he must prove the fact to be so if he intend making any use of it;—we admit no deductions from unproved assumptions. But the poet is at perfect liberty to assume this; and having done so, he paints what would be the manifestations of this sympathy. The naturalist who should describe a hippogriff would incur the laughing scorn of Europe; but the poet feigns its existence, and all Europe is delighted when it rises with Astolfo in the air. We never pause to ask the poet whether such an animal exists. He has seen it, and we see it with his eyes. Talking trees do not startle us in Virgil and Tennyson. Puck and Titania, Hamlet and Falstaff, are as true for us as Luther and Napoleon, so long as we are in the realm of Art. We grant the poet a free privilege because he will use it only for our pleasure. In Science pleasure is not an object, and we give no licence.

Philosophy and Art both render the invisible visible by imagination. Where Sense observes two isolated objects, Imagination discloses two related objects. This relation is the nexus visible. We had not seen it before; it is apparent now. Where we should only see a calamity the poet makes us see a tragedy. Where we could only see a sunrise he enables us to see 'Day like a mighty river flowing in.'

Imagination is not the exclusive appanage of artists, but belongs in varying degrees to all men. It is simply the power of forming images. Supplying the energy of Sense where Sense cannot reach, it brings into distinctness the facts, obscure or occult, which are grouped round an object or an idea, but which are not actually present to Sense. Thus, at the aspect of a windmill, the mind forms images of many characteristic facts relating to it; and the kind of images will depend very much on the general disposition, or particular mood, of the mind affected by the object: the painter, the poet, and the moralist will have different images suggested by the presence of the windmill or its symbol. There are indeed sluggish minds so incapable of self-evolved activity, and so dependent on the immediate suggestions of Sense, as to be almost destitute of the power of forming distinct images beyond the immediate circle of sensuous associations; and these are rightly named unimaginative minds; but in all minds of energetic activity, groups and clusters of images, many of them representing remote relations, spontaneously present themselves in conjunction with objects or their symbols. It should, however, be borne in mind that Imagination can only recall what Sense has previously impressed. No man imagines any detail of which he has not previously had direct or indirect experience. Objects as fictitious as mermaids and hippogriffs are made up from the gatherings of Sense.

'Made up from the gatherings of Sense' is a phrase which may seem to imply some peculiar plastic power such as is claimed exclusively for artists: a power not of simple recollection, but of recollection and recombination. Yet this power belongs also to philosophers. To combine the half of a woman with the half of a fish,—to imagine the union as an existing organism,—is not really a different process from that of combining the experience of a chemical action with an electric action, and seeing that the two are one existing fact. When the poet hears the storm-cloud muttering, and sees the moonlight sleeping on the bank, he transfers his experience of human phenomena to the cloud and the moonlight: he personifies, draws Nature within the circle of emotion, and is called a poet. When the philosopher sees electricity in the storm-cloud, and sees the sunlight stimulating vegetable growth, he transfers his experience of physical phenomena to these objects, and draws within the circle of Law phenomena which hitherto have been unclassified. Obviously the imagination has been as active in the one case as in the other; the *differentia* lying in the purposes of the two, and in the general constitution of the two minds.

It has been noted that there is less strain on the imagination of the poet; but even his greater freedom is not altogether disengaged from the necessity of verification; his images must have at least subjective truth; if they do not accurately correspond with objective realities, they must correspond with our sense of congruity. No poet is allowed the licence of creating images inconsistent with our conceptions. If he said the moonlight *burnt* the bank, we should reject the image as untrue, inconsistent with our conceptions of moonlight; whereas the gentle repose of the moonlight on the bank readily associates itself with images of sleep.

The often mooted question, What is Imagination? thus receives a very clear and definite answer. It is the power of forming images; it reinstates, in a visible group, those objects which are invisible, either from absence or from imperfection of our senses. That is its generic character. Its specific character, which marks it off from Memory, and which is derived from the powers of selection and recombination, will be expounded further on. Here I only touch upon its chief characteristic, in order to disengage the term from that mysteriousness which writers have usually assigned to it, thereby rendering philosophic criticism impossible. Thus disengaged it may be used with more certainty in an attempt to estimate the imaginative power of various works.

Hitherto the amount of that power has been too frequently estimated according to the extent of *departure* from ordinary experience in the images selected. Nineteen out of twenty would unhesitatingly declare that a hippogriff was a greater effort of imagination than a well-conceived human character; a Peri than a woman; Puck or Titania than Falstaff or Imogen. A description of Paradise extremely unlike any known garden must, it is thought, necessarily be more imaginative than the description of a quiet rural nook. It may be more imaginative; it may be less so. All depends upon the mind of the poet. To suppose that it must, because of its departure from ordinary experience, is a serious error. The muscular effort required to draw a cheque for a thousand pounds might as reasonably be thought greater than that required for a cheque of five pounds; and much as the one cheque seems to surpass the other in value, the result of presenting both to the bankers may show that the more modest cheque is worth its full five pounds, whereas the other is only so much waste paper. The description of Paradise may be a glittering farrago; the description of the landscape may be full of sweet rural images: the one having a glare of gaslight and Vauxhall splendour; the other having the scent of new-mown hay.

A work is imaginative in virtue of the power of its images over our emotions; not in virtue of any rarity or surprisingness in the images themselves. A Madonna and Child by Fra Angelico is more powerful over our emotions than a Crucifixion by a vulgar artist; a beggar-boy by Murillo is more imaginative than an Assumption by the same painter; but the Assumption by Titian displays far greater imagination than either. We must guard against the natural tendency to attribute to the artist what is entirely due to accidental conditions. A tropical scene, luxuriant with tangled overgrowth and impressive in the grandeur of its phenomena, may more decisively arrest our attention than an English landscape with its green corn lands and plenteous homesteads. But this superiority of interest is no proof of the artist's superior imagination; and by a spectator familiar with the tropics, greater interest may be felt in the English landscape, because its images may more forcibly arrest his attention by their novelty. And were this not so, were the inalienable impressiveness of tropical scenery always to give the poet who described it a superiority in effect, this would not prove the superiority of his imagination. For either he has been familiar with such scenes, and imagines them just as the other poet imagines his English landscape—by an effort of mental vision, calling up the absent objects; or he has merely read the descriptions of others, and from these makes up his picture. It is the same with his rival, who also recalls and recombines. Foolish critics often betray their ignorance by saying that a painter or a writer 'only copies what he has seen, or puts down what he has known'. They forget that no man imagines what he has not seen or known, and that it is in the *selection of the characteristic details* that the artistic power is manifested. Those who suppose that familiarity with scenes or characters enables a painter or a novelist to 'copy' them with artistic effect, forget the well-known fact that the vast majority of men are painfully incompetent to avail themselves of this familiarity, and cannot form vivid pictures even to themselves of scenes in which they pass their daily lives; and if they could imagine these, they would need the delicate selective instinct to guide them in the admission and omission of details, as well as in the groupings of the images. Let any one try to 'copy' the wife or brother he knows so well,—to make a human image which shall speak and act so as to impress strangers with a belief in its truth,—and he will then see that the much-despised reliance on actual experience is not the mechanical procedure it is believed to be. When Scott drew Saladin and Coeur de Lion he did not really display more imaginative power than when he drew the Mucklebackits,[54] although the majority of readers would suppose that the one demanded a great effort of imagination, whereas the other formed part of his familiar experiences of Scottish life. The mistake here lies in confounding the sources from which the materials were derived with the plastic power of forming these materials into images. More conscious effort may have been devoted to the collection of the materials in the one case than in the other, but that this has nothing to do with the imaginative power employed may readily be proved by an analysis of the intellectual processes of composition. Scott had often been in fishermen's cottages and heard them talk; from the registered experience of a thousand details relating to the life of the poor, their feelings and their thoughts, he gained that material upon which his imagination could work; in the case of Saladin and Coeur de Lion he had to gain these principally through books and his general experience of life; and the images he formed—the vision he had of Mucklebackit and Saladin—must be set down to his artistic faculty, not to his experience or erudition.

It has been well said by a very imaginative writer,[55] that 'when a poet floats in the empyrean, and only takes a bird's-eye view of the earth, some people accept the mere fact of his soaring for sublimity, and mistake his dim vision of earth for proximity to heaven.' And in like manner, when a thinker frees himself from all the trammels of fact, and propounds a 'bold hypothesis', people mistake the vagabond erratic flights of guessing for a higher range of philosophic power. In truth, the imagination is most tasked when it has to paint pictures which shall withstand the silent criticism of general experience, and to frame hypotheses which shall withstand the confrontation with facts. I cannot here enter into the interesting question of Realism and Idealism in Art, which must be debated in a future chapter; but I wish to call special attention to the psychological fact, that fairies and demons, remote as they are from experience, are not created by a more vigorous effort of imagination than milk maids and poachers. The intensity of vision in the artist and of vividness in his creations are the sole tests of his imaginative power.

✳ ✳ ✳

If this brief exposition has carried the reader's assent, he will readily apply the princple, and recognise that an artist produces an effect in virtue of the distinctness with which he sees the objects he represents, seeing them not vaguely as in vanishing apparitions, but steadily, and in their most characteristic relations. To this Vision he adds artistic skill with which to make us see. He may have clear conceptions, yet fails to make them clear to us: in this case he has imagination, but is not an artist. Without clear Vision no skill can avail. Imperfect Vision necessitates imperfect representation; words take the place of ideas.

In Young's 'Night Thoughts' there are many examples of the *pseudo*-imaginative, betraying an utter want of steady Vision. Here is one:–

His hands the good man fixes on the skies,
And bids earth roll, nor feels the idle whirl.

'Pause for a moment,' remarks a critic,[56] 'to realise the image, and the monstrous absurdity of a man's grasping the skies and hanging habitually suspended there, while he contemptuously bids earth roll, warns you that no genuine feeling could have suggested so unnatural a conception.' It is obvious that if Young had imagined the position he assigned to the good man he would have seen its absurdity; instead of imagining, he allowed the vague transient suggestion of half-nascent images to shape themselves in verse.

Now compare with this a passage in which imagination is really active. Wordsworth recalls how—

In November days
When vapours rolling down the valleys made
A lonely scene more lonesome: among the woods
At noon; and mid the calm of summer nights,
When by the margin of the trembling lake
Beneath the gloomy hills homeward I went
In solitude, such intercourse was mine.[57]

There is nothing very grand or impressive in this passage, and therefore it is a better illustration for my purpose. Note how happily the one image, out of a thousand possible images by which November might be characterised, is chosen to call up in us the feeling of the lonely scene; and with what delicate selection the calm of summer nights, the 'trembling lake' (an image in an epithet), and the gloomy hills, are brought before us. His boyhood might have furnished him with a hundred different pictures, each as distinct as this; power is shown in selecting this one—painting it so vividly. He continues:–

> 'Twas mine among the fields both day and night
> And by the waters, all the summer long.
> And in the frosty season, when the sun
> Was set, and, visible for many a mile
> The cottage windows through the twilight blazed,
> I heeded not the summons: happy time
> It was indeed for all of us; for me
> It was a time of rapture! Clear and loud
> The village clock tolled six—I wheeled about,
> Proud and exulting like an untired horse
> That cares not for his home. All shod with steel
> We hissed along the polished ice, in games
> Confederate, imitative of the chase
> And woodland pleasures—the resounding horn,
> The pack loud-chiming and the hunted hare.

There is nothing very felicitous in these lines; yet even here the poet, if languid, is never false. As he proceeds the vision brightens, and the verse becomes instinct with life:–

> So through the darkness and the cold we flew
> And not a voice was idle: with the din
> Smitten, the precipices rang aloud;
> *The leafless trees and every icy crag*
> *Tinkled like iron; while the distant hills*
> *Into the tumult sent an alien sound*
> *Of melancholy*, not unnoticed while the stars
> Eastwards were sparkling clear, and in the west
> The orange sky of evening died away.
> Not seldom from the uproar I retired
> Into a silent bay, or sportively
> Glanced sideway, leaving the tumultuous throng,
> *To cut across the reflex of a star;*
> *Image that flying still before me* gleamed

Upon the glassy plain: and oftentime
When we had given our bodies to the wind
And all the shadowy banks on either side
Came creeping through the darkness, spinning still
The rapid line of motion, then at once
Have I reclining back upon my heels
Stopped short; yet still the solitary cliffs
Wheeled by me—even as if the earth had rolled
With visible motion her diurnal round!
Behind me did they stretch in solemn train,
Feebler and feebler, and I stood and watched
Till all was tranquil as a summer sea.

Every poetical reader will feel delight in the accuracy with which the details are painted, and the marvellous clearness with which the whole scene is imagined, both in its objective and subjective relations, i.e., both in the objects seen and the emotions they suggest.

What the majority of modern verse writers call 'imagery', is not the product of imagination, but a restless pursuit of comparison, and a lax use of language. Instead of presenting us with an image of the object, they present us with something which they tell us is like the object—which it rarely is. The thing itself has no clear significance to them, it is only a text for the display of their ingenuity. If, however, we turn from poetasters to poets, we see great accuracy in depicting the things themselves or their suggestions, so that we may be certain the things presented themselves in the field of the poet's vision, and were painted because seen. The images arose with sudden vivacity, or were detained long enough to enable their characters to be seized. It is this power of detention to which I would call particular notice, because a valuable practical lesson may be learned through a proper estimate of it. If clear Vision be indispensable to success in Art, all means of securing that clearness should be sought. Now one means is that of detaining an image long enough before the mind to allow of its being seen in all its characteristics. The explanation Newton gave of his discovery of the great law, points in this direction; it was by always thinking of the subject, by keeping it constantly before his mind, that he finally saw the truth. Artists brood over the chaos of their suggestions, and thus shape them into creations. Try and form a picture in your own mind of your early skating experience. It may be that the scene only comes back upon you in shifting outlines, you recall the general facts, and some few particulars are vivid, but the greater part of the details vanish again before they can assume decisive shape; they are but half nascent, or die as soon as born: a wave of recollection washes over the mind, but it quickly retires, leaving no trace behind. This is the common experience. Or it may be that the whole scene flashes upon you with peculiar vividness, so that you see, almost as in actual presence, all the leading characteristics of the picture. Wordsworth may have seen his early days in a succession of vivid flashes, or he may have attained to his distinctness of vision by a steadfast continuity of effort, in which what at first was vague became slowly definite as he gazed. It is certain that only a very imaginative mind could have seen such details as he has gathered together in the lines describing how he

> Cut across the reflex of a star;
> Image that flying still before me gleamed
> Upon the glassy plain.

The whole description may have been written with great rapidity, or with anxious and tentative labour: the memories of boyish days may have been kindled with a sudden illumination, or they may have grown slowly into the requisite distinctness, detail after detail emerging from the general obscurity, like the appearing stars at night. But whether the poet felt his way to images and epithets, rapidly or slowly, is unimportant; we have to do only with the result; and the result implies, as an absolute condition, that the images were distinct. Only thus could they serve the purposes of poetry, which must arouse in us memories of similar scenes and kindle emotions of pleasurable experience.

❋ ❋ ❋

Having cited an example of bad writing consequent on imperfect Vision, I might consider that enough had been done for the immediate purpose of the present chapter; the many other illustrations which the Principle of Vision would require before it could be considered as adequately expounded, I must defer till I come to treat of the application of principles. But before closing this chapter it may be needful to examine some arguments which have a contrary tendency, and imply, or seem to imply, that distinctness of Vision is very far from necessary.

At the outset we must come to an understanding as to this word 'image', and endeavour to free the word 'vision' from all equivoque. If these words were understood literally there would be an obvious absurdity in speaking of an image of a sound, or of seeing an emotion. Yet if by means of symbols the effect of a sound is produced in us, or the psychological state of any human being is rendered intelligible to us, we are said to have images of these things which the poet has imagined. It is because the eye is the most valued and intellectual of our senses that the majority of metaphors are borrowed from its sensations. Language, after all, is only the use of symbols, and Art also can only affect us through symbols. If a phrase can summon a terror resembling that summoned by the danger which it indicates, a man is said to *see* the danger. Sometimes a phrase will awaken more vivid images of danger than would be called up by the actual presence of the dangerous object;

because the mind will more readily apprehend the symbols of the phrase than interpret the indications of unassisted sense.

Burke is his 'Essay on the Sublime and Beautiful', lays down the proposition that distinctness of imagery is often injurious to the effect of art. 'It is one thing,' he says

> to make an idea clear, another to make it *affecting* to the imagination. If I make a drawing of a palace or a temple or a landscape, I present a very clear idea of those objects; but then (allowing for the effect of imitation, which is something) my picture can at most affect only as the palace, temple, or landscape would have affected in reality. On the other hand the most lively and spirited verbal description I can give raises a very obscure and imperfect *idea* of such objects; but then it is in my power to raise a stronger *emotion* by the description than I can do by the best painting. This experience constantly evinces. The proper · manner of conveying the *affections* of the mind from one to the other is by words: there is great insufficiency in all other methods of communication; and so far is a clearness of imagery from being absolutely necessary to an influence upon the passions, that they may be considerably operated upon without presenting any image at all, by certain sounds adapted to that purpose.

If by image is meant only what the eye can see, Burke is undoubtedly right. But this is obviously not our restricted meaning of the word when we speak of poetic imagery; and Burke's error becomes apparent when he proceeds to show that there 'are reasons in nature why an obscure idea, when properly conveyed, should be more affecting than the clear.' He does not seem to have considered that the idea of an indefinite object can only be properly conveyed by indefinite images; any image of Eternity or Death that pretended to visual distinctness would be false. Having overlooked this, he says, 'We do not anywhere meet a more sublime description than this justly celebrated one of Milton, wherein he gives the portrait of Satan with a dignity so suitable to the subject.

> He above the rest
> In shape and gesture proudly eminent
> Stood like a tower; his form had not yet lost
> All her original brightness, nor appeared
> Less than archangel ruined and the excess
> Of glory obscured: as when the sun new risen
> Looks through the horizontal misty air
> Shorn of his beams; or from behind the moon
> In dim eclipse disastrous twilight sheds
> On half the nations; and with fear of change
> Perplexes monarchs.[58]

Here is a very noble picture,' adds Burke, 'and in what does this poetical picture consist? In images of a tower, an archangel, the sun rising through mists, or an eclipse, the ruin of monarchs, and the revolution of kingdoms.' Instead of recognising the imagery here as the source of the power, he says, 'The mind is hurried out of itself [rather a strange result!] by a crowd of great and confused images; which affect because they are crowded and confused. For, separate them, and you lose much of the greatness; and join them, and you infallibly lose the clearness.' This is altogether a mistake. The images are vivid enough to make us feel the hovering presence of an awe-inspiring figure having the height and firmness of a tower, and the dusky splendour of a ruined archangel. The poet indicates only that amount of concreteness which is necessary for the clearness of the picture,—only the height and firmness of the tower and the brightness of the sun in eclipse. More concreteness would disturb the clearness by calling attention to irrelevant details. To suppose that these images produce the effect because they are crowded and confused (they are crowded and not confused) is to imply that any other images would do equally well, if they were equally crowded. 'Separate them, and you lose much of the greatness.' Quite true: the image of the tower would want the splendour of the sun. But this much may be said of all descriptions which proceed upon details. And so far from the impressive clearness of the picture vanishing in the crowd of images, it is by these images that the clearness is produced: the details make it impressive, and affect our imagination.

It should be added that Burke came very near a true explanation in the following passage:—

> It is difficult to conceive how words can move the passions which belong to real objects without representing these objects clearly. This is difficult to us because we do not sufficiently distinguish between a clear expression and a strong expression. The former regards the understanding; the latter belongs to the passions. The one describes a thing as it is, the other decribes it as it is felt. Now as there is a moving tone of voice, an impassioned countenance, an agitated gesture, which affect independently of the things about which they are exerted, so there are words and certain dispositions of words which being peculiarly devoted to passionate subjects, and always used by those who are under the influence of passion, touch and move us more than those which far more clearly and distinctly express the subject-matter.

Burke here fails to see that the tones, looks and gestures are the intelligible symbols of passion—the 'images' of the true sense—just as words are the intelligible symbols of ideas. The subject-matter is as clearly expressed by the one as by the other; for if the description of a Lion be conveyed in the symbols of admiration or of terror, the subject-matter is *then* a Lion passionately and zoologically considered. And this Burke himself was led to admit, for he adds,

> We yield to sympathy what we refuse to description. The truth is, all verbal description, merely as naked description, though never so exact, conveys so poor and insufficient an idea of the thing described, that it could scarcely have the smallest effect if the speaker did not call in to his aid those modes of speech that work a strong and lively feeling in himself. Then, by the contagion of our passions, we catch a fire already kindled in another.

This is very true, and it sets clearly forth the fact that naked description, addressed to the calm understanding, has a different subject-matter from description addressed to the feelings, and the symbols by which it is made intelligible must likewise differ. But this in no way impugns the principle of Vision. Intelligible symbols (clear images) are as necessary in the one case as in the other.

❋ ❋ ❋

By reducing imagination to the power of forming images, and by insisting that no image can be formed except out of the elements furnished by experience, I do not mean to confound imagination with memory; indeed, the frequent occurrence of great strength of memory with comparative feebleness of imagination, would suffice to warn us against such a conclusion.

Its specific character, that which marks it off from simple memory, is its tendency to selection, abstraction, and recombination. Memory, as passive, simply recalls previous experiences of objects and emotions; from these, imagination, as an active faculty, selects the elements which vividly symbolise the objects or emotions, and either by a process of abstraction allows these to do duty for the wholes, or else by a process of recombination creates new objects and new relations in which the objects stand to us or to each other (*invention*), and the result is an image of great vividness, which has perhaps no corresponding reality in the external world.

Minds differ in the vividness with which they recall the elements of previous experience, and mentally see the absent objects; they differ also in the aptitudes for selection, abstraction, and recombination: the fine selective instinct of the artist, which makes him fasten upon the details which will most powerfully affect us, without any disturbance of the harmony of the general impression, does not depend solely upon the vividness of his memory and the clearness with which the objects are seen, but depends also upon very complex and peculiar conditions of sympathy which we call genius. Hence we find one man remembering a multitude of details with a memory so vivid that it almost amounts at times to hallucination, yet without any artistic power; and we may find men—Blake was one—with an imagination of unusual activity, who are nevertheless incapable, from deficient sympathy, of seizing upon those symbols which will most affect us. Our native susceptibilities and acquired tastes determine which of the many qualities in an object shall most impress us, and be most clearly recalled. One man remembers the combustible properties of a substance, which to another is memorable for its polarising property; to one man a stream is so much water-power, to another a rendezvous for lovers.

In the close of the last paragraph we came face to face with the great difficulty which constantly arrests speculation on these matters—the existence of special aptitudes vaguely characterised as genius. These are obviously incommunicable. No recipe can be given for genius. No man can be taught how to exercise the power of imagination. But he can be taught how to aid it, and how to assure himself whether he is using it or not. Having once laid hold of the Principle of Vision as a fundamental principle of Art, he can always thus far apply it, that he can assure himself whether he does or does not distinctly *see* the cottage he is describing, the rivulet that is gurgling though his verses, or the character he is painting; he can assure himself whether he hears the voice of the speakers, and feels that what they say is true to their natures; he can assure himself whether he sees, as in actual experience, the emotion he is depicting; and he will know that if he does not see these things he must wait until he can, or he will paint them ineffectively. With distinct Vision he will be able to make the best use of his powers of expression; and the most splendid powers of expression will not avail him if his Vision be indistinct. This is true of objects that never were seen by the eye, that never could be seen. It is as true of what are called the highest flights of imagination as of the lowest flights. The mind must *see* the angel or the demon, the hippogriff or centaur, the pixie or the mermaid.

Ruskin notices how repeatedly Turner,—the most imaginative of landscape painters,—introduced into his pictures, after a lapse of many years, memories of something which, however small and unimportant, had struck him in his earlier studies.[59] He believes that all Turner's 'composition' was an arrangement of remembrances summoned just as they were wanted, and each in its fittest place. His vision was primarily composed of strong memory of the place itself, and secondarily of memories of other places associated in a harmonious, helpful way with the now central thought. He recalled and selected.

I am prepared to hear of many readers, especially young readers, protesting against the doctrine of this chapter as prosaic. They have been so long accustomed to consider imagination as peculiarly distinguished by its disdain of reality, and Invention as only admirable when its products are not simply new by selection and arrangement, but new in material, that they will reject the idea of involuntary remembrance of something originally experienced as the basis of all Art. Ruskin says of great artists,

> Imagine all that any of these men had seen or heard in the whole course of their lives, laid up accurately in their memories as in vast store-houses, extending with the poets even to the slightest intonations of syllables heard in the beginning of their lives, and with painters down to minute folds of drapery and shapes of leaves and stones; and over all this unindexed and immeasurable mass of treasure, the imagination brooding and wandering, but dream-gifted, so as to summon at any moment exactly such a group of ideas as shall justly fit each other.

This is the explanation of their genius, as far as it can be explained.

Genius is rarely able to give any account of its own processes. But those who have had ample opportunities of intimately knowing the growth of works in the minds of artists, will bear me out in saying that a vivid memory supplies the elements from a thousand different sources, most of which are quite beyond the power of localisation,—the experience of yesterday being strangely intermingled with the dim suggestions of early years, the tones heard in childhood sounding through the diapason of sorrowing maturity; and all these kaleidoscopic fragments are recomposed into images that seem to have a corresponding reality of their own.

As all Art depends on Vision, so the different kinds of Art depend on the different ways in which minds look at things. The painter can only put into his pictures what he sees in Nature; and what he sees will be different from what another sees. A poetical mind sees noble and affecting suggestions in details which the prosaic mind will interpret prosaically. And the true meaning of Idealism is precisely this vision of realities in their highest and most affecting forms, not in the vision of something removed from or opposed to realities. Titian's grand picture of 'Peter the Martyr' is, perhaps, as instructive an example as could be chosen of successful Idealism; because in it we have a marvellous presentation of reality as seen by a poetic mind. The figure of the flying monk might have been equally real if it had been an ignoble presentation of terror—the superb tree, which may almost be called an actor in the drama, might have been painted with even greater minuteness, though not perhaps with equal effect upon us, if he had arrested our attention by its details—the dying martyr and the noble assassin might have been made equally real in more vulgar types—but the triumph achieved by Titian is that the mind is filled with a vision of poetic beauty which is felt to be real. An equivalent reality, without the ennobling beauty, would have made the picture a fine piece of realistic art. It is because of this poetic way of seeing things that one painter will give a faithful representation of a very common scene which shall nevertheless affect all sensitive minds as ideal, whereas another painter will represent the same with no greater fidelity, but with a complete absence of poetry. The greater the fidelity, the greater will be the merit of each representation; for if a man pretends to represent an object, he pretends to represent it accurately: the only difference is what the poetical or prosaic mind sees in the object.

Of late years there has been a reaction against conventionalism which called itself Idealism, in favour of *detailism* which calls itself Realism. As a reaction it has been of service; but it has led to much false criticism, and not a little false art, by an obtrusiveness of Detail and a preference for the Familiar, under the misleading notion of adherence to Nature. If the words Nature and Natural could be entirely banished from language about Art there would be some chance of coming to a rational philosophy of the subject; at present the excessive vagueness and shiftiness of these terms cover any amount of sophism. The pots and pans of Teniers and Van Mieris are natural; the passions and humours of Shakespeare and Molière are natural; the angels of Fra Angelico and Luini are natural; the Sleeping Fawn and Fates of Phidias are natural; the cows and misty marshes of Cuyp and the vacillations of Hamlet are equally natural. In fact the natural means *truth of kind.* Each kind of character, each kind of representation, must be judged by itself. Whereas the vulgar error of criticism is to judge of one kind by another, and generally to judge the higher by the lower, to remonstrate with Hamlet for not having the speech and manner of Mr Jones, to wish that Fra Angelico could have seen with the eyes of the Carracci, to wish verse had been prose, and that ideal tragedy were acted with the easy manner acceptable in drawing-rooms.

The rage for 'realism', which is healthy in as far as it insists on truth, has become unhealthy, in as far as it confounds truth with familiarity, and predominance of unessential details. There are other truths besides coats and waistcoats, pots and pans, drawing-rooms and suburban villas. Life has other aims besides those which occupy the conversation of 'Society'. And the painter who devotes years to a work representing modern life, yet calls for even more attention to a waistcoat than to the face of a philosopher, may exhibit truth of detail which will delight the tailor-mind, but he is defective in artistic truth, because he ought to be representing something higher than waistcoats, and because our thoughts on modern life fall very casually and without emphasis on waistcoats. In Piloty's much-admired picture of the 'Death of Wallenstein' (at Munich), the truth with which the carpet, the velvet, and all other accessories are painted, is certainly remarkable; but the falsehood of giving prominence to such details in a picture representing the dead Wallenstein—as if they were the objects which could possibly arrest our attention and excite our sympathies in such a spectacle—is a falsehood of the realistic school. If a man means to paint upholstery, by all means let him paint it so as to delight and deceive an upholsterer; but if it means to paint a human tragedy, the upholsterer must be subordinate, and velvet must not draw our eyes away from faces.

I have digressed a little from my straight route because I wish to guard the Principle of Vision from certain misconceptions which might arise on a simple statement of it. The principle insists on the artist assuring himself that he distinctly sees what he attempts to represent. *What* he sees, and *how* he represents it, depend on other principles. To make even this principle of Vision thoroughly intellligible in its application to all forms of Literature and Art, it must be considered in connection with the two other principles—Sincerity and Beauty, which are involved in all successful works. In the next chapter we shall treat of Sincerity.

Auguste Comte

From *Fortnightly Review* (January 1866)

Auguste Comte was born at Montpellier on 19 January, 1798, in a modest house still to be seen facing the church of St Eulalie. His father was treasurer of taxes for the department of Hérault. Both father and mother were strict Catholics and ardent royalists; but any influence they may have exercised over the direction of their son's thoughts was considerably neutralised by his own insurgent disposition on the one hand, and by his early education on the other. He was not docile to authority; but in after life he strenuously preached the virtue of docility. At the age of nine he became a boarder in the Montpellier Lycée; and there quickly distinguished himself by his ardour in study and his resistance to discipline. Small and delicate in frame, loved by his comrades although he seldom joined in their sports, full of veneration for his professors, he was intractable, tiresome, and argumentative with his masters; those who could teach him found him docile; those who had to restrain him found him rebellious. His professors praised, his masters punished him.

At the age of twelve he had learned all that the Lycée prescribed in the way of instruction, and the Director begged that he might be permitted to begin mathematics. Consent was given; and the result may be told in one significant sentence: in four years he had gained a first place at the École Polytechnique, although the rules of that institution did not then allow of his admission, because he was still under age. He had to wait a whole year before the doors were opened to him; and in that year he displayed his acquirements by taking the place of his old professor (who was in failing health), and giving a course of mathematics to his former comrades, and some of his former masters.

At the age of seventeen he was admitted to the École Polytechnique, and there he found republican sentiments and scientific tendencies eminently suited to his rebellious and inquiring disposition. By the time he was fourteen he is supposed to have entirely disengaged himself from all royalist and all theological opinions; and he was now occupied with the writings which in the eighteenth century discussed the fundamental axioms of social, ethical, and religious systems. He began seriously to meditate on the revolutions of modern history. His comrades respected and admired him. His professors recognised his eminent capacity. A brilliant career seemed certain, when it was arrested by a characteristic action of his own. One of the masters had

244

insulted the younger students by his manners; the elder students took up the case, and after mature deliberation decided that the master was unworthy of continuing in his office. They drew up the following notification:–

Monsieur, quoiqui'il nous soit pénible de prendre une telle mesure envers un ancien élève de l'École nous vous enjoignons de n'y plus remettre les pieds.

This notification, drawn up by Comte, had his signature at the head of the list. The result was his expulsion. His official career was at an end. He was forced to return home; and remained there some time under the surveillance of the police.

We do not learn, but we may imagine, what was his reception at home, and of what nature were the debates as to his possible future. He remained some months at Montpellier, pursuing his studies with passionate devotion, and attending the various lectures at the Faculty. But this could not last. Paris allured him. In vain were the remonstrances and threats of his troubled parents; in vain their refusal to give him a penny if he quitted his native city without an assured position; the desire for freedom and the manifold attractions of the great intellectual centre were all powerful; and he found himself lonely in the crowded capital, ready to begin that eternal struggle in which year after year so many noble intellects equipped with nothing but a little knowledge and an immense ambition fight for bread and distinction, are wounded and worsted, are wounded and conquer. A greater intellect moved by a loftier ambition has rarely fought that noble fight.

He supplied his very modest wants by giving private lessons in mathematics. Two illustrious men of science befriended him—Poinsot, who had been his professor at the École Polytechnique, and knew his mathematical power; De Blainville, who early recognised his philosophical calibre. By their aid a few pupils were obtained; one of them was the Prince de Carignan. The bread was scanty, but he wanted little more than bread. He was not one of those who flounder on the sunken rocks of Parisian life.

A brief experience of a less independent position seems to have sufficed. He became private secretary to Casimir Périer; but quickly found that the paid servant was expected to be a blind admirer. Called upon to make some comments on the public labours of his master, 'elles ne furent pas goutées'; and after a trial of three weeks the connection ceased. From Casimir Périer he passed over to the celebrated St Simon. This was in 1818. The young philosopher hoped that he might live in harmony with a philosopher; and for some years he did so. I cannot ascertain precisely the footing on which they stood together. M Littré says that Comte was first secretary, then pupil, then collaborateur and friend. Dr Robinet says that the secretaryship was practically an honorary one, for although three hundred francs a month were promised, only the first quarter's salary was ever paid. Whatever the nature of the relation, it subsisted for six years, beginning with great enthusiasm on Comte's part, continuing for some time with affectionate veneration, and ending in a violent rupture which was the culmination of a growing dissidence in opinion.

There have been angry accusations and angry recriminations from the disciples of St Simon and the disciples of Comte which render the task of an impartial biographer somewhat difficult. But whatever may have been the personal influence of St Simon, for good or evil, on the direction of Comte's aims, a superficial acquaintance with the Positive Philosophy will detect its essential independence of, and divergence from, St Simonianism. When, therefore, writers sarcastically or indignantly assert that Comte 'borrowed St Simon's ideas', they disclose a complete misapprehension of all that characterises the Positive Philosophy. On the other hand it is unnecessary to assail St Simon, and accuse him of being an ignorant charlatan, in order to prove what his own language and the express declaration of his editor unequivocally establish, namely, that he not only disapproved, he failed even to understand, the doctrines of his young collaborateur.

As a point in the history of philosophical evolution it is clear that Comte does not proceed from St Simon, but from the eighteenth century: he resumed its twofold movement towards destruction and reconstruction in one grand synthesis by means of a thorough application of the Methods of science. Nevertheless, as a point in the biographical evolution of Comte's own mind, it is, I think, undeniable that the influence of St Simon was decisive. By which I mean that through personal contact with this reformer his mind received the stimulus, if not the bias, which at that peculiar stage of his development was a determining one. At the age of twenty, familiar with all the inorganic sciences (Biology he had not then studied, and Sociology had not been conceived), well read in history, fervent in republicanism, and ambitious of mastering the great laws of social existence, this inheritor of the eighteenth century spirit, seeing in philosophy and science little beyond the dissolution of theological superstitions and feudal inequalities, came into affectionate and reverential contact with one whom some regard as a turbulent charlatan, and others as a prophetic thinker, but whom all must admit to have been impressed with the urgent need and possibility of replacing the critical and destructive spirit by a positive and constructive spirit; and the immediate consequence of this contact was, that Comte learned to look upon the revolutionary work as completed, and saw that the effort of the nineteenth century must be towards the reconstruction of society upon a new basis. The old faith was destroyed; a new faith was indispensable.

Such is the fact. Probably most readers will agree with M Littré, that so potent an intellect as Comte's might easily have passed from the revolutionary to the organic attitude without any impulse from one so manifestly his inferior as St Simon: but 'what might have been' is an idle hypothesis when we know what was; and in Biography, as elsewhere, we should guard against the tendency to substitute a possible evolution for an actual evolution. The simple biographical fact is, that in his youth Comte passed from the negative to the positive attitude while under the influence of a teacher whose special aim was constructive. He called himself a disciple of St Simon; and it is not clear what he could have learned from such a master, except the necessity of a constructive attitude.

An attitude however, is not a doctine; an aim is not a philosophy. The impulsion may have come from St Simon; the doctrine assuredly came from Comte, and from him only. It was probably owing to his keen perception of the irreconcilability of his ideas with the ideas of St Simon, and the pardonable exasperation he felt at ungenerous accusations, that made him in his later years speak of his old master with excessive bitterness. His tone was that of a man who feels himself to have been deeply injured. So far from acknowledging any intellectual debt, he, who was nobly scrupulous in acknowledgment of all such obligations, however trifling, always affirmed that St Simon's influence had been a serious retardation of his development. What the truth may be cannot now be ascertained. It is certain that his development was surprisingly rapid, and that four years after his first meeting with St Simon, namely in 1822, he laid the solid basis of the new philosophy, which he called 'positive', because it was the generalisation of the method which each positive science had employed in particular. Like Bacon, he schemed in his youth what a laborious life was devoted to work out.

St Simon had vast aspirations, but he misconceived the fundamental conditions of social reorganisation. He was, moreover, altogether unprepared for a system based upon positive science, because unacquainted with the methods of science; and accordingly, when Comte, in 1822, having discovered the laws of social evolution, drew up his memorable *Plan des travaux nécessaires pour réorganiser la Société*, it must have dawned upon St Simon that his young assistant had become his rival and superior. He published the essay, but even in publishing it disclaimed agreement in its peculiar views. Others thought more highly of it; among these were Humboldt and Guizot. In writing to a friend, the young philosopher could say,

J'ai été agréablement affecté (je ne dis pas supris) de l'effet que ce travail a produit sur M Guizot; il m'en a témoigné par écrit une profonde, et sincère satisfaction, et depuis j'ai pu voir par sa conversation que ces idées agissent sur lui.

He also mentions its effect on Flourens, adding,

Je dois avoir avec lui un entretien important sur l'idée fondamentale de mon travail, l'application de la méthode positive à la science sociale.

The open rupture with St Simon took place in 1824. The next year may be considered the year when the Positive Philosophy was constituted; for, as M Littré reminds us, the essay of 1822, republished in 1824, only sets forth the laws of social evolution, but does not give even an outline of the Positive Philosophy, which is for the first time expressly announced in the 'Considérations Philosophiques sur les Sciences et les Savants'[60] (published in the *Producteur* in 1825). In the two pregnant essays which thus form, as it were, the inaugural theses of the young philosopher, it is shown (i) that all phenomena, even those of politics, are subject to invariable laws; (ii) that the human mind passes from initial theological conceptions to final positive conceptions, through the transition of metaphysical conceptions; (iii) that human activity, in like manner, passes through three phases, from the conquering military régime to the pacific industrial régime, through the transitional state of a defensive military régime; (iv) that everywhere, and at all times, the state of opinions and manners determines the institutions, and that the nature of the general beliefs determines a corresponding political scheme; (v) that philosophy (or general beliefs) in passing from the theological to the positive stage must bring about the substitution of the industrial for the military régime; and finally, that the spiritual reorganisation, which is the necessary condition of all social reorganisation, must repose upon the authority of demonstration, it must be based upon science, with a priesthood properly constituted out of the regenerated scientific classes. In other words, the spiritual authority must issue from a Philosophy which can be demonstrated, not from a Philosophy which is imagined.

※ ※ ※

The year 1825 is memorable on other grounds; it is the date of his marriage with Caroline Massin, bookseller, then (as I infer from a phrase in one of his letters to me) in her twenty-fourth year. There is no graver event in a man's life than marriage. It may prove an inestimable blessing, the subtle influences of which will permeate every hour of the day, strengthen every fibre of his moral being, and by its satisfying repose to the affections, give his intellect a calmer and more continuous sweep. It may also prove a desolating evil, numbing the sympathies, irritating and scattering the intellectual energies, distorting his life. In Comte's case the marriage was unhappy. In spite of mutual admiration there was some essential cause of disunion, which led to much unhappiness and a final separation. Into the very delicate question of culpability I do not feel inclined to enter. The relations of man and wife are too complex and too obscure for a bystander to appreciate, even when he has personal knowledge to aid him. I have no knowledge of Comte in his domestic relations; and MM Robinet and Littré are so transparently in the position of partisans, one vehemently reviling Madame Comte, the other artfully pleading her cause in suggestive passages, that no reliance should be placed on either. M Littré is more measured in his judgments than Dr Robinet, whose imputations cannot be sustained in presence of the documentary evidence of letters from De Blainville, Comte, and Madame Comte; but M Littré, who has long been the intimate friend of Madame Comte, suppresses important facts, and uses others with insidious effect. In presence of such *ex parte* versions we shall do well entirely to suspend judgment.

Enough for us here to know what Comte was initiated into domestic life at a time when there seemed very little prospect of his being able to earn more than a precarious subsistence. His family at first opposed the match, but finally gave a reluctant consent; though to their grief the religious ceremony was resolutely declined, and a civil marriage was all that Comte would accept. We shall hear more of this presently. meanwhile we must think of the young couple as dependent entirely on the proceeds of lessons in mathematics. At the time of the marriage Comte had but one pupil: that pupil was the 'Bayard of our day', as his admirers style General Lamoricière. With the small sum of money brought by his wife, a modest lodging was furnished in the Rue de l'Oratoire. Here M de Narbonne proposed to place his son as boarder and pupil. Other aristocratic families would, it was hoped, follow the example. To receive these pupils a more dignified apartment was taken in the Rue de l'Arcade, at the corner of the Rue St Lazare; and fresh furniture had to be bought. But when the small stock of ready money was thus invested, the pupils never came, and the apartment was a burden. In a few months the solitary boarder was sent back, and the young couple had to migrate to more modest lodgings in the Rue Montmartre (No. 13). Here Comte, although unwilling to divert his attention from the working out of his great scheme which he was then meditating, was persuaded to earn a little money by publishing an occasional essay in the *Producteur*. To this we owe the 'Considérations Philosophiques sur les Sciences et les Savants', and the 'Considérations sur le nouveau pouvoir spirituel'.

By the month of April, 1826, the system was sufficiently matured in his mind for a dogmatic exposition, which he announced in a course of seventy-two lectures to be delivered in his private rooms. There is something imposing in the magnitude of the attempt. One hears with surprise of a young and obscure thinker proposing to expound the philosophy of all sciences, having for his aim the reconstruction of the spiritual power, and calling upon his auditors for a year's severe attention to his scheme. One is still more surprised to hear the names of the auditors who were prepared to give this attention: Humboldt, Poinsot, De Blainville, Montebello, Carnot, d'Eichthal, Cerclet, Allier, and Mongéry. A scheme so gigantic might, indeed, have originated in a colossal vanity unimpeded in its pretensions by any definite knowledge of what the scheme implied; for the ignorant are often seduced by their ignorance into pretensions which a little knowledge would repress. It is as easy to write a check for ten millions as for ten pounds—when you have nothing at your banker's. But the presence of an audience such as I have named, and in such a place, proves that the pretensions were recognised by competent judges, and that the lecturer had inspired men of position with the conviction that he had something important to say.

It will be readily understood, by any one acquainted with the intense cerebral excitement which attends the elaboration of great conceptions in their systematic co-ordination, that the strain on Comte's mind, amid various vexations, and particularly in the agitation of vehement personal quarrels, proved too much for him. After the delivery of three or four lectures, an attack of insanity abruptly closed the course. For some weeks previously he had displayed an irritability and violence of temper which alarmed his wife. She, not unnaturally, attributed to malignity what was in fact disease. On Friday, 24 April, he went out and did not return home. On Monday a letter came, dated from St Denis, whither his wife hastened, but found him no longer there. Remembering that he was very fond of Montmorency, she went there on the chance of finding him; and found him in a pitiable condition. A physician was sent for, who confessed the case to be alarming, but dared not bleed the agitated man. The excitement subsided, and he expressed a wish to go out for a walk. She imprudently consented, and accompanied him. As they came to the edge of the lake of Enghien, he suddenly declared that although he could not swim he should not be drowned if he walked into the lake, and he began to drag his wife with him. She was young and strong, struggled, and caught hold of a tree, and saved them both.

But now came the difficulty of getting him back to the inn. His excitement rapidly increased. The peasants refused all offers tempting them to act as guardians while his wife hurried to Paris to seek the assistance of De Blainville; and she was forced to leave him under the charge of two gens-d'armes. She returned from Paris to find him in a worse condition. In the morning De Blainville arrived followed by M Cerclet. They contrived by stratagem to get him to Esquirol's establishment for the insane; and there his exaltation was so great, that it was regarded by Esquirol as a favourable prognostic of an early recovery. Unhappily the recovery was slow, and would probably have been impossible had he not quitted the madhouse, with its incessant irritations, for the soothing influences of domestic quiet. On hearing the melancholy news, Comte's mother at once came to Paris to attend on him; and she remained there till he quitted the Asylum. De Blainville, after seeing summer and autumn pass away without sensible improvement, conceived that hatred of his keepers and the system of treatment perpetuated the excitement. Comte's father hereupon proposed that he should be removed to Montpellier. But the wife wished to have her husband under her care, and this plan was adopted.

A grotesque and lugubrious farce was played on the day of his quitting the establishment. I have already mentioned the pain and indignation of his family at his refusal to give his marriage the religious sanction of a Church ceremony; and this refusal was now regarded by his parents as the origin of the calamity which had fallen on him. The confidence with which people see the 'finger of God' in human afflictions, and see their own anger confirmed by his 'judgments', is too constantly exemplified for us to think harshly of a man like Lamennais being mixed up with what followed, namely, the attempt to make peace with offended Heaven by inducing the insane heretic to submit himself to the dictates of the Church he detested, and ask for a religious ceremony to sanction his marriage. By what arts the consent was gained, is not said; but in a lonely chamber of Esquirol's madhouse this gloomy farce was played. The officiating priest was deficient in tact, and instead of shortening the ceremony, lengthened it by a prolix discourse which excited Comte; and the shocking spectacle was presented of a priest pouring forth pious exhortations, extremely unsuited to the mental condition of the maniac, who kept up a running commentary of anti-religious incoherencies! The state of his mind was exhibited when he came to affix his signature,—after his own name he added Brutus Bonaparte. But the ceremony was performed; the Church was satisfied; the tender consciences were at peace.

He left the establishment for ever. His nurses were now his mother and his wife. Iron bars were placed before the windows of his lodging, and Esquirol sent a keeper to help and protect them. But at the end of a week it was found necessary to do away with these precautions, which made the unhappy man still imagine himself in the establishment he hated. From that moment his recovery began. In three weeks' time he was left alone with his wife. His violence at first caused anxiety. Twice a day, at meals, he would try to plant his knife in the table, in imitation, he said, of Sir Walter Scott's highlander; and he would call for a succulent pig, in imitation of Homeric heroes. More than once he threw his knife at Madame Comte—not, as she believes, with any intention of injuring her, but merely to frighten her into compliance with his wishes.

At the end of six weeks all immediate danger was over. A new danger emerged in the profound melancholy which gradually overclouded him, as with returning health there came upon him the conviction that he could no longer live that life of intellect which had once been his. Life could in future be nothing but a weariness, now that his powers were gone. The idea of suicide arose. One day, during his wife's absence, he slipped out, hurried to the Seine, and threw himself into it from the bridge. A soldier plunged in and saved him. The shock seems to have roused his energies; perhaps by determining a different direction to his circulation. He expressed great regret for his attempt, and the grief he had thereby caused his wife. From this time there was no relapse. In the month of July he was well enough to visit his parents at Montpellier.[61]

※ ※ ※

It was not without a purpose that I have told this story of the severe cerebral attack in all its painful details. The fact that he had been insane was openly avowed by himself, in anticipation of the ignoble pretext which he foresaw that it might furnish to his adversaries, who would find it easier to dismiss his philosophical ideas as the reveries of a madman than to point out incoherencies and refute arguments. We are so ready to see in any departure from our ways of thought the love of singularity, the distorted conceptions of eccentricity, or the illusions of a 'heat-oppressed brain', that when a man comes before us with opinions we do not understand, or understanding do not like, and that man is known to have been actually insane at one time, the temptation to charge his opinions on his insanity is very strong indeed. But it is only necessary to remark that, although Comte was really out of his mind for one brief period, he was perfectly sane and sound when he first conceived, and when he finally executed, the scheme of his philosophy. With this fact we push away all equivoque. Had the work been elaborated in a madhouse, or published while the author was insane, there would be an excuse for dismissing it unexamined; in such a case, however, examination would have disclosed something like a miracle which would have revolutionalised all our ideas about insanity. Every one must see that a body of doctrine so compact and originally related in its parts, could only have been wrought out in the plenitude of mental power. Call that doctrine mischievous, erroneous—what you please—only not incoherent. The intense concentration it demanded may have been the predisposing cause of the insanity, but the insanity had nothing to do with production of the philosophy. Nor will any one who is even superficially acquainted with the phenomena of mental disease, and who understands that all disease whatever is only a disturbance of equilibrium in the functions, suppose that when the disease has passed and the equilibrium restored, the functions will not resume their normal activity, the insane man becoming perfectly sane, and capable of as accurately co-ordinating ideas as before. The fevered pulse becomes normal in its beats, the inflamed mucous membrane becomes normal in its power of secretion, and the over-stimulated brain becomes normal in its action, when once the disturbing causes are removed.

There is, therefore, nothing remarkable in the fact that Lucretius and Cowper wrote their immortal poems during lucid intervals of frequent cerebral attacks. The philosophy of Lucretius has indeed been often affiliated on his insanity; but the sweet piety, the delicate humour, and the sustained excellence of Cowper, have not been thus branded; and they show that the mind *is* lucid in its lucid intervals. The list of illustrious madmen is a long one. Lucretius, Mahomet, Loyola, Peter the Great, Haller, Newton, Tasso, Swift, Cowper, Donizetti, spontaneously occur as the names of men whose occasional eclipse by no means darkens the splendour of their achievements. To these we must add the name of Auguste Comte, assured that if Newton once suffered a cerebral attack without thereby forfeiting our veneration for the 'Principia' and the 'Optics', Comte may have likewise suffered without forfeiting his claims on our veneration for the *Philosophie Positive*. But the best answer to this ignoble insinuation is the works themselves. If they are the products of madness, one could wish that madness were occasionally epidemic.

Let us hear him on this point:–

Après que la médicine m'eut enfin heureusement déclaré incurable, la puissance intrinsèque de mon organisation, assistée d'affectueux soins domestiques, triompha naturellement, en quelques semaines, au commencement de l'hiver suivant, de la maladie, et surtout des remèdes. Ce succès essentiellement spontané se trouvait, dix huit mois après, tellement consolidé que, en Août, 1828, appréciant dans un journal le célèbre ouvrage de Broussais sur L'Irritation et la Folie, j'utilisais déjà philosophiquement les lumières personnelles que cette triste expérience venait de me procurer si chèrement envers le grand sujet.

✳ ✳ ✳

I return to the narrative of his life. In 1828 he recommended that oral exposition of his system which we have seen so cruelly interrupted. This time it was in his lodgings, Rue Saint Jacques, No. 159. The great geometrician Fourier, and the celebrated physician Broussais, with De Blainville, Poinsot, and Mongéry, were among the small audience. He completed the course, and also gave a brief public exposition of his historical views at the Athénée. In 1830 he published the first volume of his Course; but the second volume, owing to the commercial crisis, did not appear till 1835; the sixth and last in 1842. I should add that in 1830 he began to give the gratuitous course of public lectures on Astronomy which was repeated for seven years, and afterwards (1844) published under the title of 'Traité Philosophique d'Astronomie Populaire.'

These twelve years (1830-42), embracing the publication of the 'Cours de Philosophie Positive', form what M Littré justly calls 'the great epoch' in his life:—

Un labeur infini l'attendait; il se soumit sans réserve à cet infini labeur. Douze ans se passèrent pendant lesquels il ferma courageusement sa vie à tout ce qui aurait pu le distraire. Jamais le besoin d'une publicité prematurée ne fit invasion dans don âme.... Sévère, persévérant, sourd aux bruits du dehors il concentra sur son oeuvre tout ce qu'il avait de méditation. Dans l'histoire des hommes voués aux grandes pensées, je ne connais rien de plus beau que ces douze années.

It would be well that we should bear this in mind. Although the world is called upon to judge results, not efforts—to accept or reject works on their own pretensions, and not on any pretensions claimed for the disinterestedness and labour of the worker—it is but just that, in speaking of the worker, we should remember his claims. Whether it is a system or a sonnet, we agree with the Misanthrope of Molière, 'Monsieur, le temps ne fait rien à l'affaire'; but the serious worker is regarded with very different feelings from those which are excited by the vain and presumptuous sciolist. Reject the Positive Philosophy if your mind refuses to accept it, but speak of Comte as one who gave a life to its elaboration; as one who believing that he was commissioned to impart a new faith, accepted the burden with a severe courage, and thought and toiled, relinquishing all other aims, steeling himself against all other seductions, and with a noble disinterestedness devoting himself to the task which he well knew was certain to bring obloquy on him while living, to be followed by an immortal fame.

Shortly after 1830 he refused to join the National Guard. He was cited before the municipality, and was condemned to an imprisonment of three days. He thus proclaimed his reasons. 'The law declares that the National Guard is instituted to defend the government which France has given herself. If it was simply a question of maintaining order I should not refuse to bear my part; but I refuse to share in political struggles. I shall never attack the government by force. But, being a republican in mind and heart, I cannot swear to defend, at the peril of my life and that of others, a government which I should attack were I a man of action.' Such language as this would have led to a criminal indictment had not the authorities dreaded the publicity of such a defence. As it was, he remained unmolested.

In 1833 he obtained an office in the École Polytechnique, which with another that soon came to him, and a mathematical class in a private educational establishment, brought ease into his domestic circumstances, and enabled him to dispense with private pupils. From this time, and for some years, he enjoyed an income of 10,000 francs. Hitherto his sole relaxations had been long walks, and what he called his *flâneries philosophiques*. Now he was enabled to indulge his passion for music, and every season had his stall at the Italian Opera. Although without musical culture, he was exquisitely sensitive to music; had a fine voice, and sang certain songs with great effect, particularly *La Marseillaise*, which he gave with vibrating revolutionary fervour.

He read absolutely nothing on philosophy or science; and he abstained on system. In his early years he had read immensely, and his memory was of extraordinary tenacity. English, Italian, and Spanish he taught himself simply by taking a book and a dictionary of each language. Gifted with such a memory, his neglect of books was perhaps a greater advantage to the integrity of his philosophising than it would be in most cases. All his knowledge was organised; whatever he had once read was always available.

M Littré describes his method of composition, which is truly remarkable.

He meditated the subject without writing a word. From the general conception he passed to the great divisions, and from those to the details. When this elaboration, first of the *ensemble* and then of the parts, was finished, he considered that his volume was completed. And this was true, for on sitting down to write he recovered without loss every one of the ideas which formed the tissue of his work, and recovered them in their order and connection, although not a word had been committed to paper. In this way he composed the course of lectures which embraced the whole positive philosophy, and the catastrophe which followed (in 1826) proves that the method was as dangerous as it was puissant.

When once he began to write he was hurried along by the impetuous current of his thoughts; and the dates which he has given of the composition of various parts of his writings prove the almost incredible rapidity with which he wrote. The sheets were sent to press as fast as they were written; so that the printing of each volume was completed almost as soon as he laid down the pen.

The last of his private pupils, whose name has not transpired, has given an interesting glimpse of his illustrious teacher, in a paper which appeared in *Chambers's Journal* (19 June, 1858). After narrating how he found himself in this position, he adds:–

Daily as the clock struck eight on the *horloge* of the Luxembourg, while the ringing hammer on the bell was yet audible, the door of my room opened, and there entered a man, short, rather stout, almost what one might call sleek, freshly shaven, without vestige of whisker or moustache. He was invariably dressed in a suit of the most spotless black, as if going to a dinner party; his white neckcloth was fresh from the laundress's hands, and his hat shining like a racer's coat. He advanced to the arm-chair prepared for him in the centre of the writing-table, laid his hat on the left-hand corner, his snuff-box was deposited on the same side beside the quire of paper placed in readiness for his use, and dipping the pen twice into the ink-bottle, then bringing it to within an inch of his nose, to make sure it was properly filled, he broke silence: 'We have said that the chord A B,' etc. For three-quarters of an hour he continued his demonstration, making short notes as he went on, to guide the listener in repeating the problem alone; then, taking up another *cahier* which lay beside him, he went over the written repetition of the former lesson. He explained, corrected, or commented till the clock struck nine; then, with the little finger of the right hand brushing from his coat and waistcoat the shower of superfluous snuff which had fallen on them, he pocketed his snuff-box, and, resuming his hat, he as silently as when he came in made his exit by the door which I rushed to open for him. This man of few words was the Aristotle or Bacon of the nineteenth century.

Naturally the pupil at first regarded this silent and automatic teacher with a certain vague fear. He learned at length to love him. Not, as he candidly says, that he knew anything of the hidden greatness of the man, but because he instinctively felt the smothered kindliness beneath that cold exterior. Years afterwards he saw him, when he was celebrated, and in poverty. 'He recalled one of those pictures of the middle ages representing St Francis wedded to poverty.' But I must refer to the narrative itself, which is too long for extract here.

The year 1842 is doubly memorable: it saw the termination of his great work and of his conjugal life. I have already said that into the domestic question I cannot enter. Be the blame of the failure chiefly hers or chiefly his, the failure sprang from conditions we cannot accurately appreciate. That the separation was her deed, and not his, seems indisputable; and in one of his letters to Madame de Vaux he writes:–

An indispensable separation, all the more irrevocable on my side because I in no way provoked it, completely relieved me of an intolerable domestic oppression, now happily converted into a simple pecuniary charge which my character forbids my feeling in its true weight. In truth, the two first years of that new situation, during the interval between the close of my first great elaboration and the opening of the second, were passed in enjoyment of the negative happiness resulting from this unhoped-for calm succeeding the long and daily agitation.

It is clear from many indications that they quarrelled frequently and violently; their views of life were different, and probably the wordly views of the one were a continual exasperation to the other; but it is also clear that he did not regard her as having done anything to forfeit his respect and admiration; in one of his letters he lays the principal stress on the fact of her having never loved him. He continued for some years to correspond with her on affectionate terms.

※ ※ ※

With the publication of the *Philosophie Positive* he assured his place among the great thinkers of all ages, but drew upon himself the bitter hatred of rivals and humiliated professors, which, being supported by the indignation of theologians, metaphysicians, and journalists, who were irritated at his dangerous doctrines and sweeping scorn, ended in driving him from his official position. He was turned adrift once more to seek a laborious existence as a teacher of mathematics. The story is told by him in the preface to the sixth volume of the *Philosophie Positive*, and in fuller detail by M Littré. It need not be repeated here; the sad result is enough. To mitigate the blow, three Englishmen—Mr Grote, Mr Raikes Currie, and Sir W. Molesworth—through the intervention of Mr John Mill, offered to replace the official salary for one year, understanding that at the end of the year Comte would be either reinstated or would have resolved on some other career. The year passed, but his re-election was again refused. At first this troubled him but little. He had learnt to regard the 'subsidy' of his admirers as his right. It was due from the rich to the philosopher; and the philosopher could more effectively use his powers if all material anxieties were taken from him. This, however, was by no means the light in which the case was seen in England. Mr Grote sent an additional six hundred francs, but a renewal of the subsidy was declined. He was dreadfully exasperated. I remember hearing him speak of the refusal as if some unworthy treachery had been practised on him. I tried to explain as delicately as I could what I conceived to be the point of view of his friends, who declined to be his bankers; but he had so entirely wrought himself into the persuasion that the refusal was a moral dereliction, and that no excuse could be offered for men who had wealth withholding a slight portion of it from thinkers whose lives were of importance to the world, that I saw it was useless. He had a fixed idea on the subject; and it may be seen expressed in haughty terms in his letter to Mr Mill.[62] If there is much to be said (and I think there is) in favour of his idea of the duty of the rich towards thinkers whose aims they approve, there is also not a little to be said on the other side, and not a little blame attributable to his manner of urging his claims. He chose to assume a 'haute magistrature morale' which others would not recognise. He professed to speak solely as a philosopher, but showed too much personal preoccupation. It is sad to hear that the result of this was a coolness on the part of Mr Mill, and the cessation of a correspondence which he had valued, and to which Comte himself attached great value (as appears in one of his letters to me, inquiring into the cause of the silence, and showing anxiety on the subject).

This idea of a subsidy replacing the 'infamous spoliation', became, as I said, a systematic conception, and he now boldly relinquished all efforts at providing for himself, and made a public appeal to his admirers for an income. The appeal was responded to during the rest of his life. The circulars which he yearly sent forth are printed in the prefaces to his 'Système de Politique Positive'.[63]

Meanwhile he was to learn the unspeakable influences of a deep affection. We have seen St Simon giving a bias to his intellect which determined the creation of the *Philosophie Positive*; we have now to see the bias given to his thoughts by a passionate love, which carried him into sentimental and mystical regions little foreseen by his early adherents.

It was in the year 1845 that he first met Madame Clotilde de Vaux. There was a strange similiarity in their widowed conditions. She was irrevocably separated from her husband by a crime which had condemned him to the galleys for life; yet although morally free, she was legally bound to the man whose disgrace overshadowed her. Comte also was irrevocably separated from his wife by her voluntary departure; and although morally free, was legally bound. Marriage being thus unhappily impossible, they had only the imperfect, yet inestimable, consolation of a pure and passionate friendship. He was fond of applying to her the lines of his favourite Dante—

Quella che imparadisa la mia mente
Ogni basso pensier dal cor m'avulse.

Every one who knew him during this brief period of happiness will recall the mystic enthusiasm with which he spoke of her, and the irrepressible over-flowing of his emotion which led him to speak of her at all times and to all listeners. It was in the early days of this attachment that I first saw him; and in the course of our very first interview he spoke of her with an expansiveness which greatly interested me. When I next saw him he was as expansive in his grief at her irreparable loss; and the tears rolled down his cheeks as he detailed her many perfections. His happiness had lasted but one year.

Her death made no change in his devotion. She underwent a transfigura-tion. Her subjective immortality became a real presence to his mystical affection. During life she had been a benign influence irradiating his moral nature, and for the first time giving satisfaction to the immense tenderness which had slumbered there; she thus initiated him into the secrets of emo-tional life, which were indispensable to his philosophy in its subsequent elaboration. Her death rather intensified than altered this influence, by purifying it from all personal and objective elements.

In one of his letters to her we read:–

Le charmant bonjour auquel je n'ai pu répondre avant hier me laissera le souvenir permanent d'une affectueuse expression caractéristique dont j'éprouve le besoin de vous remercier spécialement, quand vous y avez daigné mentionner votre bonheur de *m'acquérir*. En effet, c'est bien là, ma Clotilde, le mot qui nous convient mutuellement, pour désigner à chacun de nous sa meilleure propriété. Plus notre intimité se développe et se consolide, mieux je sens journellement que cette chaste union est devenue chez moi la principale condition d'un bon-heur que j'avais toujours ardemment rêvé, mais sans pouvoir hélas! l'éprouver jamais avant d'avoir subi votre bienfaisant empire.

The remainder of his life was a perpetual hymn to her memory. Every week he visited her tomb. Every day he prayed to her, and invoked her continual assistance. His published invocations and eulogies may call forth mockery from frivolous contemporaries—intense convictions and disinter-ested passions easily lending themselves to ridicule—but posterity will read in them a grave lesson, and will see that this modern Beatrice played a considerable part in the evolution of the Religion of Humanity. Philosophic students will admit that to act powerfully on the sentiments of others the philosopher must have first participated in them himself; and that the elaboration of a system in its emotional relations could only be accomplished by a thinker who had been profoundly moved. This initiation was gained through Madame de Vaux. In one of his letters to her he says:–

Mon organisation a reçu d'une très tendre mère certaines cordes intimes, éminemment féminines, qui n'ont pu assez vibrer faute d'avoir été convenablement ébranlées. L'epoque est enfin venue d'en développer l'activité, qui, peu sensible directement dans le premier volume, essentiellement logique, de mon prochain ouvrage, caractérisera fortement le tome suivant, et encore plus le quatrième ou dernier. C'est de votre salutaire influence que j'attends, ma Clotilde, cette inestimable amélioration, qui doit dignement écarter les reproches de certains critiques sur le prétendu défaut d'onction propre à mon talent, où quelques âmes privilégiées ont seules reconnu déjà une profonde sentimentalité implicite, en m'avouant avoir pleuré à certains passages philosophiques, ceux là même que j'avais, en effet, écrit tout en larmes.

It may be useful here to remark that Comte is frequently written against by those who know him only at second hand, as offensively dry, hard, materialistic, and irreligious; while by those who have more or less acquainted themselves with his writings, he is frequently condemned as a mystical, sentimental, and despotically moral pontiff. One class objects to him because he allows no place to the emotions; another because he makes philosophy too emotional. One class fulminates against his denial of religion; another class is more disposed to echo the apostrophe of Billaud Varennes to Robespierre, 'Avec ton Être suprême, tu commences à m'embêter!' He is called an atheist; and no one was ever more contemptuous towards atheism. He is called a materialist; and no great thinker was ever less amenable to the objections which that term connotes. The contradictory charges are grounded upon a misapprehension of the scope and spirit of his philosophy, in the first place; and in the second upon the fact that there is a very wide divergence in Method and results between his first and second works. Up to 1842 he placed himself in the direct line of historical filiation, and subordinated his researches to the Objective method; he resumed and systematised the efforts of his scientific predecessors in one vast and compact body of doctrine, creating a Philosophy out of the various sciences by giving unity to their scattered generalities. But after 1842 a radical change took place; the philosopher brusquely assumed the position of a pontiff. He changed his Method (and was forced to change it), and coincident with this theoretical transformation, was the emotional transformation, initiated by a profound affection and a profound sorrow.

Henceforward the name of Positivist or Comtist becomes equivocal. It designates two schools, or a Right and a Left, between whom there is an essential separation. Men like Mr John Mill, Mr Grote, or M Littré may be spoken of as Positivists, because of their adherence to the principles of *La Philosophie Positive*; but it would be greatly to misstate their position unless the phrase were qualified, since they altogether reject the *Politique Positive* and the *Catechism*, which the 'true positivists', the most distinguished of whom is Mr Richard Congreve, regard as the really valuable and the only consistent deductions from the philosophy. It is as if the disciples of Dr Newman who refused to follow him to Rome, were confounded with the disciples who followed him everywhere. Obviously the name of 'Newmanites' would be equivocal. The name of 'Positivists' or 'Comtists' is so likewise.

It is not my intention in this place to discuss or expound either the Philosophy or the Religion. To obviate any misconception as to my own position, it may be enough to state that I accept with gratitude the Philosophy in all its cardinal views, and having for three-and-twenty years found it a luminous guide, believe that who ever masters it will be able to say with Giordano Bruno, 'Con questa filosofia mi s'aggrandisce l'anima e mi si magnifica l'intelletto.' But in the *Politique Positive*, and the religious cultus, I can only see a magnificent utopia, and a prophetic vision of what the Religion of the future may become. As an utopia it commands a sentiment rather than an assent. As an attempt at social reorganisation, I not only resist many of the details, but altogether impugn the Method. Whenever Comte places himself in the direct line of historical filiation, resuming and systematising the conceptions which previous ages have prepared (as in the case of the conception of Humanity, the great ideal existence), and whenever he subordinates his inquiries to the Objective Method, distinguishing between a deduction and a verified deduction, I follow as a disciple. But whenever he quits this Method, and assumes the part of pontiff, arbitrarily arranging individual and social life according to his subjective conceptions, I quit the position of disciple for that of a spectator, and, generally, of an antagonist.

✳ ✳ ✳

Before setting himself to the composition of his second great work, Comte is supposed to have had another cerebral attack, though but a slight one, and of brief duration; and it will not be without indignation that impartial readers will observe how M Littré, apparently to explain his rejection of the doctrines, insinuates that they were vitiated in their origin by that (hypothetical) cerebral attack. From unthinking and reckless adversaries such an accusation might be anticipated. From one who avows himself a disciple it could only escape moral reprobation by being at least plausibly founded. Now on what grounds can M Littré pretend that the cerebral attack, the very existence of which is a supposition of his own, and the duration of which was trivial, vitiated the *Politique* when he refuses to admit that the avowed, long continued, and violent attack which preceded the composition of the *Philosophie* in no respect vitiated that work? The contradiction is glaring. To suppose that a man issues from an attack of insanity lasting many months and characterised by extreme violence, without injury to his philosophical integrity, and many years afterwards suffers a radical metamorphosis through a very trivial attack, so trivial as to be only suspected from a passing phrase in a letter, is not indeed a supposition beyond the reach of psychological inference, and if supported by evidence would find little resistance; but for a disciple of the *Philosophie* to insinuate that the *Politique* has the taint of insanity, is a contradiction I am forced to point out. The weaknesses and extravagances which strike M Littré in the second work cannot be adduced in proof, because those who reject the first work might on equal grounds detect insanity in the ideas which to them appear as weak and extravagant. Moreover, M Littré, as a student of Comte, ought not to have overlooked the very obvious germs of these extravagances which are in the *Philosophie*—the tendencies towards despotic systematisation and arbitrary hypothesis, which in the *Politique* have all the more freedom because unrestrained by established truths. As a student of history he ought not to have overlooked the fact that the unbridled employment of the deductive Method was *inevitable* on a topic which was destitute of the requisite inductions; inevitable in the case of all who are not content to await the slow results of inductive investigation. Finally, and most conclusively, M Littré should not have failed to recognise in the *Politique* the same intellectual force, the same sustained power of conception and co-ordination, although with less successful result, as had commanded his veneration in the *Philosophie*. To reject the work, to laugh at it, may be permissible; to see in it the work of an intellect distorted by disease is an extravagance greater than any to be found in its pages. The reach of intellect and profoundly moral tone displayed in every chapter, can only be misconceived by those who estimate the force of a thinker by the immediately available truths he offers them—an estimate which would make sad havoc with the pretensions of a Plato, a Descartes, a Spinoza, or a Hegel.

I am not pleading for the *Politique Positive*. On the contrary, my dissent from its leading speculations, and above all from its scheme of sacerdotal despotism, is open and direct. All the true positivists regard me as a heretic. But I am a reverent heretic, nevertheless: that is, I profoundly admire the greatness and sincerity of the thinker, although he seems to have attempted a task for which the materials were not ready. And if men could approach the work with minds sufficiently open to receive instruction from teachers whom on the whole they refuse to follow, capable of setting aside differences, to seize upon and profit by agreements, they would carry away from the *Politique* many luminous suggestions, and that ennobling influence which always rays out from a moral conviction. They must be prepared to find passages to marvel at, passages to laugh at, and passages to fling hard words at. But they will detect even in these the presence of a magisterial intellect carried by the deductive impetus beyond the limits of common sense; they will detect nothing of the incoherence of insanity. Even the startling utopia which he propounds on the basis of what he himself calls a daring hypothesis—i.e., that of the *Vierge Mère*—is a legitimate deduction from what many regard as established data; it happens to be absurd because the data are profoundly erroneous, although they have been, and still are, accepted by many scientific men as truths. Had the data been true, the deduction would have been as admirable as it is now laughable: it would have been a geniuine scientific hypothesis.

Antagonism to the Method and conclusions of the *Politique Positive* led me for many years to regard that work as a deviation from the positive philosophy in every way unfortunate. My attitude has changed now that I have learned (from the remark of one very dear to me) to regard it as an utopia, presenting hypotheses rather than doctrines, suggestions for future inquirers rather than dogmas for adepts,—hypotheses carrying more or less of truth, and serviceable as a provisional mode of colligating facts, to be confirmed or contradicted by experience. Grave students think it no misuse of time to study the *Republic* and the *Laws* of Plato. Let them approach the 'Systeme de Politique Positive' in a similar spirit; they will find there an intellect greater than Plato's, a morality higher and purer, and an amount of available suggestion incomparably greater.

Although no importance is to be attached to the slight cerebral attack (if attack there were) which preceded the composition of this work, there is intense biographical and psychological significance in the indications of the mental modifications which accompanied what may be called the development of the pontifical spirit in Comte. The germs are visible in his earliest years. No one can study the *Philosophie* without recognising the irrepressible tendency to domination, to a systematising circumscription of our aims with a view to unity (without, as Mr Mill justly remarks, any demonstration of the necessity of such unity), and to deductive reasoning irrespective of objective verification. We see only the germs, because the soil of positive science was ill suited to their development. Obliged to employ the Objective Method throughout, he was forced to restrain these tendencies, under penalty of failure. As he grew older, and lived more and more alone, absorbed in meditation, less and less occupied with what had been effected by others, his intense self-confidence became enormously exaggerated, and the disposition to take his own feelings as a sufficient guarantee and proof, grew more and more disastrous. The very vividness of his conceptions, rising up during long and lonely meditation, rendered it difficult for him to doubt their reality; while the deductive impatience natural to a systematic intellect prevented his verifying their reality. He first struck out an hypothesis; he then overleaped the next condition of testing its conformity with fact; it became a truth in his mind, and he proceeded to deduce from it as from a verified truth. The awakening of an intense emotional life, and the welcome homage of a few ardent disciples, contributed their share. The conviction of an apostolic mission grew apace. The transformation of the systematic theorist into the imperious pontiff was rapid. Those who were subjagated by his personal influence, or fascinated by the seeming truth of his doctrines, will see a logical development in this; whereas we who stand aloof can see in it nothing but the unfortunate fatality which seems attached to deep convictions in certain powerful and arrogant natures. Those who consider Mahomet an impostor, and Loyola a malignant despot, may brand Comte with similar epithets of scorn or hatred. But if with a deeper sympathy and wider knowledge we mark the line between infirmity and strength, recognising that where the lights are brightest there the shadows are darkest, we shall be careful not to found a common infirmity with an uncommon greatness. Hundreds of men have been as vain, as arrogant, as despotic in their ideas; but how many have been as severely ascetic, as profoundly moral, as devoted to high thoughts, and as magnificetly endowed? We need not accept the errors of a great mind because of its greatness; but ought we to forget the greatness when we reject the errors?

After the publication of the *Politique* there is little of biographical importance to be added. In 1852 he had published the 'Catéchisme Positiv-iste', a little work which, I think, has done more to retard the acceptance of his views than all the attacks of antagonists. It contains many profound and noble passages, and to the thorough-going disciples is doubtless a precious work; but it should have been an esoteric work, at least for many years. Catechisms are for the converted. The objections to this one, apart from the ideas which, to all but believers, must appear without adequate foundation, are, first, that being brief and popular in form it is seized on by those who wish to 'know something about Comte' and are unwilling to take the requisite labour of reading the more serious works; secondly, because he was inca-pable of conducting a popular exposition in a dramatic form, and a perpetual sense of the ridiculous accompanies the reader, preventing his giving serious attention to the matter; thirdly, because in this unpromising and unconvincing form it puts forth ideas which could only escape ridicule and indignation by a very earnest, logical, and persuasive exposition. If my voice can have the slightest weight with the reader I beg him not to open the Catechism until he has carefully studied the two great works by which Comte will live in history.

The 'Synthèse Subjective' he did not live to finish. I am given to under-stand that some eminent mathematicians think highly of the one volume which has appeared; but I only know it at second hand.

Dr Robinet has sketched the routine of his daily life in those later years; the picture should be meditated by those whose theological irritation has led them to throw hard words at this 'materialist and scoffer'. He rose at five in the morning, prayed, meditated, and wrote until seven in the evening, with brief intervals for his two meals. Every day he read a chapter from the 'Imitation of Christ' and a canto of Dante. Homer also was frequently re-read. Poetry was his sole relaxation now that he could no longer indulge his passion for the opera. From seven to nine (and on Sundays in the afternoon) he received visits, especially from working men, among whom he found disciples. On Wednesday afternoons he visited the tomb of Madame de Vaux. At ten he again prayed and went to bed. The hour of prayer was to him an hour of mystic and exquisite expansion. Nothing could be simpler than his meals: breakfast consisted only of milk; dinner was more substantial, but rigorously limited. At the close of dinner he daily replaced dessert by a piece of dry bread, which he ate slowly, meditating on the numerous poor who were unable to procure even that means of nourishment in return for their work.

He died on 5 September, 1857, at the age of sixty, leaving behind him an immortal name, and an almost canonised position in the memory of a select few, who still carry out, with admirable energy, the efforts to establish and spread the Religion of Humanity, undismayed by the ridicule and social persecution which awaits every religious movement at its outset.

※ ※ ※

The increasing notoriety of the name of Auguste Comte is significant of a spreading sympathy and a spreading dread. In grave treatises and in periodical works his opinions are silently adopted, openly alluded to, and discussed with respect; but much oftener they furnish a flippant sentence to some jaunty journalist, or pander to the austere dishonesty of some polemical theologian. Indignation, scorn, and ridicule are poured forth with all the greater freedom because usually unhampered by any first-hand knowledge. It is with him as it used to be with Kant, who not many years ago was a standing butt: many who had never opened the 'Kritik', and more who would have understood nothing of it had they read it, laughed at the 'dreamer' and his 'transcendental nonsense', without any misgiving that they were making themselves ridiculous in the eyes of those who knew something about Kant. They are now respectful or silent. Surely it is wise to be entirely silent about that of which we know ourselves to be ignorant? As if our natural liability to error were not frequently misleading us, even in our most painstaking inquiries, we must add to it by what Mr Mill somewhere calls 'the abuse of the privilege of speaking confidently about writers whom we have never read'. Few reflect that the exercise of this privilege is foolish; still fewer that it is dishonest. There is always peril in pretence. Silence cannot commit us. And if many delusively imagine that they do know enough of Comte to form a general estimate of him, let them ask themselves whether this knowledge is anything more than the echo of what others have said, those others being for the most part antagonists? Such a question would silence the candid; nothing will silence the garrulous and ignorant, who, as Locke says,

> take the words they find in use among their neighbours, and, that they may not seem ignorant what they stand for, use them confidently without much troubling their heads about a fixed meaning: whereby, besides the ease of it, they obtain this advantage, that, as in such discourses they are seldom right, so they are as seldom to be convinced that they are wrong; it being all one to go about to draw those men out of their mistakes who have no settled notions, as to dispossess a vagrant of his habitation who has no settled abode.

That Comte is often wrong, is indubitable: he was human. That he is sometimes ridiculous and offensive, may be ungrudgingly allowed. To point out these errors is to do philosophy a service. But if we are candid and prudent, we shall first ascertain that the errors we rebuke are the opinions held by him, and not the interpretations put on his words by others. And if we are just, we shall discriminate the errors from the truths, and not speak bitterly or contemptuously of the man because on many points we reject his teaching. These two simple conditions are rarely complied with in the case of any man who has not received the consecration of Time. Comte is too near to us for justice. Men persistently charge him with holding opinions directly counter to the whole scope of his teaching. They refute 'absurdities' which are simply constructions of their own, or of those whom they echo. And even should the better-instructed point out their inaccuracy, by confronting their statements with Comte's own words, they shake their heads and retire stubbornly behind the old entrenchments. They tell you candidly that they have a distaste and a dislike to views such as his, and refuse to inquire whether their conceptions of his views are or are not accurate. Only the other day a critic of some repute declared, in *La Revue des Deux Mondes*, that Comte had attempted to create a philosophy, 'although the conclusion deducible from his principles is precisely the exclusion of all philosophy.' It does not occur to this writer that, never having studied the philosophy, he is possibly not so well acquainted with its logical bearings as the philosopher himself was. Another writer affirms that Comte banishes history from his scheme: which is a strange remark to make against one considered to be the creator of the science of history! A chorus of objectors indignantly protest against positivism 'as a belief in nothing but what can be seen and touched'; and this ineptitude is not only iterated by journalists and imbecile polemists, but is asserted in an elaborate essay by a professed philosopher, 'refuting' Comte. It is true that the philosopher in question was the feeble M Emile Saisset.

If these writers suspected how ridiculous they make themselves in the eyes of the instructed, it would be a useful lesson to them not to be so ready to flatter the secret luxury of scorn on the part of readers as ignorant as themselves. Nor can they justify themselves by a reference to acknowledged absurdities. If great thinkers are to be estimated not by their greatness, but by their weaknesses, I know of none who could retain our reverence. Plato and Aristotle, Descartes and Bacon, Newton and Leibnitz, Spinoza and Hegel, have all put forth systematic absurdities which have excited the mirth and anger of generations; but what should we think of a man who scornfully rejected the demonstrations of the *Principia* because he laughed at the absurdities of the *Chronology*, which he laughed at without having read?

I cannot be supposed to desire that Comte should be shielded from criticism. I have been criticising him for more than twenty years, and lost his friendship by my freedom. I would not have a single error or a single absurdity concealed; the more so, because I do not find that my antagonism has lessened my respect for the value of those great principles which I can accept, nor shaken my faith in the incomparable value of the positive philosophy; but it is one thing to recognise an error, another to judge a system by its accessories. Men who stand outside a doctrine, and look at it only from their own standing-place, naturally have their attention led away by some accessory detail, instead of concentrating their thoughts on the great central principles. If we stand outside Catholicism, we shall see in its teaching and its practices much that is incredible, much that is ridiculous, and some things that are revolting to us. If we stand outside Protestantism, the case will be similar. Yet we know that Catholics and Protestants, with large and acute intellects, with noble and tender consciences, have believed these *incredibilia*, and have accepted these practices, overlooking or looking away from what, to the heretic, is ridiculous or revolting. There is, I suppose, no reflecting Catholic, no reflecting Protestant, who, in his secret conscience, approves of all the teaching and all the practices of his Church; but he accepts parts of the system, illogically connected with it, or historically grown out of it. He believes the great points in that system to be true and beneficent, and will not disturb their efficacy by raising discussion on minor points. Even should he privately reject many of the doctrines which belong to his Church, it will not make him less attached to the doctrines in which he finds a response to some of his spiritual needs. He feels that some mysteries are explained; and having recognised a spiritual guide which is, on the whole, firmer and surer than any he can see elsewhere, he yields himself up to it, content that other things should be unexplained, content that some contradictions should not be reconciled. Neither Catholic nor Protestant will consent to be judged by the weak points of his Church, but only by the strong; not by what outsiders may consider absurd, but by what he feels to be vital.

Apply this to Positivism, considered either as a Philosophy or a Religion. Under either aspect it is a doctrine offering spiritual guidance only to those who accept its teaching as true. Let us look at it as we look at Spinozism or Hegelianism, at Buddhism or Islamism, and if on inspection we find it respond in any considerable degree to our spiritual condition, if it is so far in harmony with demonstrated truths as to be a guide to us in our groping search for a solution of great problems, let us boldly declare as much, and not reject so inestimable a benefit because Comte, or others, may have connected with the great central ideas certain ideas which seem false or ridiculous. Unlike the Catholic and Protestant, the Positivist need shrink from no discussion, need not hesitate to reject any idea, for fear of imperilling the system; because the system claims to rest on demonstrated truth, not on revelation or authority. If they can disregard what they are not permitted openly to reject, we can openly reject whatever we do not honestly believe. I do not say that the pontiff of the new religion would have allowed us such liberty. It is one of his capital errors to have imitated the intellectual despotism which has logically belonged to all priesthoods, but which is an inconsequence in a spiritual power reposing upon demonstration. But if Comte would not allow this liberty, Positivism proclaims it to be an essential condition.

What I wish to urge upon all my readers is, that they should ascertain for themselves, by open-minded study, what are the cardinal doctrines of Positivism, or else be silent, leaving to idle chatterers and dishonest polemists the small enjoyment of talking with a knowing air on what they do not understand, and of talking contemptuously of a great intellectual movement because of certain follies in its leaders. The publication of Mr John Stuart Mill's remarkable work on Comte will, one may hope, considerably assist such a result, partly by showing the deep respect with which so eminent a thinker regards the Philosophy, even while hostile to many of its views, and the impartial calmness with which he can praise and blame; partly, also, and more effectually, by inducing serious minds to undertake a study of the works in which the Philosophy is expounded. Yet even Mr Mill's treatise singularly illustrates the inconsiderate nature of popular appreciations; for I find his readers seizing with avidity on the ridiculous points which he has felt it a duty to notice, but ignoring entirely the great luminous ideas to which he has so emphatically stated his adherence. They chuckle complacently when Mr Mill tells them to laugh; they are wholly passive when he tells them to admire. I think more might have been said for Comte than Mr Mill has said, and that a higher idea might be given to what Comte achieved, and of what the Philosophy implies, than appears in his volume; but the very moderation of the tone ought to make his eulogies carry greater force with the public.

Philosophic antagonisms should be preceded by earnest examination. It is easy to adopt an attitude of scorn towards whatever is unlike our own views; but it is not so easy to discriminate wherein lies the difference and where begins the error. Our first impulse is to reject a novelty; whereas rejection should be the final impulse. And as Milton says in the 'Areopagitica', if it come to prohibiting 'there is not aught more likely to be prohibited than truth itself, whose first appearance, to our eyes, bleared and dimmed with prejudice and custom, is more unsightly and unplausible than many errors, even as the person is of many a great man slight and contemptible to see to'.

Benedict de Spinoza

From *Fortnightly Review* (April 1866)

About thirty years ago a small club of students held weekly meetings in the parlour of a tavern in Red Lion Square, Holborn, where the vexed questions of philosophy were discussed with earnestness, if not with insight. The club was extremely simple in its rules, and quite informal in its proceedings. The members were men whose sole point of junction was the Saturday meeting, and whose sole object was the amicable collision of contending views, on subjects which, at one time or other, perplex and stimulate all reflecting minds. On every other day in the week their paths were widely divergent. One kept a second-hand bookstall, rich in freethinking literature; another was a journeyman watchmaker; a third lived on a moderate income; a fourth was a boot-maker; a fifth 'penned a stanza when he should engross'; a sixth studied anatomy and many other things, with vast aspirations, and no very definite career before him. Although thus widely separated, these divergent paths converged every Saturday towards the little parlour in Red Lion Square, and the chimes of midnight were drowned in the pleasant noises of argument and laughter: argument sometimes loud and angry, but on these occasions always terminating in laughter which cleared the air with its explosions. Seated round the fire, smoking their cigars and pipes, and drinking coffee, grog, or ale, without chairman or president, without fixed form of debate, and with a general tendency to talk all at once when the discussions grew animated, these philosophers did really strike out sparks which illuminated each other's minds; they permitted no displays of rhetoric such as generally make debating societies intolerable; they came for philosophic talk, and they talked. It is more than probable that much nonsense was at times propounded, that much shallowness mistook itself for wisdom, and that speakers were over much of their own opinion. The meetings were, however, stimulating rather to the intellect than the vanity; and if the topic under discussion sometimes disappeared in many-voiced confusion, a witticism or a remonstrance quickly restored order.

It was in this club that I first gained some knowledge of the great Hebrew thinker named at the head of this essay. I do not know that any member of the club has since attained sufficient celebrity to justify particular notice here, yet I am tempted to single out two as remarkable specimens of the varieties which the club comprised. One of these was Mr James Pierrepoint Greaves— a name which carries with it a certain mystical halo in some American and

English circles, as that of a man whose fine personal qualities acted with ennobling influence on those around him. His philosophy, one must confess, was somewhat hazy; but there shone through its mists the radiance of that better part of wisdom which springs from sympathy. He came but rarely to our meetings, and this probably because he found the dominant tone of the club strongly opposed to his teachings, and to the tendencies of his intellect. We differed greatly amongst each other, but we all united in opposing him. He was mystical, and we were all anti-mystics. He talked a language we could not comprehend, and often exasperated us by the calm assertion that we were incompetent to follow him. One evening, after listening with unusual patience to an exposition of his views, I observed, probably with a touch of youthful arrogance, that what he said might be very true, but that really I did not in the least understand it. 'Very likely,' was his calm reply, 'I am with the clouds above, while you remain on earth.' Somewhat nettled at this assignment of our relative positions, I asked him, 'If so, can you let down some Jacob's ladder up which I may climb? If I once got up to you I shall, perhaps, be able to form an opinion of what I find there. At present you seem to me to be in the clouds, and not in an enviable position there.' Disregarding the implied impertinence and the laugh which saluted this remark, he said, with earnest gravity, 'No, you cannot ascend, for you have not been *phenomenized.*' There was a momentary pause. I was at the disadvantage of not in the least divining what being phenomenized might represent. 'Have you been phenomenized?' I asked. 'I have.' 'Perhaps you would not mind telling us what it is?' The words of his reply are still ringing in my ears, 'I am what I am, and it is out of my *Iamity* that I am phenomenized.' Another brief pause, and then a roar of laughter from the listeners! He never came again.

In striking contrast to this excellent man was a German Jew, named Cohn, or Kohn, whom we all admired as a man of astonishing subtlety and logical force, no less than of sweet personal worth. He remains in my memory as a type of philosophic dignity. A calm, meditative, amiable man, by trade a journeyman watchmaker, very poor, with weak eyes and chest; grave and gentle in demeanour; incorruptible, even by the seductions of vanity; I habitually think of him in connection with Spinoza, almost as much on account of his personal characteristics, as because to him I owe my first acquaintance with the Hebrew thinker. My admiration for him was of that enthusiastic temper which in youth we feel for our intellectual leaders. I loved his weak eyes and low voice; I venerated his great calm intellect. He was the only man I did not contradict in the impatience of argument. An immense pity and a fervid indignation filled me as I came away from his attics in one of the Holborn Courts, where I had seen him in the pinching poverty of his home, with his German wife and two little black-eyed children; indignantly I railed against society, which could allow so great an intellect to withdraw itself from nobler work, and waste the precious hours in mending watches.

But he was wiser in his resignation than I in my young indignation. Life was hard to him, as to all of us; but he was content to earn a miserable pittance by handicraft, and keep his soul serene. I learned to understand him better when I learned the story of Spinoza's life.

Cohn, as may be supposed, early established his supremacy in our club. A magisterial intellect always makes its presence felt. Even those who differed from him most widely, paid involuntary homage to his power. One night he told us that he had picked up at a bookstall a German work, in which Spinoza's system was expounded. This was particularly interesting, because at that time no account of Spinoza was accessible to the English reader; nothing but vague denunciation or absurd misrepresentation. It was the more interesting to me because I happened to be hungering for some knowledge of this theological pariah—partly, no doubt, because he was an outcast, for as I was then suffering the social persecution which embitters all departure from accepted creeds, I had a rebellious sympathy with all outcasts—and partly because I had casually met with a passage, quoted for reprobation, in which Spinoza maintained the subjective nature of evil, a passage which, to my mind, lighted up that perplexed question.[64] To our delight Cohn engaged to master a proposition every week, and then expound and discuss with us its applications and its truth. He kept his promise tolerably well; but very often three weeks would elapse before he was ready with a new proposition, partly because his time had been absorbed by other and more pressing needs, partly because he would state nothing until he had thoroughly mastered it, thinking it out for himself; and this was necessarily a slow process, for he had no copy of Spinoza, and was reduced to such a glimpses as could be gained from the controversial work in which the system was presented piecemeal. As I could not read German at that time, I was forced to submit my impatience to his necessities.

At length, oh thrilling moment! I espied on the shelves of a second-hand bookseller a small brown quarto, bearing this legend,—'*SPINOZAE OPERA POSTHUMA*'. It cost twenty shillings, and twenty shillings was a large sum to me; but no sum to be demanded for the book would have seemed beyond its value at the time, and I carried the volume home as if it had been the leaves of the sybil. I was now to 'Learn his great language, catch his clear accents' without the confusion of controversy. To impress the principles more firmly on my mind, I forthwith began a translation of the *Ethics*, which, however, I had not the patience to complete.

Some years afterwards (1843) I published in the *Westminster Review* an article on the life and works of Spinoza,[65] which, imperfect as it was, attracted attention, because it was the first attempt to vindicate the great philosopher before the English public. Since then a distinguished writer has published two remarkable essays, one in the *Oxford and Cambridge Review*, for October, 1847, narrating Spinoza's life, the other in the *Westminster Review*, for July, 1855, expounding his system. A writer in the *British Quarterly* some years ago analysed the *Tractatus Theologico-Politicus* with great care, and a translation of that work was published anonymously in 1862.[66] The *Tractatus Politicus* has been translated by Mr W. Maccall, and all the works have been translated into German by Auerbach, the novelist, and into French by M Emile Saisset. There has also been a cheap and convenient reprint of the *Opera Omnia*, edited by Bruder, and recently a supplement has appeared in Holland.[67] So that there is now no lack of accessible material from which to gain a complete view of Spinoza's doctrines.

※ ※ ※

Great among the greatest as a Thinker, Spinoza is also one of the most interesting figures in the history of Philosophy—a standing lesson of the injustice of mankind to those who are honest in their opinions when the opinions happen to be unpopular. All agree that it is ignoble to pretend to believe that which the mind rejects as false; yet men are ever ready to make the rejection a crime. You ought not to be a hypocrite; but you ought not to disbelieve what we assure you is the truth. Be honest by all means; only don't think differently from us. If you do, we must suspect your morals. It has always been known that Spinoza was as gentle in his life as he was steadfast in his philosophy; that he lived modest, virtuous, and independent, without blame among men, except for his incorrigible distrust in the wisdom of his elders. It has been known that if he had been an orrthodox Jew, or an orthodox Christian, his career would have been held up as a model, and his character canonised; but this knowledge for several generations did not arrest almost universal execration, did not prevent his name becoming a brand of infamy; so that the accusation of Spinozism was another name for atheism, and deliberate yielding of the soul to Satan.

But the temper of opinion has changed. The detested atheist is now commonly spoken of as if he were a saint; the 'devil's ambassador' is listened to as if he were a prophet. Men vie with each other in exaggeration of his merits. He was good, he was wise, he was gentle, he was generous; and it is only polemical intolerance, or the uneasy vanity which seeks display in paradox, that will now deny him these qualities. We owe the change to Lessing and Mendelssohn, whose sincerity and penetration at once discerned in the execrated writings a massive grandeur and a lucid depth, and in the man a moral elevation and serenity which claimed all honour. Herder, Goethe, Novalis, Schleiermacher, Schelling, Hegel—each had his emphatic protest to utter against the vulgar outcry. France followed: and it would now be deemed as great a mark of ignorance to speak with reprobation of Spinoza as to shudder at the heresy of Galileo. The man whom the pious Malebranche could designate 'a wretch' (*un misérable*), the pious Schleiermacher invoked as a saint;[68] the man whom the sceptic Bayle called a 'systematic atheist', the Catholic Novalis named 'a God-intoxicated man'. And yet, although the temper has changed, we may doubt whether Spinoza will not continue to be misunderstood by the majority: 'Les âmes mâles,' says Rousseau, 'ont un idiome dont les âmes faibles n'ont pas la grammaire.'

Let us, from the story of his life and the study of his teaching, try to form some opinion of the justice of the hatred he inspired, and of the veneration now felt for him. When scorn for what is base and false is not imperatively commanded by the evidence, admiration becomes a duty. Admiration, provided it be sincere, and not a spurious, noisy enthusiasm, partly echo, partly sham, is so noble a feeling, so healthy in its influence on the mind whose guest it becomes, that even for our own sakes we ought to give it hospitality, while on the highest grounds of justice it carries its own credentials. Blind admiration, indeed, is of no benefit; neither is blind scorn. Spinoza needs but to be known to be admired. Hence it was that his affectionate biographer, Jean Colerus, pastor at the Hague, though trembling with a vague horror at the consequences of what Spinoza taught, was so fascinated by the beauty of the life, that he devoted himself to the collection of materials which should be a lasting monument to the goodness and purity of the heretic. Nothing is more certain than that the life was one of blameless purity. Had there been any rumours to the contrary, the hatred of offended Jews and Christians would have surely preserved and magnified them. This negative evidence is stronger even than the positive details. To be famous, to be infamous, and yet give Scandal no morsel for its malignant curiosity, is the rare lot of only the rarest natures.

Baruch Despinosa, or Benedictus de Spinoza,[69] was born on the 24 November, 1632, in a house on the Burgwal of Amsterdam, behind the Synagogue. His parents were descendants of Portuguese Jews who had sought refuge in Holland from the merciless Inquisition. His father was an honourable but not wealthy merchant. There were two daughters besides Benedict. This is pretty much all we know of the family. Of Benedict himself as a child we know nothing. Early banished from the home and hearts of his relatives, there were none of those pleasant little traditions concerning the boy which are handed about with pride when the man becomes illustrious.

The first authentic glimpse we get of him is, that he was destined for the priesthood. His rabbinical education gave him such opportunities for the display of precocious power, that he soon attracted the attention of the great Talmudist, Saul Levi Morteira, who felt in him the interest a teacher feels in a promising pupil. Unhappily for teachers, promising pupils often become troublesome: the very ardour of study and vigour of intellect which carry them beyond their school-fellows, carry them also, and with increased momentum, past those boundaries which Authority has fixed. Thus eagerness becomes dangerous, earnestness heresy, and the hopeful pupil passes into the condition of a hopeless outcast. Young Benedict asked such intelligent questions, listened so appreciatively to the replies, showed so nimble an understanding, and so much eagerness for light, that we can sympathise with

Morteira's bewilderment, half dread, half pride, when the pupil hurried on with logical impetuosity, asking questions inconvenient to answer, and pointing out slight discrepancies in the answers. He was indeed a promising pupil; but of a promise that looked threatening. At fourteen he was a match for a rabbi in the extent and accuracy of biblical learning. At fifteen he puzzled the Synagogue with questions to which satisfactory answers were not forthcoming. Morteira, alarmed, endeavoured to check this inquiring spirit. The attempt was futile. How long the period of disquiet lasted is unknown. Spinoza had made enemies by his freedom; and since he would not hold his tongue, he had to listen to threat mingled with sophistications. Naturally, heterodoxy grew with discussion. At last he felt that he could no longer remain a member of the Synagogue. We can easily imagine the wrath excited by his withdrawal, not only among the rabbis, but among the members of his family circle. We can picture the storming father, weeping and reproachful mother, indignant sisters, one after another and all together, threatening, sneering, expostulating, urging irrelevant arguments: Why should he not believe what his forefathers had believed? What vanity in him to pretend to a wisdom greater than that of the wisest rabbis! What would become of him? What could be his chance of success in life? And the feelings of his family—were they to be disregarded? It was dreadful to think of; wicked, selfish; certain to come to no good.

The arguments of Morteira having failed, we need not ask what chance there was in the 'wild and whirling words' of a family (with its feelings unaccountably disregarded) making any change in his position. Threats were tried and failed. Then a bribe was tried: the suasive influence of money would surely succeed where logic failed? A pension was proposed to him of one thousand florins annually, on the condition of his appearing from time to time in the synagogue, and keeping within his own bosom certain troublesome doubts. The 'bad example' and the 'scandal' would thus be avoided. Nothing was asked of him more than is asked by all Churches, when they are not strong enough to punish, and are weak enough to wish for homage where there is no belief. 'If you are not with us, do at least pretend to be with us; give us your countenance, if not your heart.' To some sensitive consciences this is an appalling request. It is like an echo of the tempter's voice. Spinoza had one of these sensitive consciences. He not only would not pretend to believe what he did not believe; he was hurt at the supposition that he could be bribed into hypocrisy.

We can understand how the rage of the rabbis was intensified by this refusal, without, however, believing that they instigated the attempt at assassination which followed. I, for my part, distinctly refuse to believe that. I have never seen any evidence of Jews being morally inferior to Christians; and although fanatics of all sects have shown themselves remarkably indifferent to shedding the blood of opponents, they need, for the sake of their consciences, some form to legalise or legitimise the murder they decree.

They cannot look into each other's faces, and propose what each knows will be a murder. 'Même aux yeux de l'injuste un injuste est horrible.'[70] The action of public bodies must be public, and must be protected by at least the forms of legality or the sophisms of 'a higher law.'[71] On these general grounds, therefore, I acquit the rabbis of having instigated the attempt. Far more probable is the supposition that some fanatic, hearing of the scandal about to fall upon his church, should have conceived that he would do the church a service if he arrested the scandal with the knife.

Be that as it may, one evening on returning from the theatre (according to one acount), or from the synagogue (according to another), or, as Mr Froude suggests,[72] probably coming to his home, which was behind the synagogue, a man rushed on him and struck at him with a knife. The blow, slanting downwards, only tore his coat and grazed his skin. The fanatic escaped. The torn coat was preserved by Spinoza as a memento of religious amenity.

Shortly after this exhibition of individual fanaticism there was another and more imposing exhibition of corporate indignation in the solemn process of Excommunication. There was a large and agitated crowd in the synagogue as the tabernacle wherein were deposited the Books of the Law was opened; and the light of numerous candles of black wax streamed upon the long beards and beaded eyes of the angry faithful. Morteira, formerly the proud teacher, now the irritated priest, ordered a sentence of execution to be passed. The chanter rose and chanted forth in loud lugubrious accents the words of execration and of banishment. The words ran thus:–

According to what has been decreed in the Council of Angels, and definitively determined in the Assembly of Saints, we reject, and banish, and declare him to be cursed and excommunicated, agreeable to the will of God and his Church, by virtue of the Book of the Law, and of the six hundred and thirteen Precepts contained therein. We pronounce the same interdiction used by Joshua with respect to the city of Jericho; the same curse wherewith Elisha cursed those wanton and insolent children, as well as his servant Gehasi; the same Anathema used by Barak with respect to Meros: the same Excommunication used anciently by the members of the Great Council; and which Jehuda, the son of Ezekiel, did likewise thunder against his servant, as it is observed in the Gemara, under the title *Heduschim*, &c. Lastly, without excepting any of the curses, anathemas, interdictions, and excommunications which have been fulminated from the time of Moses, our Lawgiver, to this present day, we pronounce them all in the name of *Achthariel*, who is also called *Jah*, the Lord of Hosts; in the name of the great prince *Michael*; in the name of *Metateron*, whose name is like that of his master;[73] in the name of *Sardaliphon*, whose ordinary employment consists in presenting flowers and garlands to his master,—that is, in offering the prayers of the children of Israel before the throne of God. Lastly, in that name which contains forty-two letters,— namely, in the name of Him who appeared to Moses in the bush; in that name by which Moses opened and divided the waters of the Red Sea; in the name of Him who said, *I am that I am and who shall be*; by the mysterious depths of the great name of God *Jehovah*; by His Holy Commandments engraved upon the two Tables of the Law. Lastly, in the name of the Lord of Hosts, and of the Globes, Wheels, mysterious Beasts which Ezekiel saw. Let him be cursed by the Lord God of Hosts, who sits above the cherubim, whose holy and dreadful name was pronounced by the high priest in the great day of propitiation. Let him be cursed in the name of the great prince Michael, in the name of Metateron, whose name is like that of his Master. Let him be cursed in the name of *Achthariel Jah*, who presides over the battles from the Lord; in the name of those Holy Beasts and mysterious Wheels; let him be cursed by the very mouth of the seraphim; lastly, let him be cursed in the name of those ministering angels who are always in the presence of God to serve him in all purity and holiness.

Was he born in *Nisan* (March), a month the direction of which is assigned to *Uriel*, and to the angels of his company? Let him be cursed by the mouth of Uriel and by the mouth of the angels whereof he is the head.

Was he born in *Pjar* (April), a month the direction of which is assigned to *Zephaniel*, and to the angels of his company? Let him be cursed by the mouth of Zephaniel, and by the mouth of the angels whereof he is the head.

Was he born in *Siran* (May), a month the direction of which belongs to *Amniel*? Let him be cursed, &c.

Was he born in *Thammus* (June), the direction of which is assigned to *Peniel*? Let him be cursed, &c.

Was he born in *Abb* (July), the direction of which is assigned to *Barkiel*? Let him be cursed, &c.

Was he born in *Elul* (August), the direction of which is assigned to *Periel*? Let him be cursed, &c.

Was he born in *Tisri* (September), the direction of which is assigned to *Zuriel*? Let him be cursed, &c.

Was he born in *Marcheseh* (October), the direction of which is assigned to *Zachariel*? Let him be cursed, &c.

Was he born in *Hisleu* (November), the direction of which is assigned to *Adomil*? Let him be cursed, &c.

Was he born in *Tevat* (December), the direction of which is assigned to *Anael*? Let him be cursed, &c.

Was he born in *Schevat* (January), the direction of which is assigned to *Gabriel*? Let him be cursed, &c.

Was he born in *Adar* (February), the direction of which is assigned to *Rumiel*, and to those of his company? Let him be cursed by the mouth of Rumiel, and by the mouth of the angels of whom he is the head.

Let him be cursed by the mouth of the Seven Angels who preside over the seven days of the week, and by the mouth of all the angels who follow them and fight under their banners. Let him be cursed by the Four Angels who preside over the four seasons of the year, and by the mouth of all the angels who follow them and fight under their banners. Let him be cursed by the mouth of the seven principalities. Let him be cursed by the mouth of the prince of the Law, whose name is Crown and Seal. In a word, let him be cursed by the mouth of the strong, powerful, and dreadful God.

We beseech the great God to confound such a man, and to hasten the day of his destruction. May God, the God of Spirits, depress him under all flesh, extirpate, destroy, exterminate, and annihilate him. The secret judgments of the Lord, the most contagious storms and winds fall upon the head of impious men; the exterminating angels will fall upon them. Which way soever the impious man turn, he will never find anything but contradiction, obstacles, and curses. His soul at his death will forsake his body, being delivered up to the quickest sense of fear, horror, and anguish; it will then be impossible for him to avoid the blow of death and the judgments of God. God sends the sharpest and most violent evils upon him. Let him perish by the sword, by a burning fever, by a consumption, being dried up by fire within and covered with leprosy and imposthumes without. Let God pursue him till he be entirely rooted out and destroyed. The sword of the impious man shall be pierced through his own breast; his bow shall be broken. He will be like the straw which is scattered about by the wind. The angel of the Lord will pursue him in darkness, in slippery places, where the paths of the wicked are. His destruction will fall upon him at the time when he does not expect it; he will find himself taken in the snare which he had laid in private for others. Being driven from the face of the earth, he will be driven from light into darkness. Oppression and anguish will seize him on every side. His eyes shall see his condemnation. He will drink the cup of the indignation of the Lord, whose curses will cover him at his garments. The earth will swallow him up. God will extirpate and shut him for ever out of his house. Let God never forgive him his sins. Let the wrath and indignation of the Lord surround him and smoke for ever on his head. Let all the curses contained in the Book of the Law fall upon him. Let God blot him out of his book. Let God separate him to his own destruction from all the tribes of Israel, and give him for his lot all the curses contained in the Book of the Law.

As for you who are still living, serve the Lord your God, who blessed Abraham, Isaac, Jacob, Moses, Aaron, David, Solomon, the prophets of Israel, and so many good men everywhere dispersed among the Gentiles. May it please the great God to shower his blessings upon this whole assembly, and upon all other holy assemblies, and the members thereof. God keep them under his holy protection. God preserve them in his great mercy, and deliver them from all sorts of misery and oppression. God grant them all a great many years; let him bless and prosper all their undertakings. Lastly, may the great God shortly grant them that Deliverance which they with all Israel expect: and thus let his good will and pleasure be fulfilled. *Amen.*[74]

While these curses were chanted forth from one side, the thrilling sounds of a trumpet accompanied tham at intervals from the other. The black candles were reversed, and made to melt drop by drop into a huge tub filled with blood. This symbol made the spectators shudder, and when the close came, and the lights were all suddenly immersed in the blood, a cry of execration rose from all, and in that darkness rose shouts of 'Amen!' to the curses.

Amsterdam, at least the Jewish part of it, was in an uproar; but the young man who had been cursed thus particularly was probably not much troubled. Black candles melting in blood, lugubrious chantings of detailed curses, with trumpet accompaniments, might terrify those who believed that God would certainly fulfil all the intentions which Rabbis attributed to him—believed in the wrath and ferocity, the merciless lust of vengeance, which they, personifying their own passions, attributed to the Creator; but such cursings were no more than fetid breath to one whose conceptions of the Creator were of a higher kind, whose faith in the goodness of God, and placid resignation to God's will was more than a tradition, more than a profession, a deep conviction working through his life.

※ ※ ※

So much of the outward life we know; of the inward life we know nothing. Kuno Fischer is probably warranted in the assumption that it was to the influence of Descartes that Spinoza owed his emancipation from rabbinical ideas; but we have no evidence on the subject. Nor do we know how he fared when banished from the Jewish community and his family. His isolation was great. Excluded from the society of Jews he found no refuge in that of Christians; nor had he at first a select circle of sympathising friends to whom he could turn: these came later on. There were, indeed, one or two from whom he might have received sympathy: one of these was Vanden Ende, the physician and philologist, from whom he had learned Latin and (it is conjectured) philosophy, and (as I conjecture) gained that acquaintance with anatomy and physiology which, although never obtruded, is nevertheless discernible in his writings.[75] Vanden Ende had a daughter who is sometimes said to have taught Spinoza Latin, but as she was only a child of twelve at the date of the Excommunication, 1656, inexorable chronology refuses its countenance to that myth. Whether there is any truth in the story of Spinoza's having been jilted by this Clara Maria for one Kerckrinck, a Hamburg merchant, who wooed and won her with pearl necklaces (a story which has been elevated into romance by Auerbach), it would be difficult to decide. He himself spoke of the affection he had borne her; but considering that she refused to marry Kerckrinck until he had come over to her religion, we cannot suppose that she would have listened to Spinoza, who had discarded all religious forms. And what shall we say to the suggestion of his Jewish biographer, Philipson, that it was this idea of a Jew marrying a Christian which led him to meditate on Judaism, Christianity, and Religion in the abstract, whence he rose through Love to Philosophy?

Love seems to have played but a very subordinate part in this thinker's life. He tells us himself that it was another mistress to whom he was devoted. In a fragment entitled 'On the Improvement of the Intellect,' which was his first work, there is this passage, which has biographical significance:–

Experience having taught me that all the ordinary affairs of life are vain and futile; and that those things which I dreaded were only in themselves good or bad according as they moved my soul, I finally resolved on inquiring if there was anything truly good in itself, and capable of being communicated to man, a good which, everything else being rejected, could fill the soul entirely; whether, in short, that good existed which if possessed could give supreme and eternal happiness. I say, *I finally resolved*, because at first it seemed inconsiderate to renounce the good which was certain for a greater good which was uncertain. I pondered on the advantages which accrued from reputation and wealth, all of which I must renounce if I would seriously undertake the search after another object, and which, if happiness chanced to belong to these advantages, I should necessarily see escape me; and if, on the other hand, happiness belongs to other objects and I sought happiness where it is not to be found, then also should I miss it. I therefore resolved this in my mind; whether it were possible for me to regulate my life according to a new rule, or at any rate ascertain the existence of such a rule, without changing the actual order of my life—a thing which I have often in vain attempted. For those things which most frequently occur in life, and in which men, judging from their acts, think supreme happiness consists, may be reduced to three, *riches, honours*, and *pleasures of the senses*.[76] By these three the mind is so occupied it is scarcely able to think of any other good. Pleasures of sense, especially, so absorb the mind that it reposes in them, and thus is prevented from thinking of anything else. But after fruition follows sadness, which if it does not absorb the mind at least disturbs and deadens it. The search after riches and honours also occupies the mind, especially when sought for their own sake, as if they constituted happiness. Repentance does not follow riches and honours as it follows sensuous pleasures; on the contrary, the more we possess of them the greater is our pleasure, and consequently the greater our desire to increase them. Honour, or reputation, is a serious impediment, because to attain it we must direct our lives according to the wishes of others, avoiding what the vulgar avoid, seeking what men seek. When, therefore, I saw the obstacles which hindered me from following a rule of conduct different from the ordinary rule, and saw how great was the antagonism between the two, I was forced to inquire which of the two would be most useful to me; for, as I said just now, I seemed to be abandoning the certain for the uncertain. But after meditating thereupon I found, first, that in giving up the ordinary advantages I really renounced only an uncertain good for another equally uncertain, the latter, however, being only uncertain as to the possibility of my attaining it. After assiduous meditation I found that I was only quitting certain evils for a certain good. For I saw I was in the greatest danger, which forced me to seek a remedy, even an uncertain one; as a man in sickness, seeing certain death before him unless something be done, will seize at any remedy, however vague, for in that is all his hope. And, indeed, all those things which the vulgar seek were not only unable to furnish me with a remedy, but were obstacles, because they are frequently the very causes of the ruin of those who possess them, and always of those who are possessed by them. Many are the examples of those who have suffered persecution, nay, death, on account of their wealth, or who, in the hope of gain, have exposed themselves to perils, and paid for their folly with their lives. Nor are there fewer examples of men who in the pursuit of honours, or in defending them, have become most miserable. Lastly, there are innumerable examples of those who by excess of sensual pleasures have accelerated their death. Hence the evil seems to me to arise from this; that all our happiness and unhappiness depend solely on the quality of the object which we desire. For those things which are not desired arouse neither quarrels nor sorrow if they escape us, nor envy when others possess them, neither fear nor hate, in a word, no commotion of the mind; whereas all those evils belong to our attachment to perishable things, such as those just spoken of. But love of what is eternal and infinite nourishes the mind with joy only, and is never touched with sorrow, and it is *this* good so eminently desirable that all men should seek. Yet it was not without meaning that I said, *to consider the matter seriously.* For although I clearly perceived this in my mind, I could not banish all love of wealth, honours, and sensual pleasures. But I found that so long as my mind was occupied with these thoughts, so long was it turned away from passions, and seriously meditated the new rule of life, which was to me a great consolation. For thus I saw that these evils were not incurable; and, although at first these serious moments were rare and brief, yet afterwards as the *true good* became better known they became more frequent and more durable, especially when I saw that the acquisition of wealth, glory, and sensual pleasures was fatal so long as these were sought for their own sakes and not as means to an end. If, indeed, they are sought as means, then they have their value and do little hurt; on the contrary, they are very useful towards the proposed end.

Here let me say what I mean by the *true good* and what is the *supreme good*. To understand these rightly it must be noted that *good* and *evil* are only relative, so that one and the same thing may be called good or evil according to its different aspects; and the same of perfection and imperfection. Nothing considered in itself can be called perfect or imperfect; as we shall understand when we see how all things exist according to the external order and according to the certain laws of nature. But as human weakness cannot follow this eternal order by its own thought, and meanwhile man conceives a human nature much surpassing his own, to the height of which nothing seems to prevent his arriving, he is incited to seek the means of arriving at this perfection, and everything which seems to lead there is called by him the *true good*. But the *supreme good* would be for him and others, if possible, to enjoy this higher nature. And what is this? We shall hereafter show that it is the knowledge of the union of the mind with all nature. This then is the end I must seek: to acquire this higher human nature and use every effort for others to acquire it also; that is to say, it is necessary for my happiness that many others should think with me, so that their intellects and their desires should accord with mine; for which two things are necessary: *first*, to understand Nature so as to be able to acquire this higher human nature; *next*, to form such a society as will admit of the greatest number arriving easily and securely at such perfection. Therefore our tasks are a *moral philosophy* and the *education of children*; and, as health is a not unimportant means for the end we have in view, the whole science of *medicine* must be added; and, as the arts make many difficult things easy, and aid us by saving our labour and time, we must not omit *mechanics*. But above all must be sought a method of improving the understanding, and as far as possible to correct it from the beginning, so that, warned against error, it may know clearly.

This passage must not be read as mere oratorical preamble, but as the serious expression of his conviction. His life testifies to its sincerity. What he said, he did; what he wrote in philosophic treatises he tried to live in philosophic earnestness. He was very poor, and was often tempted—tempted by money, tempted by vanity, tempted by his senses; but these lures were powerless. It was not with him as it is, unhappily, with so many of us who mean to live a noble life, and wish to act up to our best convictions, but who find that the allurements which are easily vanquished while they remain at a certain distance, become our masters when they press closely on us. Spinoza was a 'God-intoxicated man' not only in the ardours of speculative activity, but in the conflict of daily life, believing in God as an ever-present reality. Amidst temptation he continued steadfast to the divinity of those aspirations which in solitude his soul had seen to be divine. Many men before and since have been poor and obscure, have despised wealth, have been careless of fame, even when they have shown no touch of vain-gloriousness in their contempt and noisy independence; but not many have been offered the opulence and glory they despised, and have continued, after the offers, to leave them disregarded and untouched. Many men have written eloquently and sincerely of quitting the perishable things of this world for Truth; but few have shown an equal earnestness in translating this eloquence into conduct. Spinoza was one of the few; and it is well that this should be known, because the deep repugnance which is felt against his speculative opinions arises less from a sense of their falsehood, than from a belief that such opinions cannot enter the mind without necessarily dissolving all moral principles. I have no hesitation in avowing that many of Spinoza's conclusions are such as must shock all Christians, and most Theists, that to him even more than to Kant should be applied the epithet of 'all shattering' (*alles zermalmende*), that logically there is but a trivial distinction between his Acosmism, which makes God the one universal being, and Atheism, which makes the cosmos the one universal existence. Observe, I say, 'logically' there is but little difference; spiritually, the difference is profound. His Acosmism may *de*note what is scarcely distinguishable from Atheism; it *con*notes something utterly opposed to Atheism; and we know that he explicitly and emphatically repudiated Atheism. The horror which many feel at his opinions is entirely due to the rooted prejudice that morality is inseparable from certain special dogmas which, if rejected, leave the man a prey to all animal and ignoble passions. But no one was more rigorous than he in the subjection of all passions and all egoisms to the love of God and obedience to the Divine will. The love of God is everywhere proclaimed the highest good, the noblest aim, the only source of permanent felicity. And when Isaac Orobio accused him of getting rid of all Religion in the escape from superstition, he gravely asked, 'Is it to cast off Religion to acknowledge God as the supreme good, and to love him with singleness of soul, which love must constitute our highest felicity, our most perfect freedom? That the reward of virtue is virtue, and the punishment of ignorance and impotence is ignorance? and that every one should love his neighbour and obey the laws?'[77] He denied that true morality has its basis in fear of punishment. To substitute that fear for the love of God is to show that we love something better than God.

Spinoza shocks those who regard him from an antagonistic standing point. No sooner is the mind disengaged from the trammels of old prejudice than we learn to look on his arguments as on the arguments of Parmenides or Algazel; we ask whether they are true or false, whether they can be taken up into our philosophy, or rejected from it? This is the attitude of Germany. To some extent it is the attitude of France. It will become the attitude of England. For myself I cannot accept Spinoza's system; but I see how it was perfectly compatible with his own pure morality, and do not fear lest it should disturb the morality of any one who could conscientiously adopt it. I reject all ontological schemes, and deny the competence of the ontological method; but if we are to employ that method and put our trust in its conclusions, the results of Spinozism are quite as capable of dovetailing with the needs of a noble life as any other system.

And here I may make a remark of general application, namely, that the incalculable importance of morality so presses itself upon consideration at every turn, and necessarily forms so large a part of every thinker's meditations, that no rational system can be constructed which does not conform itself to the highest prevalent conceptions of the moral law; and hence we may observe, as a rule, that in proportion as a speculative system departs from the principles currently accepted in philosophy, it seeks to gain increased support from morality, thus recovering the hold of men's minds in one direction which it has given up in the other. If this be so, it shows how misguided is the anger which assails a new thought from terror at its moral consequences. Our first question should never be, To what will this lead? but, Is this true?

✳ ✳ ✳

Spinoza gained his livelihood by glass polishing. The rules of the Jewish doctors enjoin the necessity of learning some mechanical art, as well as the Law. It was not enought for a Rabbi to be a scholar, he must also have at command the means of subsistence. Spinoza, fond of optics, had learned the art of polishing lenses; and he acquired a certain celebrity for the excellence of his workmanship, as we see in a letter from Leibnitz. He also relaxed his mind occasionally with employing his pencil. Colerus had a portfolio of portraits by him of several distinguished men; among these was a sketch of Spinoza himself, in the dress of Masaniello.

In 1660 we find him living in Rhynsburg, near Leyden; and there among his friends we notice Henry Oldenburg, who had been the Hague consul in London, when Cromwell was Protector. He was also the intimate friend of Robert Boyle, and helped in the foundation of the Royal Society of Great Britain. The very first paper in the Transactions of that now illustrious society bears his signature. He writes from London to Spinoza in the year 1661, recalling their pleasant discussion on God, thought, extension, the union of the body and soul, and the philosophy of Descartes and Bacon.[78]

Another friend is Simon de Vries, who was true to him through life, and whose veneration is prettily expressed in that passage of a letter wherein he exclaims, 'Thrice happy is the young man living in the same house with you, who can see you at breakfast and dinner, who can walk with you, and listen to you on the highest subjects.' Upon which Spinoza characteristically replies, 'You need not envy my young inmate, against whom I jealously guard myself, and to whom I earnestly beg that you and other friends will not communicate my opinions until he has grown more ripe for them. At present he is too childish and volatile, impelled rather by curiosity than love of truth. But I hope that he will put aside these faults as he grows older; nay, as far as I can judge of his disposition, I feel sure of this, and on this account I take great pains with him.'[79] It was this young man that Spinoza instructed in the Cartesian philosophy, and for his use he began the composition of the 'Principles of Descartes geometrically demonstrated'; not for Simon de Vries, as is commonly said. This work was afterwards completed, and an appendix added, in which Spinoza indicates his chief points of divergence from Descartes. It was published by Meyer in 1664, and produced considerable stir among the Cartesians.

He left Rhynsburg for the Hague, and there among his warm friends was the celebrated and unfortunate Grand Pensioner, Jean de Witt. 'In all Holland,' says Mr Froude, 'there were none like these two; they had found each other now, and they loved each other as only good men love. From him Spinoza accepted a pension, not a very enormous one—some thirty-five pounds a year; the only thing of the kind he ever did accept. Perhaps because De Witt was the only person he had met who exactly understood what it was, and weighed such favours at their exact worth, neither less nor more.'

This interpretation is consistent with all we know of Spinoza. On the death of his father, his two sisters, Rebecca and Miriam, tried to keep him from his inheritance, probably thinking that an excommunicated heretic had no claim on the money of the faithful. He appealed against them in a court of law; gained his cause, and having thus satisfied his sense of justice, gave up the contested property as a free gift, thus saving his sisters from fraud and himself from an indignity. Later in life his affectionate pupil, Simon de Vries, brought him a thousand florins, entreating him to accept it as a slight payment of the heavy debt the pupil owed the teacher. Spinoza laughingly assured him that he was in no need of money, and that such a sum would turn his head. Simon then made a will, bequeathing the whole of his property to Spinoza, who, on hearing of it, at once set off for Amsterdam to remonstrate against an act so unjust to Simon's brother. His arguments prevailed. The will was destroyed, and the brother finally inherited. Now came a struggle of generosity. The heir protested that he could not accept the property unless he were allowed to settle five hundred florins a year on the disinterested friend; and, after some debate, Spinoza agreed to accept three hundred.

In 1673 Karl Ludwig, the Elector Palatine, anxious to secure so illustrious a thinker, offered him the chair of philosophy at Heidelberg. But whatever allurement there might otherwise have been in such a proposal was destroyed by the intimation that the Elector hoped he would avoid collision with existing creeds. 'I have never had any intention of teaching in public,' replied the philosopher, 'and if I give my time to expounding the first questions of philosophy, I shall perhaps not be able to make any advances in its deeper questions as I desire. Nor do I exactly understand within what limits my philosophy *can* be made to avoid collision with established creeds. Schisms do not arise so much from a genuine love of religion, as from the interests and passions, and from that love of contradiction which prompts men to falsify and anathematise even what is true.'[80] And, therefore, the professorship was declined. Louis XIV offered him a pension if he would dedicate his next work to him, but received for answer that the philosopher had no intention of dedicating anything to his Majesty.

From these example we may conclude that his acceptance of the pension from De Witt was grounded on a perfect confidence in the motives and the character of his friend. There is often as much generosity in accepting as in conferring an obligation; and as much vanity as independence in its rejection. All depends upon the nature of the existing relations, and the character of the friend.

A little incident, unnoticed by his biographers, but interesting as an indication of the state of opinion in those days, may here be related. If there is an error one might have expected the clear and penetrating intellect of Spinoza to have seen through, it is the error of the Alchemists; but this expectation is grounded on a misconception. Alchemy seems absurd to us because the experimental method has abundantly shown that the processes of the alchemists were futile. In those days it seemed plausible enough; and that which conquered the assent of eminent men, was not scientific deduction, but a striking fact. J.F. Schweitzer (known in Europe by his Latinised name of Helvetius) was then physician to the Prince of Orange, and notorious as an antagonist of alchemists. It was, therefore, their interest to convert him. On the 27th of December, 1666, he received the visit of a stranger, who declined to give his name, but who came, he said, in consequence of the dispute between Helvetius and Kenelm Digby, and was prepared with material proofs of the existence of the philosopher's stone. After a sharp discussion, the stranger handed him an extremely small portion of yellow metallic powder, having the aspect of sulphur, assuring him it would transmute an ounce and a-half of lead into gold. He departed. Helvetius, in the presence of his wife, made the experiment. To his astonishment it succeeded. There was the ingot of gold, which all the goldsmiths and assayers of the Hague pronounced to be pure. He was startled into credulity. The fact mastered him, as striking facts so often master imperfect scepticism. He wrote an account of the whole adventure, and avowed his faith in the alchemy which hitherto he had derided. This made no little stir. Among the rest Spinoza was eager for precise details, and we have a letter from him dated the 25th of March, 1667, in which he says:–

Your last letter of the 14th reached me safely, but various causes prevented my replying at once. I spoke to Vossius about the Helvetius affair, and he burst out laughing, wondering how I could occupy myself about such trivialities. But I, disregarding this contempt, went to the goldsmith who had assayed the gold, and whose name is Brechtett. He assured me that, in spite of Vossius, the gold during the fusion increased in weight on some silver being thrown into the crucible; hence, as he firmly believes, this gold which changes silver into gold must contain something peculiar in itself. Not he alone, but divers other persons who were present at the time assured me that such was the case. After this I went to Helvetius, who showed me the gold and the crucible still having a little gold attached to its inside; and told me that he had strewn scarcely a quarter of a grain on the molten lead. He added that it was his intention to publish a brief history of the affair. This is what I have been able to learn of the matter.

The trick which imposed upon Helvetius was adroit, and the knowledge of chemistry was too imperfect, and the nature of experimental evidence too little understood, to suggest the presence of a trick. Spinoza, like the others, seems to have relied upon the purely irrelevant testimony of goldsmiths and bystanders; and on similar testimony spirit-rapping, witchcraft, and other delusions have been credited.

The next, and perhaps the most considerable event to be recorded in Spinoza's life is the publication in 1670 of the *Tractatus Theologico-Politicus*. It is one of the boldest books ever written; and it was written at a time when boldness was far more perilous than it has been since; when philosophers had to use elaborate precautions in advancing even small heresies, and their skill was shown in insinuating what they could not openly avow. Spinoza had for some time resisted the entreaties of his friends; he foresaw the tumult that his opinions would arouse. Oldenburg writes to him in 1662 urging him to brave the ignorant mob and rely on the sympathy of the learned (a pretty reed to lean on!); and in 1665 he is still more pressing. 'What do you fear? Why hesitate? Begin, and you may be confident of the applause of all real philosophers. I never will believe that you would write anything against the existence and providence of God; and provided that these solid grounds of religion are respected, it is easy to excuse or defend any philosophic opinions.' Yet Oldenburg himself held a very different language after publication; and proved that Spinoza's hesitation was well founded. What finally determined him is not known. Most probably a deep sense of the importance of his views at a period of widespread unrest, a period rife with sophisms. Holland was reposing on the laurels she had won in her long and desperate struggle against Spain. Having freed herself from a foreign yoke, she might now have completed her canals, extended her commerce, and enjoyed the amenities of peace, had not theological faction disturbed it. A land of political freedom, an asylum for persecuted free-thinkers, it was torn by theological strife. The persecuted Jews might flock there from Portugal and Spain; the Protestants of France and Belgium found shelter there; but on their arrival these fugitives witnessed conflicts almost as savage as those from which they fled. Toleration was awarded to political thought; various religions were allowed to erect their churches; but within the pale of the State Church there was the old strife. What Spinoza wished to teach men was, the essential nature of Religion, and the political nature of a church. He wished to see a complete separation of the temporal and spiritual powers, giving to the Church a purely political significance in outward observances, and leaving individual conscience free as to opinions. The State has a right to determine ceremonies and observances; but it violates every principle of justice if it attempts to coerce opinions or the expression of opinions. It would be impossible for men to continue to live in society unless each gave up his right of action in deference to the laws established for all. 'The right of action on his individual judgment ceases; but the right of action only, not the right of reasoning and judging.'

I shall have to speak more particularly hereafter of this book, which was everywhere condemned, interdicted, and, above all, 'refuted'. Even free thinkers were staggered; yet it found some energetic admirers, who printed it under false titles, translated, and abridged it, thus disseminating its ideas. In England an abridgment appeared in 1720, and in 1737 a complete translation. What Spinoza thought of his 'refuters' may be gathered from a passage in one of his letters.[81] 'The other day I saw the book which the Utrecht professors have been writing against me, hanging in a bookseller's window, and from the little I had time to read of it, it seemed not worth reading, much less answering. I let the book and its author alone. Mentally smiling, I thought how the men who are most ignorant, are always those most audaciously ready to write.'

This *Tracate* made Spinoza's house the house of call for lionhunters. Foreign ministers, foreign philosophers, men who admired him, men who execrated him, and men who were to 'refute him', came to occupy his leisure with their talk. He conversed very freely with them, sketching all the while, often taking their portraits. Among these visitors we shall only here note Leibnitz, who although he plagiarised his celebrated philosophical conception of the pre-established harmony from Spinoza, never spoke of him but in terms unworthy of both these great intellects. This much is to be said for Leibnitz, however, that he never thoroughly understood Spinoza, and was shocked at the results of the system he so misconceived. If he never understood the simple Locke, we need not wonder that he failed to penetrate the meaning of Spinoza; that he did fail is conclusively and almost ludicrously shown in the posthumous work published by an admiring disciple,[82] of which

I shall take no further notice. The plagiarism of the pre-established harmony has been placed beyond a doubt. Nevertheless, whether Leibnitz understood or misunderstood Spinoza, one would have been glad of some record of their meeting and conversation.

The murder of De Witt must have been a great shock to Spinoza. It was the only occasion on which he is known to have lost all control over his emotions; and it must have recurred to him with solemn feeling when, on a visit to the great Condé, the report arose that he was a political spy, and the populace surrounded the house where he lived. 'Fear nothing,' he said to his terrified landlord, 'it is easy for me to justify myself. There are those who know the object of my journey. But whatever may arrive, as soon as the mob assembles, I will go out and meet them, even though I share the fate of De Witt.'

Annoyed at being misunderstood on points which seemed to him so clear, he shrank from the publication of his Ethics; and accordingly that work only saw the light after his death. He was timid and retiring, ill suited to the world and the world's ways, especially unsuited for conflict. A severe mysticism, like his, was not for vulgar minds. It wanted even the emotion which could commend it to mystical minds. For the peculiarity about him, that which distinguishes him from all other thinkers is, that he was a mystic whose mind moved in geometrical processes; and his severe rigour of abstraction and deduction are as repellent to the vague emotional tendencies of the mystical mind, as the intense disinterestedness and passionlessness of his system are repellent to the ordinary mind.

Let us glance at his private life. Though very poor, from his scanty pittance he had something to spare for the necessities of others. On looking over his papers after his death, it was found that one day his expenses amounted to three halfpence, for a *soupe au lait* and a little butter, with three farthings extra for beer; another day, gruel, with butter and raisins, which cost him twopence halfpenny, sufficed for his epicurism; and as his biographer Colerus says, 'Although often invited to dinner, he preferred the scanty meal that he found at home to dining sumptuously at the expense of another.' In company with a few neighbours he sat at the chimney corner, smoking his pipe and talking to them of what they could understand, not disturbing their creeds by any obtrusion of his own. No vanity of proselytism made him trouble the convictions of those unfitted to receive new doctrines. When his landlady, feeling, perhaps, that the assurance of so good and great a man was almost equal to the priests, asked him whether he believed she could be saved by her religion, which she knew was not his, he replied, 'Your religion is a good one; you ought not to seek another, nor doubt that yours will procure salvation provided you add to your piety the tranquil virtues of domestic life.' Nor was this, as some might suppose, the mere evasion of one who chose not to commit himself by exposure of his heretical opinions; it was a part of the solemn earnestness with which he looked at life and accepted faith. Read the fourteenth chapter of the *Theological Political Treatise*, and see how he distinguishes between what is essential and what collateral in religion; how faith in God and love of God, with the consequent love of mankind, are in his eyes the sum of all religion; how, even regarding religious dogmas, it is not essential that they should be true, so that they be truly believed; and how it by no means follows that those who can give the best reasons for their faith are truly the most faithful, but, on the contrary, those who live most according to justice and charity. He knew his hostess was not wise, but he saw that she was virtuous.

The children all loved him, and for them he would bring one of his lenses to show them the spiders magnified. It was his amusement to watch insects. The sight of spiders fighting would make the tears roll down his cheeks with laughter; a trait which Dugald Stewart thinks 'very decidedly indicates a tendency to insanity;'[83] and satisfactorily accounts for the horrible doctrines of Spinozism(?). Hamann sees in it only the sympathy of one web-spinner for another: 'His taste betrays itself in a mode of thought which only insects can thus entangle. Spiders and their admirer Spinoza naturally take to the geometric style of building.'[84] This is only surpassed by Hegel's interpretation of his consumptive tendency as in harmony with his philosophy, in which all individuality and particularity were resolved into the One Substance.[85]

He had been a delicate child, and although at no time positively an invalid, he had always been weakly. The seeds of consumption slowly but inevitably undermined his strength, and on Sunday 22nd February, 1677, he was so feeble that his kind host and hostess left him reluctantly to attend divine service. He feared that he was sinking. But he entreated them to go to church as usual. On their return he talked with them about the sermon, and ate some broth with a good appetite. After dinner they again went to church, but left the physician by his bedside. On their return all was over. At three o'clock he had expired in the presence of the physician—who paid himself by taking a silver-handled knife and what money lay on the table, and departed.

He died in his forty-fifth year, in the maturity of his intellect, but not before he had thoroughly worked out the whole scheme of his philosophy.

Magic and Science

From *All the Year Round* (25 March 1861)

Ancient magic was ancient science. To surprise the secrets of Nature, and, by surprising them, to control phenomena and turn them to his purposes, has everywhere been the irresistible longing of man, placed amid unseen forces with nothing but his wit to aid him. How marvellously his wit has aided him need not be told; but the help came slowly, and the victories were gained only after a succession of defeats. That which mainly thwarted him was Impatience, and its offspring, Credulity; that which mainly aided him was Patience. From the first sprang Magic; from the second, Science. Passion is ever credulous, and when the mind is greatly excited, it is ready to believe almost anything which favours its desires.

The credulity of early ages has also another source. In ignorance of the true order of Nature we find no difficulty in believing that one thing takes place rather than another. What to the cultivated minds seems a physical impossibility, to the uncultivated seems as probable as anything else. It is therefore not only far from incredible, it is highly probable to the savage that the ordinary phenomena of Nature should be the actions of capricious beings, whose caprices may be propitiated. He observes the rain falling, the seed sprouting, his cattle perishing, his children sickening, all by agencies unseen, which he at once supposes to be Spirits resembling the spirit within him, though mightier: superhuman in power, they are conceived to be human in feeling, because no other conception of power is possible to him. In animating Nature, man necessarily animates it with a soul like his own. He therefore cannot help supposing that the varied phenomena which pass before him are acts of arbitrary and capricious volition. Like the potentates of his tribe or nation, these Unseen Agencies require to be flattered, or intimidated. Incense, sacrifices, ceremonies of homage, prayers and supplications, may captivate their favour. Failing this, there is the resource of incantation, exorcism, amulets, and charms; the aid of some more powerful spirit is invoked, or the secret of some weakness is surprised. Sometimes the malignity of a spirit may be thwarted by the mere invocation of the *name* of a mightier spirit; and sometimes by the mere employment of a disagreeable object—holy water, or a strong smell—before which the demon flies. This is the condition of the mind in all half-civilised peoples, and this is the condition which determines Magic.

In the slow travail of thought, and by the accumulation of experience, another condition is brought about, and Science emerges. Before it can emerge, the most important of all changes must have taken place: the phenomena of Nature, at least all the most ordinary phenomena, must have been disengaged from this conception of an arbitrary and *capricious* power, similar to human will, and must have been recognised as *constant*, always succeeding each other with fatal regularity. This once recognised, Science can begin slowly to ascertain the *order* of Nature—the laws of succession and co-existence; and having in any case ascertained this order, it can predict with certainty the results which will arrive. If I know that the order of Nature is such that air which has once been breathed becomes imperfectly adapted for a second breathing, and becomes poisonous after a repetition of the process, I do not, when I see my fellow-creatures perishing because they breathe this vitiated air, attempt to propitiate the noxious spirit by supplications, or to intimidate by charms and exorcisms. I simply let in the fresh air, knowing that the fresh air will restore the drooping sufferers, because such is the order of Nature. I have learned, O Thaumaturgus! that your Unseen Agencies, mighty as you deem them, are not free, but are fatally subject to inexorable law; they cannot act capriciously, they must act inexorably. If, therefore, I can detect these laws—if I can ascertain what is the inevitable order of succession—it will be quite needless to trouble myself about your Unseen Agencies. You promise by your art to give me power over these Agencies, by which I shall be able to bend Nature to my purpose, to harness her to my triumphant chariot. But if I can once discover the inexorable laws, I can do what you only delusively pretend. With each discovery of the actual order of Nature, it has been found that man's power *over* Nature has become greater. He cannot alter that order, but he can adapt himself to it. He cannot change the Unchangeable, but he can predict the Inexorable. And Science thus fulfils the pretensions of Magic; it is Magic grown modest.

In proportion as regularity in the succession of phenomena became ascertained, the domain of superstition and magic became restricted. When it was seen that the seed sprouted and the rain fell in spite of all incantations, and that the direction of the wind was a surer indication than the medicine-man's formula, credulity sought refuge in phenomena less understood. Long after the course of Nature was felt to be beyond the influence of magicians, there was profound belief in their influence over life and death. The phenomena of Disease seemed wholly capricious. An invisible enemy seemed to have struck down the young and heathly warrior; an enraged deity seemed to be destroying tribes. When the epidemic breaks out in the Grecian camp, Homer attributes it solely to the rage of Apollo, whose priest has been offended. Down from Olympus the far darter comes, 'like night', sits apart from the camp, and for nine days keeps pouring in his dreadful arrows. The soldiers are struck by this invisible, but too fatal, enemy. The only rescue is by appeasing Apollo's wrath. Even in our own day, men who would smile at this childish fable, found no difficulty in attributing the Irish famine to a cause no less childish: they averred it was a punishment for the 'Maynooth grant'. In both cases the cause or order of Nature was unsuspected; and ignorant imagination was free to invent the explanation which best pleased it.

The early priests were necessarily magicans. All early religions had a strong bias towards sorcery; because their priests, believing that all the forces of Nature were good and evil demons, necessarily arrogate to themselves a power over these demons, either by propitiation or intimidation. These men never attempted to make mankind better, nor to make them wiser; their object was rather to inspire terror, and to propagate the superstitions of which they themselves were dupes. Some secrets they learned, especially the effects of certain herbs in stimulating and stupifying the nervous system, so as to produce visions and hallucinations. They learned, also, how the imagination may be impressed by ceremonies, darkness, lugubrious music, and perfumes, so that the semi-delirious devotee saw whatever he was told to see.

Hecate, for example, was the personification of the mysterious rays which the moon projects into the darkness of night, and only appeared when the moon veiled her disc. To Hecate were attributed the spectres and phantoms of darkness, and all over Greece the rites were celebrated by many practices common to sorcery. Thus everything was brought together to appal the imagination, deceive the senses and foster sombre conceptions: exorcisms and weird formulas, disgusting philtres, hell-broth made of loathsome objects, such as Shakespeare describes in Macbeth:–

> Fillet of a fenny snake,
> In the cauldron boil and bake:
> Eye of newt, and toe of frog,
> Wool of bat, and tongue of dog,
> Adder's fork, and blind-worm's sting,
> Lizard's leg, and owlet's wing,
> Scale of dragon, tooth of wolf,
> Witches' mummy; maw and gulf,
> Of the ravin'd salt-sea shark.

And to these he adds, with his terrible energy of expression,

> Liver of blaspheming Jew;
> Finger of birth-strangled babe,
> Ditch-delivered by a drab.

The mind of a cultivated man in these days, unable to conceive any *direct relation* between the liver of a blaspheming Jew and control of the course of Nature, finds it difficult to believe that minds as powerful as his own, under less favourable influences, could seriously credit such incantations. Yet the history of mankind shows that no amount of failure, no argument, no ridicule, no priestly warning and exhortation, could detach men from the practices of sorcery. The temptation to penetrate the secrets of Nature was too strong. Nothing could overcome this temptation while the belief in witchcraft lasted. Nothing could destroy the belief, but the slowly growing conviction that the succession of phenomena was not capricious but inexorable—every single event being rigorously determined by its antecedent, and not to be altered, so long as the antecedent remained the same.

No one believes in Astrology now, because the order of celestial phenomena has been ascertained with remarkable precision. Yet how natural was the belief in starry influences! In the serenity of Asiatic skies, the majestic aspects of the stars would naturally attract incessant notice. It is a tendency, observable in children and savages, to suppose that whatever interests them must also be interested in them. If we look up at the stars, do they look down upon us? If we follow their course with interest, will they not likewise with interest follow ours? Hence the belief in astral influences. The child upon whose cradle Mars has smiled will be credited with a martial career; the child born under Venus will be under her protection. These are the spontaneous beliefs. Before they can be discredited men must, by a long process, have learned to check this tendency to suppose a direct relation between events which are simply *coincident*, and must have learned that the course of the stars and the course of human conduct are in *no* direct relation to each other. But this is a slow process; and until Science has been thus far established, Astrology, and all other superstitions, are unassailable.

M Maury, in a recent treatise on Magic and Astrology—which, being at once light and learned, agreeable to read and reliable when read, may safely be commended to the curious—proves that no amount of religious reprobation has been able to uproot the belief in, or check the practices of sorcery.

The early Israelites, in common with all primitive peoples, had their magic, consulted sorcerers, explained dreams, and believed in talismans. In vain Moses proscribed these superstitions. On their return from captivity they brought with them a number of Babylonian sorceries, together with the belief in angels and demons. By a natural process they came to regard certain formulas written on parchment, and containing the names of celestial spirits, as veritable talismans. Like the Egyptians, they believed that if they summoned demons by their names, these demons were thereby compelled to appear, or to obey orders.

Respecting the gods of other nations, the Jews held two different opinions. One opinion was that these gods were vain idols; the other, that they were agents of Satan; and this was the opinion which finally prevailed. Beelzebub, for example, was originally the god of the Philistines; Astaroth was the lunar goddess of the Phœnicians; Lucifer was a god of the Assyrians; and so on. The early Christians adopted this notion, and attributed all the pagan miracles to agents of Satan. In their view the ancient polytheism was but an extensive demonology. 'Idolatry,' says Eusebius, one of the great authorities among the Fathers, 'is the adoration not of good demons, but of bad and perverse demons.' The Church became very liberal in its admittance of demons among the agencies of human affairs. Not only did it attribute bad passions and criminal acts to these demons, but it also chose to detect their agency in every form of error and imposture; by which was meant every form of opinion or pretension inconsistent with the opinions and pretensions of the Church. Once grant the existence of these demons, and it is difficult to assign a limit to their agency. And who *then* questioned their existence? Dwelling in noisome retreats, among the putrid exhalations of rotting graves, they were ready at any moment to issue forth and walk among men, to tempt the saints and delude the sinners. Not only did they tempt men, they sometimes managed to get 'possession' of them, entering their bodies, and making them mad. Nay, they entered into houses and pieces of furniture. Exorcisms consequently formed a large proportion of the priestly duties. So late as Pope Sixtus V, the Egyptian obelisk, which was brought to Rome, and now adorns the Piazza del Popolo, was publicly exorcised before it was permitted to stand in a Christian city. There were many formulas of exorcism, but the sign of the cross was naturally considered the most efficacious, and was generally used in addition to all others. Holy water, also, had great virtues. 'This continual intervention of exorcism,' remarks M Maury, 'is attested by the great number of conjurations adopted in the liturgy. It was an incessant litany of anathema against Satan. He was described as a perfidious intriguer, a thief, a serpent, a wild beast, a dragon of hell, a Belial, etc.; and in order not to be forced to repeat always this long list of insults, they were engraved on amulets, which hence acquired the virtue of driving Satan away.' What wonderful ideas of causation are implied in the conception! Epidemics, meteors, and prodigies of all kinds were attributed to demons. Plagues, tempests, and hailstorms, by one party believed to be visitations of divine wrath, were by another and larger party believed to be the work of malignant demons; and this opinion was held even by so subtle and remarkable a thinker as Thomas Aquinas. It is to this belief, M Maury says, that is due the practice of ringing the church bells during violent storms—that being the readiest mode of exorcising the demons. Formerly the storm was exorcised by the presentation of the cross, and by sprinkling holy water. As the worst storm comes to an end at last, the exorcism was certain to be successful.

Curious it is to notice what multitudes of Pagan superstitions passed into the ordinary beliefs of the Christians. The neophytes were unable to disengage their minds from all the associations of childhood, from all the prejudices in which they had been reared. Among these were the belief in, and use of, amulets and enchantments. Even Saint Augustin believed that demons were to be influenced by certain signs, certain stones, certain charms and ceremonies; and if Saint Augustin could believe this, we may imagine that less vigorous intellects would be still more credulous. There was universal belief in the evocation of departed spirits, upon evidence as cogent as modern Rapping Mediums consider sufficient in 1861, and with considerably more excuse. In the ninth century we find the Bishop of Aosta excommunicating serpents, moles, mice, rats, and other beasts, because into these bestial forms the agents of Satan delighted to hide themselves—somewhat stupidly, it would seem, seeing how little fascination these beasts, generally, have for mankind;—but the demons were never held to be very wise. Saint Bernard, from the same cause, excommunicated flies, and all the flies in the district shrivelled up at once. In the year 1200, Saint Walthen, of Scotland, proclaimed that the devil assumed the forms of a pig, a bull, a black dog, a wolf, and a rat. The black dog and black cat were generally believed to have some secret understanding with the devil; and if owned by a wise man or a blear-eyed old woman, the evidence was sufficient.

There is abundant evidence to prove that the spirit of Polytheism and its sorceries survived long after the official Polytheism was extinct. Its temples were in ruins, or were converted into churches; its idols were broken, or were rebaptised as saints and angels. Many a temple of Diana or Venus is now crowded by worshippers of the Madonna, in very much the same spirit, and with not a little of the old forms. The traveller in Italy is constantly being surprised by some living tradition of Polytheism thinly veiled. In every Neapolitan hut may be seen the ancient Lares; only they assume the form of the Virgin, before whose image a lamp is kept for ever burning. Such images are transmitted from generation to generation. They are implored on every occasion, more even than the Saviour. When the superstitious Neapolitan meditates a crime, he covers these images with a veil, to hide the crime from them.

Sometimes the change from Pagan to Christian has been very slight indeed, as in the case of Aïdoneus of Epirus, who has been altered into Saint Donatus, and Dea Pelina, who has become Saint Pelino, and Felicitas Publica, who has become Santa Felicità. In festivals meant to please the populace, we expect to find the old traditions of worship, and to find the old divinities under the masks of saints. The festivals of Ceres and Vesta, for example, have been slightly changed in the Neapolitan festival of the Madonna. Murray describes it thus:–

> Their persons are covered with every variety of ornament; the heads of both men and women are crowned with wreaths of flowers and fruits; in their hands they carry garlands and poles, like thyrsi, surmounted with branches of fruit or flowers. On their return homewards, their vehicles are decorated with branches of trees, intermixed with pictures of the Madonna purchased at her shrine, and their horses are gay with ribbons of all hues, and frequently with a plume of snowy feathers on their heads. The whole scene as fully realises the idea of a Bacchanalian procession as if we could now see one emerging from the gates of old Pompeii.

M Maury notices that the processions and prayers of priests and augurs for the plantations, vines, and public health, have all been consecrated anew. The sign of the cross, the use of holy water, and the Agnus Dei, have replaced the old exorcisms, and talismans. The Hebrew names of God, or the names of the angels, and of Abraham or Solomon, took the place of the names of Pagan deities. If oracles disappeared, the tombs of martyrs and confessors were not silent, and were interrogated with the same credulity as had formerly been shown to the oracles. In vain the Church forbade sorcery and witchcraft; it encouraged many kindred superstitions, and did not destroy the source of all superstition. Paternosters were murmured over wounds, in the perfect belief that paternosters were curative, and that wounds did *not* follow any strictly inexorable course. The relics of saints were (and still are) devoutly believed to have a wonder-working power—the same power as was formerly attributed to charms and talismans. The evil spirits who caused the drought, the sickness, or the wrecks, would shrink away in terror at the sight of the relics. And when the Church *encouraged* such beliefs as this, how could it expect to warn men from believing in chaplets which had the power of arresting bleeding, or in any other superstitions?

Some of the details collected by M Maury are curious. Thus he notices that to this day the practice of placing a fee for Charon (passage money across the Styx) is not quite unknown. In some districts the money is placed in the mouth of the corpse. By the inhabitants of the Jura it is placed under the head of the corpse, attached to a little wooden cross. In the Morvan it is placed in the hands of the defunct. The statue of Cybele used annually to be plunged into the sacred bath; she is still publicly dipped, only Cybele has become a saint. In Perpignan they solemnly dip the relics of Saint Gulderic in the waters of the Têt, confident by this ceremony that they shall secure rain. Rain falls, sure enough; and if it sometimes falls too scantily, or too tardily, this is only attributed to meteoric influences by infidels and materialists.

Many are the traces of the past which scholars find in the present. The Lupercalian festivals have become our Lenten carnival—rather a dreary festival, it must be owned! The January offerings have become our New Year's gifts—pleasant enough, when they do not assume the shape of dreadfully good 'gift-books'. The salutation of 'God bless you'. when you sneeze, is thoroughly classical. No doubt the ingenious device of securing 'luck' to a newly-married couple, by throwing an old shoe after the departing post-chaise, is equally ancient, and impresses the philosophic mind with a lively sense of how men imagine the course of Nature to be determined. The evil eye is not only very ancient, but seems to be universal. The ancients believed that when any one's ears tingled it was because somebody was talking of him; they believed, also, that it was unlucky to spill the salt.

We have already said that the Church, although appropriating many of the rites and ceremonies of Polytheism, energetically repudiated many others; but in vain. The demons which could not be invoked at the altar, were invoked in secret. Magic was called upon to perform what religion refused. The Church fulminated, and assured men that they perilled their souls by commerce with demons; but it did not discredit the agency of the demons, and its menaces were futile. In vain also was the secular arm employed against those whom the fear of hell could not restrain: the superstition was ineradicable, irresistible. Curiosity, the desire of vengeance, the passion for some secret means of superiority—these motives were stronger than fear, and these motives could only cease to impel men when men ceased to believe in supernatural agency. But against this belief the Church raised no voice. The wisest of men devoutly accepted it. Gregory the Third, in his edict against the use of Magic, especially addresses himself to the clergy as well as to the laity; but his edict is against the *use* of Magic, not against the *belief* in Magic.

Magic, no less than Science, rests on the *explanation* of phenomena. The only difference is that Magic seeks its explanation in some analogy drawn from human nature, and Science seeks its explanation in some analogy drawn from *other* phenomena. No preliminary knowledge is required for the former; man instinctively dramatises the events, and interprets them by such motives as sway his own conduct. For the latter explanation it is necessary that a vast amount of knowledge shall have been accumulated; man must know a great deal about many phenomena before he can detect their laws. Let us see this illustrated in the views held about Dreams.

In Egypt, Assyria, Judæa, and Greece, there was a regular class of dream-interpreters, men who undertook to *explain* what was prefigured by dreams. No one doubted that the phenomena were supernatural. Dreams *came* to a man; they were not suspected to be the action of his brain. We see this belief naïvely exhibited in Homer, who makes Jupiter summon a dream (*oneiros*) to his presence as he would summon any other personage. He bids the dream descend to the camp of Agamemnon, and appear before that King of Men, to whom he must deliver a most delusive message. The dream departs, and repeats the very words of Jove. Nor is this conception wonderful. If you consider dreams, you will notice as one peculiarity that in them the mind is, as it were, separated into two distinct entities which hold converse with each other. We are often astonished at the statements and repartees of our double; we are puzzled by his questions, we are angered or flattered by his remarks—and yet these have been our own creation. It is natural to suppose that we have actually been visited during sleep by one of the spirit world; and until the science of psychology had learned to interpret the phenomena of dreams by the phenomena of waking thought, especially of reverie, this supernatural explanation would prevail.

The same may be said of insanity. It was necessarily regarded as supernatural, until science had shown it to be a disease of the nervous system. The dreadful aspect, the incoherent language and conduct of madmen, seemed only referable to an evil demon having got 'possession' of the man; and this belief was of course strengthened by the general tendency of

madmen to attribute their actions to some one urging or forcing them. They
fancied themselves pursued by fiends, whom they saw in the lurid light of
their own distempered imaginations. But before science could have ascertained even the simplest laws of insanity, what an immense accumulation of
knowledge on particular points was necessary! Instead of believing that a
madman is 'possessed', we say he is 'diseased'; instead of a demon within
him to be exorcised, we say there is a functional disturbance in his nervous
system which must be reduced to healthy activity once more. We know as
certainly that a disease of this nervous system will produce the phenomena
of insanity, as that an inflammation of the mucous membrane will produce
a catarrh, or that disease of the lungs will produce consumption. But what
vast labours of many generations before it could have been ascertained that
the nervous system was specially engaged in all mental phenomena, and that
insanity was a disease of this system! It was so much readier an explanation
to suppose that a demon had entered the unhappy victim; and this once
suggested, it became a question how best to get rid of the demon. Incantation
was an easy resort. Among the means of purification many nations seem to
have fancied that 'fumigation' must hold a high rank, demons decidedly
objecting to stinks. To this day the Samoyedes and Ostiaks burn a bit of
reindeer-skin under the nose of the maniac. The patient falls into a sort of
stupefaction from which he often revives considerably calmed, the action of
a narcotic on his nervous system being mistaken for an action of stinks on
the olfactories of the demon. The old superstition of hanging odoriferous
plants over the door of the house of one 'possessed' points to the same belief
that odours drive away demons.

In this rapid survey of a wide subject we hope the reader has been able to
see that magic, which was the Science of the ancients—and the only science
they could have for a long while— is wilful Nescience in moderns who have
ample means at hand for ascertaining the fundamental fact that the *order* of
Nature is not capricious but constant, and is not to be altered by incantations,
even by those powerful incantations which take place in the 'most respectable drawing-rooms' somewhat darkened. The ancient thaumaturge was to
a great extent his own dupe; if he did practise certain tricks, he had profound
belief that there *was* an art to which he pretended. But the modern thaumaturge is generally an impostor; and those who believe in him, and his
miracles, ought to be consistent, and believe in all the grossest superstitions
of the early ages. For if the order of Nature is *not* constant, as we suppose,
there is no assignable limit to the power of Magic.

Charles Darwin

Mr Darwin's Hypotheses (April 1868)

The Origin of Species made an epoch. The product of an immense series of
tentative gropings, it formed the turning-point of an entirely new series:
concentrating as in a focus the many isolated rays emitted by speculative
ingenuity to illuminate the diversified community of organic life, it propounded an hypothesis surpassing all its predecessors in its congruity with
verifiable facts, and in its wide-reaching embrace. Because it was the product
of long-continued though baffled research, and thereby gave articulate
expression to the thought which had been inarticulate in many minds,[86] its
influence rapidly became European; because it was both old in purpose and
novel in conception, it agitated the schools with a revolutionary ferment. No
work of our time has been so general in its influence. This extent of influence
is less due to the fact of its being a masterly work, enriching Science with a
great discovery, than to the fact of its being a work which at once clashed
against and chimed with the two great conceptions of the world that have
long ruled, and still rule, the minds of Europe. One side recognised a powerful
enemy, the other a mighty champion. It was immediately evident that the
question of the *Origin of Species* derived its significance from the deeper
question which loomed behind it. What is that question?

If we trace the history of opinion from the dawn of Science in Greece
through all succeeding epochs, we shall observe many constantly-reappear-
ing indications of what may be called a premonitory feeling rather than a
distinct vision of the truth that all the varied manifestations of Life are but
the flowers from a common root,—that all the complex forms have been
evolved from pre-existing simpler forms. To the early speculators such a
feeling was enough. Knowing little of the intellectual needs of our time, they
were careless of precision, indifferent to proof. But when such a point of view
had once been adopted, it revealed consequences irreconcilable with the
reigning doctrines, and was therefore challenged sharply by the defenders of
those doctrines, and called upon to produce its evidence, furnish proofs.
Unhappily, it had little evidence, no proof. The scientific intellect found no
difficulty in making what was offered as evidence appear quite inadequate.
The more precision a few ingenious advocates endeavoured to give to their
arguments, the more glaringly absurd the speculation seemed. To men largely
acquainted with the phenomena of organic life, and trained in the habits of
inductive inquiry, there was something repulsive in the crude disregard of

evidence exhibited in such theories as those of De Maillet and Robinet.[87] A certain discredit was thrown on the hypothesis by the very means taken to recommend it. So long as it remained a vague general notion, it was unassailable, or at least unrefutable; but on descending into the region of verification, it presented a meagre aspect.

Nevertheless, it survived opposition, ridicule, refutation. In the face of evidence, in the face of ridicule, in the face of orthodoxy very indignant, this idea of the evolution of complex forms from simpler forms persisted; and the reason of this persistence is that the idea harmonises with one general conception of the world—(*Weltanschauung*, as the Germans say)—which has been called the Monistic because it reduced all phenomena to community, and all knowledge to unity. This conception, under its various forms of Pantheism, Idealism, Materialism, Positivism, is irreconcilable with the rival, or Dualistic, conception, which in phenomena separates and opposes Force and Matter, Life and Body, and which in knowledge destroys unity by its opposition of physical and final causes. The history of thought is filled with the struggle between these two general conceptions. Slightly varying Schlegel's dictum, 'Every man is born either a Platonist or an Aristotelian', I think it may be said that every man is somewhat by his training, and still more by his organisation, predisposed towards the Monistic or the Dualistic conception, a predisposition which renders it easier for him to feel the force of the arguments on one side than on the other; and that, in consequence of this native bias, we may generally predict what will be his views in Religion, Philosophy, and Art—to a great extent even in Science. Be this as it may, there can be little doubt that the acceptance or the rejection of Darwinism has, in the vast majority of cases, been wholly determined by the Monistic or Dualistic attitude of the mind.

And this explains, what would otherwise be inexplicable, the surprising fervour and facility with which men wholly incompetent to appreciate the evidence for or against Natural Selection have adopted or 'refuted' it. Elementary ignorance of Biology has not deterred them from pronouncing very confidently on this question, which involves all the principles of Biology; and biologists with grim scorn have asked whether men would attack an astronomical, physical, or chemical hypothesis with no better equipment. Why not? They feel themselves competent to decide the question from higher grounds. Profoundly convinced of the truth of their general conception of the world, they conclude every hypothesis to be true or false, according as it chimes with, or clashes against, that conception. Starting from this point, each party throws its whole energy into collecting (oftener snatching at rather than collecting) evidence and arguments, flavoured with ridicule and rhetoric, for or against the hypothesis. Only desirious of vindicating a foregone conclusion, they rarely attempt a meditative and dispassionate survey of the evidence.

So it has been, so it will long continue. The Development Hypothesis is an inevitable deduction from the Monistic conception of the world; and will continue to be the battle-ground of contending schools until the opposition between Monism and Dualism ceases. For myself, believing in the ultimate triumph of the former, I look on the Development Hypothesis as one of the great influences which will by its acceptance, in conjunction with the spread of scientific culture, hasten that triumph, teaching us, to use Goethe's words,

Wie Natur im Schaffen lebt.
Und es ist das ewig Eine
Das sich vielfach offenbart.

But it is one thing to hold firmly to the Development Hypothesis, another thing to accept Natural Selection as the last word on that subject. Darwinism is undoubtedly a better explanation than any of its forerunners; but it will probably give place to some successor, as the hypotheses of Geoffroy St Hilaire, Meckel, Lamarck, Bonnet, and Robinet gave place to it. Meanwhile, it is the best hypothesis at present before the world, and has converted many naturalists who before were sceptical. For I should convey a false impression by what was said just now if I did not add that many biologists whose conception of the world was purely Monistic rejected with scorn the explanations of Lamarck and others as to the origin of the species; and although the luminous suggestion of Natural Selection has converted some of these, there still remain many unconvinced. The immense superiority of Darwinism is that it not only puts forward as the cause of *all* variation a law which is demonstrably the cause of *much* variation, but includes also the *verae causae* suggested by Lamarck and Meckel. The law of Natural Selection may indeed be said to be only a larger and more philosophic view of the law of Adaptation which Lamarck had imperfectly conceived. We must not, however, underrate the singular importance of Lamarck's hypothesis in calling attention to the modifiability of structure through modifications of adaptation; though he was led into exaggerations by a one-sided view, which made him attribute too great an influence to one set of external conditions. Naturalists before his time had been wont to consider the Organism apart from the Medium in which it existed; he clearly saw that vital phenomena depended on the relation of the two; but in his hypothesis he sacrificed the one factor somewhat to the other; he paid too little regard to the Organism and its laws of development. Meckel captivated attention by the striking illustrations from embryology[88] in proof of Kielmeyer's position that all existing organisms are modifications of a single type, all the stages of the lower types being indicated in the successive transformations of an embryo of the highest type; but a rigorous criticism showed that in this form the hypothesis was not tenable.[89] The hypothesis put forth in the *Vestiges*, though it had the merit of connecting the organic evolution with the cosmical evolution, uniting the hypotheses of Lamarck and Meckel with the nebular hypothesis of Kant and

Laplace, laboured under the great disadvantage of reposing on two principles which only a metaphysician could accept as *verae causae*. One of these was the conception of a pre-existent Plan, according to which organisms were supposed to have been formed (the υστερον τροτερον fallacy);[90] the other the conception of Time as a factor apart from all the conditions.[91] We need discuss neither here. But the helplessness of such metaphysical explanations is well exhibited in the case of rudimentary organs—perhaps the strongest case against final causes—which appear to the author of the *Vestiges* as 'harmless peculiarities of development, and interesting evidences of the manner in which the Divine Author has been pleased to work'.[92]

Minds unconvinced by all such attempts were at once subdued by the principle of Natural Selection, involving as it did, on the one hand, the incontestable Struggle for Existence, and on the other, the known laws of Adaptation and Hereditary Transmission. There still remain philosophers and theologians who have an 'intuition' of its falsehood, and naturalists who fail to see how it clears up a mass of difficulties; the legitimate opposition of these adversaries will go far towards a furtherance of the final solution. Meanwhile adherents regard Mr Darwin's work as crowning the labours of a century. There is, indeed, a curious coincidence of dates noticed by Haeckel.[93] Exactly one hundred years, he reminds us, elapsed between the *Theoria Generationis* of Wolff (1759), which by the doctrine of Epigenesis laid the foundation-stone of the theory of Development, and the *Origin of Species* (1859), which supplied the coping-stone. Nor does the coincidence of dates end here. For half a century, he says, the doctrine of Wolff remained almost dormant, till, in 1806, it was made the common property of the scientific world by Oken's exposition of the mode in which the intestinal canal was developed (which was mainly a restatement of the exposition given by Wolff in his Memoir *De Formatione Intestinorum*, 1766) In like manner the theory of Descent, which Lamarck produced in 1809, had to wait fifty years before it received its scientific consecration in the *Origin of Species*.

It would be easier to write a volume on this vast subject than a satisfactory essay; and as I cannot indulge my inclinations with writing a volume, I only propose to discuss two or three topics directly involved, especially to answer the objections which are regarded as the most serious, namely: (i) Why have Species not varied during the four thousand years of which we have record? (ii) Why are domesticated animals, when suffered to run wild, always found returning to the primitive wild type? (iii) Why are not new species constantly produced, and why are not the intermediate forms discoverable? Having answered these questions, I shall have something to say respecting Mr Darwin's hypothesis of Natural Selection as the determining cause of specific forms, and respecting his hypothesis of Pangenesis as the determining cause of inherited forms.

✲ ✲ ✲

What is meant by Species? A man unversed in and unperplexed by the *dicta* of naturalists would simply answer: A kind of plant or animal. But on turning to the authorities for a more precise definition, such as would enable him to particularise the kind, and describe the characters by which it could be identified, he would find himself in presence of strange contradictions. A little experience would disclose that even the most authoritative naturalists had one rule to be followed in theory, another and very different rule to be followed in practice. On this point we may say with Fritz Müller,[94] that as in a Christian country there is a Catechism which every one repeats and no one considers himself bound to follow, or expects others to follow, so in Zoology there are dogmas which every one's practice denies. Among a hundred writers who feel called upon to preface their treatises with a confession of faith, ninety-nine begin with a grave exposition of the rule that a natural system must not be founded on any one character, but on all the characters; it must take into consideration the whole organisation, and not estimate characters as of equal value, but according to their physiological rank, &c. But on passing to the actual work of classification, and attempting to range the animals into Species, Genera, and Families, there is probably not one of the ninety-nine who thinks of applying these philosophic rules. Thus Agassiz follows Cuvier in making the Radiata a branch of the animal kingdom, although nobody has any idea what may be the importance in the life of the animal which this radiate structure may have, and in spite of the well-known fact that the radiated echinoderms issue from bilateral larvae. Again, fishes are divided into Ctenoid and Cycloid, according as the margins of their scales are toothed or rounded—a detail which must be of infinitesimal importance in the life of the animal. Sometimes plants and animals are classed as different Species when they differ only in colour,[95] in size, in shape, in habits, or instincts; at other times, when they differ widely in any or all of these characters, they are classed together, and are called Varieties.

Not only does the practice contradict the rules, the rules themselves are contradictory, and eminently capricious. Linnaeus defines species thus: 'Species tot sunt diversae quot diversae formae ab initio sunt creatae.' But who shall say what were the forms originally created? And when Cuvier appeals to the bond of parentage, defining species as 'la réunion des individus descendant l'un de l'autre et des parents communs, et de ceux qui leur ressemblent autant qu'ils se ressemblent entre eux,' the rule would be excellent if we were always in possession of all the genealogical data; but in point of fact, even with regard to domesticated animals, we cannot always trace this family bond, and with regard to wild animals, it is wholly an assumption. An attempt is made to prove the relationship by the evidence of indefinite fertility; and this character is currently regarded as decisive of species, only those plants and animals being held to be of the same species which are indefinitely fertile with each other. So much stress is laid on this point that I would willingly accumulate pages of evidence against it, if space permitted; but three considerations must suffice. First, it is not true, and Mr Darwin has proved it not to be true, that any species is indefinitely fertile where the bond of kinship is closest; breeding in and in always terminating in sterility. Secondly, the generative system is so readily affected by slight changes in the conditions of life, that animals undeniably of the same blood are sterile under those conditions. Thirdly, animals sterile with some members of the species are fertile with others, and fertile with members of different species, 'It is a great law of nature,' says Mr Darwin, in his latest work, 'that all organic beings profit from an occasional cross with individuals not closely related to them in blood; and that, on the other hand, long-continued close interbreeding is injurious'.[96] Hence it is utterly fallacious to argue from fertility. Moreover, when a species is known to us only through one individual, how are we to determine whether it is a Species or Variety? Obviously we can only say, Here is a form which differs from all other known forms; and it is on this difference that we assign it a place in our system. By its resemblances we bring it under one group; by its distinctive traits we isolate it in that group. Thus recurs the unscientific definition: 'Species means a kind of plant or animal'. While the chemist can furnish a precise and unvarying definition of chemical species, the naturalist can only furnish a vague and varying definition. The kind of resemblance and difference which one naturalist regards as specific, another holds to be generic, and a third to be simply the mark of a variety.

Very important is it to bear in mind that Species is a subjective creation having no objective existence: it is an idea, not a thing; a systematic artifice, not a living entity. This is clearly enough expressed in the favourite definition: 'Species is a succession of individuals capable of reproducing themselves'; but when naturalists argue about fixity of species, they mostly overlook this conception of a succession and its implications, to replace it by a conception of an abstract form, an unvarying entity which is independent of the individuals. On several occasions I have called attention to the lingering remnant of Scholasticism cherished in the arguments defending the fixity of species. In the early days of speculation, when it was a first principle that what we know as General Terms had corresponding Objects existing in the external world as distinct realities, and not simply as relations, the belief in a *thing* Species was rational enough; when philosophers believed that over and above the numberless individual animals they saw around them, there existed an Animal which they did not see, but which was the norm and pattern for all individuals—when they held that over and above the good and bad actions committed by them and their fellows, there existed an Immutable Virtue and an indestructible Evil—when, in short, they held the theory of Ideas, they could have no grounds for suspecting the reality of Species. But is it otherwise in our day. Platonists are rare, and Scholasticism is a scoff. Nevertheless unconscious disciples argue about the fixity of Species as if

Species were a thing that could be mutable or immutable. They would deny the charge, no doubt; they are not sufficiently clear on the point to see their real position.

Regarded objectively, what place is held by Species? In certain fundamental traits, all plants and all animals have a community, and on this is founded the first division of the Organic and Inorganic. The next step is to divide Plants from Animals. From the microscopic formless dab of jelly which constitutes the Amoeba, up to the marvellously complex structure which we name Man, there is, underlying all diversities, a community on which we found the group Animal. In classifying these diversities we establish groups to which different names are affixed, as indications of the degrees of unlikeness. When all the animals differ but slightly, we group them as Varieties; when they differ more, as Species; when they are still more different, as Genera; and so on through Families, Orders, Classes, Sub-kingdoms. That these resemblances and diversities exist objectively—that is to say, that the corresponding phenomena are thus related—is indisputable; and it is therefore not only true, but a truism, to affirm that the Names by which we designate them have a fixed meaning; but it is not true, it is a falsism, to assert that these relations are immutable, being, as they are, the relations of variable individuals.

We should think it very irrational to insist that while bank-notes, shillings, sixpences, and pence were conventional monetary standards, sovereigns were something more than conventional, and had a monetary reality denied to other moneys. It is not less irrational to insist that while the wider divisions of genera, orders, classes, and the narrower divisions of varieties are conventional, the intermediate divisions (species) are not conventional, but real.

I will cite but four writers where it would be easy to cite forty. Buffon says: 'Les espèces sont les seuls êtres de la nature. Les individus sont les ombres dont l'espèce est le corps.'[97] Cuvier declares that Classes, Orders, and Genera are abstractions, 'et rien de pareil n'existe *dans la nature*'; but instead of logically extending this to the group of slighter differences, he maintains that Species is not an abstraction.[98] Flourens, his disciple, says: 'Les espèces sont les formes primitives de la nature. Les individus n'en sort que des représentations, des copies'.[99] To conclude with Johannes Müller: 'The species is a living form represented by individual beings, which reappears in the product of generation with certain invariable characters'.[100]

Unless men held Species to have an existence apart from individuals, the question of fixity would have no sense, because the real question is, Are individuals variable? If they are, their relations to each other must vary, and it is their relations which we designate in the terms Species and Genus. That animals *do* vary is indisputable, undisputed. And here arises the further question: Are these variations only possible within certain ascertained limits, or are the variations indefinite? The majority of naturalists answer that the limits are ascertained, and the term Species corresponds with such limits.

Their opponents, at least the more philosophical of them, while admitting that no individual organism can be greatly modified (and it is therefore correct to say of an individual that there are narrow limits of possible variation), assert that the small variations of each individual will so accumulate in the course of numerous successive generations as to transcend all specific limits, and in effect become indefinite. The divergence which is inappreciable at the apex of an acute-angled triangle becomes gradually greater, and at the base may be enormous.

It is not only a surprising simplification of the problem when we thus set aside the metaphysical figment of Species, and direct our attention solely to the facts of variation, and the accumulation of variations through inheritance; but the problem which is thus simplified is also brought from the region of Theology and Metaphysics into the region of Science: it has come within the range of Verification. How much metaphysical and theological misdirection has hitherto confused this subject may be seen in the disguised form of the scholastic conception which moderns have adopted; for I should be doing naturalists an injustice if I allowed the inference to pass that they adopt the crude notion of Species as an objective reality, which their language and arguments imply. It comes to them under two guises and disguises. One is that of the 'creative fiat'; the other, and more reasoned hypothesis, is that of 'creative plan'. According to the first, plants and animals had their forms ordained for them at the moment of their creation, and these forms are unchangeable. According to the second, the organic world is part of a general scheme, in which each Species represents an Idea in the Divine Mind, and must be taken as an item in a Plan conceived from the first in all its details, although realised in successive epochs. Each Type was impressed once for all on each group; however the individuals in each group may vary among themselves, the Type is unvarying, and constantly effaces the variations of individuals.

※ ※ ※

The first impulse of a scientific scepticism is to inquire by what means the philosophers have acquired this precise knowledge of the Ideas existing in the Divine Mind; very enviable knowledge, but needing some guarantee of its genuineness. If it was gained from the study of Nature, then it must be amenable to all the canons of scientific research; and these assure us that the utmost to be learned in such a study is the *persistence* of Types,—of their *pre-existence* nothing whatever can be rigorously ascertained; and these canons further assure us that the persistence of a type is necessarily limited to the persistence of its concurrent conditions. Any hypothesis which starts from an *à priori* construction of creative fiat, or creative plan, must first justify its origin. In science an explantation is the reduction of phenomena to a series of known conditions, thus bringing what was unknown within the circle of the known. But of creative fiats we can know nothing; we may infer them; and the validity of our inference has to be tested by that very process which constitutes a scientific explanation. To infer that Species were Ideas in the Divine Mind is on a par with the inference once firmly accepted, that anomalies and monstrosities were 'freaks of Nature', and the work of demons; or that other inference of fountains and trees being animated with Naiads and Hamadryads. Now that we have learned something of the process of organic development, we have learned that anomalous forms are deviations in the line of growth, due to arrest or excess, and are neither effects of God's wrath nor of Satan's malice.[101]

The hypothesis of creative fiats begs the question, and explains nothing. It is an hypothesis burdened with the double disadvantage of being incapable of proof, and incompetent to explain: incapable of proof, for no one can ascertain what was or was not 'ordained',—we can only ascertain what is the order of phenomena within our ken; incompetent to explain, for whenever a variation arises, the only resource is to affirm that this variation also was ordained. Andreas Wagner boldly sought this refuge, affirming (as quoted by Haeckel) that the conception of Species was not applicable to domesticated plants and animals, because they were created variable in order to subserve the purposes of man. It is the peculiarity of this kind of philosophising that its conclusions cannot be refuted because they do not admit of proof. There is always an escape from every objection through some easy supposition invented for the nonce. You think you disprove the notion of an invariable Plan by showing instances of variation? Your objection is set aside by the remark that the variations were also planned.[102] You observe that unhealthy organisms transmit their morbid states, and you are assured that Nature '*revient par des voies détournées sur la rigueur de ses décrets*', as if Nature were full of pity, and relented on the pathway of destruction. An easy phrase eludes all argument. 'A chaque type spécifique,' says a recent advocate, 'on peut rattacher des formes secondaires dérivées, produites par les influences de milieu; si l'on en méconnaît l'origine, *on sera conduit à les considérer comme espèces légitimes, tandis qu'elles sont seulement l'expression de la flexibilité organique.*'[103] If those who maintain the variability of Species are to have their illustrations disposed of by this simple process of rebaptism, it is clear that all argument becomes idle; when 'organic flexibility' has any meaning given to it other than specific variability, Language once more proves its services to Metaphysics.

The hypothesis of creative fiats having ordained the existence of Species is an evasion of the question, not an answer to it. Moreover, its limitations are strangely unwarrantable. Thus it assumes the remarkable uniformity in the number of segments recognisable in crustacea and insects under the amazing varieties of their forms to be due to conformity with Plan. And as comparative anatomists point out the existence of these twenty segments, even when they are so fused as to present little or no segmentation to the uninstructed eye, the argument seems weighty. But when Nature shows deviations from this Plan, in articulated animals having fewer than twenty segments, or more than twenty, the argument is proved to be inconsistent. 'Why,' asks Mr Spencer, 'if the skeleton of each species was separately contrived, was this bony mass (the sacrum) made by soldering together a number of vertebrae like those forming the rest of the column, instead of being made of one simple piece?' The answer is, that the sacrum is made of segments in conformity with the vertebrate Plan; but Mr Spencer then asks, 'Why does the number of sacral vertebrae vary within the same order of birds? Why, too, should the development of the sacrum be by the roundabout process of first forming its separate constituents, and then destroying their separateness?'[104] Nor does the contradiction of the hypothesis end here; it assumes that Genera and Species were produced by direct exercise of a Creative Will, whereas Varieties and Races were produced by the operation of natural laws. Such a separation of agencies is unphilosophic; and if we avoid it by the acknowledgement of every individual plant and animal being the product of a creative fiat, then indeed we get rid of the Dualistic conception of Nature, but the difference between the hypothesis of Creation and the hypothesis of Evolution becomes only a difference of terms.

I have endeavoured elsewhere[105] to expose the fallacy involved in the notion of Plan or Type as anything more than a subjective concept, a *nexus* we discover in evolved forms, and which we, by a natural infirmity, imagine to have been the *nisus* of those forms—a resultant which we imagine to be a principle. To that discussion I must refer, not having space now at command to treat of its bearing on Species. If Type means the *correlation* of parts which remains constant under all diversities among those parts—the Vertebrate Type, for example, being that correlation of parts which is found in fishes, reptiles, birds, marsupials, and mammals, so that whenever the same parts are found in different animals, the connections of such parts are the same— there are obvious advantages in our being able to use this shorthand phrase; but there are no advantages and many dangers in using the phrase as if it meant that before vertebrate structures existed, a Type existed according to which they were formed.

It is possible that the hypothesis of Natural Selection, which Mr Darwin opposes to that of creative fiat and fixity of Plan, may be an imperfect explanation, but at any rate it has the immense merit of bringing the question within the region of Research. If it leaves many difficulties unexplained, the rival hypothesis explains none. Some of these we may have to consider hereafter; at present we have to see what its opponents regard as insuperable difficulties.

'If Species are variable, why have they not varied?' This is the objection most frequently urged. Our answer simply is, that *animals* have varied, which is all that the hypothesis requires. Were it not for the unconscious influence of the belief in Species as an entity or as an unchangeable fiat, no one would have been misled by the facts which have misled even philosophic minds. It is only necessary to replace the horse before the cart, only necessary to recognise that the Type (or arrangement of parts) is the result of concurrent conditions, not the cause of their concurrence, to perceive the real value of the alleged objection. We are referred to the testimony of paintings and sculpture some four thousand years old as evidence that several well-known Species and even well-marked Races of animals and men have not changed. Nimrod hunted with horses and dogs which might be claimed as ancestors by the horses and dogs at Melton Mowbray. Semiramis and Rhamses were served by negroes in every respect similar to those who were toiling amid the sugar-canes of Alabama when President Lincoln decreed their emancipation. The fact is certain. What does it imply? According to the advocates of fixity, it implies that Species cannot be changed. If during four thousand years no change has taken place, why assume that there is an inherent tendency to change? This argument is the *cheval de bataille* of the Cuvier school, but it turns out on close inspection to be a spavined, broken-winded Rosinante.

In the first place, the testimony proves too much, for it proves that Races are as unchangeable as Species. Now Races, according to all naturalists, are not special creations, but are variations which have become permanent; and as no one holds that particular Types were created for all the variations (that being, indeed a contradiction in terms), but all hold that races are the result of modifications impressed on the original Type, the fact of such modifications remaining unchanged during four thousand years entirely robs the testimony of its argumentative value when applied to Species.

In the second place, it may be paradoxical, but it is strictly true,[106] that the fact of particular species having remained unaltered during four thousand years does not add the slightest weight to the evidence in favour of the fixity of Species. Four thousand or forty thousand prove no more than four. You would not suppose that I had strengthened my case if, instead of contenting myself with stating reasons once, I repeated those same reasons during forty successive pages; you would remind me that iteration was not cumulation and that no force could be given to my fortieth assertion which was absent from my first. Why then ask me to accept the repetition of the *same fact* four thousand times over as an increase in evidence? It is a fact that Like produces Like, that dogs resemble dogs, and do not resemble buffaloes; this fact is deepened in our conviction by the unvarying evidence we see around us, and is guaranteed by the philosophical axiom that 'like causes produce like effects'; but when once such a conception is formed, it can gain no fresh strength from any particular instance. If we believe that crows are black now, we do not hold our belief more firmly when we are shown that crows were black four thousand years ago. In like manner, if it is an admitted fact that individuals always produce individuals closely resembling themselves, it is not a whit more surprising that the dogs of Victoria should resemble the dogs of Semiramis than that they should resemble their parents; the chain of four thousand years is made up of many links, each link being a *repetition* of the other. So long as a single pair of dogs resembling each other unite, so long will there be specimens of that species, simply because the children inherit the characteristics of their parents. So long as negroes marry with negroes, and Jews with Jews, so long will there be a perpetuation of the negro and Jewish types; but the tenth generation adds nothing to the evidence of the first, nor the ten thousandth to the tenth.

All that the fact implies is that during four thousand years there has been a concurrence of conditions which has been sufficiently uniform to preserve the descendants of Species and Races from alteration. It is far from proving that simultaneously with this uniformity there has been no diversity capable of producing new Races and new Species; indeed, a slight consideration suffices to convince us that such diversity *has* existed, and that side by side with the persistent forms new forms have arisen. The testimony of Egyptian tombs is valuable as far as it reaches, but naturalists need only wander beyond the precincts of those tombs to find forms that have altered beside forms that remain unaltered. Thus let us suppose an Egyptian king to have had one hundred dogs all of them staghounds, and no other form of dog to have existed at that time. These staghounds would transmit to their offspring all their specific characters. But however dogs resemble each other, they always present individual differences in size, colour, strength, intelligence, &c. Now if any one of these differences should become marked and increase by intermarriage, on the principles of Natural Selection, or by the intentional interference of the Breeder, a new race would be formed, and might be propagated side by side with the old one. From the original staghound, which still propagated its kind, twenty well-marked varieties might be reared, each of which would transmit its type. When we find an Egyptian plough closely resembling the plough still used in some countries, we identify it as being of the same species; but we do not thereby disprove the fact that steam ploughs and ploughs of very various forms have been constructed side by side with the old form, all the new forms being modifications of the original type.

The answer to the question. Why, if species are variable, have they not varied during four thousand years? is thus extremely simple. 'Species', as a term designating a group of relations, is not variable; but the parts related are variable; and when 'Species' designates particular animals, we affirm that those animals which have been produced under similar conditions continue the type which has thence resulted, but those animals which have been produced under dissimilar conditions present corresponding variations from this type. There is one source of confusion which I shall more explicitly illustrate when treating of the relation between the Organism and its Medium; but as this would lead us too far from the course of our argument just now, I will merely say that by 'conditions' we are not to understand geographical or climatal influences simply, or even mainly; but the whole group of conditions, external and internal, physical, organic, and social, which determine the result.

❋ ❋ ❋

Passing now to the second question: Why are domesticated animals, if suffered to run wild, always found returning to the original type? This, which has been urged as a fatal objection against the hypothesis of Evolution, is, correctly interpreted, a necessary deduction from that hypothesis. I do not pause to discuss the validity of the statement itself, though Dr Hooker and Mr Darwin have pointed out the extremely imperfect evidence on which it is founded. I accept the argument as if there were no exaggeration in its data, and as if a domesticated animal suffered to run wild inevitably returned to the wild type; although, in the vast majority of cases, the animal would really perish, and instead of returning to the wild type would be supplanted by wild rivals, better suited to the medium. The argument fails even when its data are granted. Indeed, the very language of the objectors contains the terms of the answer. 'Les variétés de plantes obtenues par le semis et les variétés d'animaux domestiques, loin d'être invoquées en faveur de la variabilité des espèces, sont, à mons sens, un puissant argument à l'appui de leur fixité.' So speaks M Chevreul; and we listen to such a master with attention. What is the argument? 'Autrement,' he says 'comment concevoir les difficultés que nous éprouvons à maintenir des modifications produites par la culture et le climat, ou par la domestication, lorsque nous les jugeons propre à satisfaire nos besoins ou nos jouissances? *Dès que ces êtres modifiés cessent de se trouver dans les sphères des causes de modifications, celles-ci tendent à s'éffacer.*'[107] What more could Mr Darwin desire than the admission that modifications, *produced* by the action of certain causes, *disappear with the cessation* of that action? If a plant or an animal changes under changed conditions, why should we conclude that on restoring it to the old conditions it will not again change in obedience to the same law? We have removed it from the sphere of later modifying causes, and replaced it in the sphere of causes to which it was previously adapted by old modifications. Do you wonder that a steel spring rebounds when the pressure on it is removed? Do you wonder that it resists the pressure, and with every slackening of the pressure 'tends' to return to the straight line from which you bend it? Why does it resist and rebound? Because of a certain arrangement of its molecules. If you somewhat alter that arrangement, this alteration will give a permanent bend to the steel, and then there will be no force needed, no return to the straight line, except by the application of force. It is the same with plants and animals. A given type is the adaptation of structure to external conditions; the parts are so arranged that the organism can exist and continue its functions in this particular medium, and like the straight steel wire it can, within certain limits, be bent on the application of changed conditions. Yet, inasmuch as its arrangement of parts is one which was best adapted to the straight condition, it continually resists the forces which bend it, continually tends to recur to that state which is best adapted to its structure, and, consequently no sooner are the ill suited forces lessened or removed than we see a return to the original state. Every biologist knows that there is regressive, no less than progressive, metamorphosis; that an organ diminishes from disuse as it increases from use. It should also be remembered that in the modifications impressed on plants and animals under domestication, there is, for the most part, a change which serves our fancy and convenience rather than the advantage of the organism in its struggle for existence; and such changes difficult to be induced are naturally difficult to be maintained, so that they readily disappear when the modifying influences are removed. But those changes, which although perhaps brought about to suit our convenience, do likewise give the organism some advantage by its adaptation to the external conditions, will not readily alter when the organism is left to run wild; if it then alter, the alteration will be owing to external influences, not owing to internal tendencies regaining their old direction. Consider one example. Von Baer[108] tells us that the zoologists of the sixteenth century expressly and unanimously declare that the guinea-pig was unknown in Europe before the discovery of America, yet that now the guinea-pig, as we know it, is only found in Europe. Our species is always variegated—black, brown, and white are its colours. The American is like in size and form, but is always of a grey-brown colour. This, however, is a trifling difference. When we extend the comparison we find a wider gulf. The American loves damp places; the European perishes in them. The American supports a cold which destroys the European. The American brings forth young only once a year; the European thrice. The changes in the osseous structure are not unimportant, but the change to which I would most call attention is that which, according to zoological dogmas, would constitute a generic difference—the American and European guinea-pigs will not couple together! Such have been the modifications consequent on three centuries of domestication. If we suppose our guinea-pig, which is well adapted to its medium, suddenly replaced in the medium of its ancestors, it would be so ill-adapted to that medium that it would inevitably perish; and if by a certain pliability of organisation it could readjust itself to the new condition, that re-adjustment would be through an approximation to the ancestral structure. Nothing can be more arbitrary than to assume modifying influences or external conditions in the case of domestication, and to deny a similar influence in the case of organisms removed to another sphere. 'No one,' says Mr Darwin,

> would expect that our improved pigs, if forced during several gener-
> ations to travel about and root in the ground for their own subsistence,
> would transmit, as truly as they now do, their tendency to fatten, and
> their short muzzles and legs. Dray-horses assuredly would not long

transmit their great size and massive limbs if compelled to live on a cold, damp mountainous region; we have, indeed, evidence of such deterioration in the horses which have run wild on the Falkland Islands. European dogs in India often fail to transmit their true character. Our sheep in tropical countries lose their wool in a few generations.

The tendency to recur to the ancestral form, a tendency noticeable even under domestication, is a fact of profound significance, but it is a simple consequence of biological laws, and is invoked by the advocates of Evolution not less than by the advocates on the other side. It has, therefore, no peculiar significance in the case now under examination. All we have to deal with here is the influence of external conditions in modifying an organism; and by a curious confusion of ideas, it is this very influence which is invoked to disprove an hypothesis founded on the possibilities of change under changing conditions.

※ ※ ※

Respecting the third objection we have selected for discussion, namely, Why new species are not constantly appearing before our eyes, or why there is no evidence of such appearances in the existence of intermediate forms? it cannot conveniently be treated until we have treated of the way in which new forms arise; and for this discussion it will be necessary to expound certain biological principles. This I shall attempt in the second part. Meanwhile, if there were greater force in the objection than can be assigned to it, we should only regard it as a difficulty to be explained by future research, or to be interpreted on another form of the Development Hypothesis, not as a refutation of that hypothesis. Indeed, we must protest against the frequent assumption that Darwinism is disproved because it fails to account for all the phenomena: if it interprets truly some of the phenomena, it is valuable as a colligation of facts; if it interpreted all of them it would cease to be an hypothesis. Observe, moreover, that writers who are most contemptuous against this hypothesis because it fails—or they think so—to explain some phenomena, urge us to accept the hypothesis of creative fiats, or Divine Ideas, which absolutely explain none. They reject an attempt to trace some of the intermediate steps by following the actual processes of evolution as far as these are known to us, and prefer relying on a vague phrase, which is only a restatement of the fact to be explained, and which suggests a process altogether inconceivable by the human mind.

At any rate, we have reached one result: Animals are variable. The extent to which this variability may be carried under any given Type is fairly a question; but we should remember that a Type is not a thing, but a relation: it is the arrangement of the parts which remains constant under a diversity in the size, shape, and number of those parts. The Vertebrate Type embraces all those animals which have an internal skeleton, and a neural axis above the haemal axis. What amazing diversities it includes! Let us glance at its extreme limits—man and fish. Though both breathe air, one lives in the air and dies in the water; the other lives in the water and dies in the air. One breathes by lungs, the air entering through the nose as well as through the mouth; the other breathes by gills, the air entering only through the mouth. One is vocal, the other silent; one has limbs, the other none. One has four hearts, with double circulation and red blood corpuscles; the other two hearts, and single circulation (the *Amphioxus* has properly no heart, nor any red blood). Not only is the Vertebrate Type a purely ideal construction, representing the affinities of a large group, but it is varied in subordinate groups—mammals, marsupials, birds, reptiles, fishes; each group again having groups subordinated to it, and so on till we come to the group of Varieties, from which there are minor divergences not considered worthy of classification. 'There are crustaceans,' as Mr Darwin notices, 'at the opposite ends of the series which have hardly a character in common; yet the species at both ends, from being plainly allied to others, and these to others, and so onwards, can be recognised as unequivocally belonging to this, and to no other class of the Articulata.' How fluctuating therefore must be the crustacean Type!

To return to our point: something is gained when the discussion of variability is disengaged from the misleading conception of Types and Species, and is reduced to the question of how far individual forms can vary, and how far the accumulation of slight variations through successive generations may originate specific and generic distinctions. Naturalists, unable to deny the obvious fact of variation, have evaded the conclusion to which it points by boldly asserting that the variation is always confined to unimportant characters. It is not true, and Mr Darwin has abundantly shown that it is not true. All organs vary. When naturalists assert—and no argument is more frequently used—that by Selection we have acted solely on the exterior, without in any respect altering the internal and essential parts ('sans en changer en rien la constitution essentielle et profonde'),[109] the assertion is in one sense true, in another false; and the sense in which it is true does not oppose the Evolution hypothesis, whereas the sense in which it is false is an argument that upsets the hypothesis of fixed species. Thus it is true that the modifications, which can be impressed on an individual, or on a succession of individuals, during a brief period are necessarily slight (and at first usually external), the laws of Adaptation rendering them so; but Mr Darwin has nowhere intimated that the case was otherwise; indeed, his constant iteration of the principle that variations are slowly accumulated, ought to have prevented his adversaries from overlooking it—ought to have convinced them that the objection was beside the question. But while there is a sense in which it is true to say that the modifications are always slight, it is absurd to pretend that when these cumulate into striking alterations in the skeleton, alterations in the mode of alimentation, alteration in the modes of reproduction, alteration in the habits and instincts—of which there is overwhelming evidence—these are not essential alterations such as establish distinctions meriting the name of specific, nay also of generic. In his last work Mr Darwin gives pictures of different breeds of pigeon, and, above all, of their skulls, which every naturalist would class as belonging to different species and genera if he were unacquainted with their origin; but, being acquainted with their origin, he regards these diversities as proofs of 'organic flexibility', and the trifling variations which species may assume. 'If we could collect,' says Mr Darwin, 'all the pigeons which have ever lived from before the time of the Romans to the present day, we should be able to group them in several lines, diverging from the parent rock pigeon. Each line would consist of almost insensible steps, occasionally broken by some slightly greater variation or sport, and each would culminate in one of our present highly modified forms.' No less than one hundred and fifty distinct breeds have descended from one original stock, and these, if found in a state of nature, would have been grouped in at least five genera.

Resuming in a sentence the arguments which these pages have set forth, we admit of the fact that specific forms are persistent, but deny that this fact has the slightest value as evidence against the evolution of new specific forms through modification; and affirm that embryology furnishes the plainest testimony that such evolutions do take place. Species, except as a subjective classification of resemblances, has no existence. Only individuals with variable resemblances exist; and as these individuals propagate, the propagation is necessarily a reproduction of the parent type. But while the law of reproduction secures a continuance of the species, it also secures a continuance of any variations from the parent form which may have been produced by incident forces sufficiently prolonged; and these variations may form the starting-points of divergence, from which in time a new species will result.

Although this is a process by which all organic diversities *may* have been evolved, we are not obliged to accept it as more than an explanation of the way in which many of them have been evolved. Natural Selection, although a true cause, is, I think, only one of the causes of diversity. There are many points which it leaves obscure; and Mr Darwin, with that noble calmness which distinguishes him, admits the numerous difficulties. Whether these will hereafter be cleared away by an improvement in the Geological Record, now confessedly imperfect, or by more exhaustive exploration of distant countries, none can say; but, to my mind, the probability is that we shall have to seek our explanation by enlarging the hypothesis of Natural Selection, subordinating it to the laws of Oragnic Combination. It does not seem to me, at present, warrantable to assume Descent as the sole principle of morphological uniformities; there are other grounds of resemblance beyond those of blood-relationship; and these have apparently been overlooked; yet a brief consideration will disclose that similarity in the laws and conditions of

Organic Combination must produce similarity in organisms, independently of relationship, just as similarity in the laws and conditions of inorganic combination will produce identity in chemical species. We do not suppose the carbonates and phosphates found in various parts of the globe—we do not suppose that the families of alkaloids and salts have any nearer kinship than that which consists in the similarity of their elements and the conditions of their combination. Hence, in organisms, as in salts, morphological identity may be due to a community of casual connection, rather than community of descent. Mr Darwin justly holds it to be 'incredible that individuals identically the same should have been produced through natural selection from parents *specifically distinct*', but he will not deny that identical forms may issue from parents *genetically distinct*, when these parent forms and the conditions of production are identical. To deny this would be to deny the law of causation. And that which is true of identical forms under identical conditions is true of similar forms under similar conditions. When History and Ethnology reveal a striking uniformity in the progression of social phases, we do not thence conclude that the nations are directly related, or that the social forms have a common parentage, but that the social phases are alike because they have common causes. When chemists point out the uniformity of type which exists in compounds so diverse in many of their properties as water and sulphuretted or selenetted hydrogen, and declare phosphoretted hydrogen to be the congener of ammonia, they do not mean that the one is descended from the other, or that any closer link connects them than that of resemblance in their elements.

In the case of vegetal and animal organisms, we observe such a community of elementary substance as of itself to imply a community in their laws of combination, and under similar conditions the resulting forms must be similar. With this community of elementary substance, there are also diversities of substance and of conditions; corresponding with these diversities, there must be differences of form. Thus, although observation reveals that the bond of kinship does really unite many widely divergent forms, and the principle of Descent with Natural Selection will account for many of the resemblances and differences, there is at present no warrant for assuming that all resemblances and differences are due to this one cause, but, on the contrary, we are justified in assuming a deeper principle, which may be thus formulated: All the complex organisms are evolved from organisms less complex, as these were evolved from simpler forms; the link which unites all organisms is not always the common bond of heritage, but the uniformity of organic laws acting under uniform conditions.

It is therefore consistent with the hypothesis of Evolution to admit a variety of origins or starting-points, though not consistent to admit the sudden appearance of complex Types, such as is implied in the hypothesis of specific creations. I must reserve, however, for the second part of this essay, the gounds on which such a position may be defended.

On the Dread and Dislike of Science

From *Fortnightly Review* (June 1878)

In the struggle of life with the facts of existence, Science is a bringer of aid; in the struggle of the soul with the mystery of existence, Science is a bringer of light. As doctrine and discipline its beneficence is far-reaching. Yet this latest-born of the three great agents of civilisation—Religion, Common-Sense, and Science—is so little appreciated by the world at large that even men of culture may still be found who boast of their indifference to it, while others regard it with a vague dread which expresses itself in a dislike, sometimes sharpened into hatred.

I shall be told, perhaps, that the growing demand for popular expositions of scientific results and the increasing diffusion of scientific inquiry point to a different conclusion. It is true that there never was a time when Science was so popular. It is true that every year the attendance on lectures and the meetings of scientific associations is larger. The tide is rising. The march of Science is bit by bit conquering even the provinces which most stubbornly refuse allegiance to it. But, meanwhile, among the obstacles it has to overcome are certain prejudices and misconceptions which are the grounds of a deep-seated dread. No better illustration can be given of the general suspicion and dislike of Science as Science than the great stress which is laid on the 'iniquity of Vivisection', *because* experiments on animals are pursued for purely scientific purposes. The animating impulse of an effort to awaken a due sympathy with animal suffering and check an inconsiderate infliction of it is one which so entirely commands my esteem, that I would willingly overlook the flagrant contradiction of people tolerating without a murmur the fact that yearly *millions* of creatures are mutilated and tortured to give a few men pleasure, to make food more palatable, and domestic animals more tractable, yet are roused to fury by the fact that a few *score* creatures are mutilated (a smaller number tortured) to discover remedial agents and scientific truths. All the pain inflicted for sport or other pleasure is condoned; the pain inflicted for scientific ends is pronounced diabolical. Is it, therefore, not on account of the suffering inflicted, but on account of the scientific purpose, that Vivisection is to be reprobated? Ten thousand times the amount of suffering is disregarded if only its purpose be *not* that of acquiring knowledge. And that this is so, is manifest in another case. For suffering may be also inflicted on human beings, and on a large scale, without exciting any outcry, if the motive be commercial advantage. Not to mention wars undertaken to push commerce, let us only consider some industrial experiment which will certainly drive hundreds of families from their employment with starvation as the consequence; yet the sufferings thus occasioned, if they excite pity, weigh so little against the prospect of the general good, that if the starving workmen revolt and destroy the machinery, the philanthropist is ready to enforce on them the utmost rigour of the law. Here the social benefit is allowed to override the individual injury. That is to say, an experiment which has the prospect of enlarging *wealth* may inflict suffering on men, women, and children; but an experiment which has only the prospect of enlarging *knowledge* must be forbidden if it inflict suffering on animals! Obviously such a contradiction could not be upheld if Science were recognised as a social benefit. It is not so recognised. And one indication of this is the frequent accusation that physiologists are actuated by the 'selfish motive of acquiring reputation', not by the unselfish motive of benefiting mankind. I will not pause to discuss the question of motives, nor how far the selfish motive may further a social advantage; I will only ask whether the motive of the industrial experimenter is less selfish? Unless Science were a social benefit, no one would ardently desire a scientific reputation.[110]

Having indicated the existence of the dread and dislike of Science, let us now glance at the causes.

The primary cause is a misconception of what Science is. No rational being dreads and dislikes Knowledge. No one proclaims the superiority of Ignorance as a guide of conduct. Yet Science is simply Knowledge classified, systematised, made orderly, impersonal, and exact, instead of being left unclassified, fragmentary, personal, and inexact. Auguste Comte calls it 'Common-Sense methodised and extended.' There is plenty of knowledge which is not exact, and of exact knowledge which is not methodised. There is plenty of experience, which is personal and incapable of being communicated to others. Wanting the illumination of many minds, this store cannot do the work of Science, which is the experience of many enlarging the experience of each. If there is immense benefit in knowing what are the facts and the order of the physical world in which we live, and of the social world in which our higher life is lived, there is clearly a great advantage that this knowledge should be made orderly and communicable; and the dread of such an arrangement of knowledge is obviously irrational. Thus enlightened, we recognise in Science the deliberate effort to reduce the chaos of sensible experiences within the orderliness of ideal constructions, condensing multitudes of facts into simple laws—an effort which the Intellect acknowledges as a supreme duty, and which Conduct acknowledges as a guide.

Another source of the dislike is the opposition of our native tendencies. Science is abstract, impersonal, whereas our experiences are concrete and personal. It is systematic, and systematisation is troublesome: our native indolence renders us impatient of labour, and our impatience leads us to prefer the facile method of *guessing* to the difficult method of *observing*: we have to be trained into the preference of observing what the facts are, instead of arguing as to what the facts must be. Science, moreover, is greatly occupied with remote relations; now to feel an interest in these we must first have had them 'brought home' to us. Knowledge springs from desire. It begins when prolonged *observation*, stimulated by emotion, replaces the incurious animal *stare* at things; and for this prolongation there is needed a sustaining motive. The sustaining motive of research is the conviction of the vast increase of our power which Science creates. Measuring by a footrule and measuring by trigonometry may be taken as types of Common Knowledge and Science: the result reached may in some particular case be the same, whichever method be used; but the incomparable extent of the second method, which is applicable where the footrule cannot reach—which measures the heights of mountains and the distances of stars—furnishes the sustaining motive to the study of trigonometry.

Science demands exactness, and this demand irritates the vulgar mind. The impatience with which your cook listens to your advice that she should measure and not guess the quantities (advice you can never get her to follow), is but the same movement which rouses your resistance when any one desires to test your opinions by weighing the evidence, or endeavours to show that your traditional beliefs rest on no verifiable observations. Is not he who insists on evidence commonly styled 'a bore' by all whose opinions have been adopted quite irrespective of evidence? Is it not pronounced 'narrow' to hesitate in accepting wide conclusions without a keen appreciation of their data?

The distaste for accuracy, and the impatience at any restriction of the divine right of judging without evidence, will disappear with the advance of knowledge; and with this advance will also disappear certain mistaken pretensions of scientific men too ready to step beyond their own domain. It is this which causes the distaste of artists, men of letters, and moralists; and their opposition to the spread of scientific teaching. They do not oppose knowledge in the abstract, nor any particular knowledge; what they resist is the idea that the conclusions reached in one department of inquiry are to dictate in another. The artist is quite willing to accept the chemist's methodised experience of chemical facts, but refuses to listen to the chemist theorising about Art. The moralist will accept from the physicist equations of light, and from the anatomist relations of structure; but reserves to himself the right of deciding on a moral question.

One must admit that in the inarticulate resistance of Sentiment and Common Sense against certain applications of scientific doctrines there is often a justification. For example, there are mechanical laws and equations which admirably explain the facts of motion, yet Sentiment is shocked at the attempt to explain Nature on mechanical principles only, and is sustained by Common Sense, which sees other facts besides facts of motion, and sees that Nature is not mechanical only. Again, when the stored-up wealth of sentiments laboriously evolved in civilised life is set aside in favour of some analogy drawn from observed processes in the inorganic world, when the moral impulse to cherish the weak and sickly is condemned because Nature (which is *not* moral) cherishes the strong and pitilessly destroys the weak, Common Sense protests, and the protest helps to intensify the popular distrust of Science. Yet, in truth, the wiser heads among men of science are equally alive to the mistake of such applications.

What is to be understood by Science? It means, first, a general Method, or Logic of Search, applicable to all departments of knowledge; and secondly, a Doctrine, or body of truths and hypotheses, embracing the results of search. In this second acception there are the particular sciences—such as Mathematics, Physics, Chemistry, Biology, Psychology, etc.—which are the special applications of the general Method to special departments of knowledge; and although there is an interdependence of these sciences, each is restricted to its own class of facts, none can legislate for the others. But because the various branches of knowledge have been very unequally reduced to the exactness and orderliness of Science, those which have been most successfully reduced have acquired the almost exclusive title; so that Science is generally regarded as something apart—the peculiar study of a particular class. Hence also the opinion that there is a profound separation between the principles applicable in the Physical Sciences and the principles applicable in the Moral Sciences. What has been the consequence? It has been that the Method which is no longer regarded as a rational procedure in dealing with the phenomena of Nature, is followed without misgiving in dealing with the phenomena of Human Nature; and the supernaturalism long banished from physical theories is still invoked in psychological and social theories.

Of late years this has ceased to be the universal error, though it still remains a widespread error. We are slowly beginning to recognise that there may be a science of History, a science of Language, a science of Religion, and, in fact, that all knowledge may be systematised on a common Method. The facts of the External Order, which yield a Cosmology, are supplemented by the facts of the Internal Order, which yield a Psychology, and the facts of the Social Order, which yield a Sociology. These are all comprised in Science. However imperfect the second and third may be, in comparison with the first, the greater complication of the phenomena does not warrant the introduction of another Logic of Search. The principles which have guided us successfully in the first are to be followed in the others. The three classes of facts are all facts of Experience, so far as they are known, and must all be tested, classified, and systematised by the same rules.

This being so, we can separate the rational from the irrational antagonism against Science. It is rational when protesting against the misplaced application of the results reached in one department to problems belonging to a different department—for this is an offence against scientific Method. It is irrational when protesting against the rigorous application of one Logic to all inquiries. Those, therefore, who sneer at Science, and would obstruct its diffusion, are sneering against the effort to make all Knowledge systematic, and are obstructing the advance of civilisation.

The notion, implied or expressed, of two Logics, two Methods of Search, two systems of explaining phenomena, the natural and the supernatural, is the foundation of the great conflict between Science and Theology. And since in the majority of minds, Theology is identified with Religion, and Religion is of supreme importance to man, it is natural that Science should be regarded with dread and dislike. Before proceeding to dissipate the confusions on this subject, it will be needful to glance at the attitude of sincere theologians in our day, and at the reasons which justify to their minds the acceptance of scientific doctrines side by side with the acceptance of theological doctrines. It would be equally ungenerous and short-sighted to suggest that a mind which is deeply impressed with the truth of certain theological opinions may not be also deeply impressed with the beneficence of Science in general, and the truth of scientific doctrines which do not directly embrace moral and religious questions. We have too many conspicuous examples of men eminent in Science and sincere in their theological professions, not to admit that the mind *can* follow two Logics, and can accept both the natural and the supernatural explanations. Whether the mind *ought* to do so, is another question. Let no one therefore suspect me of a doubt as to the sincerity of theologians who proclaim that the sphere of Science is limited to the processes of the physical world, and may be frankly accepted in all that it teaches respecting such processes, without in the least involving the moral world which Theology derives from a source independent of experience. Science, they say, systematises whatever experience reveals; its test is Reason. Theology systematises what had been revealed from a higher source; its test is Faith. Between Reason and Faith there is an absolute demarcation; and between Science, which relies on observation and induction, and Theology, which relies on precept and intuition, there is no conflict. As the artist appeals to the chemist for a theory of salts, and to the mathematician for a theory of singular integrals, but declares both chemist and mathematician to have no voice in a theory of Art, so the theologian accepts the teaching of mathematician, physicist, chemist, and biologist, in their respective departments, but peremptorily excludes each and all from the supreme department of moral and religious duties founded on a theory of the relations of the world to its creator.

Thus stated, one must admit a sufficient logical consistency in the present condition of compromise, and need suppose no kind of insincerity, no conscious equivocation in the acceptance of both the natural and the supernatural modes of explaining phenomena. Nor, indeed, could the fundamental inconsistency of such a compromise have been even recognised, until the quite modern extension of scientific method to moral questions had come to complete the disintegrating effects of historical and philosophical criticism applied to the Sacred Books on which Theology relied. In the earlier stages of development, although the natural explanation was adopted in reference to the most familiar experience, and framed the rough theories of Common Sense for the habitual guidance of conduct, both in relation to the physical world and to society, the supernatural was adopted in reference to whatever was unusual and unseen; and the wider range of this speculative method was due to the immensity of ignorance. The slow progress of positive knowledge has more and more enlarged the domain of natural explanation, more and more restricted the domain of the supernatural. Yet even now the majority of cultivated men regard the facts of human nature as only partly explicable without aid drawn from the supernatural; and resist, as impiety, the attempt to assign natural causes in explanation of moral relations. That is to say, there where the operation of natural causes escapes our penetration, supernatural causes are invoked. Just as to men ignorant of natural conditions thunder was the fury of the storm-demon, or an eclipse was God's anger, so nowadays men ignorant of natural conditions interpret epidemics as 'visitations,' and regard 'intuitions' as of divine origin. The inconsistency, then, of the acceptance of theological side by side with scientific principles, is only a continuation of the primitive mental state, and must vanish when there is a general conviction that Science is orderly Knowledge, and is co-extensive with Experience. If we can have no knowledge transcending Experience in the widest sense, and if Faith is the vision of things unknown—dealing with what transcends knowledge—then the conflict between Science and Theology is the conflict between Knowledge and Ignorance.

Unless this be the character of Faith, I dispute the claim of Theology to the exclusive possession of Faith as a principle of guidance. Science also has its Faith, and by it must all men to a great extent be guided. But the Faith of Theology amd the Faith of Sciences are very different in their *credentials*. The former is reliance on the truth of principles handed down by Tradition, of which no verification is possible, no examination permissible; the latter is reliance on the truth of principles which have been sought and found by competent inquirers, tested incessantly by successive generations, are always open to verification in all their details, and always modifiable according to fresh experiences. We believe in the law of gravitation, though we never opened the *Principia*, and could not, perhaps, understand it; but we rely on those who can understand it, and who have found its teachings in harmony with fact. We believe in the measurement of the velocity of light, though ignorant of the methods by which the velocity is measured. We trust those who have sought and found. If we distrust them, the search is open to us as to them. The mariner trusts to the indications of the compass without pretending to know how these indications were discovered, but assured by constant experience that they guide the ship safely. That also is Faith.

But if the mental attitude is one of the same obedience as the Theological

Faith, its justification is different. Its credentials are conformity with experience. Those of Theology are the statements of the Sacred Books: the Vedas, Zendavesta, Bible, Koran. The statements therein made concerning the divine nature, its relations with the human, and the providential government of the world, are not open to the verification of Experience, for they were not sought and found in Experience. If we ask for their credentials, we are told that they are of divine origin. If we ask for evidence of this divine origin, we are referred to History or to our Moral Consciousness. Tradition has handed down these statements through successive generations; yet if we ask, as we ought to ask, how the tradition itself originated, we are brought face to face with this twofold difficulty: we cannot recognise that those who first promulgated the statements *had any better means of knowing the truth than we have;* and we are struck with the fact that the statements thus handed down by tradition do not agree. That of the Hindoos is not that of the Jews; the Persians reject the traditions of both.

Modern historic criticism has made such havoc with the historical pretensions, that theologians are now throwing all the emphasis on Moral Consciousness. The doctrine of our Sacred Books is said to be unequivocally ratified by our intuitions: we feel their truth, and we see in their moral influence on mankind the verification of their divine origin. But here again the scientific method, which applied to the historical evidence has shattered its claim, applied to the evidence of Moral Consciousness is equally destructive. Psychology not only enlightens us as to the genesis of the intuitions, but in a comparison with other nations and the earlier stages of human development, shows how they vary. If the intuitions of the savage are not those of the civilised, if precepts which the Hindoo feels to be divine are opposed to precepts which the Chinese, the Jew, the Mohammedan, and the Christian feel to be divine, we need a criterion beyond these varying standards.

There is a widespread superstition which regards whatever is innate, or otherwise unexplained, as of a higher authority and diviner sanction than what is acquired through individual experience or is explicable on known laws. Our religious instincts are appealed to, as if Instinct were the infallible guide in conduct; although a moment's reflection will show that it is the great aim of civilisation to correct and repress many instincts. If the developed music of our day is of a higher order and more adapted to our sensibilities than the music of the Middle Ages; if our theories of natural phenomena are of a higher order and approximate more nearly to the truth than the corresponding theories of Aquinas and Albertus Magnus, why should our theories of moral phenomena be deemed inferior to those of Judaism or the Councils? Is the nursery a school of riper wisdom than the laboratory?

So much as to Method; now as to results. The Sacred Books of all theologians claim to expound a theory of the universe and a theory of human life and destiny. Their theories of the universe, both as general conceptions and particular explanations, are in such flagrant contradiction with the teachings of Science, that nowadays no one who is worth a moment's consideration seeks astronomical, geological, or physiological explanations in the Sacred Books. There has arisen the assertion that the Sacred Books were never intended to teach man scientific truths, but only to teach him his duties. The answer is twofold: first, that man's duties are comprised among scientific truths: secondly, that the Books *do* teach, not scientific truths, but doctrines which science shows to be erroneous. We ask, therefore, if their dicta are proved to be erroneous on points where the control of observation is possible, what authority can they claim on points beyond all such verification? If their astronomical, geological, and biological statements are false, why are we to believe their statements respecting the origin of the universe, the laws of its evolution, the nature of man, and the conduct of man?

The escape from this dilemma which is attempted by giving up the physical world to Science, reserving the moral world for Theology, is only a temporary escape. Let it be granted that the authority of the Sacred Books refers solely to the phenomena of Human Nature in the double aspect of the relations of Man to God and his relations to Society. If they contain explicit statements which are at variance with our moral culture—such as that God is 'jealous' and 'vindictive', or that sinners will be consigned to everlasting torment—they must have some other guarantee of their truth than the ratification of Moral Consciousness, since that rejects them; and if they contain statements respecting man's nature which are at variance with experience when they can be verified, how shall we accept their authority when the statements are beyond verification?

When the statements are ratified by experience and moral culture, Theology can give these no *extra* sanction; when they are not so ratified, Theology cannot make them acceptable. By way of illustration of the conflict between Science and Theology, in their explanations of human phenomena, with the precepts which are founded upon each, let us take the case of Disease.

Very little is accurately known of its causes; but whatever they are, Science, recognising Disease as the result of some disturbance of the organic functions, seeks the unknown causes in the known properties of the substances composing the organism. Theology, which uniformly explains the unknown by the unknown, invokes a supernatural cause for this natural effect. It declares that God sends diseases as chastisements and lessons. Nor is this declaration withdrawn when common sense objects that the chastisement is often an injustice and the lesson an enigma. The innocent are seen to suffer even more than the guilty, and no one knows why they suffer; no one can regard the punishment of the child for the sin of its father as in agreement with human justice. But you say 'all men are guilty'? Then why are not all punished? And why are animals and plants also afflicted with diseases? Have they, too, the burden of Adam's disobedience? There was a time when such explanations reconciled the doctrine with observation; but nowadays cultivated minds shrink from the conception of 'imputed sin' as a rational explanation of human and animal suffering.

In applauding this progress we must also point out the logical inconsistency of those who maintain the absolute authority of the Texts of which such conceptions are the necessary applications. Theology maintains its doctrine even when theologians set aside the practice which that doctrine ordains. To claim absolute submission to the physician's formulas, and yet refuse to follow his prescriptions, is surely irrational? Yet this is the case nowadays. When the supernatural theory of Disease was undisturbed by positive knowledge, prayers and incantations were the remedies in vogue; but now even those who will not acknowledge the theory to be an antiquated error practically disavow it, for they replace prayers and incantations by drugs and diet. Only the small sect called 'The Peculiar People' trust entirely to prayer; and Christian magistrates are so outraged at this trust that they punish it as a crime! In vain are epidemics declared to be visitations, in vain are books written with such titles as *God in Disease*; the practical sense of the nation decides that Cholera or Cattle Plague are not to punish landlords and farmers for the scepticism of a few speculative minds, and hence that we had better seek to avert them by a course of treatment and 'an order in council', than by pulpit eloquence and a 'day of humiliation'.

I have taken the case of Disease because it is less open to the ambiguities and difficulties which beset a moral problem, but a similar discrepancy might be pointed out between the theological precepts and the moral practices. Here, as everywhere, it is patent that as knowledge advances, Theology loses its hold; and Morality, instead of remaining stationary like Theology, advances with an enlarging insight into the healthy conditions of human relations. Science is often taunted with its imperfections and its inability to explain the mysteries of life. Imperfect it is, and that is why we should all strive to make it less so. Mysteries will doubtless for ever encompass us. But science may answer the taunt by challenging Theology to show that its explanation of the mysteries has any claim to our acceptance. The question is not whether *an* explanation can be given, but whether the given explanation has any verifiable evidence. Kant has truly said that now Criticism has taken its place among the disintegratory agencies, no system can pretend to escape its jurisdiction. The Church has its texts, and has decided once for all what meaning these texts must bear. But the criticism of scientific method asks for the evidence which can prove these texts to be of divine origin, and the evidence which can prove these interpretations to be in agreement with fact. In both respects the answer is unequivocal. There is no evidence to prove the texts. The interpretations are discordant with experience. Thus the Catholic who accepts Galileo and Newton must give up the texts, or take the first step towards Protestantism, which asserts the right of interpreting the texts according to private judgment. And the Protestant who asserts this right of interpretation, and forsakes the literal meaning of the texts, has taken a step towards Rationalism, and implicitly disavowed the authority of the texts, since what he obeys is not their teaching, but the teaching of the culture of his day and sect. The Rationalist, in turn, has taken a step towards the scientific position; he regards the texts as symbols of an earlier stage of culture, which need the interpretation of our present culture; and when he learns—as easily he may learn—that all the facts of the moral world are to be investigated and systematised on the same principles as the facts of the physical world, setting aside in the one as in the other all supernatural and metempirical conceptions, because these cannot enter into the framework of Knowledge, he will learn that Science, in the true meaning of the term, embraces Nature and Human Nature, and moreover that it expresses what is *known* of both, whereas Theology is only 'the false persuasion of knowledge'.

Many readers may vehemently deny the assertion just made. They will maintain the validity of theological explanations, all the more because, persisting in the old confusion of Theology with Religion, they refuse to acknowledge that a science of Nature and Human Nature, if truly expressing the facts, must be a better foundation for Religion than a Theology which untruly expresses those facts. The whole contest lies between the two modes of explanation and the results reached by such modes. I accept the appeal to History. This shows how in proportion as knowledge became exact and orderly in each department of inquiry, the supernatural and metempirical explanations were silently withdrawn in favour of natural and experiential explanations. Nowadays, among the cultivated minds of Europe, it is only in the less-explored regions of research, where argument is made to do duty for observation, that the supernatural and metempirical explanations hold their ground. When science has fairly mastered the principles of moral relations as it has mastered the principles of physical relations, all Knowledge will be incorporated in a homogeneous doctrine rivalling that of the old theologies in its comprehensiveness, and surpassing it in the authority of its credentials. 'Christian Ethics' will then no longer mean Ethics founded on the principles of Christian Theology, but on the principles expressing the social relations and duties of man in Christianised society. Then, and not till then, will the conflict between Theology and Science finally cease; then, and not till then, will the dread and dislike of Science disappear.

Notes and References

Lewes' own footnotes, given exactly as they are in the original, are preceded by *L*.

'Vivian': Dramatic Criticism in the *Leader*

p. 33   1. *Not so Bad as We Seem*, a comedy by Bulwer Lytton, written for amateur performances in aid of the Guild of Literature and Art, was first performed before Queen Victoria and Prince Albert at Devonshire House, 27 May 1851, with Dickens, Wilkie Collins and Douglas Jerrold among the cast.

p. 34   2. *Every Man in his Humour* was performed at Manchester and Liverpool in July 1847, for the benefit of Leigh Hunt. Dickens played Bobadil, John Forster, Kitely, and Lewes, Old Knowell. *The Merry Wives of Windsor* was put on in London, Liverpool, Manchester, Birmingham, Edinburgh and Glasgow between April and July 1848, for the benefit of the playwright Sheridan Knowles. Lewes played Sir Hugh Evans.

p. 35   3. Sophocles, *Philoctetes*, ll. 257-9. 'The men whose unholy hands have cast me out laugh and speak not of it; while my affliction has grown fat and climbs ever higher.'

The Miseries of a Dramatic Author – *Cornhill Magazine*, VIII (October 1863)

p. 53   4. James Sheridan Knowles (1784-1862), actor and dramatist.

5. Astley's Royal Amphitheatre, a theatre in which equestrian and acrobatic shows were put on. It specialised in dramatisations of the battle of Waterloo.

Charles Dickens – *National Magazine and Monthly Critic*, I (December 1837); *Leader* (11 December 1852); *Leader* (5 February 1853); *Fortnightly Review*, XI (February 1872)

p. 58   6. Washington Irving (1783-1859), American humourist.

7. Theodore Hook (1788-1841), wit and writer of fashionable novels.

p. 60   8. William Cobbett (1763-1835), political writer.

p. 62   9. snapdragon, a Christmas game of plucking raisins from a dish of burning brandy.

p. 64   10. Justus von Liebig (1803-73), distinguished German chemist, discoverer of chloroform, whom Lewes visited in Munich in the 1860s. Richard Owen (1804-92), comparative anatomist at Royal College of

Surgeons, later founder and designer of the Natural History Museum. Thomas Graham (1805-69), professor of chemistry at University College London, 1837-55. August Wilhelm von Hofmann (1818-92), professor of chemistry at Bonn, then at the Royal School of Mines.

p. 70 11. Louis-François Lélut (1804-77), French doctor, specialising in mental illnesses.

p. 77 12. Lewes was in Berlin in July 1838, moving on to Vienna in June 1839, and returning home in July 1839.

p. 79 13. Francis, Lord Jeffrey (1773-1850), Scottish judge and editor of *Edinburgh Review* from its founding in 1802 until 1829.

Charlotte Brontë and Mrs Gaskell – *Fraser's Magazine*, XXXVI (December 1847); Charlotte Brontë, letters to G.H. Lewes, 1847-8, in Elizabeth Gaskell, *The Life of Charlotte Brontë* (1857, repr. 1984), pp. 233 ff.; *Westminster Review*, III (April 1853)

p. 81 14. Henry Colburn, publisher of fashionable novels.

p. 84 15. Jean Paul (Johann Paul Friedrich Richter, 1763-1825), German Romantic humourist, a favourite of Carlyle's.

p. 87 16. 'Was die Weiber lieben und hassen,/Das wollen wir ihnen gelten lassen;/Wenn sie aber urteilen und meinen,/Da will's oft wunderlich erscheinen.' ('Whenever women love or hate,/We'll let them have their will;/But when they dare to judge and think,/That's much too strange, we feel'), Goethe, *Zahme Xenien* (1815-27), a series of mildly polemical epigrams.

W.M. Thackeray – *Morning Chronicle* (6 March 1848); W.M. Thackeray, letter to G.H. Lewes in *Letters and Private Papers*, ed. G.N. Ray, 4 vols (Cambridge, MA, 1945-6); *Leader* (21 December 1850)

p. 108 17. 'Ridentem dicere verum quid vetat', Horace, *Satires*, I, i, 24. 'What is to prevent a person from telling the truth and laughing as well?'

p. 109 18. blackleg. A late eighteenth-century term for a dishonest gambler.

p. 111 19. Archdeacon Hare and his brother Augustus, *Guesses at Truth* (1827), describe the use of the word 'individual' to mean 'man, woman or child' as 'a strange piece of pompous inanity'.

p. 113 20. 'Tis distance lends enchantment to the view', Thomas Campbell, *The Pleasures of Hope* (1799), I, 7.

p. 114 21. 'La popularité? C'est la gloire en gros sous', Hugo, *Ruy Blas* (1838), III, 4.

p. 116 22. 'tapis franc', pub, dive, joint.

23. Triboulet and Borgia, in Hugo's *Le Roi s'amuse* (1832) and *Lucrèce Borgia* (1833) respectively.

Robert Browning – *Leader* **(27 April 1850)**

Alfred Tennyson – *Leader* **(22 June 1850)**

p. 124   24. 'Begin, Sicilian Muses, begin the lament', *Lament for Bion* (wrongly attributed to Moschus).

p. 125   25. 'Si vis me flere, dolendum est primum ipsi tibi' (If you wish me to weep, you must first feel grief yourself'), Horace, *Ars Poetica*, l. 102.

Elizabeth Barrett Browning – *Leader* **(30 November 1850)**

p. 129   26. 'Work-day world', a phrase used also by George Eliot in her essays and novels. See Introduction, p. 9.

p. 130   27. 'Years that bring the philosophic mind', Wordsworth, 'Ode: Intimations of Immortality from Recollections of Early Childhood' (1807), l. 190.

Matthew Arnold – *Leader* **(26 November 1853);** *Leader* **(3 December 1853)**

p. 132   28. Alexander Smith (1830-67), minor Scottish poet.

29. 'Et quasi cursores vitae lampada tradunt' ('And like runners they pass on the torch of life'), Lucretius, *De Rerum Naturae*, II, 79.

p. 135   30. 'principium et fons' ('source and fountain').

31. Benjamin Robert Haydon (1786-1846), historical painter, friend of Keats and Hazlitt.

p. 138   32. 'Sohrab and Rustum' ll. 110-6 are an imitation of the *Iliad*, ii, 459-66.

Charles Lamb – *British Quarterly Review*, **VII (May 1848), repr. in the** *Bulletin of the Charles Lamb Society*, **CLXIX, (January 1963).**

p. 140   33. Translated in a footnote in the original as follows: ' "A man's personal appearance is the text for all that can be said of him or felt about him" – *Stella*'.

p. 141   34. 'a friend of ours.' Leigh Hunt (1784-1859), friend of Shelley and Byron, encourager of Lewes and other young writers. See Introduction, p. 5.

p. 142   35. The footnote in the original quotes from Lamb's *Essays of Elia*: *On Imperfect Sympathies*: 'I have been trying all my life to like Scotchmen, and am obliged to desist from the experiment in despair'.

36. 'And as round mountain-tops...', Wordsworth, 'Written after the Death of Charles Lamb' (1835), ll. 18-22.

p. 144   37. Cockletop and Ritson, antiquaries. Scott consulted Joseph Ritson (1752-1803) when preparing his Border Minstrelsy.

p. 145   38. *L*.: 'Compare his beautiful essay on New Year's Eve.'

39. *L*.: 'No one, we hope, will misinterpret this into any disparagement of Plato; it is only saying, that read by the light which Plato himself

helped to spread abroad, his works are less important to us than they were to those for whom he wrote them'.

p. 153 40. 'And let him grieve...', Wordsworth, 'Written after the Death of Charles Lamb', ll. 72-86.

Benjamin Disraeli – *British Quarterly Review*, X (August 1849)

p. 158 41. collet monté (strait laced).

T.B. Macaulay – *British Quarterly Review*, XXIII (April 1856)

p. 176 42. The anatomist referred to is probably Richard Owen of the Royal College of Surgeons, with whom Lewes was friendly.

p. 186 43. 'Where freedom slowly broadens down/From precedent to precedent' – Tennyson, 'You ask me why, though ill at ease' (1842), ll. 11-12.

p. 187 44. *L*.: *'British Quarterly* No. XVII.'

Alexandre Dumas – *British Quarterly Review*, VII (February 1848)

p. 203 45. *L*.: 'This speech and the rejoiner are so intensely national, that no reader can thoroughly relish them unless he be acquainted with French life. The *mot* flew over France like lightning and a few days after, a cattle dealer, on his trial, in Normandy, being asked his profession, replied "*Je dirais marchand de boeufs, si je n' étais dans la patrie de Corneille*". Corneille is a great cattle-dealer of France.'

p. 208 46. *L*.: 'It is respectfully hoped that no one will demand an explanation of the meaning of the above'.

p. 209 47. Lewes refers the reader to *Les Mystères de Paris* by Eugène Sue.

p. 213 48. Even as Lewes wrote this article, the French were about to enact their February 1848 revolution.

Johann Wolfgang von Goethe – *The Life and Works of Goethe* (1855, rev. 1875), Book VI, ch. 2

p. 219 49. *L*.: '*Charakteristiken und Kritiken*, p. 168. Schlegel's review is well worth reading as an example of ingenious criticism, and praise artfully presented under the guise of analysis.'

p. 220 50. *L*.: 'See especially Book I., cap. 15, for his idea of the private life of players, as if they carried *off* the stage something of their parts *on* the stage.'

p. 221 51. Lewes points out that the story has been translated by Carlyle.

p. 222 52. *L*.: (quotes from *Schriften*, II, p. 367): '*Das Buch handelt bloss von gewöhnlichen Dingen, die Natur und der Mysticismus sind ganz vergessen. Es ist eine poetisirte bürgerliche und häusliche Geschichte; das Wunderbare darin wird ausdrücklich als Poesie und Schwärmerei behandelt. Künstlerischer Atheismus ist der Geist des Buchs.*'

The Principles of Success in Literature – *Fortnightly Review*, I (15 July 1865), ch. 3

p. 227 53. Cisterns and fountains, an echo of Coleridge's defence of poets against the charge of plagiarism: 'There is amongst us a set of critics, who seem to hold, that every possible thought and image is traditional; who have no notion that there are such things as fountains in the world, small as well as great; and who would therefore charitably derive every rill they behold flowing, from a perforation made in some other man's tank', Preface of 1816 to *Christabel*.

p. 232 54. Coeur de Lion and Saladin appear in Scott's *The Talisman* (1825), and Mucklebackit in *The Antiquary* (1816).

55. The 'imaginative writer' is George Eliot, 'Worldliness and other-Worldliness: the Poet Young' (*Westminster Review*, January 1857), *Essays of George Eliot*, p. 367.

p. 233 56. 'A critic.' Ibid.

57. 'In November days…', Wordsworth, 'The Influence of Natural Objects in Calling Forth and Strengthening the Imagination in Boyhood and Early Youth' (1798-9, later incorporated into *The Prelude*, Book I).

p. 237 58. 'He above the rest…', Milton, *Paradise Lost*, Book I, ll. 589-99.

p. 240 59. Ruskin, *Modern Painters*, IV (1856), ch. 2.

Auguste Comte – *Fortnightly Review*, III (January 1866)

p. 248 60. Lewes' footnote here directs the reader to the fourth volume of the 'Système de Politique Positive' for 'an excellent introduction to the study of Comte'.

p. 251 61. *L*.: 'I have followed M. Littré in this narrative of the attack, because it is confirmed, to a great extent, by documentary evidence, though of course the story proceeds from Madame Comte'.

p. 257 62. *L*.: [quotes from Comte]: 'Je somme tous les Occidentaux capables de sentir, d'une manière quelconque, la vraie portée de mes travaux, de concourir loyalment, suivant leur moyens respectifs, au digne protectorat institué pour moi. Si les positivistes incomplets persistaient à motiver leur *coupable indifférence* sur leurs divergences partielles envers l'ensemble de ma doctrine, *je dévoilerais aisément l'égoisme mal caché* sous ce vain pretexte.' – *Système de Politique Positive*, 3, preface, p. 25. Not only were partial adherents thus summoned to contribute to his support under the penalty of very hard terms, but even adversaries if they expressed any admiration were considered as eligible subscribers. There is something very droll in the *naïveté* with which in the preface to the *Politique*, vol. 2, he tells us of an American Methodist, who had reviewed the *Philosophie* in language of sympathy, which 'sans dissimuler aucune dissidence forme un heureux contraste avec celui de nos psycologues ou idéologues:' adding that this language 'm'inspira bientôt une démarche exceptionnelle, pour faire concourir ouvertement de pareils adversaires au libre subside qui jusqu'ici ne garantit pas suffisament mon existence matérielle.'

63. Lewes' footnote informs the reader that after his death, Littré sent round a circular 'appealing to the generosity of Positivists in favour of Madame Comte – which was, however, under all the circumstances, so excessively ill-judged, that its failure prevented a repetition'.

Benedict de Spinoza – Fortnightly Review, IV (April 1866)

p. 271 64. *L.*: 'I forget where it was, and forget what the passage was, but have little doubt that it was a more or less distorted version of the appendix on Final Causes which occurs in the Ethics.'

65. *L.*: 'Reprinted in a separate form and incorporated in the *Biographical History of Philosophy* (1846)'. The reference in the previous paragraph is to the translation of the *Ethics* which Lewes offered to do for Bohn, and which Marian Evans completed in Germany in 1855. See introduction, p. 7.

p. 272 66. Lewes refers to *Tractatus Theologico-Politicus* by Benedict de Spinoza (Trübner and Co., 1862).

67. Lewes refers to Vloten, *Ad B. de Spinoza Opera quae supersunt Omnia Supplementum* (Amstelod, 1862).

68. Lewes refers to Malebranche, *Méditations Chrétiennes, IX., 13.* Schleiermacher, *Rede über die Religion*, p. 47.

p. 273 69. *L.*: 'In the Royal Library at Hanover there is a letter from Spinoza to Leibnitz in which he signs himself B. Despinoza. But when he published his Abridgment of Descartes he wrote his name Spinoza; and this is the spelling adopted in the Excommunication. Such minor variations were little thought of in early days, and even at the present day in France we sometimes see a similar indifference.'

p. 275 70. Lewes' footnote ascribes this quote to Boileau.

71. Lewes quotes Spinoza's next passage from the *Tractatus Theologico-Politicus* XII: 'Ita enim hominum naturam constitutam videmus ut unusquisque (sive rex sive subditus sit) si quid turpe commisit factum suum talibus circumstantiis adornare studeat ut nihil contra justum et decorum commisisse credatur'.

72. J.A. Froude (1818-94), historian of Elizabethan England and biographer of Carlyle, had published the article on Spinoza in the *Westminster Review* in 1855 mentioned by Lewes on p. 271.

73. *L.*: 'The letters of the word *Metateron* make up the same number with the word *Schadai*, the Almighty, namely three hundred and fourteen.'

p. 278 74. *L.*: 'The formula of excommunication I have found nowhere but in the little work called *An Account of the Life and Writings of Spinoza*, published in London, 1720, which none of the latter writers seem to have known. It contains an abbreviation of the Life by Colerus, and a slight analysis of the *Tractatus Theologico-Politicus*. It has only ninety-six pages of large print; and was published for one shilling. The form of excommunication printed by Vloten in the *Supplementum*, is only an abridgment of that quoted in the text; whether this abridgment were made in the copy paper to Spinoza or whether it were made by the chief Rabbi at the ceremony, is not clear.'

75. *L.*: 'There are many slight indications scattered through his works, but the best evidence is that he never commits himself by ignorant statements in these matters.'

p. 279 76. Lewes points out in his footnote that Spinoza's language is stronger here 'but to translate more literally would, perhaps, mislead; he says: *Divitias, honorem, atque libidinem.*'

p. 282 77. Here Lewes quotes from *Epist.* XLIX., p. 294: 'An quaeso, ille omnem religionem exuit, qui Deum summum bonum agnoscendum statuit, eundemque libero animo ut talem amandum? et quod in hoc solo nostra summa felicitas summaque libertas consistit? porro quod praemium virtutis sit ipsa virtus, stultitiae autem et impotentiae supplicium sit ipsa stultitia: et denique quod unusquisque proximum suum amare debet et mandatis summae potestatis obedire?'

p. 283 78. Lewes gives the reference: 'Spinoza: *Epist.* I'.

p. 284 79. Lewes gives the reference: 'Vloten: *Supplementum*, p. 295.

p. 285 80. Lewes quotes from *Epist.* LIV., p. 304: 'Quippe schismata non tam ex ardenti religionis studio oriuntur quam ex vario hominum affectu vel contradicendi studio, quo omnia etsi recte dicta sint, depravare et damnare solent.'

p. 287 81. Lewes refers the reader to *Epist.* L., p. 299.

82. The reference given is: '*Refutation Inédite de Spinoza. Par Leibnitz. Précédée d'une Mémoire par M. Foucher de Careil* (Paris, 1854)'.

p. 289 83. Dugald Stewart, *Dissertation Prefixed to Encyclopaedia Brittanica.* Lewes' footnote reads as follows: 'So readily are accusations made that even this amiable writer thinks it probable that Spinoza learned his irreligious principles from the chief school of Atheism, the Synagogue of Amsterdam, "where without any breach of charity (!) a large proportion of the more opulent class may be reasonably presumed to belong to the Sadducees".'

84. The footnote refers the reader to Hamann's *Schriften* I, p. 406.

85. *L.*: 'The play on words cannot be rendered in English: "diese Schwindsucht über einstimmend war mit seinem System, in dem auch alle Besonderheit und Einzelheit in der Einen Substanz verschwindet".'

Magic and Science – *All the Year Round* (25 March 1861)

Charles Darwin – *Fortnightly Review*, III (April 1868)

p. 299 86. Lewes quotes Von Baer in his footnote: 'Mir scheint die ganze Lehre mehr eine Entwickelungsstufe der Naturwissenschaft als das Eigenthum eines einzelnen Mannes.'

p. 300 87. Lewes' footnote refers to Robinet, *De la Nature* (Amsterdam, 1766). Lewes informs the reader that he had reviewed this book in *Fraser's Magazine* in November 1857.

p. 301 88. Lewes' footnote refers to Meckel, 'Traité d'Anatomie Comparée' (French translation, 1828, vol. I).

89. *L.*: 'Compare Von Baer, "Ueber Entwickelungsgeschichte", 1828'.

p. 302 90. The fallacy referred to is that of putting first what should logically follow, of philosophically putting the cart before the horse.

91. Lewes' footnote refers to *Vestiges of the Natural History of Creation* (10th edition, 1853, pp. 117-18), published anonymously by Robert Chambers.

92. In his footnote Lewes also refers the reader to Agassiz' 'Essay on Classification' (1859) and quotes from it as follows: 'Does not the existence of a rudimentary eye in the blindfish show that these animals, like all others, were created with their peculiarities by the fiat of the Almighty, and that this rudiment of eye was left them *as a remembrance of the general plan of structure of the great type to which they belong?*'.

93. Lewes is referring to Haeckel's *Generelle Morphologie der Organismen* (1866). His footnote reads: 'Many readers will be grateful for having their attention directed to this work, one of the most instructive contributions to the philosophy of Biology which has appeared in our time. It will assuredly give great offence to many by the way it rides rough-shod over dogmas theological and biological, and by its widesweeping scorn of systematists and specialists; but it is rich in special knowledge and suggestive ideas. Mr Darwin has reason to be proud of his disciple'.

p. 303 94. The reference is to Fritz Müller's *Für Darwin* (1864).

95. In his footnote Lewes quotes from Geoffroy St Hilaire's *Principes de Philosophie Zoologique* (1830): 'Une légère nuance dans la couleur suffit même quelquefois pour la distinction de deux êtres, comme cela se voit l'égard de la fouine et de la martre; deux espèces que l'on ne confond jamais, et qui cependent ne different guère que par la teinte de leur gorge lavée de jaune chez la martre, et entièrement blanche chez la fouine.'

p. 304 96. *L.*: '[Darwin] mentions the case of a sow who would not breed at all to her sire, but bred at once to a stranger in blood. Another sow, the product of close interbreeding for three generations, when paired with her own uncle (known to be productive with other sows), produced a litter of only six, and another litter of only five weak pigs; but paired with a boar of a small black breed (which produced seven swine with a sow of his own breed), she who had been so unproductive with her uncle, yielded twenty-one, and in a second litter, eighteen pigs'

p. 305 97. *L.*: 'Buffon, *Hist. Nat.* III.'

98. *L.*: 'Cuvier, *Lettres à Pfaff*, p. 179.'

99. *L.*: 'Flourens, *Cours de physiologie Comparée*, 1856.'

100. *L.*: 'Müller, *Physiology*, English translation, II, p. 1,662.'

p. 307 101. *L.*: ' "Les monstres," said Ambrose Paré, "ont choses qui apparaissent contre le cours de la nature, et sont le plus souvent signes de quelque malheur à advenir' (quoted by Isidore Geoffroy St Hilaire, *Histoire des Anomolies*, 1832, I, p. 71). Aristotle acutely saw that although contrary to the ordinary course of nature, these monsters were produced by the same laws as those which formed the ordinary type (*Gen. Animal.*, iv. 3). M St Hilaire is, therefore, wrong in classing the Stagirite with Ambrose Paré.'

102. Lewes points out that on this subject Müller quotes the Portuguese proverb, that 'God writes straight in crooked lines'.

103. *L.*: 'Faivre, *La Variabilité des Espèces et ses Limites*, 1868, p. 25.'

p. 308 104. *L.*: 'Spencer, *Principles of Biology*, 1864, i. 383.'

105. *L.*: 'In the Prolegomena to the *History of Philosophy*, 3rd edition, 1867, p. lxxxv.'

p. 309 106. *L.*: '*Studies in Animal Life*, p. 149.'

p. 311 107. *L.*: 'Chevreul, *Histoire des Connaissances Chimiques*, 1866, i. 186.'

p. 312 108. *L.*: 'Von Baer, *Das allgemeinste Gesetz der Natur in aller Entwickelung. See his Reden*, 1864, p. 53.'

p. 314 109. *L.*: 'Faivre, op. cit. p. 83.'

On the Dread and Dislike of Science – *Fortnightly Review*, XXIII (June 1878)

p. 318 110. *L.*: 'When one observes those who believe Hospitals and Colleges to be important institutions, socially beneficial, threatening to withdraw all support unless the teachers openly declare what they do not believe, namely, that vivisection for scientific ends is unjustifiable, one is reminded of the recent outbreak of fanaticism on the part of the Jains. This Hindoo sect has such a horror at the destruction of animal life that a group of the most fervent murdered all the Mussulman butchers in the neighbourhood.'

Index